Christopher T. Baglow, Ph.D.

FAITH SCIENCE & REASON

THEOLOGY ON THE CUTTING EDGE

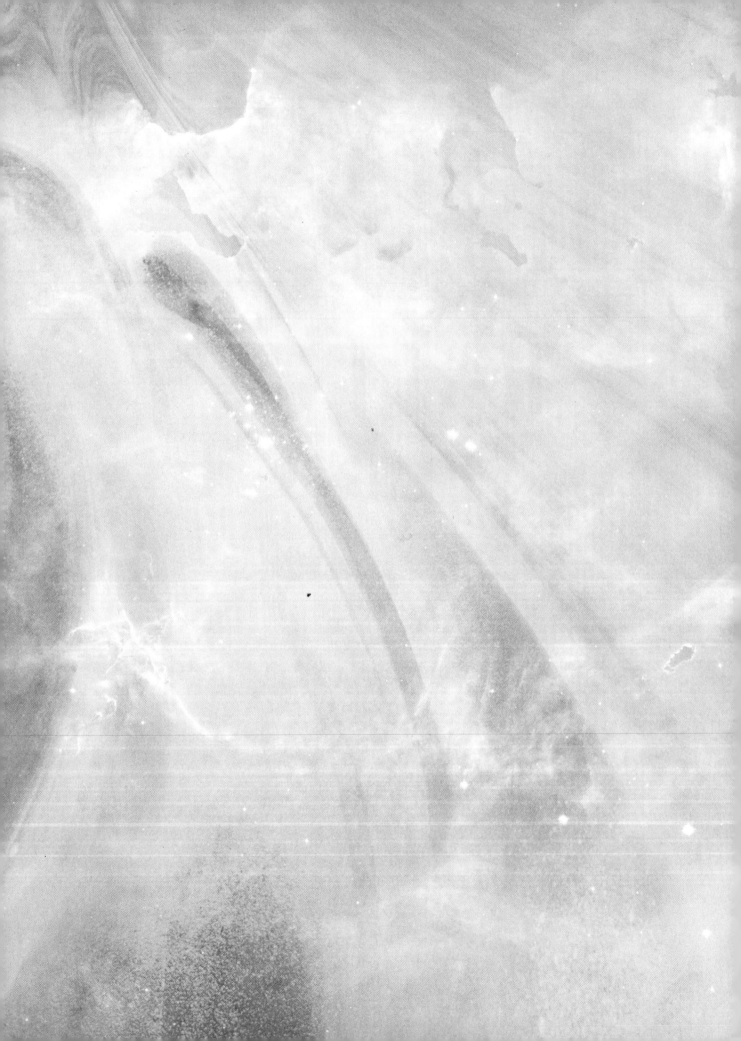

FAITH SCIENCE & REASON

THEOLOGY ON THE CUTTING EDGE

REDISCOVERING FAITH ON THE FRONTIERS OF SCIENCE

By
Christopher T. Baglow, Ph.D.

AN EDUCATIONAL PROGRAM OF THE
POPE BENEDICT XVI INSTITUTE
FOR
FAITH, ETHICS AND SCIENCE

MCGILL-TOOLEN CATHOLIC HIGH SCHOOL
MOBILE, ALABAMA

"Scientia Pro Amore Dei"
(Knowledge for the Love of God)

MIDWEST THEOLOGICAL FORUM

Published in the United States of America by

MIDWEST THEOLOGICAL FORUM
1420 Davey Road, Woodridge, IL 60517
www.theologicalforum.org

AUTHOR: Christopher T. Baglow, Ph.D.

GENERAL AUTHOR: Rev. James Socias

EDITOR-IN-CHIEF: Jeffrey S. Cole

SCIENTIFIC EDITOR AND CONTRIBUTOR: Stephen M. Barr, Ph.D.

SCIENTIFIC CONTRIBUTORS: Dermott J. Mullan, Ph.D.; Mary Beth Porter, Ph.D., M.T.S.; Charles Brockhouse, Ph.D.

THEOLOGICAL CONTRIBUTORS: J. David Franks, Ph.D.; Cory Hayes, M.A.

DESIGN AND PRODUCTION: Jerzy Miszczyszyn, Lyndon Studio, Downers Grove, Illinois

ACKNOWLEDGEMENTS

English translation of the Catechism of the Catholic Church for the United States of America copyright ©1994, United States Catholic Conference, Inc.–Libreria Editrice Vaticana. English translation of the Catechism of the Catholic Church: Modifications from the Editio Typica copyright ©1997, United States Catholic Conference, Inc.–Libreria Editrice Vaticana.

Scripture quotations contained herein are adapted from the Revised Standard Version of the Bible, copyright ©1946, 1952, 1971, and the New Revised Standard Version of the Bible, copyright ©1989, by the Division of Christian Education of the National Council of the Churches of Christ in the United States of America, and are used by permission.
All rights reserved.

Citations of official Church documents from Neuner, Josef, SJ, and Dupuis, Jacques, SJ, eds., The Christian Faith: Doctrinal Documents of the Catholic Church, 5th ed. (New York: Alba House, 1992). Used with permission.

Excerpts from Vatican Council II: The Conciliar and Post Conciliar Documents, New Revised Edition edited by Austin Flannery, O.P., copyright ©1992, Costello Publishing Company, Inc., Northport, NY, are used by permission of the publisher, all rights reserved. No part of these excerpts may be reproduced, stored in a retrieval system, or transmitted in any form or by any means—electronic, mechanical, photocopying, recording or otherwise, without express permission of Costello Publishing Company.

Disclaimer: The editor of this book has attempted to give proper credit to all sources used in the text and illustrations. Any miscredit or lack of credit is unintended and will be corrected in the next edition.

Library of Congress Cataloging-in-Publication Data	
Baglow, Christopher T., 1968-	
Faith, science, and reason : theology on the cutting edge / by Christopher T. Baglow. -- 1st ed.	
p. cm.	
Includes index.	
ISBN 978-1-936045-25-9 (hardcover : alk. paper)	
1. Religion and science. I. Title.	
BL240.3.B34 2009	
201'.65--dc	222009036075

Table of Contents

Table of Contents

Table of Contents

Table of Contents

Table of Contents

Abbreviations

Books of the Bible

Old Testament

Gn	Genesis	Neh	Nehemiah	Dn	Daniel
Ex	Exodus	Tb	Tobit	Hos	Hosea
Lv	Leviticus	Jdt	Judith	Jl	Joel
Nm	Numbers	Est	Esther	Am	Amos
Dt	Deuteronomy	Jb	Job	Ob	Obadiah
Jos	Joshua	Ps	Psalms	Jon	Jonah
Jgs	Judges	Prv	Proverbs	Mi	Micah
Ru	Ruth	Eccl	Ecclesiastes	Na	Nahum
1 Sm	1 Samuel	Sg	Song of Songs	Hb	Habakkuk
2 Sm	2 Samuel	Wis	Wisdom	Zep	Zephaniah
1 Kgs	1 Kings	Sir	Sirach	Hg	Haggai
2 Kgs	2 Kings	Is	Isaiah	Zec	Zechariah
1 Chr	1 Chronicles	Jer	Jeremiah	Mal	Malachi
2 Chr	2 Chronicles	Lam	Lamentations	1 Mc	1 Maccabees
Ezr	Ezra	Bar	Baruch	2 Mc	2 Maccabees
		Ez	Ezekiel		

New Testament

Mt	Matthew	Eph	Ephesians	Heb	Hebrews
Mk	Mark	Phil	Philippians	Jas	James
Lk	Luke	Col	Colossians	1 Pt	1 Peter
Jn	John	1 Thes	1 Thessalonians	2 Pt	2 Peter
Acts	Acts of the Apostles	2 Thes	2 Thessalonians	1 Jn	1 John
Rom	Romans	1 Tm	1 Timothy	2 Jn	2 John
1 Cor	1 Corinthians	2 Tm	2 Timothy	3 Jn	3 John
2 Cor	2 Corinthians	Ti	Titus	Jude	Jude
Gal	Galatians	Phlm	Philemon	Rev	Revelation

Other Sources

CCC — *Catechism of the Catholic Church*

CPG — *Solemn Profession of Faith*: Credo of the People of God

DH — *Dignitatis humanæ* (Declaration on Religious Freedom)

DS — Denzinger-Schonmetzer, *Enchiridion Symbolorum, definitionum et declarationum de rubus fidei et morum* (1985)

DV — *Dei verbum* (Dogmatic Constitution on Divine Revelation)

GS — *Gaudium et spes* (Pastoral Constitution on the Church in the Modern World)

ITC — International Theological Commission

LG — *Lumen gentium* (Dogmatic Constitution on the Church)

PL — J.P. Migne, ed., *Patrologia Latina* (Paris: 1841-1855)

Foreword

The most important goal of education is to give the student a framework for understanding reality. For a Catholic, of course, the overarching framework is the Catholic Faith and the revealed truths which it teaches about God, man, and the world. There is another order of truths, however, that we know, not by divine revelation, but by reason and experience. Of this kind are the truths discovered by science. How do these fit into the framework? A truly educated Catholic is one who is able to integrate the different kinds of knowledge he or she has, and keep them in proper balance and perspective. In other words, he or she is a person who does not compartmentalize life but has a coherent view of it. This is the primary reason for a textbook such as this. But there is another reason, which makes this textbook by Dr. Baglow of especially urgent importance.

A Catholic student going out into the world will face challenges to his or her faith. Some of these will be in the form of sharp questions about Christian beliefs. These questions may come from those who wish to mock or from those who sincerely wish to learn. In either case, the questions will not always be easy to answer for someone who has never thought much about them. Or maybe the Catholic student has thought about them, but has been left in a state of confusion. For example, he or she may be asked, How does the biblical account of Creation relate to the Big Bang theory? How do Adam and Eve relate to what we have learned about the evolution of modern humans from *Australopithecus afarensis* and *Homo habilis?* How do spiritual realities, such as the soul, fit into the world of matter described by physics, chemistry, and biology? Is it possible to believe in miracles and also the laws of nature? Is scientific reason compatible with religious faith? Do the discoveries of modern science really imply that we are just material beings without free will, as some scientists have claimed? Does the case of Galileo show that the Catholic Church is hostile to science?

Some people, perhaps, avoid these questions because they are afraid that the answers may be unsettling. But avoidance only means that students will grow up nursing secret doubts and fears and be easy prey for the first scientific atheist they meet in college or later life. Nor is avoiding questions compatible with our nature as rational beings made in the image of God. We are seekers after truth. That indeed is what leads us to God, who is Truth itself. What we have to fear is not truth, but rather half-truths and untruths. And, sadly, when it comes to the relation between science and Christian doctrine, what many people are told consists largely of half-truths and untruths. That is why this book by Dr. Baglow is so urgently needed.

There is hardly any subject about which there is more widespread ignorance and misinformation than the relationship between the Catholic Faith and science. This ignorance extends to all sectors of society, from the "man on the street" to the professor at the elite university; and it has taken a terrible toll. Gross misconceptions about the Church's teachings and about her historical record with regard to science have undermined the faith of many believers and have created suspicion towards religion in many non-believers.

It would be easy to blame this state of affairs entirely on the hostility of militantly atheist or anti-Catholic people. And indeed, for well over two centuries there has been relentless propaganda about the supposed warfare between Catholicism and science. However, it is also the case that Catholics have not been vigorous enough in confronting these issues and telling our side of the story.

Talk to any audience of Catholics, whether of adults or high school students, and ask them what name comes to mind when they think of the relationship of the Catholic Church to science and the result is always the same: "Galileo!" they shout out. That is almost all they have been taught on the subject. Have they heard of Niels Stensen? Francesco Grimaldi? Georges Lemaître? Every educated Catholic should—and yet almost none have. (No, I won't tell you who they are. You will have to read Dr. Baglow's wonderful book to find out!) Looking over my oldest daughter's shoulder one day, I saw that there was a paragraph in her high-school biology textbook about the experiments of Lazzaro Spallanzani, one of the greatest biologists of the eighteenth century. I asked her, "Did you know that he was a Catholic priest?" She didn't. How could she? The textbook didn't mention it, and her teacher had never heard it either.

And it is not just on questions of history that Catholics have not been given an accurate or full story. Too often, what they know about scientific discoveries is filtered through the interpretations of scholars or journalists who are at best indifferent to religion and sometimes deeply hostile. Fortunately, in recent years many scientists who are Christian believers have undertaken to write about science from a theologically informed perspective. This includes Catholics, such as Fr. Michał Heller, a scientist at the Vatican Observatory who does research in quantum gravity; Peter E. Hodgson, who prior to his death in late 2008 was a professor of nuclear physics at Oxford University; and Kenneth R. Miller, a professor of biology at Brown University. It includes non-Catholic Christians as well, such as Dr. Francis Collins, former Director of the Human Genome Project; Prof. Owen Gingerich of the Harvard-Smithsonian Center for Astrophysics; and the Rev. John Polkinghorne, formerly a professor of particle physics at Cambridge University, and now an Anglican theologian. Dr. Baglow has drawn upon the insights of these and other scientists to produce a textbook that is impressively sophisticated in its treatment of science while remaining highly accessible to students.

But it is not only the relevant history and science that have often been neglected in the education of our students. Much of the rich tradition of Catholic theology and philosophy has been neglected as well. What does the Church mean by "creation"? What has she historically taught about evolution and human origins? What is meant by saying we have "spiritual souls"? How does God govern the universe, and what is meant by Divine Providence? In what sense is God the "First Cause," and what is meant by "secondary causes"? What is "faith" and what is its relation to reason and general and scientific inquiry in particular? One cannot begin to discuss science and its discoveries from a Catholic perspective without the proper theological tools. Here again, Dr. Baglow has done a masterful job of presenting the crucial doctrines and the theological and philosophical insights of Catholic tradition in an engaging and illuminating way.

There are so many ways that a book on science and religion can go wrong.

Some authors think it is necessary to jettison or radically revise doctrines of the faith to be consistent with what science says. Others think it is necessary to dismiss well-established truths of science to be faithful to Scripture. Some put Catholic theology and science into a blender and end up with a pseudo-mystical mush that is neither genuinely Catholic nor genuinely scientific. Some retreat into what amounts to nature worship.

Not this book! Dr. Baglow takes authentic and unadulterated Catholic teaching and authentic and unadulterated science and shows them to be in wonderful harmony. He makes his own the words of a great scientist, whom he quotes:

> Many people think that modern science is far removed from God. I find on the contrary, that… in our knowledge of physical nature we have penetrated so far that we can obtain a vision of the flawless harmony which is in conformity with sublime reason.

Dr. Baglow's careful analysis and lucid exposition make one apparent difficulty after another melt away. He shows that the record of the Church in relation to science is one to be proud of, and indeed quite glorious. The student will come away with a deeper understanding of the Catholic faith, of science, and of their coherence with one another.

We are all deeply in Dr. Baglow's debt. There has been a terrible drought of classroom instruction in this area. This book is not just a few drops of water on the parched earth—which itself would have been welcome—but a drenching, reviving rain.

Prof. Stephen M. Barr, Dept. of Physics and Astronomy, University of Delaware

Introduction

If it had not been for Hurricane Katrina, this book would probably have never been written.

Over many years of study I had developed an interest in the relationship between the Catholic Faith and modern science. In the summer of 2005, a widely televised public debate was sparked over issues closely related to this topic. Evolution, Intelligent Design Theory, and their respective places in the public school curricula throughout the United States were making headlines. Even President George W. Bush offered an opinion in the debate. But with a very busy job as the Coordinator of a new undergraduate theology program in my hometown of New Orleans, Louisiana, I could not even afford to think about more reading, much less any writing, in the subject area. Time was a resource that I did not have.

In early September 2005, Hurricane Katrina saw to it that I had plenty of time. Our hurried evacuation landed my wife, my children and myself in the tiny, central Louisiana town of Bunkie. The flooding of our beautiful city had shut down the Fall 2005 semester and with it, my administrative and teaching responsibilities. Contracting the rebuilding of our own flooded home was now the only thing occupying my time and effort.

While I was still in Bunkie, a call came from Thomas McDonald, a close friend and a religion teacher at McGill-Toolen Catholic High School in Mobile, Alabama, regarding an intriguing and exciting possibility: the development of a senior-level high school theology curriculum regarding faith and science from the Catholic perspective. The proposal and planning process was quick, and by October 1 had undertaken the writing of this textbook.

As the chapters began to unfold, my fascination and my sense of reverence and excitement regarding the Creator and his creation as revealed in faith and science continued to grow. I became more and more convinced that this curriculum could serve Catholic students beyond McGill-Toolen. I had recently reviewed the Didache Series published by Midwest Theological Forum (MTF), and had been impressed with the quality of these texts. With the permission of Fr. Shields, president of McGill-Toolen, I contacted MTF. Fr. James Socias, General Editor of MTF, surprised me by revealing that he had already hoped to start a textbook project in the area of faith and science.

Since I began research and writing in October 2005, the development of this textbook has seen the rebuilding of my home, the proposal and inauguration of a graduate program in theology, the birth of my third child (Peter George), the death of my beloved grandmother, and the slow and still-unfinished recovery of my city and my region. Much of it was written in the Eucharistic Adoration Chapel of St. Catherine of Siena Parish in Metairie, Louisiana, one of the few places where I could find both silence and the Presence of Our Lord through this long period of change.

Many thanks are in order to many people. But first and foremost, glory and praise are due to Christ in the Eucharist. *Thanks be to you, Lord Jesus Christ, for the grace to begin this project and to see it to completion. It is dedicated to you, Savior of Humanity and Savior of its science.*

Among all those who supported me and endured my efforts, all of my love and thanks go to Christine Kelly Baglow, Margaret Jane Baglow, John Trevor Baglow and Peter George Trevor Baglow. I could not have done it without you, and I did it all for you.

I am grateful to Mr. Joseph C. Canizaro, Mrs. Sue Ellen M. Canizaro and Fr. Neal W. McDermott, O.P. of the Donum Dei Foundation. Their generous endowment of the Sue Ellen M. Canizaro Chair in

Catholic Theology at Our Lady of Holy Cross College in New Orleans, which I was honored to hold through the entire period of the writing of this book, have made this and many good things possible.

Special thanks go to Fr. Bry Shields, President of McGill-Toolen Catholic High School, whose bold vision for McGill-Toolen inspired me to look past Katrina losses and towards the exciting possibilities of integrating faith and science in high school catechesis and college theological instruction, and also to Thomas McDonald for recommending me for this project. I offer my sincere gratitude to the excellent students, faculty and administration of McGill-Toolen, especially Ms. Michelle Haas, Principal; Mr. Gary Blackburn, Assistant-Principal; Mr. Bill McAtee, Assistant-Principal; Mr. Blake Stein, Assistant-Principal; Mr. Patrick Arensberg, Chair of the Theology Department; Mr. Joseph Arensberg, Senior Theology Teacher; Dr. Tim Burgess, Chair of the Science Department; and Dr. Faustin Neff Weber, Physics Teacher.

Finally, continued heartfelt thanks and admiration go to the staff of MTF, especially Fr. James Socias for seeing the merit of this idea long before I did and for privileging me with this endeavor; to Mr. Jeffrey S. Cole, Editor-in-Chief, who piloted the book in its long journey to publication; and to Mr. Jerzy Miszczyszyn and his staff at Lyndon Studio, whose exceptional artistry is evident on every page of the text.

May Christ and Our Lady be with us all as we journey on the road of discovery that leads to our Heavenly Father.

Christopher T. Baglow, Ph.D.
Notre Dame Seminary
New Orleans, Louisiana
Feast of the Assumption
15 August 2009

Part One

A FRIENDLY REUNION:
THE RELATIONSHIP BETWEEN NATURAL SCIENCE AND SUPERNATURAL FAITH

Chapter One

Faith and Science: At the Crossroads of Nature and Spirit

THE LOVE OF GOD AND OF SPIRITUAL REALITIES, ESPECIALLY THE DEEP DEVOTION TO THOSE MOMENTS AND TRUTHS THROUGH WHICH GOD HAS MANIFESTED HIMSELF IN OUR WORLD, HAVE POWERFULLY SHAPED OUR CULTURE AND OUR WAY OF LIFE....

"Faith and reason are like two wings on which the human spirit rises to the contemplation of truth; and God has placed in the human heart a desire to know the truth—in a word, to know himself—so that, by knowing and loving God, men and women may also come to the fullness of truth about themselves."

—John Paul II, *Fides et ratio,* Prologue

A. Truly, Madly, Deeply: A Tale of Two Loves

This textbook is, from beginning to end, about two love-affairs that have powerfully shaped human history. Anyone who knows about that history knows that the effects of these two loves are so powerful that they touch our individual lives at every moment.

The first of these loves is *the love of God and of spiritual realities,* especially the deep devotion to those moments and truths through which God has manifested himself in our world. Above all, this is the love of Jesus Christ, the person who is true God and true man, who was and ever will be the full appearing of the supernatural in history. By "supernatural" we mean that fullness of being and goodness that is beyond every created nature: the intimacy of God's inner life that we desire but cannot obtain by our natural powers. Our families, our national form of life, our culture—all of these have been touched and shaped by people whose lives and hearts were passionately directed toward the "One Beyond the World;" the very One who created and sustains history and the universe.

Faith and science are both essential to the human quest for understanding and fulfillment, and reason is essential to both. In faith, reason makes possible a deeper grasp of spiritual realities. In science, reason unaided by faith discovers the truth about nature, "an adventure God has left to us ourselves." (Pope Benedict XVI)

...AS HAS THE LOVE OF NATURE, THE VISIBLE, PHYSICAL COSMOS AND EVERYTHING IN IT, INCLUDING THE HUMAN SPECIES.

THE KIND OF KNOWLEDGE INVOLVED IN THE LOVE OF GOD IS CALLED *FAITH*, AND THE KIND OF KNOWLEDGE INVOLVED IN THE LOVE OF NATURE IS CALLED *SCIENCE*.

The second kind of love that touches and steers history as well as our individual lives is *the love of nature*. By nature we mean the visible, physical cosmos and everything in it, but especially the strange and marvelous phenomenon of living things, including the human species. This love is the most recent and most potent form of love that shapes our world at present. Scientific discovery and the benefits we derive from it shape every facet of our lives.

For instance, in your own circle of family and friends, there are almost certainly some who, had you and they been born just one hundred years ago, would not have survived to share your life today. In fact, you yourself might only be alive today thanks to the passionate lovers of nature who study it and learn its secrets. The love of nature is, without a doubt, a vital force or energy that has made modern life possible.

But how well do we understand these two loves? Where do they come from? Why do they exist? We cannot have sufficient knowledge of our own destinies if we do not understand, at least basically, these two great love-affairs which are like two hands that shape and steer our history. Only if we have some knowledge of both, can we begin to say where we fit into that history and how we should respond to its changes. If one of these loves is an empty love, a wishful thinking about something unreal or imaginary, then we must know to avoid it. If either one is valid, real, or worthwhile, then we must know it, so we can participate in it. Knowledge of both gives us the power to respond correctly to both.

So what can be known about these two great loves? The first thing we should recognize about both of these passionate love-affairs is that they involve the human mind, the human ability to know. It is sometimes said that love is blind. But really, it is impossible to love anything that is unknown or unseen. For example, to love someone you have never met or at least seen is impossible. Even in a fantasy, a person "loves" something or someone imagined on the basis of other things or people that he or she knows. If I were to develop a total case of amnesia, losing all of my personal knowledge, my love for my family and friends would cease, because I would not know them in order to love them.

Therefore, in order to understand the two great love-affairs with God and with nature that shape human history, we have to start with knowing who God is and knowing what nature is. That is, we have to examine both the spiritual and natural in order to know why they evoke such powerful responses in human beings.

We must also study the kind of knowledge involved in the love of God, the knowledge called Faith, and the kind of knowledge involved in the love of nature, the knowledge called *Science*. Only then can we examine how the two might be related, and the issues involved in that relationship.

B. Nature and Spirit: Defining and Exploring the Levels of Reality

What objects could be so great that the love and effort they inspire could literally move and shape the whole history of humanity? Much of this text is devoted to examining the characteristics of nature and spirit. Defining either of them is a massive task because both are massive realities. In this short introduction, we will begin to examine the basic traits that help us identify and distinguish the natural realm from the spiritual realm. In many ways, the rest of this text will simply be about expanding and refining our definitions of nature and spirit.

THIS TEXT IS DEVOTED TO EXAMINING THE CHARACTERISTICS OF NATURE AND SPIRIT. DEFINING EITHER OF THEM IS A MASSIVE TASK BECAUSE BOTH ARE MASSIVE REALITIES. IN THIS SHORT INTRODUCTION WE WILL BEGIN TO EXAMINE THE BASIC TRAITS THAT HELP US IDENTIFY AND DISTINGUISH THE NATURAL REALM FROM THE SPIRITUAL REALM.

NATURE: THE MYSTERY OF VISIBLE REALITY

When we speak of nature, we are referring to the visible world, which is also called "the universe" or "the cosmos." The priest and physicist Stanley Jaki has given an excellent definition of *nature*—nature is "the true and specific totality of all coherently and consistently contingent [physical] interacting beings."[1] I have added the word "physical" because we must distinguish nature from immaterial beings, such as angels.

Let us break Jaki's definition down in order to understand it:

Because it is the organ of sight, the human eye is a classic symbol for the human ability to discover truth.

A True and Specific Totality:

Simply put, this phrase refers to nature as the sum total of all that exists in it, the universe taken "as a whole."

Coherently and Consistently Contingent:

All that exists in nature is characterized by *coherence* (order and harmony), and, therefore, *intelligibility,* which is the ability of a thing to be understood. Here we can speak of the laws of nature, which govern each and every part of it, describing how natural things exist and act.

The beings within nature are also *contingent.* They are beings which exist because of other beings. *To be contingent is to lack a sufficient explanation for your existence within yourself.* No thing in nature has ever been located or identified which is not somehow dependent for its existence on things that are independent of it.

For instance, a human being is dependent on his or her parents when his or her bodily existence is considered from its beginning;

AMONG THE MANY BREAKTHROUGHS INTO UNDERSTANDING THE MYSTERY OF VISIBLE REALITY, COPERNICUS' TREATISE ON THE MOVEMENT OF THE EARTH AROUND THE SUN IS ONE OF THE EARLIEST AND MOST IMPORTANT TO MODERN SCIENCE.

when it is considered at any moment, the bodily existence of a human being is dependent on a stable atmosphere and a hospitable environment and temperature range. Just as in the case of human existence, all natural things are also contingent, even the universe itself.

In a later chapter, we shall see that nature as a whole and everything in it requires a Creator. Nature itself is contingent, and therefore it is correct to add another title for it besides universe and cosmos: nature is God's *creation. Creation* refers to all realities that are contingent. Creation is a category which transcends nature and is applicable to the realm of spirit as well; in fact, it is applicable to all beings except God.

Physical:

Nature as we are defining it here only refers to those beings that are thoroughly physical or *material,* that are made up of matter. It includes many things that we can see, hear, touch, and smell, as well as many others that are not accessible directly through our senses. Such things have some common characteristics:

a) they are made up of parts and therefore occupy space;

b) they are destructible and changeable, which means that they exist in time, which is the measurement of change;

c) they can be experienced and known directly and/or indirectly through our senses: sight, smell, hearing, touch, and taste.

Interacting Beings:

The word *universe (uni-versum)* means "turned towards unity." This title points to the fact that everything in nature is interrelated. Nature is a vast system of real beings joined together simply by the fact that they all exist.[2] Even more fundamentally, nature is also unified in the fact that all of its members have a physical existence. Another element of nature's unity is found in its laws, which are consistent and universally unbreakable by the things which exist within nature.

Finally, the interactions that occur within nature create the great systems we find in the visible cosmos: solar systems, galaxies, atoms, and, above all, biological life, the most complex and unified kind of existence within the material universe. Although we cannot experience all of the parts of the universe, such as very distant objects, the beings that we cannot experience interact with beings that we can, thereby forming a unified system.

As noted above, the visible and physical reality we call nature is not the only reality that exists. We now turn to the realm of spiritual reality.

Copernicus's De Revolutionibus Orbium Caelestium, 1543

Astronomer Copernicus: Conversation with God

SPIRIT: THE MYSTERY BEYOND VISIBLE REALITY

Human history has been shaped by a deep fascination with nature. Before we consider the process of knowledge and exploration that first fueled and continues to fuel that fascination, we must look at a second realm of reality, the love of which also shapes life as we know it—the realm of spirit.

For the sake of completeness and accuracy, we can define *spirit or spiritual reality* as "all that really exists and transcends nature; all that is not contained by visible reality." This is the realm of the *supernatural,* and, above all, the reality of God, who is the Creator of all other natural and spiritual things that are not himself.[3] Creatures existing within this realm are angels and humans. Angels are pure spirit. Human beings are a composite of the spiritual and the natural, of soul and body.

We saw above that nature and everything within it is characterized by specific characteristics. The same is true of spirit; any and every spiritual reality has some important attributes that characterize it as such. Let us look at some of these characteristics:

Reason (Intellect):

The physical cosmos, nature, is comprised of things that are thoroughly understandable, orderly, and harmonious. Spiritual reality is the realm of beings who are not simply intelligible, but also intelligent; in other words, of beings that are capable of reason. A natural reality is knowable; a spiritual reality is both knowable and knowing.

God is the highest spiritual reality, and therefore God is the Perfect Knower. One theologian even defines God as "the unrestricted act of understanding."[4] This means that God knows all realities, both natural and spiritual, fully and without limit;

Will (Free Will):

Nature is comprised of beings that follow unvarying, universal laws. Spiritual reality is the realm of beings that are able to determine themselves and other things in real ways; to be "first causes" of chains of events. This is what it means to be free—to be able to act on the basis of reason.

This does not mean that spiritual beings are entirely self-determining, but that they are able to freely direct their own existences. Another way of saying this is to say that spiritual beings are *moral;* they are responsible for their actions and are consciously capable of good and evil. When they choose what truly fulfills them in right order and proportion, then they do good. When they do not, then they do evil. Something that simply belongs in nature as we have defined it above is not free and therefore is not capable of moral choices.

SPIRIT IS "ALL THAT REALLY EXISTS AND TRANSCENDS NATURE; ALL THAT IS NOT CONTAINED BY VISIBLE REALITY." THIS IS THE REALM OF THE SUPERNATURAL, AND, ABOVE ALL, THE REALITY OF GOD, WHO IS THE CREATOR OF ALL OTHER NATURAL AND SPIRITUAL THINGS THAT ARE NOT HIMSELF.

A PRIME EXAMPLE OF SPIRIT IS THE ANGELS, WHOSE EXISTENCE IS A TRUTH REVEALED BY GOD IN SACRED SCRIPTURE AND IN THE CONSTANT TEACHING OF THE CHURCH. AS THE *CATECHISM OF THE CATHOLIC CHURCH* TEACHES, ANGELS ARE PURELY SPIRITUAL CREATURES, PERSONAL AND IMMORTAL, WHOSE PERFECTION IS GREATER THAN ANY OF THE CREATURES WE FIND IN NATURE.

God is the highest spiritual reality, and therefore is not simply free to be good, but is Perfect Goodness. In fact, because love is the perfection of freedom, it is accurate to say that God is the unrestricted act of loving, just as he is the unrestricted act of understanding.

Superior to and Governing Nature:

To be a spiritual being means to transcend determination by the laws of nature—at least to some extent. Man as a union of body and spirit is partially subject to the laws of nature. God and his angels do not fall under these laws. Rather, the spiritual has a governing relationship to nature; it can make nature subject to its influence.

A prime example of spirit is the angels, whose existence is a truth revealed by God in Sacred Scripture and in the constant teaching of the Church. As the *Catechism of the Catholic Church* teaches, angels are purely spiritual creatures, personal and immortal, whose perfection is greater than any of the creatures we find in nature.[5] Although sacred art often depicts them as having wings and human forms, these depictions are symbolic, not literal—their greatness is to be found in the fact that they are superior to the physical realm—they are *non-corporeal* (i.e., non-physical).

In nature's relationship to God the Creator, we see this superiority of spirit to nature most clearly. Nature needs spirit for its very existence, because God is the source of all existence.

Personal:

Because all spiritual beings possess reason and will, they exist in a much higher way than individual physical beings exist in nature. They are self-directing and self-shaping, and so have an interiority, a personhood or personality.

God is Supreme Personhood: in fact, God is three Divine Persons in a perfect unity of love—Father, Son, and Holy Spirit.

Personhood is a great bridge from our definitions of nature and spirit to the question of how we know natural and spiritual things. We know from experience that it is possible to know another person in a superficial way, and yet not *really* know them. Whether a person reveals himself or herself to me is a matter of that person's freedom, and only in trust can I experience that person's true self. Natural things, on the other hand, lie open to anyone who has the intelligence and will to investigate them.

In other words, both natural beings and spiritual beings can be known, and therefore, can be loved. But *how* they are known involves two different kinds of knowledge. To know a natural being involves an act of reason called *science*. To know a spiritual being involves an act of reason and will called an *act of faith,* or of believing. Let us look more closely at these two paths of knowledge that lead us to the crossroads of nature and spirit.

C. Faith and Science: The Two Paths of Knowledge

As we study the two paths of knowledge, the one that leads to knowledge of the natural universe called science, and the one that leads to knowledge of God and angels called faith, we should begin by identifying what they both have in common. Both kinds of knowledge can be described as "thinking with assent."[6] That is, both are the use of reason by which one reaches a conclusion about reality—"thinking." And both of them involve an assent to truth, a response of "yes, this is true."

What makes them different from each other is the order in which thinking and assent occur. In science, thinking occurs first and makes assent possible and even necessary. But in faith, assent and thinking walk hand in hand; they balance each other.[7]

The key to the riddle at the heart of this difference can be understood if we recall one essential element of spirit: the element of freedom. In science, nature is explored through the use of strict demonstration, involving experimentation and repeatability. Once a scientific possibility is convincingly shown to be the case, however, the honest person must assent to it. The will is forced by the obviousness of what is demonstrated by science; we are not free to refuse it and remain honest with ourselves.

But in knowing a spiritual reality, one is always dealing with another free, intelligent person. Here one may search and strive and get a little knowledge, but only if the other person "opens up" a way for us, and only if we assent freely to his/her invitation, is true and profound knowledge of that person possible. In this kind of knowing, the will is not forced. It is invited by another will; and if my will responds to that invitation, then it can advance in knowledge. This is exactly how love between two persons "works"—one can be drawn to another by beauty or by what one perceives of the person through his or her words and actions. But at a point, only if the two wills are mutually open can knowledge progress to a deep intimacy.[8]

So science reveals knowledge of things that do not have freedom and does so in a way in which the evidence compels us to assent to certain conclusions. But knowing another intelligent, free person—a spiritual reality—involves a constant *openness to know and an openness to being known.* At each and every step, thinking and assent walk hand-in-hand in an act of trust. This is why one definition of faith is trust, as when one person says, "I have *faith* in you" to another person.

In the case of knowing God, however, we are dealing with the same problem on an entirely different level. God is a reality that completely transcends our minds and wills. Through reason, we can

KNOWING A SPIRITUAL REALITY INVOLVES A CONSTANT *OPENNESS TO KNOW* AND AN *OPENNESS TO BEING KNOWN*. THE WILL IS NOT FORCED, AS IT IS IN SCIENCE. IN FAITH, THINKING AND ASSENT WALK HAND-IN-HAND IN AN ACT OF TRUST.

know that God exists, but to "know God"—intimately— requires that he reveal himself to us and that he empower our wills to embrace the reality he offers us. God must give us a new kind of trust in order for us to progress in our knowledge of him. This is *faith* in the strict supernatural sense; through God's grace and our voluntary cooperation with it, we are made capable of trusting and knowing God himself.

Unlike science, in which knowledge "forces" the assent of the will by its undeniability, the path of faith is walked when our wills, empowered by God, travel hand-in-hand with our minds, and when our love and knowledge of God increase together. In the words of Pope Benedict XVI:

> Believing is not an act of the understanding alone, not simply an act of the will, not just an act of feeling, but an act *in which all the spiritual powers of man are at work together* [emphasis added]. Still more: man in his own self, and of himself, cannot bring about this believing at all; it has of its nature the character of a dialogue. It is only because the depth of the soul—the heart—has been touched by God's Word that the whole structure of spiritual powers [knowing, willing, and feeling] is set in motion and unites in the "Yes" of believing.[9]

Here we see that the two kinds of knowledge which fuel the two powerful loves that shape human history are not in opposition to each other. They are simply different, as different as analyzing a tissue sample is different from knowing someone whom you love deeply.

Which Love to Choose?

You may be saying to yourself, "Yes, this description of faith makes sense, but why bother? Is not knowing and loving nature enough?" The answer is that only by loving God and other persons can perfect and lasting happiness be found. All of our free choices are ultimately about seeking fulfillment in which our thirst for happiness is fully and continually quenched. In the words of St. Augustine, "You have made us for yourself, O Lord, and our heart is restless until it rests in you." Faith promises the will perfect rest and the mind perfect knowledge by offering God, the source of all goodness and truth. That is why faith is not a lack of knowledge. Instead, it is "the certainty on which our life is based."[10]

But this is not to disrespect science. Both faith and science are legitimate forms of knowing, and both are part of God's loving plan for his human creatures. To the question, "Which love to choose, love of nature or love of God?" the answer is a clear "both/and," not a restrictive "either/or." God created nature "to show forth and communicate his glory," so that his creatures can share in his "truth, goodness, and beauty."[11] To know the universe is a path to knowing God. But as we will see later, to try to know the world without knowing God, to try to study science while rejecting faith, is to miss the truest meaning of the universe.

Theology on the Cutting Edge

The task of this book is to introduce students to the harmony that can and should exist between faith and science and to the exciting relationship that exists between nature and spirit. Nature is a limited but real reflection of the abundance of spirit. Although we can become confused about one or the other, to really know them both is key to being on the cutting edge of either.

Faith involves assenting to God's truth even prior to our total understanding of it; in this sense, it is the reverse of science. God's self-revelation in Scripture and in Church Tradition requires the *obedience of faith,* which is "a personal adherence of the whole man to God... an assent of intellect and will to the self-revelation God has made through his deeds and words."[12]

But oftentimes our assent still leaves us with questions, especially when there seems to be a disagreement between what we experience and what God has revealed. According to Pope Benedict XVI, in faith "struggling and questioning thought remains present, which ever and again has to seek its light from that essential light which shines into the heart from the Word of God."[13] In addition, the infinite richness of the knowledge of God made available through faith summons our reason to explore those riches.

Therefore faith, like science, seeks deeper knowledge. According to St. Anselm, *theology* is "faith seeking understanding," the study of God and his Revelation using human reason in order to understand it more deeply and live in accord with it more fully. This use of reason never rejects God or his truth, but takes God and his revealed truth as its basis, its first principles, much like a chemist approaches the periodic table of the elements. Theology can and must inquire into the relationship between the knowledge given through faith and the knowledge acquired through reason and experience, including scientific knowledge, in order to be a cutting edge theology.

To inquire into nature, spirit, and their relationship is the heart of our quest in this book—to rediscover faith on the frontiers of science, relying on theological study to give us a deeper understanding of both.

THE TASK OF THIS BOOK IS TO INTRODUCE STUDENTS TO THE HARMONY THAT CAN AND SHOULD EXIST BETWEEN FAITH AND SCIENCE AND TO THE EXCITING RELATIONSHIP THAT EXISTS BETWEEN NATURE AND SPIRIT.

Science and the Arts

D. Conclusion:
Standing at the Crossroads

The subtitle of this chapter is "At the Crossroads of Nature and Spirit." As we end our introduction to the two great loves that shape our history and the paths of knowledge that inspire them, we can say that the *human person* is truly the crossroads of science and faith. Our bodies are physical and subject to the laws of nature, and yet we are also spiritual, intelligent, free persons. Applying the definitions of nature and spirit to human beings, we can see at once that human beings are intrinsically natural and spiritual—in the universe but not entirely of the universe. Later, we will see that to be human is actually to be the link between nature and spirit.

Therefore, to be a human being is to be a knower and a lover of nature and spirit, because to be human is to be both natural and spiritual. As humans we are called to live in and care for the visible universe for the sake of a supernatural destiny.

As we saw earlier, God knows himself and all things perfectly, without restrictions. An angel knows itself without reference to the visible and physical universe, because an angel is purely spiritual. But man must travel two roads, the road of science and the road of faith, to know his true meaning. The crossroads of science and faith is where every human being "lives and moves and has his being" (Acts 17:28), for God is the source of the truths of both nature and spirit.

But of all human beings who stand at the crossroads, one human being above all stands there: *Jesus Christ,* true God and true man;

- Son of God from all eternity, Christ is the goal of faith, the one who reveals God to us;
- Son of Mary and fully human in his Incarnation, Jesus Christ is also all that we are. He has a human body, a human mind, and a human will;
- Savior of the world through his Cross, Christ is the one who promises to renew the natural world and bring humanity into the heart of God.

As we engage in our "cutting-edge" theological investigation of reality, nature, and spirit, we will re-encounter Jesus Christ over and over again. Savior of humanity, he is also the Redeemer of science and the giver of faith—"the Way, the Truth, and the Life" for all believers. As we begin our journey, may he be with us in the power of his Spirit.

THE HUMAN PERSON IS TRULY THE CROSSROADS OF SCIENCE AND FAITH. OUR BODIES ARE PHYSICAL AND SUBJECT TO THE LAWS OF NATURE, AND YET WE ARE ALSO INTELLIGENT, FREE PERSONS.

THEREFORE, TO BE A HUMAN BEING IS TO BE A KNOWER AND LOVER OF NATURE AND SPIRIT, BECAUSE TO BE HUMAN IS TO BE BOTH NATURAL AND SPIRITUAL.

Supplementary Reading

Defining Faith and Science

(excerpted from Paul Haffner, Mystery of Creation [Herefordshire, UK: Gracewing, 1995], pp.156–157).

An introduction to the vast area of relations between faith in God the Creator and modern science may be obtained by considering various meanings of faith and science:

FAITH

1. The act of believing.
2. The consequences of faith, religious practice as a way of life.
3. Statements of faith (creeds, theologies).
4. Faith organized institutionally and communities of faith.

SCIENCE

1. The method of knowing in science.
2. The scientific enterprise; its technological application and practice.
3. The... growing [body] of tested and acknowledged propositions and hypotheses in science.
4. Science organized institutionally and the scientific communities.

Any approach to relating faith in God the Creator with science must take into account the multi-faceted meanings of both faith and science. Science consists of many branches, and often physics is taken to be the prime model of the exact sciences beca use of its phenomenology which can be clearly traced, its mathematical structure, its power of describing reality, and its precision. The question then arises as to how the [numerous] dimensions of faith relate to the various aspects of science. It is soon perceived that science and religion make up, even from a linguistic point of view, two different systems. Corresponding to the differences between scientific and religious language, there is also a difference in *method*. Essentially, while science deals with human investigation of creation, Christian Faith treats of the initiative taken by God in revealing that which is beyond the reach of the human mind, and also that which, as a result of the Fall, the human mind would have great difficulty in [discovering].

However, it is insufficient to consider the issue of relations between faith and science from a merely linguistic viewpoint; rather the question must be faced of what lies beneath language and gives it meaning and its foundation:

> Belief in the Word (Logos), eternally uttered by the Father, has become the salvation of human words as well. Only in that perspective have these words remained immune to being degraded into mere tools of facile intellectual games, all aimed at undermining the intellect itself.

Supplementary Reading

Thus, language cannot simply be defined in terms of its use, nor solely with regard to the individuals or community who express themselves with it, nor simply considering the interrelation between the various words which make it up.... In this sense, religious language and scientific language will have points of contact to the extent that they both deal with created reality. However, scientific language cannot approach God the Creator, for he is beyond its sphere of competence.

The *Catechism of the Catholic Church* on Nature and Natural Things: ON THE VISIBLE WORLD

337   God himself created the visible world in all its richness, diversity, and order. Scripture presents the work of the Creator symbolically as a succession of six days of divine "work," concluded by the "rest" of the seventh day.[14] On the subject of creation, the sacred text teaches the truths revealed by God for our salvation,[15] permitting us to "recognize the inner nature, the value, and the ordering of the whole of creation to the praise of God."[16]

338   *Nothing exists that does not owe its existence to God the Creator.* The world began when God's word drew it out of nothingness; all existent beings, all of nature, and all human history are rooted in this primordial event, the very genesis by which the world was constituted and time begun.[17]

339   *Each creature possesses its own particular goodness and perfection.* For each one of the works of the "six days" it is said: "And God saw that it was good." "By the very nature of creation, material being is endowed with its own stability, truth, and excellence, its own order and laws."[18] Each of the various creatures, willed in its own being, reflects in its own way a ray of God's infinite wisdom and goodness. Man must therefore respect the particular goodness of every creature, to avoid any disordered use of things which would be in contempt of the Creator and would bring disastrous consequences for human beings and their environment.

340   God wills the *interdependence of creatures.* The sun and the moon, the cedar and the little flower, the eagle and the sparrow: the spectacle of their countless diversities and inequalities tells us that no creature is self-sufficient. Creatures exist only in dependence on each other, to complete each other, in the service of each other.

Supplementary Reading

341   *The beauty of the universe:* The order and harmony of the created world results from the diversity of beings and from the relationships which exist among them. Man discovers them progressively as the laws of nature. They call forth the admiration of scholars. The beauty of creation reflects the infinite beauty of the Creator and ought to inspire the respect and submission of man's intellect and will.

342   The *hierarchy of creatures* is expressed by the order of the "six days," from the less perfect to the more perfect. God loves all his creatures[19] and takes care of each one, even the sparrow. Nevertheless, Jesus said: "You are of more value than many sparrows," or again: "Of how much more value is a man than a sheep!"[20]

343   *Man is the summit* of the Creator's work, as the inspired account expresses by clearly distinguishing the creation of man from that of the other creatures.[21]

344   There is a *solidarity among all creatures* arising from the fact that all have the same Creator and are all ordered to his glory:

> *May you be praised, O Lord, in all your creatures, especially brother sun, by whom you give us light for the day; he is beautiful, radiating great splendor, and offering us a symbol of you, the Most High.*
>
> *May you be praised, my Lord, for sister water, who is very useful and humble, precious and chaste.*
>
> *May you be praised, my Lord, for sister earth, our mother, who bears and feeds us, and produces the variety of fruits and dappled flowers and grasses.*
>
> *Praise and bless my Lord, give thanks and serve him in all humility.[22]*

Supplementary Reading

The *Catechism of the Catholic Church* on Faith (and Science): ON THE CHARACTERISTICS OF FAITH

"And [Abraham] believed the LORD; and the LORD reckoned it to him as righteousness." Genesis 15:6

Faith is a Grace

153   When St. Peter confessed that Jesus is the Christ, the Son of the living God, Jesus declared to him that this Revelation did not come "from flesh and blood," but from "my Father who is in heaven."[23] *Faith is a gift of God, a supernatural virtue infused by him.* "Before this faith can be exercised, man must have the grace of God to move and assist him; he must have the interior helps of the Holy Spirit, who moves the heart and converts it to God, who opens the eyes of the mind and 'makes it easy for all to accept and believe the truth." [24]

Faith is a Human Act

154   Believing is possible only by grace and the interior helps of the Holy Spirit. But it is no less true that believing is an authentically human act. Trusting in God and cleaving to the truths he has revealed is contrary neither to human freedom nor to human reason. Even in human relations it is not contrary to our dignity to believe what other persons tell us about themselves and their intentions, or to trust their promises (for example, when a man and a woman marry) to share a communion of life with one another. If this is so, still less is it contrary to our dignity to "yield by faith the full submission of . . . intellect and will to God who reveals,"[25] and to share in an interior communion with him.

155   In faith, the human intellect and will cooperate with divine grace: "Believing is an act of the intellect assenting to the divine truth by command of the will moved by God through grace."[26]

Supplementary Reading

FAITH AND UNDERSTANDING

156   What moves us to believe is not the fact that revealed truths appear as true and intelligible in the light of our natural reason: we believe "because of the authority of God himself who reveals them, who can neither deceive nor be deceived."[27] So "that the submission of our faith might nevertheless be in accordance with reason, God willed that external proofs of his Revelation should be joined to the internal helps of the Holy Spirit."[28] Thus the miracles of Christ and the saints, prophecies, the Church's growth and holiness, and her fruitfulness and stability "are the most certain signs of divine Revelation, adapted to the intelligence of all"; they are "motives of credibility" *(motiva credibilitatis),* which show that the assent of faith is "by no means a blind impulse of the mind."[29]

157   Faith is *certain.* It is more certain than all human knowledge because it is founded on the very word of God who cannot lie. To be sure, revealed truths can seem obscure to human reason and experience, but "the certainty that the divine light gives is greater than that which the light of natural reason gives."[30] "Ten thousand difficulties do not make one doubt."[31]

158   "Faith *seeks understanding*":[32] it is intrinsic to faith that a believer desires to know better the One in whom he has put his faith and to understand better what He has revealed; a more penetrating knowledge will in turn call forth a greater faith, increasingly set afire by love. The grace of faith opens "the eyes of your hearts"[33] to a lively understanding of the contents of Revelation: that is, of the totality of God's plan and the mysteries of faith, of their connection with each other and with Christ, the center of the revealed mystery. "The same Holy Spirit constantly perfects faith by his gifts, so that Revelation may be more and more profoundly understood."[34] In the words of St. Augustine, "I believe, in order to understand; and I understand, the better to believe."[35]

159   *Faith and science:* "Though faith is above reason, there can never be any real discrepancy between faith and reason. Since the same God who reveals mysteries and infuses faith has bestowed the light of reason on the human mind, God cannot deny himself, nor can truth ever contradict truth."[36] "Consequently, methodical research in all branches of knowledge, provided it is carried out in a truly scientific manner and does not override moral laws, can never conflict with the faith, because the things of the world and the things of faith derive from

A tinted engraving from Tycho Brahe's 1598 publication **Astronomiae instayrata mechanica.** The illustration shows Tycho and his Great Quadrant at Uraniborg. The accuracy of this instrument, based on comparison with eight reference stars, has been estimated to 34.6 seconds of arc.

Supplementary Reading

the same God. The humble and persevering investigator of the secrets of nature is being led, as it were, by the hand of God in spite of himself, for it is God, the conserver of all things, who made them what they are."[37]

The freedom of faith

160   To be human, "man's response to God by faith must be free, and … therefore nobody is to be forced to embrace the faith against his will. The act of faith is of its very nature a free act."[38] "God calls men to serve him in spirit and in truth. Consequently they are bound to him in conscience, but not coerced… This fact received its fullest manifestation in Christ Jesus."[39] Indeed, Christ invited people to faith and conversion, but never coerced them. "For he bore witness to the truth but refused to use force to impose it on those who spoke against it. His kingdom… grows by the love with which Christ, lifted up on the cross, draws men to himself."[40]

The necessity of faith

161   Believing in Jesus Christ and in the One who sent him for our salvation is necessary for obtaining that salvation.[41] "Since 'without faith it is impossible to please [God]' and to attain to the fellowship of his sons, therefore without faith no one has ever attained justification, nor will anyone obtain eternal life 'but he who endures to the end.'"[42]

Perseverance in faith

162   Faith is an entirely free gift that God makes to man. We can lose this priceless gift, as St. Paul indicated to St. Timothy: "Wage the good warfare, holding faith and a good conscience. By rejecting conscience, certain persons have made shipwreck of their faith."[43] To live, grow, and persevere in the faith until the end we must nourish it with the word of God; we must beg the Lord to increase our faith;[44] it must be "working through charity," abounding in hope, and rooted in the faith of the Church.[45]

Faith—the beginning of eternal life

163   Faith makes us taste in advance the light of the beatific vision, the goal of our journey here below. Then we shall see God "face to face," "as he is."[46] So faith is already the beginning of eternal life:

> When we contemplate the blessings of faith even now, as if gazing at a reflection in a mirror, it is as if we already possessed the wonderful things which our faith assures us we shall one day enjoy.[47]

164   Now, however, "we walk by faith, not by sight";[48] we perceive God as "in a mirror, dimly" and only "in part."[49] Even though enlightened by him in whom it believes, faith is often lived in darkness and can be put to the test. The world we live in often seems very far from the one promised us by faith. Our experiences of evil and suffering, injustice and death, seem to contradict the Good News; they can shake our faith and become a temptation against it.

165   It is then we must turn to the witnesses of faith: to Abraham, who "in hope … believed against hope;"[50] to the Virgin Mary, who, in "her pilgrimage of faith," walked into the "night of faith"[51] in sharing the darkness of her son's suffering and death; and to so many others: "Therefore, since we are surrounded by so great a cloud of witnesses, let us also lay aside every weight, and sin which clings so closely, and let us run with perseverance the race that is set before us, looking to Jesus the pioneer and perfecter of our faith."[52]

Study Guide

Faith and Science:
At the Crossroads of Nature and Spirit

VOCABULARY

Define the following terms:

1. Nature
2. Coherence
3. Intelligibility
4. Contingency
5. Material
6. Time
7. Universe (*universum*)
8. Spirit
9. Reason (Intellect)
10. Will (Free Will)
11. Person (personal, personhood)
12. Science
13. Faith
14. Obedience of Faith
15. Theology
16. Human Person (crossroads)
17. Jesus Christ (crossroads)

STUDY QUESTIONS

1. Think of an example of a living non-rational being; one that inhabits nature. Briefly explain how the characteristics given in the definition of nature apply to it.
2. Using the natural example in (1) above, explain how this natural creature fails to meet the characteristics given in the definition of spirit.
3. How are faith and science alike? How are they different?
4. Explain, focusing on free will, how faith involves a different path or process of knowing than the one involved in science.
5. Is faith possible without the help of God? Why or why not?
6. Why does faith (believing) involve thinking and assent simultaneously?
7. Why is love of God superior to the love of nature?
8. Is knowing and loving nature incompatible with knowing and loving God? Why or why not?
9. If we have faith, then why is theology still necessary?
10. Explain why the human person is the crossroads of nature and spirit, science and faith.
11. Explain why, above all others, Jesus Christ is the crossroads of nature and spirit, science and faith.

Study Guide

PRACTICAL EXERCISES

1. Reread the quote from John Paul II that begins the chapter. Describe a situation in your own life in which faith and reason (especially the reasoning involved in science) were necessary to arrive at the fullness of the truth about that situation.

2. Imagine that your school had a new principal who decided that only natural realities would be studied. What would your classes be like? What would change, and what would remain the same?

3. Faith is a gift, but it also requires our cooperation with God's grace in order for it to be the certainty on which our lives are based. To deepen your cooperation with God's grace, ask God for the gift of faith. Say the following prayer once a day for the next week:

> *O my God, I firmly believe that you are one God in three Divine Persons:*
> *Father, Son, and Holy Spirit. I believe that your Divine Son became man,*
> *and died for our sins, and that He will come to judge the living and the dead.*
> *I believe these and all the truths which the Holy Catholic Church teaches*
> *because You have revealed them, who can neither deceive nor be deceived. Amen.*

Endnotes

1. Stanley Jaki, *God and the Cosmologists* (Edinburgh: Scottish Academic Press, 1989), 84.
2. W. Norris Clarke, T*he One and the Many: A Contemporary Thomistic Metaphysics* (Notre Dame: University of Notre Dame, 2001), 304.
3. Our definition of the supernatural does *not* pertain to magic or the occult.
4. Bernard J.F. Lonergan, *Insight: A Study of Human Understanding* (New York: The Philosophical Library, 1967), 639–677.
5. CCC 330.
6. Joseph Ratzinger, "Faith and Theology," in *Pilgrim Fellowship of Faith: The Church as Communion* (San Francisco: Ignatius Press, 2005), 22. This term originally comes from St. Augustine.
7. Ibid., 22–23.
8. Idem.
9. Ibid., 24.
10. Ibid., 20.
11. CCC 319.
12. Ibid., 476.
13. Ratzinger, "Faith and Theology," 25.
14. Gn 1: I—2:4.
15. Cf. DV 11.
16. LG 36 § 2.
17. Cf. St. Augustine, *De Genesi adv. Man.* 1, 2, 4: PL 34, 175.
18. GS 36 § 1.
19. Cf. Ps 145:9.
20. Lk 12:6–7; Mt 12:12.
21. Cf. Gn 1:26.
22. St. Francis of Assisi, *Canticle of the Creatures.*
23. Mt 16:17; cf. Gal 1:15; Mt 11:25.
24. DV 5; cf. DS 377; 3010.
25. *Dei Filius* 3: DS 3008.
26. St. Thomas Aquinas, STh II–II, 2, 9; cf. *Dei Filius* 3: DS 3010.
27. *Dei Filius* 3: DS 3008.
28. *Dei Filius* 3: DS 3009.
29. *Dei Filius* 3: DS 3008–3010; Cf. Mk 16:20; Heb 2:4.
30. St. Thomas Aquinas, STh II–II, 171, 5, obj. 3.
31. John Henry Cardinal Newman, *Apologia pro vita sua* (London: Longman, 1878), 239.
32. St. Anselm, *Prosl. prooem.*: PL 153, 225A.
33. Eph 1:18.
34. DV 5.
35. St. Augustine, *Sermo* 43, 7, 9: PL 38, 257–258.
36. *Dei Filius* 4: DS 3017.
37. GS 36 § 1.
38. DH 10; cf. CIC, can. 748 § 2.
39. DH 11.
40. DH 11; cf. Jn 18:37; 12:32.
41. Cf. Mk 16:16; Jn 3:36; 6:40 et al.
42. *Dei Filius* 3: DS 3012; cf. Mt 10:22; 24:13 and Heb 11:6; Council of Trent: DS 1532.
43. 1 Tm 1:18–19.
44. Cf. Mk 9:24; Lk 17:5; 22:32.
45. Gal 5:6; Rom 15:13; cf. Jas 2:14–26.
46. 1 Cor 13:12; 1 Jn 3:2.
47. St. Basil, *De Spiritu Sancto*, 15, 36: PG 32, 132; cf. St. Thomas Aquinas, STh II–II, 4, 1.
48. 2 Cor 5:7.
49. I Cor 13:12.
50. Rom 4:18.
51. LG 58; John Paul II, RMat 18.
52. Heb 12:1–2.

Chapter Two

Science and the Christian Faith: Renewing an Old Relationship

SCIENCE AND THE CHRISTIAN FAITH ARE NOT STRANGERS TO EACH OTHER. IN FACT, MANY GREAT SCIENTISTS ARE ALSO CHRISTIAN BELIEVERS.

A. New Rumors about an Old Friendship

Have you ever encountered a rumor that you and an old friend are no longer on speaking terms? Perhaps someone heard about a disagreement between you and your friend, one that was settled weeks or even months ago. The person at the source of the rumor concluded that what was a momentary, real conflict has actually become the status quo, and that you and your friend have actually become sworn enemies.

If you have had this experience, then you have a solid insight into a common misunderstanding concerning the relationship between natural science and the *Christian Faith,* the truth God has revealed in Sacred Scripture, Sacred Tradition, and the teaching of the Church. This misunderstanding is a matter of crucial importance at this moment in history.

Science and the Christian Faith are not strangers to each other. In fact, many great scientists, even today, are also Christian believers. However, this is not always apparent to many, especially to some who have important roles as opinion-makers in society. Many actually claim that growth in scientific knowledge is a process which makes belief in God difficult or unnecessary. They assume that to be friendly with science means to lose one's acquaintance with religion. Many also assume that to believe in God, especially as he is revealed in Sacred Scripture and in the teaching of the Church, is to cease being scientific.

Many scientists have arrived at the conclusion that to be scientific necessarily excludes any kind of faith. One example is the famous biologist E.O. Wilson, who left behind his Baptist upbringing as soon as he discovered the theory of evolution in his scientific studies in college. "I knew the healing power of Redemption," he tells his readers in his book *Consilience*. "But... I chose to doubt."[1] Doubt about God, not faith in him, Wilson tells us, made it possible for him to arrive at a truly scientific outlook on the world.

It should not surprise anyone that, just as Wilson rejected faith in his quest to be scientific, so others have rejected contemporary science in an attempt to maintain a religious outlook. Debates have long raged over how much of the findings of modern science can be accepted by a genuine believer, especially in the area of biological evolution. Some believers have thrown doubt on scientific findings that seem to them to threaten what they find in the pages of the Bible. Some try to use *miracles* (that is, direct interventions by God in the universe) to explain gaps in scientific data. Other believers have pointed to the inability of science to achieve absolute certainty as a sign that science is on shaky ground in all cases.

It is not surprising, then, that the opinion that science and faith are basically incompatible has become a rarely challenged principle in our society. A letter published in *Time* magazine a few years ago captures the thoughts of many. Commenting on the debate over teaching Intelligent Design Theory in American public schools, the author states as a matter of fact that believers in the Christian Faith have been at war with science for centuries.[2]

Why are so many convinced that these two old friends, science and the Christian Faith, are actually enemies? In order to understand why, we must first recognize the truth—that the Christian Faith and science have a harmony that can truly be called a friendship.

B. Fighting for the Friendship: Credibility and Affirmation[3]

The remedy for the misconception that science and the Christian Faith are enemies is to take a closer look at both, which we shall do in this text. As we do so, it will be clearly demonstrated that the Faith of the Church *affirms* and supports the value of the scientific investigation of the universe. It will also become apparent that the discoveries of science have not harmed the *credibility* of the Christian Faith (i.e., its believability on the basis of natural reason); rather, in many cases those discoveries directly support that credibility. For now, let's briefly summarize what we mean when we declare that science supports the credibility of the Christian Faith, and that the Church thoroughly affirms science as a path of knowledge.

THE FAITH OF THE CHURCH AFFIRMS AND SUPPORTS THE VALUE OF THE SCIENTIFIC INVESTIGATION OF THE WORLD.

CREDIBILITY: SCIENCE CORRECTING ITSELF

In the last two centuries a growing number of thinkers came to the conclusion that groundbreaking new scientific discoveries had damaged the credibility of the Christian Faith, including belief in God. Of course, science had not disproved the Christian Faith, but it had posed important challenges to it. Furthermore, the answers to those challenges were not very clear at the time. In the twentieth century, however, the situation began to change. Some of the conclusions of earlier scientific inquiry that had seemed difficult to reconcile with Christian belief were called into question and were even overturned by newer discoveries.

In fact, these newer discoveries, far from undermining Christian doctrines, actually began to point in a direction that made those doctrines more credible. (We will explore several examples later. One you may have already heard about is the Big Bang theory, which is now the generally accepted account of the beginnings of the universe. But there are other examples of discoveries that strengthen the credibility of religion, and we shall discuss them at length.) So, in the twentieth century the story of science did not go in the direction that some had expected: there were several "twists in the plot," so to speak. These helped to overcome some of the challenges to the credibility of the Christian Faith that had once seemed so formidable. There is an important lesson in all of this: while God's truth cannot change, the conclusions of science can and do, and often in quite unexpected ways. This should teach us not to jump to hasty conclusions about supposed "conflicts" that may later turn out to be illusory.

These new discoveries of science began to change the minds of some people. This is reflected in the title of a best-selling book, *God and the New Physics,* by the theoretical cosmologist Paul Davies. Another well-known scientist who has argued for the importance of recent discoveries for the relationship between science and religion is Sir John Polkinghorne. Polkinghorne, who was a professor of physics at Cambridge University, gave up a very successful scientific career to become an Anglican priest. He is convinced that the findings of his first career offer *credibility* to the Faith he professes in his new one.

AFFIRMATION: FAITH FOSTERS SCIENCE

The misconception that science and the Christian Faith are enemies is contradicted by a second fact, namely that the teaching of the Christian Faith regarding God and creation, above all as it is found

SOME OF THE CONCLUSIONS OF EARLIER SCIENTIFIC INQUIRY THAT HAD SEEMED DIFFICULT TO RECONCILE WITH CHRISTIAN BELIEF WERE CALLED INTO QUESTION AND WERE EVEN OVERTURNED BY NEWER DISCOVERIES.

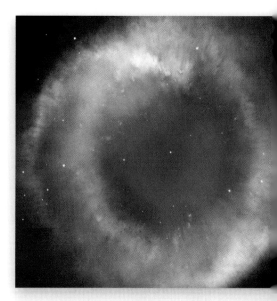

in the Bible, actually played an enormous role in fostering the development of modern science from its birth. This may surprise some people, but this is a historical fact. In studying ancient civilizations, such as Greece, China, Egypt, and the Aztec Empire of Mexico, historians discovered that many of them had achieved some impressive results in science and *technology* (the practical application of mathematics and science). But of all the world's cultures and civilizations, only the Christian culture of Western Europe made the breakthrough to a total, lasting, and far-reaching scientific approach to the world. It was from there that modern science spread to the rest of the world.

This was a puzzling fact, especially to those who assumed that Christian belief and natural science do not mix. Why would a society based on the Christian Faith, a Faith some claim to be science's enemy, be the very society that formed the cradle for the natural sciences? The answer is so surprising that it is still often overlooked. According to some leading historians, it was the *centrality of Sacred Scripture* to European culture and learning which had offered the perfect atmosphere for modern science to emerge.

This makes more sense if we give a little thought to what the Bible teaches about God and the universe. Sacred Scripture insists that the universe reflects the wisdom and goodness of its Creator. Indeed, it was created by a God who, according to Christian belief, is both Wisdom and Goodness itself. Because of this, Christian culture had confidence the world could be understood and was worthy of understanding *on its own terms.* The world was the product of a Mind, and so could be understood by minds. God, according to Scripture, had given laws to the universe "which will not pass away" (Ps 148:6). Since other civilizations lacked a strong notion of a personal and creative God, they also lacked confidence in the importance and fruitfulness of searching for principles and laws in the universe.[4]

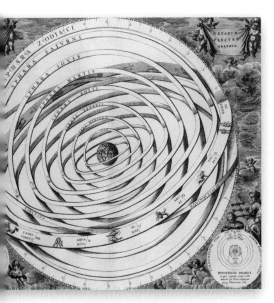

...OF ALL THE WORLD'S CULTURES AND CIVILIZATIONS, ONLY THE CHRISTIAN CULTURE OF WESTERN EUROPE MADE THE BREAKTHROUGH TO A TOTAL, LASTING, AND FAR-REACHING SCIENTIFIC APPROACH TO THE WORLD. IT WAS FROM THERE THAT MODERN SCIENCE SPREAD TO THE REST OF THE WORLD.

The scriptural and Christian belief that the universe is created by an all-good, all-powerful Creator implies that it has limits that can be found, order which can be marveled at, and a goodness that makes it valuable. It is this outlook which gave and still gives affirmation to science, and which nurtures it and encourages it to begin and continue its quest for more knowledge.[5] For those who still dream that science and the Christian Faith are enemies, history has a wake-up call. Not only has the Christian Faith been the friend of science, it actually helped to bring modern science to birth. And, as we shall see in Chapter Four, the Church has continued to play an active and positive role in the development of science for over eight hundred years.

We should bear these things in mind as we now consider some common misconceptions about the relationship between the Christian Faith and science.

C. Scientific Atheism and Scientific Creationism: Some Misconceptions about Faith and Science

False rumors about the end of a friendship are often started by people who cannot believe that the friendship could ever have been real. It should not surprise us then that those most responsible for spreading the science versus religion myth have denied that the two had anything in common in the first place. They hold belief systems that lead them to conclude that a positive relationship between science and the Christian Faith is unlikely, if not impossible.

MATERIALISM, REDUCTIONISM, SCIENTISM: WHAT YOU SEE IS *ALL* YOU GET!

One such belief system is called *materialism,* the notion that "lifeless and mindless 'matter' alone is real."[6] Put another way, materialism is the conviction that only the visible universe, that is, things that are capable of being seen, smelled, touched, heard, and tasted (or at least capable of being measured by instruments) are actually real. Materialists believe that only natural science is capable of getting in touch with reality, because only natural science makes physical, touchable, measurable things the main object of study. Closely related to materialism is *reductionism,* the idea that all of reality is reducible to its smallest physical parts. In this belief system, what seem to be higher levels of existence (like animals and humans) are merely new collections of smaller elements, arranged in a different order. Perhaps the most famous statement of reductionism came from the well-known American scientist Carl Sagan, who once said, "I, Carl Sagan, am nothing but a collection of atoms bearing the name 'Carl Sagan.'"[7]

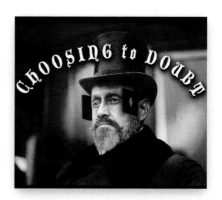

Of course, most people recognize that physical creatures are made up of atoms, just as Sagan said. However, reductionism is the belief that physical creatures, humans included, are *nothing but* collections of atoms.

The reductionist and materialist worldviews can be summarized in one term—scientism, which can also be called *scientific atheism. Scientism* is the view that "science alone can put us in touch with the ultimate depths of the world."[8] Scientistic (vs. scientific) worldviews obviously allow no room for the Christian Faith as a

Carl Sagan (1934–1996, third from left) was an American scientist, author, and television celebrity who became famous through "Cosmos," his popular 1980 TV series.

source of truth. As the Christian Faith is concerned ultimately with God, who is spiritual and not physical, those who deny that there are any non-physical realities have little patience with the claims made by the Christian Faith. Since reductionists and materialists see science as the only way to gain knowledge of things as they really are, they consider religion to be inherently incompatible with scientific thought. In particular, scientific atheism finds fault with the Christian Faith because it involves *dogmas* and *mysteries.*[9] A closer look at both will help us understand why. It will also show that scientific atheism involves a flawed understanding of what dogmas and mysteries are.

Dogmas (also known as *doctrines*) are truths revealed by Christ which, because they come from God himself, cannot be changed or challenged.[10] An example of a dogma would be the Christian belief that the eternal Son of God became man in the womb of the Virgin Mary: the dogma of the Incarnation. Scientific atheists see the believer's acceptance of dogmas as *anti-rational.*

But this objection is incorrect. To believe in a dogma on God's own authority is perfectly rational—if God does exist and has really revealed it. And dogmas, once accepted on those grounds, can be rationally explored: we can examine them by means of our naturally derived knowledge in order to understand how they fit together to form a coherent and consistent picture of reality. This is the task of theology.[11]

In fact, the Church teaches that what we believe as Christians as well as our act of believing it are in harmony with reason, as well as that God desires us to see the reasonableness of the things he has revealed, so that we can better understand the world, ourselves, as well as God himself. The Church, therefore, invites us to approach dogmas intelligently—to ponder them and penetrate more deeply into them, just as Mary "kept all these things and pondered them in her heart" (Lk 2:51). In the words of Vatican I (1869–1870), "The assent of faith is *by no means* a blind impulse of the mind."[12]

Mysteries are aspects of reality that transcend our ability to fully grasp them because they are so closely connected to the reality of God, who is infinite. An example of a mystery would be, believe it or not, *yourself.* Because the human person is made in the image of God, our own reality as human beings transcends our ability to entirely understand it.[13]

Scientism sees the Christian respect for mysteries as anti-rational because it involves the assertion that some things transcend our intellectual capacity. To say that there are things that are beyond our full comprehension, according to scientism, is to give up on thinking, to end the struggle for deeper understanding. But that which lies beyond our mental grasp does not necessarily put an end to thought.

...THE CHURCH TEACHES THAT WHAT WE BELIEVE AS CHRISTIANS AND OUR ACT OF BELIEVING IT ARE IN HARMONY WITH REASON, AND THAT GOD DESIRES US TO SEE THE REASONABLENESS OF THE THINGS HE HAS REVEALED, SO THAT WE CAN BETTER UNDERSTAND THE WORLD, OURSELVES, AND GOD HIMSELF.

In the words of physicist Stephen Barr,

> [Mysteries] do not shut off thought, like a wall. Rather they open the mind to vistas that are too deep and too broad for our vision. A mystery is what cannot be seen, not because there is a barrier across our field of vision, but because the horizon is so far away. [To name something a mystery] is a statement not of limits, but of limitlessness. The reason that there are mysteries is that God is infinite and our intellects are finite.[14]

Let us go back to the mystery of a human being. It is possible to know a human being on many levels: one can study human biology or physiology, or the range of human emotions, or even human brain waves. But in such an attempt, we begin to realize that there are activities, actions, accomplishments, and desires that go beyond the purely physical. As we realize this, what Pope John Paul II once called "the immensity of the human spirit"[15] becomes apparent, an immensity and dignity that cannot be reduced to the biological level.

In summary, the acknowledgement of mysteries does not close the human mind. Rather, it exposes it to an infinite horizon.

We will spend a good deal of time in this text discussing, and even debating with, the worldview of scientific atheism. What should be noted now is that scientism is a *belief system,* a conviction about reality. Scientism must be clearly distinguished from science as such. Science, which examines the elements of the visible world, is not the same thing as materialism, which holds that the elements of the visible world are the only things that really exist. Nor is it the same thing as reductionism, which says that all things are reducible to their physical, visible parts. In short, *science is not scientism.* Belief that only science can reveal the truth (scientism) is not a requirement for the study of science, just as the study of paintings does not require denying that other forms of art are also valuable.

The second thing that should be noted is that *scientism* involves a fatal logical flaw—it is based on an assertion that contradicts itself. As we said above, scientism is based on the belief that only science, which observes and measures physical realities, can put us in touch with truth. And yet the very statement "only science can put us in touch with truth" is itself not able to be verified by science.

If you are having a hard time grasping this, think about this statement, which is similar because it is also logically inconsistent: "Nobody goes there anymore, because it is too crowded."

In the same way, if the statement "only science can put us in touch with truth," is true, then it must be scientifically verifiable. But that assertion cannot be observed or measured through science. Thus, the very logical foundations of scientism, or scientific atheism, are a contradiction in terms and, consequently, must be recognized as inherently flawed or false.

IN ANY ATTEMPT TO KNOW A HUMAN BEING, WE BEGIN TO REALIZE THAT THERE ARE ACTIVITIES, ACTIONS, ACCOMPLISHMENTS AND DESIRES THAT GO BEYOND THE PURELY PHYSICAL.

Plato and Aristotle

SCIENTIFIC CREATIONISM

Tree of Truth

Another source of the rumor that science and faith are enemies is actually a very vocal group of believers. They are often referred to as *scientific creationists,* because of their belief that God created the universe in exactly (or almost exactly) the way described in the first creation account found in the Book of Genesis (Gn 1:1–31). Some common beliefs among scientific creationists are that the universe is only 6,000 years old and that all species were created by God directly from matter in a sudden and miraculous process. In regard to such ideas, Christoph Cardinal Schönborn, the general editor of the *Catechism of the Catholic Church* and the Archbishop of Vienna, Austria recently had this to say:

> The Catholic position on [scientific creationism] is clear.
> St. Thomas [Aquinas] says that "one should not try to defend the Christian Faith with arguments that are so patently opposed to reason that the Faith is made to look ridiculous." It is simply nonsense to say that the world is only 6,000 years old. To try to prove this scientifically is what St. Thomas calls provoking the *irrisio infidelium,* the scorn of the unbelievers. It is not right to use such false arguments and to expose the Faith to the scorn of unbelievers.[16]

Cardinal Schönborn

Before we continue, however, we should look a little more closely at scientific creationism, because it is often misunderstood and too easily dismissed. In fact, the name itself is a little misleading for two reasons. First, many believers do not hold to the exact details of the biblical creation account, and would give some room to some scientific evidence. For example, they might allow that the process of bringing the universe into its initial existence took longer than six days.

Second, the name *scientific creationism* does not get to the real reason these Christians reject some scientific data and theories. This reason is based on two truths that all believers would agree with—namely, that God is not capable of error, and that his Word given in Sacred Scripture cannot be wrong. Unfortunately, from these truths they draw a false conclusion. It is one thing to say that the purpose of the Bible is to reveal truth; it is quite another to say that it is directly concerned with the kinds of truth about the physical world that natural science investigates. Maybe unconsciously, "scientific creationists" have absorbed some of the errors of scientism, by ascribing to truths about the natural world a kind of ultimate importance, instead of realizing that the truths with which Scripture is primarily concerned are of a much higher order.

In Chapter Three, we will look more closely at the issue of *how* God's Word is without error in order to explain how it is possible to accept both science and Scripture. We will examine how Sacred Scripture itself gives indications that it does not mean to give an account of the

SCIENTIFIC CREATIONISTS RISK MAKING CHRISTIANITY SEEM RIDICULOUS IN THEIR UNNECESSARY ATTEMPTS TO INTERPRET THE BIBLE AS A SCIENTIFIC TREATISE, AN ACT THAT ST. THOMAS AQUINAS CALLS PROVOKING THE *IRRISIO INFIDELIUM,* THE SCORN OF THE UNBELIEVERS.

scientific details of the physical world, but rather shows itself open to changing views of the universe that become deeper and more accurate with time. In short, we will see that Scripture shows itself to be open to science.

D. Separation Anxiety:
A False Solution

In large part, one can trace the opinion that science and the Christian Faith are irreconcilable to the groups we just examined. But while they have fueled the rumor that science and faith are enemies, another group has attempted to dispel the rumor by asserting that science and faith have *no relationship.* In other words, while scientific atheists and scientific creationists are spreading the rumor that science and faith are not on speaking terms because they are in conflict, this third group holds that they are not speaking because they have really never met!

In their anxiety to end the rumor that science and faith are irreconcilable, many thinkers—some of whom are scientists, some of whom are believers, and some of whom are both—have argued that science and faith are really too different to be in conflict. Ian Barbour gives an excellent explanation of this position, which he calls the "Independence Model"—"Proponents of this view say there are two jurisdictions [i.e., science and faith] and each party must keep off the other's turf. Each must tend to its own business and not meddle in the affairs of the other."[17] We will refer to this approach as separationism, because it maintains that science and the Christian Faith must always be kept separate in every way possible.

According to separationism, a person can embrace both scientific discoveries and religious customs and values without having to worry about contradictions, because their jurisdictions never intersect.

GOING FOR THE GOULD?

One influential separator of science and faith is the late biologist *Stephen Jay Gould.* According to Gould, science and religion are actually concerned with two entirely different kinds of truths. Science, he tells us, is about facts; religion is about "values and meaning." No war can exist between them, because they dwell on separate continents with no way of crossing from one to the other.[18]

Euclid of Alexandria

...WHILE SCIENTIFIC ATHEISTS AND SCIENTIFIC CREATIONISTS ARE SPREADING THE RUMOR THAT SCIENCE AND FAITH ARE NOT ON SPEAKING TERMS BECAUSE THEY ARE IN CONFLICT, SEPARATIONISTS HOLD THAT THEY ARE NOT SPEAKING BECAUSE THEY HAVE REALLY NEVER MET!

Stephen Jay Gould

Sir Isaac Newton (1643–1727), one of the greatest scientists of all time, saw clearly that science and the Christian Faith cannot be neatly separated. As he put it, "Gravity explains the motions of the planets, but it cannot explain who set the planets in motion. God governs all things and knows all that is or can be done."

St. Thomas Aquinas (ca. 1225–1274), one of the greatest theologians in the history of the Church, also recognized that science and the Christian Faith are concerned with many of the same realities, although they approach them in different ways.

Gould's approach is attractive to many people. By separating science and all religious beliefs, including the Christian Faith, into their own compartments and keeping them neatly tucked away from each other, Gould intends to resolve potential problems and conflicts before they even begin.

However, this very tidy separationist approach has a big problem—it involves a complete misunderstanding of the Christian Faith.

GETTING THE FACTS ABOUT THE CHRISTIAN FAITH

Contrary to the view held by the separationists, the Christian Faith is not just interested in values and meaning, but in facts as well. The problem with separationism can be explained in a single sentence: *the Christian Faith considers facts as having value and meaning, and values and meaning as factual.* Let us look more closely at what this sentence means, and why it makes the separation approach to science and faith a dead-end.

The Christian Faith considers facts as having value and meaning. The full value of facts can only be understood in the light of faith in God. Faith in God involves the recognition that all things are *Theocentric*—that is, they are centered on God because (a) they were created by God, and (b) they were created for a purpose known to God. To know about a thing without knowing (a) and (b) is to know it in a limited sense. This does not mean that science must involve faith—as a method, it must not. But it does mean that the two really are talking about the same things, contrary to separationism.

But there is more. The Christian Faith, like science, also reveals certain facts, and calls us to put our faith in them. The Incarnation of the Son of God, who became man in the womb of the Virgin Mary, is proclaimed by both Scripture and the Church to be a real event. It is a fact, something that really happened in history, although it is certainly not a fact that can be proven by science.

This is also true of other elements of faith as well, such as the belief that God is a Trinity of Persons, that Jesus rose from the dead, and that his mother was assumed body and soul into Heaven. But it does mean that the Christian Faith and science really do talk about many of the same realities, contrary to separationism.

The Christian Faith considers values and meaning as factual. That is, they are not mere opinions, which change from person to person. Values and meaning are not human daydreams projected onto a neutral landscape of facts which science lays out for us. The statement "murder is evil" is no less true than the statement "the water molecule contains two hydrogen atoms." Its truth just happens to be known in a different way than by looking into a microscope.

The objectivity and factuality of values and meaning has often been overlooked by the modern world, but has never been overlooked by the Catholic Church. In the words of Joseph Cardinal Ratzinger, now Pope Benedict XVI:

> We must again learn to understand that the great ethical insights of mankind are just as rational and just as true as—*indeed more true than*—the experimental knowledge of the realm of the natural sciences and technology. They are more true, because they... have a more decisive significance for the humanity of man.[19]

At a recent conference on the human genome project, Camillo Cardinal Ruini expressed exactly this point in relation to science's new ability to map out the entire genetic information present in human beings. The map of the human genome is being drawn, he told his audience, just at the point when it seems that humans may have lost the map of the meaning and value of life itself.[20]

The point is clear—there is a real map to life, just as there is now a real map of the human genome. Science and the Christian Faith both really tell us about *what is*—not just what we happen to feel or imagine.

In an effort to make peace between science and religion, separationists actually make them strangers. In the process, they correctly understand science, but entirely misunderstand the Christian Faith.

E. Looking Ahead

We have looked at some mistaken ideas of the relation between science and religion. Some want to put science and faith into a no-holds-barred cage match, while others want to put each in its own little airtight box where they can do no harm to each other. But what is the right relationship? There must be a way of looking at the universe that respects both science and the Christian Faith, a way which unites facts, values, and meaning. Can we really let science be science, let faith be faith, and yet still celebrate the places where they meet? If not, then even if science and the Christian Faith seemed to be friends, their friendship would be false.

In the next chapter, we will find guidance on this question from a source that some might find surprising—Sacred Scripture. As we discussed above, the Christian Faith and its predominance in Western culture made Europe an excellent incubator for the natural sciences in their infancy. But more specifically, *it was the Christian belief that Sacred Scripture is God's Word that made Western civilization a perfect place for science to grow.*

The Bible, which has often been rumored to be thoroughly anti-scientific, holds many surprises between its covers. But perhaps the most unexpected surprise the Bible has for our culture today is this: the very "DNA" of science itself, the "genome" of scientific investigation, is written across its ancient pages.

To stay on the cutting edge of the relationship between faith and science, therefore, we too must open the covers of the Bible, God's own Word written in the words of men.

Supplementary Reading

"The Christian Faith and the Birth of Science"

(excerpted from Peter E. Hodgson, Theology and Modern Physics [Ashgate Publishing, 2006], pp.19–21)

Viewed in the widest historical perspective, the explosive development of science in seventeenth-century Europe is one of the most astonishing events in the whole of human history. It makes that civilization unlike any other. For the first time people all over the world are joined together by rapid communications, easy travel and extensive trade. Why did this understanding of the detailed structure of the world that we call science develop and come to maturity just when and where it did? This is a question that can lead us to the heart of the relation between science and the Christian basis of our civilization.

...Science as we know it is based on certain definite beliefs about the world. Many of them were first formulated by the ancient Greeks but were not sufficient to establish science as a continuing enterprise. Modern science began only when they were reinforced and extended by the religious beliefs of the Hebrews and finally brought to completion by the theology of Christian Europe.

If we look at the great civilizations of the past, in China and India, in Babylon and Egypt, in Greece and Rome, we frequently find well-developed social structures, magnificent artistic and architectural achievements, imperishable drama and philosophy, but nothing remotely equivalent to modern science. We find great skill in the working of wood and metal, ingenious mechanical contrivances and perceptive philosophical speculations about the world, but not the detailed quantitative understanding of matter, from quarks to galaxies, expressed as the solution of a few differential equations, that is the hallmark of the more developed areas of modern science.

Supplementary Reading

Most of the great civilizations of the past were able to provide all the material requirements for the growth of science. There was a leisured class, technical skills, and systems of writing and mathematics. Obviously this by itself is not enough. What was lacking was the attitude towards the material world that is the essential precondition of science, and in some cases a social structure that allows new ideas to flourish.

What do we have to believe before we can hope to become scientists? We must believe that the world is in some sense good, so that it is worthy of careful study. We must believe that it is orderly and rational, so that what we find out one day will still be true on the next day. We must believe that this order is open to the human mind, for otherwise there would be no point in trying to find it. We must believe that this order is not a necessary order that could be found out by pure thought like the truths of mathematics, but is rather a contingent or dependent order that can only be found by making experiments.

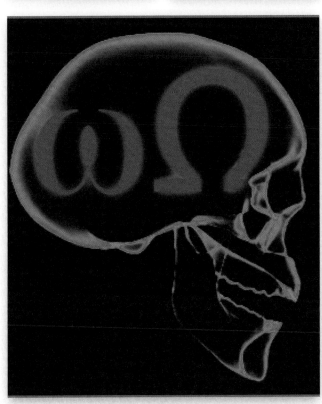

In addition to these beliefs about the world itself, the development of science depends on moral convictions such as the obligation freely to share any knowledge that is gained. Furthermore, once it becomes clear that scientific understanding can be applied to grow more food to cure diseases, then its further development is encouraged if we believe that we should do these things to help our fellow men.

These beliefs may seem obvious to us, but in the context of human history they are very special. They are not found in the ancient civilizations, and that is why science in the modern sense never developed among them. In some cases, particularly in ancient Greece, an impressive start was made by a few individuals of genius, but they lacked the support of a coherent set of beliefs shared by the whole community, and science never became a self-sustaining enterprise....

A new beginning, a fresh style of scientific thinking, was made possible by the Judeo-Christian vision of the world.

Supplementary Reading

"The Voice of Materialism, Reductionism and Scientism"

(excerpted from Stephen M. Barr, Modern Physics and Ancient Faith
[Notre Dame: University of Notre Dame Press, 2003], pp. 19–21)
(Note: The following is Barr's summary of the materialist view of nature, not the expression of his own view of nature.)

The Scientific Materialist's View of Nature

"The world revealed by science bears little resemblance to the world as it was portrayed by religion. Judaism and Christianity taught that the world was created by God, and that things therefore have a purpose and meaning, aside from the purposes and meanings we choose to give them. Moreover, human beings were supposed to be central to that cosmic purpose. These comforting beliefs can no longer be maintained in the face of scientific discoveries.

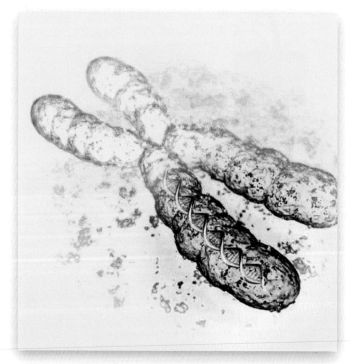

"The universe more and more appears to be a vast, cold, blind, and purposeless machine. For a while it appeared that some things might escape the iron grip of science and its laws—perhaps Life or Mind. But the processes of life are now known to be just chemical reactions, involving the same elements and the same basic physical laws that govern the behavior of all matter. The mind itself is, according to the overwhelming consensus of cognitive scientists, completely explicable as the performance of the biochemical computer called the brain. There is nothing in principle that a mind does that an artificial machine could not do just as well or even better. Already, one of the greatest creative chess geniuses of all time has been thrashed by a mass of silicon circuitry.

"There is no evidence of a spiritual realm, or that God or souls are real. In fact, even if there did exist anything of a spiritual nature, it could have no influence on the visible world, because the material world is a closed system of physical cause and effect. Nothing external to it could affect its operations without violating the precise mathematical relationships imposed by the laws of physics. The physical world is 'causally closed,' that is, closed off to any non-physical influence.

Supplementary Reading

"All, therefore, is matter: atoms in ceaseless, aimless motion. In the words of Democritus, everything consists of 'atoms and void.' Because the ultimate reality is matter, there cannot be any cosmic purpose or meaning, for atoms have no purposes or goals.

"Once upon a time, scientists believed that even inanimate objects did have purposes or goals: 'ends' which they sought or toward which they tended. For example, heavy objects were said to fall because they sought their proper place at the center of the earth. That was the idea in Aristotelian physics. It was precisely when these ideas were overthrown four hundred years ago that the Scientific Revolution took off. With Galileo and Newton, science definitively rejected 'teleology' in favor of 'mechanism.' That is, science no longer explains phenomena in terms of natural purposes, but in terms of impersonal and undirected mechanisms. And, of course, if there are no purposes anywhere in nature, then there can be no purpose for the existence of the human race. The human race can no longer be thought of as 'central' to a purpose that does not exist.

"Science has dethroned man. Far from being the center of things, he is now seen to be a very peripheral figure indeed. Every great scientific revolution has further trivialized him and pushed him to the margins. Copernicus removed Earth from the center of the solar system. Modern astronomy has shown that the solar system itself is on the edge of a quite ordinary galaxy, which contains a hundred billion other stars. That galaxy is, in turn, one of billions and perhaps even an infinite number of galaxies. Earth is an insignificant speck in the vastness of space: its mass compared to all the matter in the observable universe is less than that of a raindrop compared to all the water in all the oceans of the world. All of recorded history is a fleeting moment in the eons of cosmic time. Even on this cozy planet, which we think of as ours, we are latecomers. Homo sapiens have been around at most a few hundred thousand years, compared to the 4 billion years of life's history. The human species is just one branch on an ancient evolutionary tree, and not so very different from some of the other branches—genetically we overlap more than ninety-eight percent with chimpanzees. We are the product not of purpose, but of chance mutations. Bertrand Russell perfectly summed up man's place in the cosmos when he called him 'a curious accident in a backwater.'"

Study Guide

Science and the Christian Faith: Renewing an Old Relationship

VOCABULARY

Define the following terms:

1. The Christian Faith
2. Credibility
3. Affirmation
4. Technology
5. Scientism (Scientific Atheism)
6. Materialism
7. Reductionism
8. Dogma (Doctrine)
9. Mystery
10. Scientific Creationism
11. Independence Model
12. Separationism
13. Stephen Jay Gould
14. Theocentric

Dialogo di Galileo

STUDY QUESTIONS

1. How is the relationship between the Christian Faith and science much like a human relationship that is plagued by false rumors?
2. What is the truth about the relationship between the Christian Faith and modern science? What roles do each play in the relationship?
3. How does the history of science reveal the closeness between the Christian Faith and science?
4. Explain the two key elements of the Christian Faith which scientism rejects. Why is this rejection misguided?
5. Why is scientism a flawed position from the perspective of logic?
6. What motivates scientific creationism to reject modern science?
7. Why is separationism a false approach to "reconciling" the Christian Faith and science from the perspective of facts?
8. Why is separationism a false approach to "reconciling" the Christian Faith and science from the perspective of values and meaning?

Study Guide

PRACTICAL EXERCISES

1. The various positions on the relationship between faith and science discussed in this chapter are present in our society today, and reveal a widespread disagreement about that relationship. Speak with someone outside of your class about the relationship between faith and science. List the various positions, and ask him/her what position most closely resembles his/her own. Without judging or identifying the person, explain their reasons for their answer to the class.

2. Think of some realities in human life that all humans experience and that cannot be fully explained by science. Make a list of these realities. With this list in mind, can scientism do full justice to the fullness of human experience? Explain.

3. The human person is a mystery of faith because, although the human body can be completely understood by science in terms of physical processes, the highest human realities cannot, especially the human desire for union with God. Describe another mystery of faith that cannot be completely comprehended by human reason.

4. The statement "Only science can uncover the truth about the world" is a logically inconsistent statement. Make a list of other logically inconsistent statements.

Endnotes

1. E.O. Wilson, *Consilience: The Unity of Knowledge* (New York: Knopf, 1998), 6.
2. "Letters," *Time*, September 5, 2005.
3. John F. Haught, *Science and Religion: From Conflict to Conversation* (New York/Mahwah: Paulist, 1995), 9. Haught's original terminology is "confirmation" and "credibility;" I have altered the former term to "affirmation."
4. Stephen M. Barr, *Modern Physics and Ancient Faith* (Notre Dame: University of Notre Dame Press, 2003), 66–68 (hereafter referred to as *Modern Physics*); cf. Wilson, 31.
5. Haught, *Science and Religion*, 22.
6. John F. Haught, *God After Darwin: A Theology of Evolution* (Boulder: Westview, 2000), 1.
7. Clarke, 247.
8. John F. Haught, *Deeper than Darwin: The Prospect for Religion in an Age of Evolution* (Boulder: Westview, 2003), 32.

9. Barr, *Modern Physics*, 11–15.
10. Cf. CCC 88.
11. Barr, *Modern Physics*, 11–12.
12. *Dei Filius*, 3: DS 3009, as quoted by Barr, *Modern Physics*, 12.
13. By the way, these two examples are closely related; as the Church teaches in the *Catechism*, "'In reality it is only in the mystery of the Word made flesh that the mystery of man truly becomes clear.'" (CCC 359; cf. Vatican II, *Gaudium et spes*, 22).
14. Barr, *Modern Physics*, 14–15.
15. John Paul II, "Address to a group of scientists gathered to honor the centenary of the birth of Albert Einstein" (September 28, 1979).
16. Christoph Cardinal Schönborn, "In the Beginning God Created..." Internet. Available from http://stephanscom.at/edw/katechesen/articles/2005/12/02/a9719/; accessed April 2, 2007. This has been reproduced as part of *Chance*

or *Purpose? Creation, Evolution, and a Rational Faith*, trans. Henry Taylor, ed. Hubert Philip Weber (San Francisco: Ignatius Press, 2007), 37–38.
17. Ian G. Barbour, *Religion and Science: Historical and Contemporary Issues* (New York: HarperCollins, 1997), 84.
18. Stephen J. Gould, *Dinosaur in a Haystack* (New York: Harmony, 1995), 48.
19. Joseph Ratzinger, *A Turning Point for Europe? The Church in the Modern World—Assessment and Forecast* (San Francisco: Ignatius Press, 1994), 35–36.
20. "Genome Known, but Meaning of Life Lost," in Zenit: *The World Seen from Rome Daily Dispatch*, November 28, 2005. Internet. Available from www.zenit.org; accessed April 11, 2007.

Chapter Three

The Big Bang about Creation: Is Sacred Scripture Anti-Science?

FROM THE VERY BEGINNING OF THE CHURCH'S HISTORY, SACRED SCRIPTURE HAS ALWAYS BEEN RECOGNIZED AND REVERED AS THE WORD OF GOD.

A. The Bible: God Reaching Down, Humanity Reaching Up

For a Christian, there can be no doubt about the importance of the Bible. From the very beginning of the Church's history, Sacred Scripture has always been recognized and revered as the Word of God. The *Catechism of the Catholic Church* strikingly formulates the importance of Sacred Scripture for faithful believers, comparing its veneration to that of the Eucharist, which is nothing less than Jesus Christ himself: "The Church has always venerated the divine Scriptures as she venerated the Body of the Lord: *both* nourish and govern the whole Christian life [emphasis added]."[1] A perfect illustration of this truth can be seen at Mass, during which only two things are raised up by the priestly minister: the consecrated Host, and the Book of the Gospels.

Therefore, like the Eucharist, Sacred Scripture is divine. And yet the Eucharist is not simply divine; it is also a human reality. Jesus Christ, who is really present in the Eucharist, is the Word who became flesh. He is fully God and fully human, a unity of both in his one Divine Person. It should not surprise us, then, that the Bible is fully human also—it has God as its Author, but he is its Author only through human instruments: "God is the author of Sacred Scripture because he inspired its human authors; he acts in them and by means of them."[2] God "writes" the Bible by divinely inspiring

"And the Lord God said, 'Let there be light'; and there was light." (Genesis 1:3)

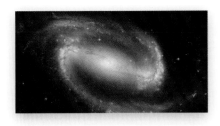

THE BIBLE REFLECTS TWO HISTORIES AT ONCE: IT IS THE HISTORY OF GOD REACHING DOWN TO HUMANITY, AND IT IS HUMANITY REACHING BACK, STRIVING TO UNDERSTAND AND LIVE ACCORDING TO THE TRUTH THAT GOD REVEALS.

Moses the teacher and lawgiver, one of the many to whom God entrusted his fully divine message found in the Old Testament.

members of his People to write it. And this means that the Bible reflects a long human process—it has a history.

Joseph Ratzinger, now Pope Benedict XVI, once put it this way:

> …Scripture is not a meteorite fallen from the sky… Certainly Scripture carries **God's thoughts** within it; that makes it unique and constitutes it an authority. Yet it is **transmitted by a human history.** It carries within it the life and thought of a historical society that we call the "People of God."[3]

The Bible reflects, therefore, two histories at once: it is the history of God reaching down to humanity with his truth and his saving grace, and it is humanity reaching back, striving to understand and live according to the truth that God reveals. In regard to God's reaching down, Sacred Scripture is *inerrant*—the writings it contains "teach without error his [God's] saving truth."[4] As the Second Vatican Council clearly affirmed, "we must acknowledge that the books of Sacred Scripture *firmly, faithfully, and without error* teach that truth which God, *for the sake of our salvation,* wished to see confided in the Sacred Scriptures [emphasis added]."[5]

But because the Bible is also the history of his People reaching back up to him, God's truth is transmitted through the concrete conditions of God's People in their own history: their level of learning, "the conditions of their time and culture," even their own style of writing.[6] This is why the Bible requires interpretation; above all, so that what God wants to reveal for our salvation is clearly understood even though the writings through which it comes to us are from a culture quite different and distant from our own. As the *Catechism* notes, "What comes from the Spirit is not fully 'understood except by the Spirit's action'"[7] —God's help is needed to make a correct interpretation of Sacred Scripture.

This important fact, that Scripture is divine and human, the divine Word in human words, must guide us as we approach the relationship of science and Sacred Scripture, and in particular as we approach the biblical accounts of creation found in the Book of Genesis and other parts of the Bible. This will help us avoid two opposite errors that lead to dead-ends and misconceptions. The first error is scientific creationism, which defends the divinity of God's Word, but loses sight of its humanity. The opposite error, popular with those who embrace materialism, reductionism, and scientism, sees only the human aspects of the Bible and therefore dismisses it as the product of pre-scientific ignorance. If we instead take an approach that respects both the human and the divine elements of Sacred Scripture—with the understanding that the divine truth comes to us *through* the human—we will understand Scripture properly and see that its truth allows us, and indeed encourages us, to be open to modern scientific insights.

If we take a "both/and" approach, respecting both aspects of Scripture, we will really understand it and understand how its truth is not a barrier to our openness to modern scientific insights. A "both/and" approach means embracing all three of the following points:

1) The Bible tells us, without error, all we need to know for the sake of our salvation about the world God created;

2) The Bible tells us this truth using language and images about the physical world that are not scientific; *and*

3) The way in which this truth is transmitted in the Bible has something to teach us.

Keeping this in mind, we should not expect from the Bible the precise scientific description of the world's origins that only became possible once modern scientific approaches were developed. Yet, for all the conditions that are natural to its human character, Scripture, as God's Word, truly contains a saving message about creation that remains valid for all time. Moreover, that message, by elevating our minds and teaching us to value both the world that God made and the spiritual intellect with which God endowed human beings, helped Western civilization to give birth to a scientific approach to the world.

To consider Sacred Scripture in relation to modern science we must go back to Genesis 1, the very text that has provoked so many of the debates on this issue. There we find an account of the beginning of the world and the origin of its creatures, including man, an account in which the creation of all things is completed by God in less than a week—six days, to be exact. Is this story, and the Bible as a whole, anti-scientific? Does it stand as a barrier to believers who wish to embrace the valid insights of modern science regarding the age of the universe and other crucial points? Or is there something that is being missed in the noisy debate over it?

To answer these questions about Genesis 1 is to answer the question of the whole relationship between God's Word and modern science. Let us begin by going to the creation accounts themselves— "accounts," not "account," for as we shall see later, there are several creation accounts in Sacred Scripture.

WE SHOULD NOT EXPECT FROM THE BIBLE THE PRECISE SCIENTIFIC DESCRIPTION OF THE WORLD'S ORIGINS THAT ONLY BECAME POSSIBLE ONCE MODERN SCIENTIFIC APPROACHES WERE DEVELOPED. YET IT TRULY DOES CONTAIN A SAVING MESSSAGE ABOUT CREATION THAT REMAINS VALID FOR ALL TIME.

Galileo Galilei

Albert Einstein

B. "In the Beginning": The Genesis Story of Creation (Genesis 1:1—2:4a)

The first creation account in Genesis is a piece of literature that is familiar to many people but is not often studied with care and attention. It must be read closely and in full in order to be understood.

CHAPTER ONE

1   *In the beginning God created the heavens and the earth.*

2   *The earth was without form and void, and darkness was upon the face of the deep; and the Spirit of God was moving over the face of the waters.*

3   *And God said, "Let there be light"; and there was light.*

4   *And God saw that the light was good; and God separated the light from the darkness.*

5   *God called the light Day, and the darkness he called Night. And there was evening and there was morning, one day.*

6   *And God said, "Let there be a firmament in the midst of the waters, and let it separate the waters from the waters."*

7   *And God made the firmament and separated the waters which were under the firmament from the waters which were above the firmament. And it was so.*

8   *And God called the firmament Heaven. And there was evening and there was morning, a second day.*

9   *And God said, "Let the waters under the heavens be gathered together into one place, and let the dry land appear." And it was so.*

10 *God called the dry land Earth, and the waters that were gathered together he called Seas. And God saw that it was good.*

11 *And God said, "Let the earth put forth vegetation, plants yielding seed, and fruit trees bearing fruit in which is their seed, each according to its kind, upon the earth." And it was so.*

12 *The earth brought forth vegetation, plants yielding seed according to their own kinds, and trees bearing fruit in which is their seed, each according to its kind. And God saw that it was good.*

13   *And there was evening and there was morning, a third day.*

14   *And God said, "Let there be lights in the firmament of the heavens to separate the day from the night; and let them be for signs and for seasons and for days and years,*

15   *and let them be lights in the firmament of the heavens to give light upon the earth." And it was so.*

16   *And God made the two great lights, the greater light to rule the day, and the lesser light to rule the night; he made the stars also.*

17   *And God set them in the firmament of the heavens to give light upon the earth,*

18   *to rule over the day and over the night, and to separate the light from the darkness. And God saw that it was good.*

19   *And there was evening and there was morning, a fourth day.*

20   *And God said, "Let the waters bring forth swarms of living creatures, and let birds fly above the earth across the firmament of the heavens."*

21   *So God created the great sea monsters and every living creature that moves, with which the waters swarm, according to their kinds, and every winged bird according to its kind. And God saw that it was good.*

22   *And God blessed them, saying, "Be fruitful and multiply and fill the waters in the seas, and let birds multiply on the earth."*

23   *And there was evening and there was morning, a fifth day.*

24   *And God said, "Let the earth bring forth living creatures according to their kinds: cattle and creeping things and beasts of the earth according to their kinds." And it was so.*

25   *And God made the beasts of the earth according to their kinds and the cattle according to their kinds, and everything that creeps upon the ground according to its kind. And God saw that it was good.*

26   *Then God said, "Let us make man in our image, after our likeness; and let them have dominion over the fish of the sea, and over the birds of the air, and over the cattle, and over all the earth, and over every creeping thing that creeps upon the earth."*

27   *So God created man in his own image, in the image of God he created him; male and female he created them.*

28   *And God blessed them, and God said to them, "Be fruitful and multiply, and fill the earth and subdue it; and have dominion over the fish of the sea and over the birds of the air and over every living thing that moves upon the earth."*

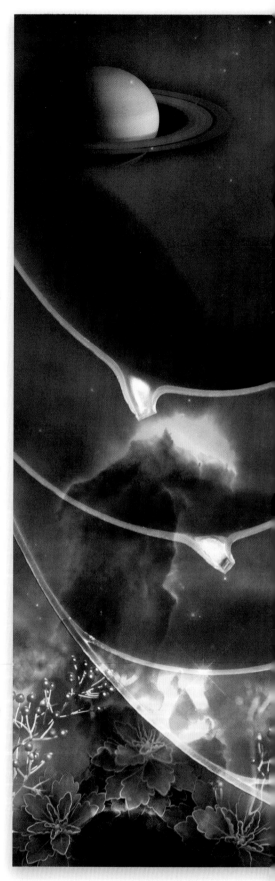

29 And God said, "Behold, I have given you every plant yielding seed which is upon the face of all the earth, and every tree with seed in its fruit; you shall have them for food.

30 And to every beast of the earth, and to every bird of the air, and to everything that creeps on the earth, everything that has the breath of life, I have given every green plant for food." And it was so.

31 And God saw everything that he had made, and behold, it was very good. And there was evening and there was morning, a sixth day.

CHAPTER TWO

1 Thus the heavens and the earth were finished, and all the host of them.

2 And on the seventh day God finished his work which he had done, and he rested on the seventh day from all his work which he had done.

3 So God blessed the seventh day and hallowed it, because on it God rested from all his work which he had done in creation.

4a These are the generations of the heavens and the earth when they were created.

When one reads this passage closely and carefully, one is able to see both its power and its beauty. But more background is necessary to fully grasp its truth. Some people, who regard themselves as scientific, dismiss this story as a primitive myth, the product of "a Bronze Age desert kingdom." Ironically, they have this dismissive attitude, in many cases, not because they know more history than the theologians do, but because they know far less. They see the apparent human limitations of the men who set down these words so long ago. Yet it is precisely because they do not really understand the human history and the human context in which the story was written that they cannot hear God's voice within it. For if God really acts *in and through* the human, as we noted above, and not merely alongside the human, then one cannot hear the divine voice unless one truly understands the human voice through which it speaks. There is a further irony: the scientific atheist dismisses the Genesis 1 account of creation as myth and superstition, not realizing that it was actually written, among other things, in order to dismiss myth and superstition.

In order to understand this, let us look at the story *behind* the story we just read—a story both human and divine, a story about God's People.

Imagine that you are a Jew, living more than five hundred years before Christ. You are a priest, with a duty of religious leadership bestowed by God upon your family line, a duty that you take as the primary purpose of your life. Your responsibilities are vital: offering sacrifices, leading the congregation in prayer, and maintaining a close adherence to the Law given by Moses, whom God raised up long ago to lead his People out of slavery in Egypt and into a land flowing with milk and honey—the Promised Land.

But you are no longer living in that land. It has been devastated by an invading empire. You, and all of God's People, have been forcibly removed from it, and have been deported to live in the land of the very empire that took it from you—Babylon. The Temple, the place of God's Presence, has been reduced to rubble. You now have a new duty—you must help your people hold on to their faith in God and to the way of life he gave to them, and you must do it against all odds.

It is in that place, during that terrible time which generations to come will call the Exile, that you first hear these words:

> *When in the height heaven was not named,*
> *And the earth beneath did not yet bear a name,*
> *Apsu, Fresh-Water, the Father of the Gods,*
> *And Tiamat, Salt-Water, Chaos, the mother of the Gods,*
> *Mingled their waters together…*
> *Then, in the midst of heaven, the gods were created…*

These words begin the *Enuma elish,* the Babylonian story of the world's creation and the central myth of the Babylonian religion. It begins with a father god, Apsu, and a mother god, Tiamat, attempting to kill their own children. It continues with them being killed by their offspring instead, and with the leader of those offspring, Marduk, making the earth and sky out of his mother's body parts. It ends with Marduk killing the demon Kingu who instigated the murderous plot As the blood of the demon drips out onto the newly formed earth, human beings are formed out of the droplets. Marduk then makes man to be a slave to all the gods, including the sun-god, the moon-god, and the star-gods.

It is a story of violence and death, filled with deeds that are the polar opposite of the way the one and true God, Yahweh, acts. Slowly, but surely, a response is growing within you and within the other priests to this dreadfully warped picture of divinity and of the origin of man and the universe. Thanks to you, a different story will be heard by the people, a story with a very different beginning: *"Bereshit bara Elohim et hashamayim ve'et ha'arets"*—"In the beginning, God [not Apsu, nor Tiamat] created heaven and earth.…"

THE GENESIS 1 ACCOUNT OF CREATION WAS WRITTEN IN ORDER TO DISMISS MYTH AND SUPERSTITION. IN ORDER TO UNDERSTAND THIS, WE MUST LOOK AT THE STORY BEHIND THE STORY—A STORY BOTH HUMAN AND DIVINE, A TRUE STORY ABOUT GOD'S PEOPLE.

The Confusion of Tongues

THE UNIVERSE WAS CREATED
BY A GOD WHO IS ONE, WHO IS
ALL-POWERFUL, WHO IS PERFECTLY
INTELLIGENT, AND WHO IS
PERFECTLY GOOD.

C. The Divine Message of the Creation Story

THE PLAIN MESSAGE: GOD, THE CAUSE OF THE COSMOS

Perhaps it is only with the bloody events of the *Enuma elish* still floating in our minds that we can best interpret all of the amazing details of the Genesis account of creation. In this beautiful picture of the origins of the world, the violence of the *Enuma elish* is utterly rejected. We see an enlightened, indeed an inspired, people responding to superstition and ignorance regarding the nature of the world and humanity.

Now that we have this background, we can get a better understanding of the first creation account's true meaning. Scholars tell us that this meaning is communicated to us in two ways: both by certain important assertions, and in the way those assertions are made. We must look at both the message and the medium, both the statements in the story and the structure of the story, to catch its total meaning.

Let us give our attention first to the message itself. We can summarize it as follows: *The universe was created by a God who is one, who is all-powerful, who is perfectly intelligent, and who is perfectly good.*

The clearest element of the creation drama of Genesis 1 is that it has a single actor. In contrast to the *Enuma elish,* there is only *one God.* Everything else that exists has God as its source and designer. In the Babylonian religion, the sun, moon, and stars were all considered to be gods who had to be worshipped. In this story, they are lights which God turns on to illuminate the earth and to measure time for the sake of humanity. God has no rival in the universe or in any of its parts. Just as no stream can rival the spring from which it flows, so no creature can be compared with the Creator. Because the world and all that it contains have been created by God out of nothing, they cannot be divine themselves.

Perhaps the most interesting element of the account is the way creation comes about. It is not the accidental by-product of a divine brawl. It is, very clearly, a planned event—there is one God, and he makes all that exists according to his deliberate intention.[8] The world exists because God willed it to be.

But God is not simply a feeling or a force in the story. His *astonishing power* is also revealed by the account, and it is infinitely greater than that of Marduk. God does not even have to exert himself in the making of the world in Genesis 1. He just speaks his word and the world springs into being, so that the universe can be defined simply as "the event of God's personal word."[9] He burns no calories, nor flexes any muscles, in the series of events, because calories and muscles are part of the creation, not of the Creator. Nothing disrupts his perfect tranquility, and a tranquil creation pours out of his own tranquility as he wills it to do so.

If there is anything active about God in the account, it is his mind. Just as the *Enuma elish* is saturated with violence, the Genesis account is saturated with intelligence, what many have called *divine rationality.* God is a profound architect, structuring and setting up a masterpiece of design:

> There is no confusion; light is distinguishable from darkness, the land from the sea. Vegetation is abundant and guarantees a rich array of food for humanity. The categorization of animals, fish and birds reflects [an] appreciation for order.[10]

And the world God creates is good, a reflection of its *perfectly good Creator.* This goodness is both manifested in its order and explicitly declared by God. Seven times he sees and declares its goodness, a number which in the Bible signifies completion and perfection.

At one point, God's goodness and rationality reach a peak of intensity in his creative action—at the creation of his image, man and woman.

The author portrays God in deep reflection and planning only once— when he creates human beings. It is as if God is looking into a mirror as he speaks. Only human beings are called God's image and likeness. While God sees each part of his creation as good, only after man and woman are present in it does he call it "very good." The message is clear—humans are not the spawn of Kingu's blood, but the reflection of God himself, "man and woman equally and in union with each other."[11]

God sees the goodness of all that he creates, but he speaks directly to his human creation, describing his will for them and the tasks they must fulfill. Only they are given the command to subdue the earth, and only they are given dominion over all the other creatures. In every way humans are to be part of the creation, but also a very unique part. *Humans are the summit of the perfection of God's creation.*

The Creator's oneness, power, rationality, and goodness are clear from the straightforward message of the account. Now we can look at the account's structure and see how it enriches the story and deepens its message.

Ezra thanks God for his help

IN EVERY WAY HUMANS ARE TO BE PART OF THE CREATION, BUT ALSO A VERY UNIQUE PART. *HUMANS ARE THE SUMMIT OF THE PERFECTION OF GOD'S CREATION.*

THE MEDIUM HAS A MESSAGE: READING THE SHAPE OF CREATION

Biblical scholars who have looked carefully at the creation account have some important details to add to our understanding of it that we might otherwise have overlooked. The rationality and goodness of the production of the world by God has a more fundamental layer

NOTE THAT WHAT IS STRESSED IN
THIS DEEPER ORDER IS NOT SO
MUCH WHAT IS MADE FIRST,
SECOND AND THIRD, BUT THAT
EACH PART OF CREATION
CORRESPONDS TO OTHER PARTS.
THE WHOLE THING FITS, AND FITS
TOGETHER PERFECTLY.

than just the events of the account. It also has a deeper order below its surface—*symmetry* (i.e., equality of measure) and proportion even characterize the way the story is told. The medium reinforces the written message and even carries its own message.

First, the six days of making (Gn 1:1–31) actually interact with each other, making two columns of events. When the days are considered in two sets, Days 1–3 and Days 4–6, each day in the first column matches the corresponding day in the second column.

On Day 1, God makes light; on Day 4, he makes lights (sun, moon and stars). On Day 2, he makes sky and sea; on Day 5 he makes birds (sky creatures) and fish (sea creatures). On Day 3 he makes the dry land and vegetation (green plants and fruit trees); on Day 6 he makes the land creatures and humans who eat these plants and fruits.

Note that what is stressed in this deeper order is not so much what is made first, second and third, but that each part of creation corresponds to other parts. The whole thing fits, and fits together perfectly. Horizontally (that is, among its creatures), the world is symmetrically interdependent, just as it is vertically dependent on God.

Looking even more closely, we can detect *another* layer of meaning— *the world God is creating is being set up precisely to support life.* In the first three days things are made that are needed for the life created in the last three days. On Day 1 and Day 4 God makes light and the sources of light that benefit all living things. On Day 2 he makes sky and sea; on Day 5 the life forms that inhabit sky and sea. On Day 3 he makes land; on Day 6 the life forms that inhabit land. The fitting together of Days 1–3 with Days 4–6 reveals that the non-living world is made for the benefit of living creatures. As we shall see in Chapter Seven, this layer of meaning fits beautifully with what modern science has discovered, namely that the very structure of the universe in its fundamental laws seems specifically designed to bring about and support living things.

If the two sets of days run side-by-side perfectly like two columns, the seventh day is the arch that completes their unity: the *Sabbath,* God's day of rest (Gn 2:1–4a). This particular aspect of the story offers a detail that science itself cannot teach or know about. It is that the world is ordered toward fulfillment, rest, and worship. God's rest is reflected in his later command to his people to keep the Sabbath (which will later become the "eighth day" of Christ's Resurrection) holy; that is, to order the Sabbath toward the One who gave rise to all things through intelligence and love.

The Sabbath, the majestic arch that binds all parts of the creation into one, is a clue for man as to what God's creation is all about. At least one thousand years after Genesis was written, St. Benedict of Nursia, the father of Western monastic life, captured this idea in his great Rule of Life, in which he says, *"Operi Dei nihil praeponitur"*—"Nothing should be put before the service of God."[12] And one thousand years after that, St. Ignatius of Loyola would write these words: "Human beings are created to praise, reverence and worship God, and by means of this to save their souls. The other things on the face of the earth are created for human beings to help them in pursuit of this goal for which they are created." In other words, all the columns of creation point toward the arch, which is the possibility of finding fulfillment in God. As the Christian mystic Meister Eckhart once put it, "God enjoys himself, and wants us to join him."

The medium is the message, or at least, it is a vital part of the message—God's architectural masterpiece, the universe, is a unity, one which reflects God's glory so that man can know God in it and serve him through it for the sake of man's own happiness.

GOD'S ARCHITECTURAL MASTERPIECE, THE UNIVERSE, IS A UNITY, ONE WHICH REFLECTS GOD'S GLORY SO THAT MAN CAN KNOW GOD IN IT AND SERVE HIM THROUGH IT FOR THE SAKE OF MAN'S OWN HAPPINESS.

D. Obstacle or Origin? Genesis 1 and Modern Science

The picture of creation drawn by the author of Genesis 1 seems a perfect picture; in fact, it seems too perfect to some. As we noted above, many dismiss it as a religious daydream. Nice try, they say, but scientifically speaking, Genesis 1 is simply a primitive, unenlightened myth.

Yet we have already seen that the Genesis view of the world was a major part of the climate necessary for science to be born and to thrive. In rejecting it outright, scientific thinkers actually are sawing away at the very branch they are sitting on. The notion of an all-good, all-powerful, intelligent Creator implies that the universe he created has discoverable limits, order, and value. Without limits, order, and value, scientific investigators would have nothing to investigate.

So what are the difficulties raised by those who wish to dismiss the creation account? The devil is in the details. Here are a few problems that are often pointed out:

1) **The Superdome Sky**—Genesis 1:6 describes the sky as an upside-down bowl which has been submerged in water, having water on all sides and above it. But, of course, we now know that the sky is not shaped like a bowl.

2) **The Order of Production**—God makes plants before he makes the sun. The problem is obvious: how could they grow?

3) **The Duration of Creation**—Although the sun and moon are not created until the fourth day, it seems as if the whole production of the universe occurs in seven, twenty-four hour periods. Modern science, however, has shown the earth itself to be at least 4.5 *billion* years old and the universe to be 13.7 billion years old.

The details of the account are clearly contradicted by modern science. How can the words that describe them be divinely inspired? There are two ways that believers have tried to answer this question. The first one is wrong—let us begin by dissecting it.

CONCORDISM: DRESSING UP THE DETAILS

In response to the growth of scientific knowledge of the details of the beginning of the universe and of the earth, some believers have tried to create a harmony between every detail of the Genesis 1 creation account and the *cosmogony* (i.e., the theory of the origin and evolution of the universe) offered by modern science. This is called *concordism*; and believers who have attempted to match up details in this way have fallen into two serious mistakes.

First, the concordists are trying to hit a moving target: science keeps changing. Later we will look at some important ways that it has changed in the last century. (See Parts II–III). As a result, concordists in the past succeeded by great ingenuity in matching the Bible to science, only to have that science later proven to be false. Here is the tragic irony: what was an attempt to strengthen faith in God actually resulted in jeopardizing that faith—the divine truth of the Bible was incorrectly tied to a discarded theory.[13]

A classic and somewhat ludicrous example occurred in the case of *Archbishop Ussher*, a seventeenth century Anglican thinker who attempted to reconcile the six-day creation account with the physics of Sir Isaac Newton. In his strained attempt at harmonization, he announced that the creation began in the year 4004 BC on Sunday, October 23, at 9:00 a.m.[14]

> SOME BELIEVERS HAVE TRIED TO CREATE A HARMONY BETWEEN EVERY DETAIL OF THE GENESIS 1 CREATION ACCOUNT AND THE COSMOGONY OFFERED BY MODERN SCIENCE. THIS THEOLOGICAL ERROR IS CALLED CONCORDISM.

The second mistake involved in concordism is even more significant than the first. In artificially trying to tie the cosmogony of the Bible to a modern, scientific one, concordism actually misses the whole point of the account. To see this, we must look more closely at Genesis 1. Let us do so now with the help of a leading theologian of our day, Pope Benedict XVI.

DEALING WITH THE DAYS: WHAT GOD IS NOT TELLING US IN GENESIS 1

The beauty of the six-day account can be appreciated by anyone with a taste for ancient literature and poetic description. And its meaning can be discovered through its plain message and its structure, as we saw above. But to interpret what it means also requires discovering

Archbishop Ussher

what it does not mean. And this requires reading it in the context of the entirety of Sacred Scripture.

The Bible, the Christian Faith tells us, is a unity—it is one Book. As Pope Benedict XVI pointed out, "[The creation account in Genesis 1] is not, from its very beginning, something that is closed in on itself... Hence, the theme of creation is not set down once in only one place...."[15] In fact, there are several other creation accounts in the Bible, including a much older one which immediately follows Genesis 1 (see Gn 2:4b–25). By reading these other accounts alongside Genesis 1, we discover that certain details vary from one account to another (as the authors of the later accounts would obviously have realized), showing that, even to the authors themselves, such details were secondary to the heart of the message that God's Word was conveying. These details simply serve as different ways of grasping hold of that deeper message.

For instance, whereas in Genesis 1 man is created last, in Genesis 2 God creates man before the other living things (Gn 2:4b–7). If the details of the order of creation in Genesis 1 were part of Scripture's divine message, it would make no sense for the second story to be included. Clearly, we are dealing with the literary dimension of the story when we deal with such poetic details as the dome sky, the exact sequence of events, and the duration of creation.

CLEARLY, WE ARE DEALING WITH THE LITERARY DIMENSION OF THE STORY WHEN WE DEAL WITH SUCH POETIC DETAILS AS THE DOME SKY, THE EXACT SEQUENCE OF EVENTS, AND THE DURATION OF CREATION.

Here is another example. In Genesis 1, the message is proclaimed using the details of pagan mythology in order to correct them, to purify them of religious errors, and to orient them toward God. But Psalm 104, the great psalm of praise to the Creator, narrates God's production of the world using different details. For instance, it speaks of the sun and moon only after the man and animals. Birds and fish are referred to separately from each other, while in Genesis 1 they are created together on Day 4. As Pope Benedict XVI points out,

> Thus we can see how the Bible itself constantly readapts its images to a continually developing way of thinking, how it changes time and again... In the Bible, the images [e.g., the six days, the sky dome, etc.] are free and they correct themselves accordingly. In this way they show, by means of a gradual and interactive process, that they are only images, which reveal something deeper and greater.[16]

Is Pope Benedict XVI saying that the Bible is wrong? Obviously not. What he is saying is that Sacred Scripture has something to teach every age of history, regardless of the level of science any age may have reached. Its truth is "deeper and greater" than science, and it adopts the cosmogony of its age to express that truth. That is why, even in Scripture, the scientific details vary from creation account to creation account.

IN SCRIPTURE, SOMETHING LIKE SCIENCE IS GOING ON. THERE IS A PROCESS BY WHICH THE PEOPLE OF ISRAEL (THE HUMAN ELEMENT) INTERACT WITH VARIOUS SOURCES OF INSIGHT AND WISDOM AND PRODUCE NEW WAYS OF EXPRESSING THAT "DEEPER AND GREATER" DIVINE TRUTH, WHICH DOES NOT CHANGE AND "WILL NOT PASS AWAY."

THE DEEPER, GREATER TRUTH: SCIENCE AND SCRIPTURE

Now we can formulate the final response to the skeptic who would dismiss the Bible as anti-scientific. The images of the world and its creation given in Scripture are there to bear witness to "a deeper, greater" truth—that God creates the world in Reason and therefore establishes it as orderly, true, and good. The images are there to express this. Even in Scripture, something like science is going on. There is a process by which the people of Israel (the human element) interact with various sources of insight and wisdom and produce new ways of expressing that "deeper and greater" divine truth, which does not change and "will not pass away."

Another example of the openness of Scripture to new ways of expressing revealed truth can be found in the Book of Wisdom. The author of that Book refers to his desire and prayer for the gift of wisdom. He then describes the wisdom he was given *in scientific terms:* "For he gave me sound knowledge of existing things, that I might know the organization of the universe and the force of the elements, the beginning and end and midpoint of times..." (Gn 7: 17–18a). Here, a biblical author, inspired by God and writing centuries after the Book of Genesis was written, goes on a quest for knowledge concerning the "beginning." If the details of the Book of Genesis were to be taken as if they were scientific textbook facts, why would this inspired biblical author need knowledge of different details? As a Jew, he revered the Torah (including Genesis) as God's Word. His desire for and openness to new insights leave no doubt that "sticking to the old images such as the seven days"[17] *is to miss the picture for the frame that holds it.*

Of course, there is a major issue we have not yet touched upon: Has science overthrown the "deeper and greater" truth to which the human images in Scripture are pointing? Has God's eternal Reason (which Scripture calls his Wisdom and his Word) been shown to be absent from creation—or magnificently pervasive throughout it? Is Divine Rationality really the final word on the world and the universe?

Most of this book will be spent answering this question. For now we can say this: the more deeply the sciences have penetrated the universe, the more its rich and wonderful rationality has been revealed. Albert Einstein, perhaps the greatest scientist of the twentieth century and even of human history, was himself taken aback by this fact. "In the laws of Nature," he declared, "there is revealed such a superior Reason that everything significant which has arisen out of human thought and arrangement is, in comparison with it, the merest empty reflection."[18]

Here the notion of the six days from Genesis 1 can be rediscovered as having an enduring significance even today in our scientific age The process described there—the creation of light, of earth and sky, of celestial lights and living things—is the result of an intelligent plan, not haphazard but ordered. Its deeper, greater truth is confirmed every time scientists uncover new and deeper levels of the order of nature—from the vastness uncovered by astronomy all the way down to the minute order found in subatomic particles.

THE FINAL WORD ON CREATION: THE WORD WAS GOD

The last creation account given in Sacred Scripture was written by a Jew who was also a Christian; it is found in the New Testament in Chapter One of St. John's Gospel. In it and through it we reach down so deeply into the truth of the world that we are allowed to reach right into the identity of the Creator:

1   *In the beginning was the Word [Logos], and the Word was with God, and the Word was God.*

2   *He was in the beginning with God;*

3   *all things were made through him, and without him was not anything made that was made.*

4   *In him was life, and the life was the light of men.*

5   *The light shines in the darkness, and the darkness has not overcome it.*

10   *He was in the world, and the world was made through him, yet the world knew him not.*

14   *And the Word became flesh and dwelt among us, full of grace and truth; we have beheld his glory, glory as of the only Son from the Father.*

16   *And from his fulness have we all received, grace upon grace.*

17   *For the law was given through Moses; grace and truth came through Jesus Christ.*

18   *No one has ever seen God; the only Son, who is in the bosom of the Father, he has made him known.*

The Greek word "Logos," which is usually translated "Word," also means "Reason." So this famous passage also bears this meaning: "In the beginning was Reason, and Reason was with God, and Reason was God. He was in the beginning with God. All things came to be through him...." Thus, Divine Reason, the blueprint of the universe, becomes flesh in Jesus Christ. All things flow, not from a divine What, but a divine Who—the Son, the Image of the Father who is one with and equal to the Father, brings the universe about as an expression of God's goodness.

"IN THE BEGINNING WAS REASON, AND REASON WAS WITH GOD, AND REASON WAS GOD. HE WAS IN THE BEGINNING WITH GOD. ALL THINGS CAME TO BE THROUGH HIM...." THUS, DIVINE REASON, THE BLUEPRINT OF THE UNIVERSE, BECOMES FLESH IN JESUS CHRIST.

Clio

The Father loves the Son from all eternity, and the universe is a free overflow of that love. It is created by the Father, the power behind its existence, for and through the Son, the source of its rationality and order, in the Divine Love they share—the Holy Spirit, who is the source of its goodness. How far we have come from the *Enuma elish,* with its foreboding, terror-filled chaos of murderous deities and demons, can be seen in the words of the Christian mystic Meister Eckhart, who once declared that "the world is created out of the laughter of the Trinity."

E. The Whole Picture

For the sake of summarizing, let us go back to the three points with which we began our explanation and interpretation of Genesis. Noting that Scripture was both human and divine, we developed a *holistic (*a complete, "both/and") approach to Scripture which respects both:

~1~

The Bible tells us, without error, all we need to know for the sake of our salvation about the world God created. And in the specific case of the creation account in Genesis, we see that the story does exactly that: it reveals that the world has an all-powerful, all-good, perfectly intelligent God as its source (reflected in the logically ordered and perfectly symmetrical "six days") and its unifying summit (the "seventh day"). Its plain message and its structure both point confidently to a creation that flows from eternal Reason and reflects it. The words of St. Thomas Aquinas make this point, and then lead us to our second principle:

> With respect to the origin of the world, there is one point that is a matter of faith, that is, to know that it began by creation.... *But the manner and order according to which creation took place concerns the faith only incidentally,* in so far as it has been recorded in Scripture, and of these things [the fathers of the Church and Christian theologians], safeguarding the truth by their various interpretations, *have reported different things.*[19]

~2~

The Bible tells us this truth using language and images about the physical world that are not scientific. In regard to this aspect of Genesis 1, we see that, when we read it in the light of the rest of Sacred Scripture, we do not need to strain the details to fit modern scientific discoveries. These details are not there to give us an exact, scientific cosmogony; they are images that are open and freely adaptable to new contexts, especially to the context of new knowledge. Here we should remember that this principle is an ancient one; we can see it in Scripture itself in the Book of Wisdom.

To those believers who would demand some kind of concordism, or even worse, a strict literal interpretation that rejects modern science, we can offer the response of St. Augustine:

> [It] is a disgraceful and dangerous thing for unbelievers to hear a Christian, presumably giving the meaning of Holy Scripture, talking nonsense on [scientific subjects]… If they find a Christian mistaken in a field which they themselves know well and hear him maintaining his foolish opinions about our books, how are they going to believe those books in matters concerning the resurrection of the dead, the hope of eternal life, and the kingdom of heaven…?

> For then, to defend their utterly foolish and obviously untrue statements, [some believers] will try to call upon Holy Scripture for proof and even recite from memory many passages which they think support their position, *although they understand neither what they say nor the things about which they make assertion.*[20]

~ 3 ~

The literary way in which this truth is transmitted in the Bible has something to teach us. In regard to the creation account in Genesis 1, we saw that the total story, even in its pre-scientific details, gives a wonderful way of approaching the vastness of the universe "in a nutshell"—all of its beauty, its vastness, its incredible detail, all boils down to the glory of its Creator offered freely to humanity, finding its summit in the fulfillment which God offers it in a Sabbath rest and worship that ultimately leads to union with himself. The gift is great, but the Giver is even greater.

If the purpose of the creation accounts in the Book of Genesis had been to give us scientific knowledge about how the universe began, how stars and planets formed, and how life started on earth, we would have to judge them miserable failures. But that was obviously not their purpose. The priests of the Jewish people had other things on their minds during their woeful exile in Babylon besides physics, chemistry, astronomy, geology, and biology. Their concerns were entirely religious. And so if we think of the details of Genesis 1 as scientific details, we will be reading into them a kind of meaning of which the authors never dreamed.

The details do indeed have meaning. They were painstakingly chosen and arranged, but to teach religious truths, not scientific ones. What mattered to the authors was not whether the moon was made by the condensation of a dust cloud as once was thought, or by the impact of a large object striking the earth as is now thought, or by some other

THE AUTHORS OF GENESIS HAD
SOMETHING TO TELL US ABOUT THAT
PURPOSE. THE UNIVERSE DOES NOT
ONLY EXIST FOR ITS OWN SAKE,
BUT SO THAT THERE COULD BE LIFE.
AND LIFE DOES NOT EXIST ONLY
SO THAT THERE COULD BE PLANTS
AND ANIMALS, BUT SO THAT THERE
COULD BE RATIONAL BEINGS MADE
IN THE IMAGE OF GOD.

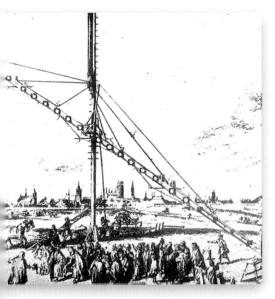

WE MUST LOOK INTO THE DISTANT
PAST AND FIRST EXPLORE THE
MARVELOUS HISTORY OF THE
CHURCH'S SUPPORT OF THE
SCIENCES. THEN WE MUST LOOK
DIRECTLY AT THAT BLEMISH AND
INTO THE LIFE OF A SCIENTIST
WHOSE NAME IS ALMOST A
SYNONYM FOR SCIENTIFIC
DISCOVERY—GALILEO GALILEI.

mechanism; what mattered to them was just that it *was* made, that it is a part of God's creation and not itself a god. They were not proposing a theory about how the universe is ordered, but calling attention to the gigantic fact that it is ordered and that its orderliness points to a divine plan. The pattern of the Six Days is not the kind of pattern that the modern physicist would capture with an equation or a graph, but the kind of pattern that reveals a purpose. And the authors of Genesis had something to tell us about that purpose. The universe does not only exist for its own sake, but so that there could be life. And life does not exist only so that there could be plants and animals, but so that there could be rational beings made in the image of God. And these beings have not been made only for themselves, but so that they could have a relationship with God, a relationship expressed in the notion of a Sabbath and in the notion of a "rest" that stands for completion and fulfillment: the eternal rest we shall have with God, the rest of which St. Augustine spoke when he said, "Our hearts are restless until they rest in Thee."

F. Looking Ahead

Sacred Scripture is not only compatible with science, but it fosters it and offers it a transcendent goal. What is true of biblical cosmogony is also true of other pre-scientific details. Throughout this text, we will return to Sacred Scripture: miracles, the second creation account in Genesis, and many other biblical topics will emerge as we continue our quest to rediscover faith on the frontiers of science.

The Bible is not simply a divinely inspired Book; as we saw at the beginning of this chapter, it is also the Book of the Church. God's Book is certainly compatible with science, but what about his Church and her teachings? For some people, the fact that the Catholic Church is pro-science is almost as surprising as the fact that Scripture is pro-science. There is a reason for this; while she has defended and promoted science for centuries, the Catholic Church also has a serious blemish on her history, one that explains why many in modern society consider her to be a harsh persecutor of scientific pioneers. To understand this, we must look into the distant past and first explore the marvelous history of the Church's support of the sciences. Then we must look directly at that blemish and into the life of a scientist whose name is almost a synonym for scientific discovery—Galileo Galilei.

Supplementary Reading

"The Voice of Vatican II:
The Human and Divine Elements
of Sacred Scripture"

*(Vatican II, The Dogmatic Constitution on Divine Revelation, Chapter III,
"Sacred Scripture, Its Inspiration and Divine Interpretation")*

11. Those divinely revealed realities which are contained and presented in Sacred Scripture have been committed to writing under the inspiration of the Holy Spirit. For holy mother Church, relying on the belief of the Apostles (see Jn 20:31; 2 Tm 3:16; 2 Pt 1:19–20; 2 Pt 3:15–16), holds that the books of both the Old and New Testaments in their entirety, with all their parts, are sacred and canonical because written under the inspiration of the Holy Spirit, they have God as their author and have been handed on as such to the Church herself. In composing the sacred books, God chose men and while employed by him they made use of their powers and abilities, so that with him acting in them and through them, they, as true authors, consigned to writing everything and only those things which he wanted.

Therefore, since everything asserted by the inspired authors or sacred writers must be held to be asserted by the Holy Spirit, it follows that the books of Scripture must be acknowledged as teaching solidly, faithfully, and without error that truth which God wanted put into sacred writings for the sake of salvation. Therefore "all Scripture is divinely inspired and has its use for teaching the truth and refuting error, for reformation of manners and discipline in right living, so that the man who belongs to God may be efficient and equipped for good work of every kind" (2 Tm 3:16–17, Greek text).

12. However, since God speaks in Sacred Scripture through men in human fashion, the interpreter of

Supplementary Reading

Sacred Scripture, in order to see clearly what God wanted to communicate to us, should carefully investigate what meaning the sacred writers really intended, and what God wanted to manifest by means of their words.

To search out the intention of the sacred writers, attention should be given, among other things, to "literary forms." For truth is set forth and expressed differently in texts which are variously historical, prophetic, poetic, or of other forms of discourse. The interpreter must investigate what meaning the sacred writer intended to express and actually expressed in particular circumstances by using contemporary literary forms in accordance with the situation of his own time and culture. For the correct understanding of what the sacred author wanted to assert, due attention must be paid to the customary and characteristic styles of feeling, speaking and narrating which prevailed at the time of the sacred writer, and to the patterns men normally employed at that period in their everyday dealings with one another.

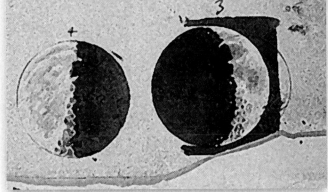

But, since Holy Scripture must be read and interpreted in the sacred spirit in which it was written, no less serious attention must be given to the content and unity of the whole of Scripture if the meaning of the sacred texts is to be correctly worked out. The living tradition of the whole Church must be taken into account along with the harmony which exists between elements of the faith. It is the task of exegetes to work according to these rules toward a better understanding and explanation of the meaning of Sacred Scripture, so that through preparatory study the judgment of the Church may mature. For all of what has been said about the way of interpreting Scripture is subject finally to the judgment of the Church, which carries out the divine commission and ministry of guarding and interpreting the word of God.

13. In Sacred Scripture, therefore, while the truth and holiness of God always remains intact, the marvelous "condescension" of eternal wisdom is clearly shown, "that we may learn the gentle kindness of God, which words cannot express, and how far he has gone in adapting his language with thoughtful concern for our weak human nature." For the words of God, expressed in human language, have been made like human discourse, just as the word of the eternal Father, when he took to himself the flesh of human weakness, was in every way made like men.

Supplementary Reading

"The Bible and Modern Science"

*(excerpted from Peter E. Hodgson,
Theology and Modern Physics
[Ashgate Publishing, 2006], pp.21–24)*

A new beginning, a fresh style of scientific thinking, was made possible by the Judeo-Christian vision of the world. The God of the Hebrews is very different from the God of Plato or the Prime Mover of Aristotle. In sharp contrast, the God of the Hebrews freely created a world completely distinct from himself, and his actions are inscrutable to men unless he freely chooses to reveal his plans.

The book of Genesis bears witness to the Hebrew belief in a transcendent creator from its opening phrases: "In the beginning God created the heavens and the earth... And God saw all that he had made, and indeed it was very good" (Gn 1:31). The Hebrew word translated as "good" also means "beautiful", and beauty is one of the most important characteristics of a scientific theory. In contrast to the confused creation myths of the surrounding nations, the creation story in Genesis has a clear logical structure, expressed in poetic form. It clearly expresses the belief in the absolute sovereignty, rationality and benevolence of God, who brings everything into being by his command and communicates his own goodness to them. Although not expressed in modern language, it contains the essential beliefs about the world that must be held if science is to flourish.

The earliest psalms tell us how God made the world and prepared it for man: He sets the heavens, the moon and the stars in their places, obeying a law that is fixed forever (Ps 148). He makes man the ruler over his works, ordering everything "in measure, number and weight" (Wis 11:20). In his reply to Job, Yahweh asks:

Where were you when I laid the foundation of the earth?
Tell me, if you have understanding.
Who determined its measurements—surely you know!
Or who stretched the line upon it?

Supplementary Reading

*On what were its bases sunk,
    or who laid its cornerstone,
when the morning stars sang together,
and all the sons of God shouted for joy? (Job 38: 4–7)*

[In the Bible, n]othing comes into being, nothing remains in being, without being loved and willed by God:

*For thou lovest all things that exist,
and hast loathing for none of the things
    which thou hast made,
for thou wouldst not have made anything
    if thou hadst hated it.
How would anything have endured
    if thou hadst not willed it?
Or how would anything not called forth by thee
    have been preserved?
Thou sparest all things, for they are thine,
O Lord who lovest the living. (Wis 11: 24–26)*

The heroic mother of the seven martyred brothers in Maccabees (2 Mc 7: 22–23) likewise expressed her belief in creation when she exhorted her sons to stand firm, saying to them:

*I do not know how you came into being in my
womb. It was not I who gave you life and breath,
nor I who set in order the elements within each
of you. Therefore the Creator of the world, who
shaped the beginning of man and devised the
origin of all things, will in his mercy give life and
breath back to you again, since you now forget
yourselves for the sake of his laws.*

When it came to the last son, Antiochus tried to persuade him to abandon the traditions of his ancestors, and appealed to his mother to advise the young man to save his life. She finally agreed to persuade her son, but she fooled the cruel tyrant with the words:

*I beseech you, my child, to look at the heaven and the earth and see everything that is in them, and recognize
that God did not make them out of things that existed. Thus also mankind comes into being. Do not fear this
butcher, but prove worthy of your brothers. Accept death, so that in God's mercy I may get you back again
with your brothers. (2 Mc 7: 28–29)*

Supplementary Reading

[In the Book of Jeremiah,] the faithfulness of God to Israel is compared with the reliability of natural phenomena (Jer 31:35). [Ps 119 does the same:]

> *For ever, O LORD, thy word*
> *   is firmly fixed in the heavens.*
> *Thy faithfulness endures*
> *   to all generations;*
> *thou hast established the earth,*
> *   and it stands fast. (Ps 119: 89–90)*

The order and stability of natural phenomena are taken for granted with the same quiet certainty as shown by the mother of the seven brothers:

> *The works of the Lord have existed*
> *   from the beginning by his creation,*
> *   and when he made them,*
> *   he determined their divisions.*
> *He arranged his works*
> *   in an eternal order,*
> *and their dominion for all generations;*
> *they neither hunger nor grow weary,*
> *and they do not cease from their*
> *   labors. (Sir 16: 26–27)*

Matter is entirely passive and it consequently endures, obedient to God's will. It is a perfect model for us. Thus according to Judeo-Christian beliefs, the world is the free creation of God from nothing. The structure of the world cannot therefore be deduced from first principles; we have to look at it, to make observations and experiments to find out how God made it.

Supplementary Reading

The *Catechism of the Catholic Church* on the Sabbath

345   The sabbath—the end of the work of the six days. The sacred text says that "on the seventh day God finished his work which he had done," that the "heavens and the earth were finished," and that God "rested" on this day and sanctified and blessed it.[21] These inspired words are rich in profitable instruction:

346   In creation God laid a foundation and established laws that remain firm, on which the believer can rely with confidence, for they are the sign and pledge of the unshakeable faithfulness of God's covenant.[22] For his part man must remain faithful to this foundation, and respect the laws which the Creator has written into it.

347   Creation was fashioned with a view to the sabbath and therefore for the worship and adoration of God. Worship is inscribed in the order of creation.[23] As the rule of St. Benedict says, nothing should take precedence over "the work of God," that is, solemn worship.[24] This indicates the right order of human concerns.

348   The sabbath is at the heart of Israel's law. To keep the commandments is to correspond to the wisdom and the will of God as expressed in his work of creation.

349   The eighth day. But for us a new day has dawned: the day of Christ's Resurrection. The seventh day completes the first creation. The eighth day begins the new creation. Thus, the work of creation culminates in the greater work of redemption. The first creation finds its meaning and its summit in the new creation in Christ, the splendor of which surpasses that of the first creation.[25]

Study Guide

The Big Bang about Creation:
Is Sacred Scripture Anti-Science?

VOCABULARY

Define the following terms:

1. Inerrant
2. Genesis 1:1—2:4a
3. Divine Rationality
4. The Exile
5. *Enuma elish*
6. Sabbath
7. Symmetry
8. Cosmogony

9. Concordism
10. Archbishop Ussher
11. Genesis 2:4b–25
12. Psalm 104
13. Wisdom 7:17–18a
14. Torah
15. John 1:1–8
16. *Logos*

The Tower of Babel

STUDY QUESTIONS

1. What are the implications of the fact that Sacred Scripture is both divine and human?
2. Does the divine and human status of Sacred Scripture have any important implications for the issue of modern science and Sacred Scripture?
3. What three principles should guide our approach to the creation account in Genesis 1?
4. What is the human background of the creation account in Genesis 1?
5. What is the message about God in the creation account found in Genesis 1?
6. What is its message about the world and humanity?
7. What does the structure of the creation account in Genesis 1 reveal?
8. Why do some scientific thinkers dismiss the creation account in Genesis 1?
9. What is concordism, and why is it the wrong approach for believers to use in defending Sacred Scripture as God's Word?
10. What is God *not* telling us through the creation account in Genesis 1?
11. Why are the pre-scientific details of the creation account not a threat to the inerrancy of Sacred Scripture?
12. What "deeper, greater truth(s)" is God really trying to tell us through the creation account and other biblical passages which refer to the world?

Study Guide

PRACTICAL EXERCISES

1. Consider each of the following Scripture verses. Explain what each has to say about the "deeper, greater truth" of creation: Isaiah 40:12–14, 18–20; Isaiah 42:25–31; Job 28:20, 23–28; Psalm 95:1–7; Psalm 8; Sirach 24:1–7; Wisdom 13:1–7; Romans 1:18–21; Colossians 1:15–18; Hebrews 1:1–3.

2. Using the data from exercise (1) above, define the "deeper, greater truth" of creation in your own words.

3. Read St. Augustine's quote on page 54. Write a paragraph in which you attempt to persuade a skeptic that the Bible is not anti-science.

Endnotes

1. CCC 141; cf. Vatican II, *Dei Verbum*, 21.
2. Ibid., 136.
3. Joseph Ratzinger, "What in Fact is Theology?" in *Pilgrim Fellowship of Faith: The Church as Communion*, translated by Henry Taylor (San Francisco: Ignatius Press, 2005), 33.
4. CCC 136.
5. Vatican II, *Dei Verbum*, 11; cf. CCC 107.
6. Ibid., 12; cf. CCC 110.
7. CCC 137; cf. Origen, *Hom. in Ex.*, 4, 5: PG 12, 320.
8. Michael Duggan, *The Consuming Fire: A Christian Guide to the Old Testament.* San Francisco: Ignatius, 1991), 74.
9. Ibid., 74.
10. Ibid., 75.
11. Ibid., 75.
12. As quoted in Joseph Ratzinger, *In the Beginning: A Catholic Understanding of the Story of Creation and the Fall*, translated by Boniface Ramsey (Grand Rapids: Eerdmans, 1986), 27–28, 38.
13. Paul Haffner, *Mystery of Creation* (Herefordshire, UK: Gracewing, 1995), 11.
14. Ibid.
15. Ratzinger, *In the Beginning*, 8–9.
16. Ibid., 15.
17. Ibid., 15.
18. Ibid., 23.
19. St. Thomas Aquinas, *Commentary on the Sentences* II.12.3.1, as quoted in Barr, *Modern Physics*, 6.
20. St. Augustine, *De Genesi ad litteram*, I. 19.
21. Gn 2:1–3.
22. Cf. Heb 4:3–4; Jer 31:35–37; 33:19–26.
23. Cf. Gn 1:14.
24. St. Benedict, *Regula* 43, 3: PL 66, 675–676.
25. Cf. *Roman Missal*, Easter Vigil 24, prayer after the first reading.

Chapter Four

Patroness or Persecutor? The Catholic Church and Scientific Discovery

A. The Catholic Church, Patroness of Science

As we begin our investigation of the Church's relationship to the sciences, we are faced with a question—is the Church a patroness (that is, a "sponsor" and a "supporter"[1]) of the sciences, or is she a persecutor of scientists? As we will clearly see, the Church is a patroness of the sciences—her history is full of examples of her sponsorship and support of the sciences. First, she has formally nurtured the sciences in her teaching and in her actions. Second, members of the Church throughout her history have been inspired to enter into the scientific arena and have made momentous contributions to the progress of the sciences.

Later, we will consider a sad event in this otherwise positive history in which some Church officials made the mistake of persecuting a scientist. It is an event modern historians refer to as "the Galileo affair." But as we shall see, it is really a rare exception to an otherwise excellent relationship.

GREAT CATHOLIC MOMENTS IN FAITH AND SCIENCE: THE "PRE-NATAL PERIOD"

Science as a formal, systematic, mathematical study of the natural world is a rather recent development, and did not fully blossom until the latter half of the second Christian millennium. But the Church's patronage predates the birth of modern science. In fact, certain moments in Catholic teaching actually laid the groundwork for the birth of modern science, and occurred during the "pre-natal period"

Galileo's telescope

just before the emergence of the scientific approach to the universe. We have seen in Chapter Three how Sacred Scripture, which the Church recognizes as the Word of God,[2] is front and center in this history. Now let's consider the role played by the Church herself.

The first moment of direct importance to science in Church history occurred at the *Fourth Lateran Council (Lateran IV)*, an ecumenical council of the bishops in union with the pope (and therefore an infallible council) in the year 1215. It was there that the Church solemnly taught that God created the world "out of nothing" (*ex nihilo* in Latin) and that his creation, unlike God himself, had a beginning in time.[3] Both of these ideas are biblical,[4] and both are crucial to a scientific outlook.

First, by teaching that the universe was created out of nothing, the Church dispelled a popular idea, born in ancient times, that the world was somehow divine, supernatural in itself, and not subject to discoverable principles and laws, such as the Law of Gravity. This allowed people to approach the world scientifically and not as if it had its own will and mysterious personality.[5] In fidelity to Genesis 1, the Church at the Fourth Lateran Council continued to oppose false ideas such as those we saw gruesomely illustrated in the *Enuma elish*.

The Lateran IV declaration that the universe had a real starting point, a beginning in time, was another crucial ingredient in the soil which the seeds of modern science needed to germinate and grow. Many in the ancient world thought that the universe was caught up in an ongoing cycle, a great hamster wheel in which all events repeat themselves over and over again. But the revelation that there was a real beginning encouraged believers to think in terms of real starting points, to look for causes in the past for things in the present, and to discover patterns that are there not simply because the "Great Cycle" always brings them back, but because they have some real relationship to other things.[6]

God made the world out of nothing, and so the world was free to be itself—not a disguised form of divinity. And it had a beginning in time, which meant that cause and effect relationships were of the utmost importance in understanding it from its beginning to its end. *These key beliefs created questions. Science grew out of the intelligent attempt to answer those questions.*

Only sixty-two years after Lateran IV, another teaching moment in Church history contributed further to the birth of science. In the year 1277, Bishop Stephen Tempier of Paris rejected the Aristotelian idea that God had to create the universe as we see it now. Aristotle had taught that the universe could not be different than we find it to be; that it "had" to be the way it is or not at all. For example, the Aristotelians said that a true "vacuum" is an absolute impossibility. But this kind of limit on God, Bishop Tempier said, contradicts the doctrine of God's omnipotence. Since God is all-powerful, He could have made a world where vacuums exist. This teaching stimulated people to think about vacuums and how they would behave if they did exist.

Similarly, Tempier condemned the Aristotelian idea that there could not possibly be other worlds. So questions such as whether other worlds exist or vacuums exist could not be answered except by seeing what God had actually chosen to create. In other words, by rejecting certain Aristotelian ideas in his authoritative role as a bishop, Tempier pushed Western thought away from the idea that we can know what the universe is by *pure logic without experimentation*.[7] Because God is free in creating the world, we have to take the world on its own terms—we have to explore it to know it.

Results of scientific importance were quick to follow—only fifty-three years after Tempier's decree, in 1330, *John Buridan*, a professor at the Sorbonne in Paris, originated the principle of *impetus*—the notion that God set in motion the heavenly bodies, but that they remained in motion without further divine (or angelic) action. With Buridan we are one step away from a sentence you may well be familiar with from your own physics (or physical science) classes: "a body, once in motion, tends to remain in motion." That sentence is Sir Isaac Newton's First Law of Motion, a foundation stone for modern physics, though relativity theory and quantum mechanics have since added new depth to this old and important insight.[8]

THE CHURCH AND THE GROWTH OF THE SCIENTIFIC AGE

The Church declared these teachings before the scientific age began. When science finally got going, it found the Church ready to embrace it. Perhaps the most important moment in this long history occurred at the *First Vatican Council* (Vatican I) in 1869–1870, particularly in the Vatican I Dogmatic Constitution on the Catholic Faith, entitled *Dei Filius*.

This important proclamation asserted a number of teachings of significance for the relationship between the Christian Faith and the sciences. It repeated earlier statements that the world was created out of nothing, in time, as an act freely undertaken by God.[9] But it also helped to establish a certain "rule of thumb" regarding how a believer should approach the difficulties which may arise in the "dialogue" between science and faith:

> …there can never be a real conflict between faith and reason, since the same God who reveals mysteries and infuses faith has bestowed the light of reason on the human mind, and **God cannot deny himself**, nor can truth ever contradict truth.[10]

In other words, science, which comes from the use of God-given reason, and the Christian Faith, which comes to us through the Church established by God, cannot really be at odds. If they seem to be, then

Science, it is widely agreed, originated from two main sources. One was the need to develop practical knowledge and to pass it from generation to generation. The other was a more spiritual concern with the nature and origin of the world. Common to both of these well-springs of science was an appreciation of the regularity of Nature. One of the first scientists to make frequent use of the concept of a law of Nature, in the sense that we now use that term, was the Franciscan friar and scholar Roger Bacon (c. 1214–1292).

In Ephesus, St. Paul performed miracle after miracle, and conversions were many. The new converts brought their books of magic and burned them in public. (cf. Acts 19: 1–20)

This event dramatizes the effect the Christian Faith had on superstitious and paganistic views of nature, paving the way for the Scientific Revolution.

we have not fully understood one or the other. God the Revealer is none other than God the Creator.

The *Second Vatican Council* (Vatican II) of 1962–1965 would apply what Vatican I had decreed in general about the relationship of faith and reason to the sciences in particular. In this regard, it taught specifically about the freedom of science, for which it uses the word *autonomy*—that is, the freedom to engage in scientific discovery and speculation without artificial constraints. It begins by deploring those situations, such as in the Galileo case, where this autonomy was not respected by believers:

> We cannot but deplore certain attitudes (not unknown among Christians) deriving from a shortsighted view of the rightful autonomy of science; they have occasioned conflict and controversy and have misled many into thinking that faith and science are opposed.[11]

In this statement, Vatican II revealed the distance between the Catholic position and positions like scientific creationism, which we discussed in Chapter Two. Then it lays out the proper understanding:

> …there are "two orders of knowledge" which are distinct, namely faith and reason; and … the Church does not forbid that "the human arts and disciplines use their own principles and their proper method, each in its own domain;" therefore "acknowledging this just liberty," this Sacred Synod affirms the legitimate autonomy of human culture and **especially of the sciences**.[12]

Once again, the respect with which the Church approaches the sciences is reaffirmed. Now that the Church's teaching has been considered, let us look at her actions. In this regard, we have a picture that paints a thousand words.

THE PONTIFICAL ACADEMY OF SCIENCES

In 1603, the *Academy of Lynxes* named after a wild feline with extremely large eyes was founded in Rome under the patronage of Pope Clement VIII. The purpose of the Academy was to develop "a method of research based upon observation, experiment, and the inductive method"—in other words, a truly *scientific* method. Its unusual name came from *Federico Cesi*, the Roman prince who started the Academy, and referred to his desire that the scientists who worked there have eyes as sharp as wildcats in order to penetrate the secrets of nature, on both the tiniest and the largest levels.[13] It predates all other existing scientific societies, including the English Royal Society and the French Academy of the Sciences.[14]

The leader of the Academy of the Lynxes was a very well-respected scientist—Galileo Galilei, whose story we shall consider shortly.

Although it has seen periods of inactivity and even dissolution, the Academy has always been refounded, and in 1937 received its present name from Pope Pius XI—the *Pontifical Academy of Sciences* ("pontifical" refers to the pope, who is also known as the Roman *Pontiff*). Its goal is "the promotion of the progress of the mathematical, physical, and natural sciences, and the study of related... questions and issues."[15] Since 1908, it has had thirty-six Nobel Prize winners among its members.[16]

As should be expected on the basis of the Church's teaching, the Pontifical Academy of the Sciences enjoys autonomy as a scientific organization.[17] It includes scientists without regard to their membership in the Catholic Church, recognizing that all human beings are capable of reason, and therefore, of good science.

In this great and internationally esteemed Academy, the Church offers a clear example of her love and respect for the sciences. It is a respect which has not just been a blessing to the sciences in general, but has also given the members of the Church, the blessing to engage in scientific discovery. The number and variety of Catholics who have responded to this blessing are living proof that faith and science both share a home in the Church's heart.

Let us turn to these great Catholics now, but with a special focus: let us consider only priests and bishops who have engaged in scientific discovery. By doing so, we focus our attention on a group that by their very vocation are at the heart of the Church's life.

B. Priest-Scientists throughout the Ages[18]

In response to the popular misconception that the Church seeks to suppress the natural sciences, rather than foster them, the French scientist and Catholic Pierre Duhem (1861–1916) often referred to the "extreme liberty" which the Church offers to Catholics who are engaged in scientific discovery.[19] Perhaps there is no better way to see this extreme liberty than to observe how many great scientists the Church has had within the ranks of her bishops and priests throughout history.

THE MIDDLE AGES

It was once believed that very little original scientific work was done in the Middle Ages. The thought was that medieval scientists just repeated whatever Aristotle and other ancient scientists had said without questioning it, and that new ideas had to wait for the time of such figures as Copernicus, Kepler, and Galileo. Historians such as

Pierre Duhem, A.C. Crombie, and Edward Grant have shown that this is not true. Medieval scientists took vitally important steps that led the way to the great breakthroughs of the 1600's. Most of those medieval scientists who took these steps were members of the clergy. Here are the most important ones:

Robert Grosseteste (1168–1253) was bishop of the City of Lincoln in England in the thirteenth century. His originality lay in the fact that he used both mathematical analysis and experimentation in the study of the behavior of light (the branch of science called "optics"). These were vitally important steps in the development of truly empirical science. Grosseteste formulated a geometric law for the refraction of light that was qualitatively correct, and used it to explain (correctly) how lenses magnify images.

Roger Bacon (c. 1214–1294) was a student of Grosseteste and an English Franciscan monk. Some credit Roger Bacon with the invention of the telescope. Whether he actually constructed a telescope or not, his writings certainly predicted the construction of devices that would make distant objects look very near. Like his teacher Grosseteste, Roger Bacon strongly emphasized in his writings the importance of both experimentation and mathematics in science, and so helped lay the groundwork for modern scientific methods.

St. Albert the Great (1200–1280) (also known Albertus Magnus) was a German Dominican priest and later a bishop. He is famous for being the teacher of St. Thomas Aquinas. St. Albert played an important role in introducing the science of the ancient Greeks and the Arabs into the curriculum of medieval universities. Like Grosseteste and Bacon, he emphasized in his writings the importance of an experimental approach to science. And he practiced what he preached, by doing a great amount of original observational work in botany and zoology, especially in the classification of plants, flowers, and fruits; in animal reproduction and embryology; and in the study of insects. For example, he was the first to distinguish between thorns and prickles on the basis of their formation and structure, to note the influence of light and heat on the growth of trees, to establish that sap is tasteless at the root of a plant but becomes flavored as it ascends, and to discover that ants lose their sense of direction when their antennae are removed. *The Dictionary of Scientific Biography* calls his work *On Vegetables and Plants* "a masterpiece for its independence of treatment, its accuracy and range of detailed description, its freedom from myth, and its innovation in systematic classification."

Thomas Bradwardine (1290–1349), who became Archbishop of Canterbury in England, analyzed Aristotle's ideas on motion and showed that they were mathematically inconsistent. He then attempted to develop a mathematical law that related the force acting on a body, the body's resistance to force, and the resulting velocity of the body. Even though Bradwardine's law was not correct, it was the first attempt to formulate a mathematical law of motion. And it illustrates both the creativity of medieval scientists and their willingness to criticize the mistakes of the science that they inherited from the ancient world.

Nicholas Oresme (1329–1392), who was bishop of the City of Lisieux in France, was the most brilliant scientist of the Middle Ages. Oresme was not only very original, but also remarkably broad in his interests and accomplishments. He made contributions to musicology, psychology, physics, and mathematics, and is considered the greatest economist of the Middle Ages.

In mathematics, Oresme discovered the rules for combining "exponents," and even discussed fractional exponents and irrational exponents. He developed the use of simple graphs to plot physical quantities, thus anticipating by three centuries some of the ideas of Cartesian "analytic geometry." He used such graphical methods to prove the "Merton theorem," which gives the distance traversed by a uniformly accelerating body. Oresme proposed that the speed of a falling body is proportional to the time it has fallen, which is correct and is equivalent to the famous "law of falling bodies," which Galileo discovered almost three hundred years later. Oresme argued that the apparent motion of the stars could be explained by the earth's rotation on its axis, and the analysis by which he refuted common physical objections to this was superior in some ways to those later given by Copernicus and Galileo, because he understood how to decompose motion into horizontal and vertical components.

Nicholas of Cusa (1401–1464) was a German Cardinal who died nine years before Copernicus was born. Cusa (also called Cusanus) was an important figure in medieval philosophy. In fact he was really more of a theologian and philosopher than a scientist. For theological and philosophical reasons, Cusa suggested that the universe is infinitely large and has no center and that all bodies in the universe, including both the earth and the sun, are in motion in infinite space. He also theorized favorably about the existence of intelligent life on other planets, which he thought was probable due to God's creativity.

Historians of science rightly admire the boldness of Copernicus and Galileo in suggesting that the earth was in motion and that the sun rather than the earth was at the center of the universe, and rightly disapprove of those who attempted to quiet them. Yet it is not often mentioned that even before them, Nicholas of Cusa had proposed even bolder ideas.

Nicolaus Copernicus (1473–1543), the great Polish astronomer, was probably never ordained a priest. However, we include him in this list, because he did hold ecclesiastical office: he was the "canon" of Frauenberg Cathedral. It was his great book *De revolutionibus orbium coelestium* ("On the Revolutions of the Heavenly Spheres") that sparked the Scientific Revolution.

Nicholas Oresme

Nicholas of Cusa

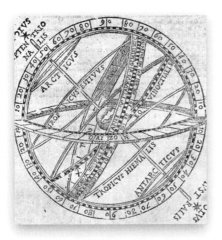

A diagram of an armillary sphere created by Christoph Clavius.

THE JESUITS WERE AMONG THE LEADERS IN ASTRONOMY IN THE 1600'S AND FOR QUITE A WHILE AFTER THAT. IN FACT, AT THE TIME OF THE AMERICAN REVOLUTION, THIRTY OUT OF THE WORLD'S 130 ASTRONOMICAL OBSERVATORIES WERE OPERATED BY THE JESUIT ORDER.

A chart of sunspots by Christoph Scheiner. Notice the Jesuit logo, with the letters "IHS," at the top.

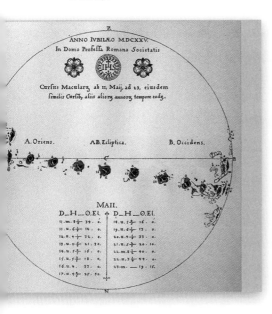

THE TRADITION OF JESUIT ASTRONOMY

The Jesuit Order was founded in 1540, and within a few decades its members were already in the forefront of scientific research, particularly astronomy. One of the earliest contributions of Jesuit astronomy is the very calendar we use today, the so-called Gregorian calendar, named after Pope Gregory XIII, who promulgated it in 1582. This calendar was proposed by the Jesuit astronomer **Christoph Clavius**. The Jesuits were among the leaders in astronomy in the 1600's and for quite a while after that. In fact, at the time of the American Revolution, thirty out of the world's 130 astronomical observatories were operated by the Jesuit order.

The Jesuits astronomers of the 1600s made a number of noteworthy discoveries. Four of these priest-scientists are worthy of particular mention: Christoph Scheiner, Niccolo Zucchi, Giambattista Riccioli, and Francesco Grimaldi.

Christoph Scheiner (1573–1650) was one of five people who discovered sunspots independently of each other, and practically at the same time. (The others were Thomas Herriot, Johannes and David Fabricius, and Galileo.) To be more precise, these men were the first to discover them *with telescopes*. Sunspots were actually seen with the naked eye as early as 165 BC by Chinese astronomers, and also by the ancient Greeks. The first drawing of a sunspot was by an English monk, John of Worcester, in 1128. However, the scientific investigation of sunspots only began when they were rediscovered with telescopes in the 1600's. It was Galileo who first figured out what sunspots were, but it was Scheiner who made the most sustained and systematic observations of them, published in his massive treatise, *Rosa Ursina*, in 1640. Scheiner tracked sunspots as they moved across the face of the sun, and showed from this data that the sun was rotating on an axis that is tilted with respect to the earth's orbit. Scheiner's extensive sunspot data is still of use to scientists today.

Niccolo Zucchi (1586–1670) made no great discovery. However, he was the first person to build a *reflecting telescope* (i.e., telescopes which use a mirror to gather light, rather than a lens.) Zucchi constructed his telescope in 1616, or perhaps even earlier—more than fifty years before Isaac Newton, who is often credited with building the first reflecting telescope. Zucchi used his telescope to make accurate observations of spots on Mars's surface in 1640, and his data contributed to Cassini's discovery in 1666 that Mars rotates on its axis.

Giambattista Riccioli (1598–1671) has the distinction of being the first person to observe a binary star. We now know that most stars are not single stars like the sun, but orbit around other stars in binary systems. Riccioli also perfected the pendulum as an instrument to measure time precisely, which was important for later scientific research. With his fellow Jesuit, Francesco Grimaldi, he mapped the surface of the moon. A copy of their map stands at the entrance to the lunar exhibit at the Smithsonian Museum in Washington, D.C. Thirty five of the moon's craters are named after Jesuit astronomers, including several of the largest craters. For example, a crater 250 miles in diameter is named after Grimaldi.

Francesco Grimaldi (1618–1663), who helped Riccioli map the surface of the moon, made his greatest discovery in physics not astronomy. It is one of the truly great discoveries in the history of science. He discovered (and named) the very important phenomenon of the "diffraction of light." Grimaldi studied the shadows cast on a screen by objects of various shapes illuminated by a thin beam of sunlight that he allowed to enter a darkened room through a small aperture in the wall. He discovered that within the shadow region on the screen there were faint fringes of light, and in the illuminated region there were faint fringes of shadow. Grimaldi not only discovered these "diffraction fringes," he made very careful observations of their number, intensity, and coloration, and how they looked for objects of different shapes. Grimaldi's pioneering work was known by later investigators, including Hooke and Newton. However, it was not until almost two centuries later that the significance of the diffraction effect was understood: it shows that light is a wave. In the twentieth century it was discovered that all matter is made up of waves, and consequently the phenomenon of diffraction is important in many branches of physics—entire chapters are devoted to it in college and graduate-level physics textbooks. If you have ever wondered why CDs and DVDs have those bands of bright color, it is a diffraction effect. So when you see those colors, think of Fr. Grimaldi.

THE 1600'S, THE CENTURY OF THE SCIENTIFIC REVOLUTION

The century of the Scientific Revolution—the century of Kepler, Galileo, Boyle, Hooke, and Newton—was also the golden age of priest-scientists. We have already heard about four of them, Scheiner, Zucchi, Riccioli, and Grimaldi. We will now look at four others, Mersenne, Castelli, Cavalieri, and Steno, all of whom were founders of entire branches of science.

Marin Mersenne (1588–1648) was a French priest of the Minimite Order. In our day, scientists and mathematicians learn about new developments in their fields and share their discoveries with other researchers in several ways: through professional journals, international conferences, and, more recently, by the internet. However, in the 1600's, when the scientific revolution began, there were no professional journals; there were no international

THE CENTURY OF KEPLER, GALILEO, BOYLE, HOOKE, AND NEWTON—WAS ALSO THE GOLDEN AGE OF PRIEST-SCIENTISTS.

MARIN MERSENNE'S CONVENT IN PARIS BECAME A MEETING PLACE OF SCIENTISTS. HIS REGULAR VISITORS INCLUDED SUCH MAJOR FIGURES OF SCIENTIFIC HISTORY AS DESCARTES, GASSENDI, FERMAT, PASCAL, AND ROBERVAL. IN 1653, MERSENNE ORGANIZED THE *ACADEMIA PARISIENSIS* (I.E., THE PARIS ACADEMY), ONE OF THE EARLIEST SCIENTIFIC ORGANIZATIONS IN EUROPE. HE WAS THUS ONE OF THE "ARCHITECTS OF THE EUROPEAN SCIENTIFIC COMMUNITY," ACCORDING TO THE *DICTIONARY OF SCIENTIFIC BIOGRAPHY*.

MERSENNE MADE EVEN GREATER CONTRIBUTIONS TO THE STUDY OF SOUND AND VIBRATIONS. ONE OF THE BASIC FACTS TAUGHT IN COLLEGE PHYSICS COURSES IS HOW THE FREQUENCY OF VIBRATION OF A STRING IS RELATED TO ITS LENGTH, ITS MASS-PER-UNIT-LENGTH, AND ITS TENSION THESE RELATIONSHIPS WERE FIRST DISCOVERED BY MARIN MERSENNE.

Marin Mersenne

conferences; and, of course, there was no internet. What they did have, at least in France, was Marin Mersenne.

Mersenne carried on volumes of correspondence with the leading scientists of his day. They would inform him by letters of their new results and he would disseminate the information by letters to other scientists. His convent in Paris became a meeting place of scientists. His regular visitors included such major figures of scientific history as Descartes, Gassendi, Fermat, Pascal, and Roberval. In 1653, Mersenne organized the *Academia Parisiensis* (i.e., the Paris Academy), one of the earliest scientific organizations in Europe. He was thus one of the "architects of the European scientific community," according to the *Dictionary of Scientific Biography*.

Today, Mersenne's name is most well-known in the mathematical world, because of so-called "Mersenne prime numbers." Every so often one sees a story in the newspapers or on the internet that a new Mersenne prime has been discovered. Finding new and larger Mersenne primes has become an ongoing worldwide competition. The results are even listed in the *Guinness Book of World Records*. But Mersenne's really significant contributions to science lay elsewhere, in particular in the sciences of optics and acoustics.

In optics, Mersenne contributed to the theory and design of reflecting telescopes. According to a technical book on the subject, which devotes several pages to discussing his contributions, "Mersenne's work is often referred to, [but] its full significance is rarely appreciated.... Mersenne must be accorded the credit for inventing, on paper, the definitive basic geometrical form of the modern telescope."

However, Mersenne made even greater contributions to the study of sound and vibrations. One of the basic facts taught in college physics courses is how the frequency of vibration of a string is related to its length, its mass-per-unit-length, and its tension. These relationships were, in fact, first discovered by Mersenne. He also measured the speed of sound and showed that it was independent of frequency and loudness. He showed that the intensity of sound fell off with distance by an inverse-square law. He showed that sounds of the same pitch had the same frequency, no matter what musical instruments produced them. For these and other discoveries Mersenne has been called the "father of acoustics." Mersenne also discovered that the frequency of a pendulum is inversely proportional to the square root of its length. This was also one of Galileo's most famous discoveries. However, Mersenne discovered it independently and published it a year before Galileo did.

Benedetto Castelli (1578–1643) was a priest of the Benedictine Order. He had a famous teacher and two famous pupils. Castelli was a student of none other than Galileo himself. Castelli defended Galileo and Copernicanism throughout Galileo's troubles. At a critical moment in these troubles, when Galileo decided to defend himself publicly against some of his accusers, he chose to do so by means of an open letter addressed to Castelli.

At Galileo's recommendation, Castelli was made professor of mathematics at the University of Pisa in 1613. There he began to study water in motion. In 1628, he published his *magnum opus, On the Measurement of Water Currents*, which is considered the beginning of modern hydraulics. By this time, he had been called to Rome by Pope Urban VIII to be a consultant on hydraulics and a professor at the University of Rome. There he taught his famous student Evangelista Torricelli, who carried Castelli's work on fluid motion much further. Torricelli was the first person to create a sustained vacuum and to discover the principle of the barometer. He discovered the law known as Torricelli's Theorem, and was the first person to give the correct explanation of wind. In honor of such contributions, one of the standard units of pressure, the "Torr," is named after him. Torricelli also made substantial contributions to mathematics, along with another of Castelli's pupils, a priest named Cavalieri.

Bonaventura Cavalieri (1598–1647) was a priest of the Jesuate order (not to be confused with the Jesuit order). He is a significant figure in the history of mathematics. His great contribution was his so-called "method of indivisibles." This was a technique for computing the volumes and areas of geometric figures by dividing them into infinitesimal parts, and it was an important step on the road to the discovery of calculus later by Newton and Leibniz. Leibniz himself later wrote, "In the sublimest of geometry, the initiators and promoters, who performed a yeoman's task, were Cavalieri and Torricelli. Later others progressed even further, using their work." Galileo wrote, "few, if any, have delved as far and as deep into the science of geometry as Cavalieri."

Bl. Nicholas Steno (1638–1686), also known as Niels Stensen, was a remarkable figure in many ways. He made fundamental contributions to four branches of science: anatomy, paleontology, geology, and crystallography. While still in his twenties he was already recognized as one of the leading anatomists in Europe. His anatomical studies greatly increased knowledge of the glandular-lymphatic system. Various parts of the body are named after him, including Stensen's duct, Stensen's gland, Stensen's vein, and Stensen's foramina. He also did important work on heart and muscle structure, brain anatomy, and embryology. He was a Dane by birth, but eventually ended up in Florence, where he worked in a research institute that included some of Galileo's pupils. In 1666, while he was dissecting the head of a Great White shark that had been caught near Livorno, he noticed that the teeth of the shark bore a strong resemblance to the so-called tongue-stones that were common on the island of Malta. This led him to develop, after much further investigation, a detailed theory of the origin of fossils and of sedimentary rock that was very controversial at that time, but was essentially correct. He is thus regarded as the founder

BL. NICHOLAS STENO MADE FUNDAMENTAL CONTRIBUTIONS TO FOUR BRANCHES OF SCIENCE: ANATOMY, PALEONTOLOGY, GEOLOGY AND CRYSTALLOGRAPHY. HE IS THE FOUNDER OF THE BRANCH OF GEOLOGY KNOWN AS STRATIGRAPHY.

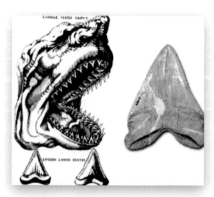

BL. NICHOLAS STENO'S SKETCH OF A SHARK (LEFT) AND A FOSSIL SHARK TOOTH (RIGHT).

Bl.Nicholas Steno: Bishop, Scientist and Catholic Saint

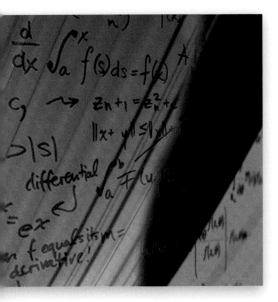

IN EVERY CENTURY UP TO OUR OWN DAY THERE HAVE CONTINUED TO BE IMPORTANT SCIENTISTS WHO WERE CATHOLIC PRIESTS.

of the study of fossils and is often listed first among the founders of the science of geology, in particular of the branch of geology called "stratigraphy." Steno's theory of how geological strata were laid down allowed people to begin to understand the history of the earth.

The study of geology led Steno to the study of crystals, where he discovered the basic fact, known as Steno's Law, that in all crystals of the same mineral the angles are the same.

Steno was raised as a Lutheran, but after a deep study of theology and early Church history, he converted to Catholicism. He left scientific research to become a priest, and was soon elevated to the rank of bishop. In his last public lecture as a scientist, he offered to history one of the greatest descriptions of the relationship between nature, our grasp of truth, and the absolute mystery of God:

> *Beautiful is what we see.*
> *More beautiful is what we comprehend.*
> *Most beautiful is what we do not comprehend.*

As bishop, he was known as an ardent advocate for the poor, for whom he sold all of his belongings, even his bishop's ring. He practiced rigorous asceticism, constantly praying and fasting. On October 23, 1988, he was beatified by Pope John Paul II.

LATER CENTURIES

As science became more specialized, it became harder and harder for people to make important discoveries without first spending years in technical training. Since priests also have to spend years studying theology, philosophy, and other matters required for the priesthood, it is not surprising that the number of priest-scientists tended to decline over time. Nevertheless, in every century up to this day there have continued to be important scientists who were priests.

Lazzaro Spallanzani (1729–1799) is regarded as one of the top biologists of the eighteenth century. He investigated digestion, the dynamics of blood circulation, regeneration of limbs in lower animals, fertilization, respiration in plants and animals, and the senses of bats. He disproved the idea of spontaneous generation, the idea that some living things are generated from non-living matter. When Louis Pasteur had to do the same thing a hundred years later, he based his own experiments on those of Spallanzani.

Rene-Just Haüy (1743–1822) is regarded as the founder of the science of crystallography.

Giuseppe Piazzi (1746–1826) was the director of the Palermo Observatory. On January 1, 1801 (the first day of the nineteenth century), he discovered the first known (and also the largest) asteroid, which he named Ceres.

Bernhard Bolzano (1781–1858), a Czech priest, is an important figure in nineteenth century mathematics. He helped put calculus, the "theory of real numbers," and the "theory of functions" on a more rigorous foundation. Anyone who studies advanced mathematics will encounter the "Bolzano function" and the "Bolzano-Weierstrass theorem."

Pietro Angelo Secchi (1818–1878) continued the great tradition of Jesuit astronomy into the nineteenth century. He is one of the founders of modern astrophysics. He pioneered the study and classification of stars using spectroscopy, or color classification. His classification of stars was the standard one for two decades, until a somewhat improved one was developed at Harvard University in the early twentieth century. Perhaps nothing so dramatizes the positive relation of faith and science as the fact that Secchi did much of his research using a telescope that was set up on the roof of Sant Ignazio, one of the most beautiful churches in the city of Rome, right above the sacred space where he and his fellow Jesuits daily celebrated Mass.

Pietro Angelo Secchi

Gregor Mendel (1822–1884), an Augustinian priest and monk, is so famous that his contributions do not have to be explained here. He is universally honored as the founder of the science of genetics.

Henri Breuil (1877–1961) was for decades one of the leading paleontologists in the world. In particular, he was considered the foremost authority on cave paintings and prehistoric art. In a humorous take on to his religion, he is often called "the pope of prehistory."

Julius Nieuwland (1878–1936), a priest of the Holy Cross Order, was a professor of chemistry at the University of Notre Dame. His work led to the development of "neoprene," the first synthetic rubber.

A sketch of Fr. Secchi's telescope when it was located in a tower of the Church of St. Ignatius in Rome.

Georges Lemaître (1894–1966), a Belgian priest, was one of the two originators of the Big Bang theory, now accepted as the correct account of the beginnings of the universe. One might say that the Big Bang theory was too revolutionary for Einstein, even though it was based on Einstein's own theory of gravity, the Theory of General Relativity. Einstein published this in 1916. In 1922, a Russian mathematician Alexander Friedmann and, independently a few years later, Georges Lemaître found solutions of Einstein's theory that described a universe in which space itself is expanding. Einstein and others at first resisted the idea, but in 1929, the astronomers Edwin Hubble and Milton Humason confirmed that the universe is indeed expanding, and physicists began to accept Lemaître's idea. Lemaître also served as the Director of the Pontifical Academy of the Sciences. His great discovery will be discussed in more detail in Chapter Seven.

Fr. Georges Lemaître with Albert Einstein. It was Lemaître who developed the Big Bang theory based on Einstein's equations.

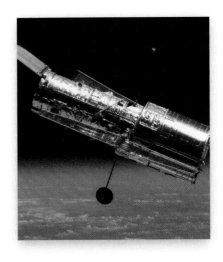

SUMMARY

We see that important priest-scientists existed in every century from the 1100's to the 1900's. They had significant firsts to their credit: the discovery of the first binary star, the first asteroid, the building of the first reflecting telescope, the first synthetic rubber. They were "founding fathers" of entire branches of science: acoustics, hydraulics, stratigraphy, paleontology, crystallography, genetics, and Big Bang cosmology.

Our recognition of these priest-scientists leaves us with an important question: had the Church been opposed to science, or if the Christian Faith were somehow incompatible with scientific inquiry, how could so many priests have found the time and freedom to rank among the greatest of scientific pioneers?[20]

These many priest-scientists are proof-positive of the harmony between the Christian Faith and the sciences, as well as the enthusiasm the Church has always shown for scientific discovery. Yet perhaps the best example of this enthusiasm is a nonscientist, Pope John Paul II. A brief tour of his papacy shows that this "Witness to Hope" was and remains the model witness to the Church as patroness of the sciences.

IF THE CHRISTIAN FAITH WERE SOMEHOW INCOMPATIBLE WITH SCIENTIFIC INQUIRY, HOW COULD SO MANY PRIESTS HAVE FOUND THE TIME AND FREEDOM TO RANK AMONG THE GREATEST OF SCIENTIFIC PIONEERS?

C. The Example of Pope John Paul II

Less than thirteen months after he stunned the world by becoming the first Polish pope in history, Karol Wojtyla, now John Paul II, gave a birthday speech at the Pontifical Academy of the Sciences. He was not honoring the birthday of a former pope, or of an important Catholic figure. This day, he wished to give tribute to someone for "the eminent contribution he made to the progress of science."[21] In this important moment of a papacy filled with important moments, John Paul II revealed a key feature of his leadership of the Church—his desire to nurture an even greater intimacy between the Church and the world of scientific discovery.

So what was this exalted occasion to which John Paul II wished to draw attention? It was the 100th birthday of the renowned genius Albert Einstein, and the pope's celebration of it signaled that the Church's long respect for the sciences was about to be taken to a whole new level.

In the twenty-six years of his papacy, John Paul II would give dozens addresses on the relationship between faith and science. He would express his esteem for the sciences in his writings. He would weigh in on specific matters that touch the relationship between science and

John Paul II

the Christian Faith. And he would forever set a precedent for fruitful dialogue and collaboration between the international community of scientists and the Catholic Church.

Karol Wojtyla demonstrated a love for the sciences long before he became Pope John Paul II. A key friendship with a young physicist, Jerzy Janik, developed into a study group with a number of scientists. Janik, for his part, was fascinated by the young priest's "instinctive grasp of physics" and his ability to connect philosophical ideas with scientific findings. He "could speak… in a connected way about everything," from ski poles to deep scientific theory to God.[22] Already his mind showed the expansiveness necessary to connect what was under the microscope to the ultimate Truth of reality, which is God. He would continue to meet with this group well after his elevation to the rank of archbishop and then cardinal.[23]

THE PAPACY: REUNITING THEOLOGY AND SCIENCE[24]

Wojtyla's love for science would continue during his papacy, as would his dialogue with scientists. Through this dialogue, important insights emerged that would further outline the intersections of science and faith, the key role of ethics in science, and the importance for believers of keeping the sciences in view. He also respectfully pointed to some important insights that religious faith has to offer scientists.

The most important contribution the Pope would make would be his insight into the need for a unified view of the world, one which includes the truths of the Christian Faith and the truths discovered by science. These truths are distinct but inseparable; if one wishes to have a total view of reality, including the source of reality, which is God, then both must be respected.

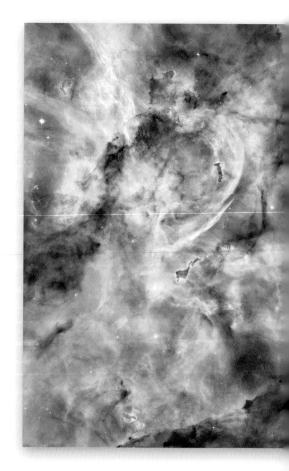

Because the two are distinct, John Paul II saw that one could have insights into one order and not the other. But this fractured view of the universe is something to be avoided, a point he would frequently reiterate.

At the intersection of the two orders of truth, the Pope repeated over and over again, is man. The human person links the order of natural science with the highest order, that of the total meaning of the universe. Man cannot be reduced to mere matter, and so he is a sign to himself that the meaning of the universe cannot be reduced to just its physical elements. Man is a marriage between the aspect of reality seen through scientific investigation and the aspect of reality seen in philosophy and in God's Revelation. As we noted earlier, the human person is the crossroads of faith and science.

Slowly over the course of centuries, the worlds of theology and science have drifted apart, each speaking only to itself and forgetting how to speak in the language of the other. What is needed is a more intense and lively communication between the two—one that would resemble a dialogue between friends. To a large extent, as a result of the efforts of scientists like Fr. Stanley Jaki, Stephen M. Barr, Peter E. Hodgson, Paul Davies, Ian Barbour, Rev. John C. Polkinghorne, Fr. Michal Heller, Kenneth R. Miller, Francis S. Collins, and Owen Gingerich, this conversation has indeed been reinvigorated in recent decades. Pope John Paul II, even before he became pope, played a significant role in fostering this dialogue. As Archbishop of Cracow, he held meetings in his episcopal residence that brought together scientists (including some of those just listed), theologians, and philosophers. After his elevation to the papacy, these meetings continued under the leadership of the Polish priest-physicist Fr. Michael Heller, who held them on a more regular basis.

In the next chapter, we will look at four principles that guided Pope John Paul II in his efforts to renew the dialogue between science and faith. But before we leave our historical investigation, we must consider one Catholic who did not receive a blessing for his scientific insights—Galileo Galilei. The Galileo Affair is also a part of the history of the Church's relationship to science. Getting all the facts of this story will show that it was and is a negative exception, and not the rule, of the Church's sponsorship and support of the sciences.

D. A Misleading Moment: The Galileo Affair

Galileo Galilei (1564–1642) was a trailblazer, a man who was unafraid to look at things in a new way. His insights into the workings of the universe using mathematics and the power of careful experimentation have led many to call him "the Father of Modern Science."[25]

As he forged his new path, he found himself on trial and then condemned for one of his major achievements—his recognition that an earlier thinker (Copernicus) was right when he asserted that the earth moves around the sun.

The court which condemned him was none other than a panel of cardinals; a panel which punished him for disobeying an earlier command "not to hold, teach, or defend in any way whatsoever that the earth moves."[26] As George Weigel paints his picture of this moment, we see a stunning event that has become for many a symbol of the relationship between the Catholic Church and the natural sciences:

In the second half of the second Christian millennium, no incident has done more to sustain the image of the Catholic Church as an authoritarian enemy of human progress than the seventeenth century Galileo case, in which the pioneering Florentine scientist was condemned by the Church for holding and teaching Copernicus' theory that the sun, not the earth, was the center of the solar system. Galileo, who would spend the last eight years of his life under house arrest, was forced to make a humiliating public retraction.[27]

What could be a more embarrassing situation for the Church, which claims to have a unique relationship to God the Creator, than to have condemned a scientist for doing nothing more than accurately describing God's creation? It seems that the story of this unjust blunder is the only chapter that needs to be read before closing the book on the Catholic Church and her relationship to modern science—until one realizes that the story of Galileo is one page of one chapter of a book with many chapters.

"HOW TO GO TO HEAVEN, NOT HOW THE HEAVENS GO": THE SITUATION BEFORE GALILEO

To assume that the sun, moon, and stars move around the earth (an idea called *geocentrism*) is perhaps the most forgivable of errors. After all, we still use geocentric language today whenever we speak of the sun "rising" and "setting." And without the benefit of scientific instruments and precise observation, nearly everyone before Galileo assumed that the appearance was the reality. Some, such as the ancient philosopher Aristotle and the ancient astronomer Ptolemy, had actually theorized that the whole universe had the earth as its central point.

And yet the possibility that the earth moves had been considered before Galileo, and had even been asserted by the great Copernicus. Experiments had been performed to investigate the issue, but no decisive proof had ever been discovered to uproot the conception that seems so obvious—the sun moves, the earth does not.

The Catholic Church had never attempted to settle the matter. In fact, up until the time of Galileo, the Church had never condemned or proclaimed a scientific theory. Not once, in the 1500 years of its existence prior to Galileo, had it ever pronounced anything about botany, zoology, astronomy, or any other science.[28]

In fact, the Church had adopted an open approach to intelligent investigation of the natural world, one based on its understanding of God's Revelation in Sacred Scripture. The Church recognized that the Bible, in the words of a cardinal whom Galileo himself quoted in defense of his position, "is to teach us how one goes to heaven, not

how the heavens go."[29] From that perspective, the Church had always seen the fallacy in assuming that God had revealed in Scripture things already accessible to the human mind about the world he created. God, when inspiring the writers of the Bible, did not seek to give a preview of coming astronomical discoveries. He had bigger fish to fry.

St. Augustine (354–430), the great Catholic bishop, philosopher and theologian, probably put the Church's position best: "One does *not* read in the Gospel that the Lord said: 'I will send you the Paraclete [the Holy Spirit] who will teach you about the course of the sun and the moon. For he willed to make them *Christians*, not *mathematicians*.'"[30]

So why was Galileo condemned? The entire tragedy of Galileo's condemnation actually revolved around a lack of evidence: Galileo was defending the right position without sufficient proof.

THE CONDEMNATION

That the earth goes around the sun (a scientific position called heliocentrism) is a fact no sane person would argue with today. But most people are not aware that Galileo did not have solid proof of it. The conclusive evidence only came decades after Galileo died. This created a situation in which the authorities to whom he appealed were left with little more than Galileo's word on the matter.

This was pointed out to Galileo's close friend Paolo Foscarini by Robert Cardinal Bellarmine, head of the Holy Office of the Roman Inquisition, which later condemned Galileo after Bellarmine's death:

> If there were a real proof that the Sun is in the center of the universe, ... and that the Sun does not go around the Earth but the Earth round the Sun, then we should have to proceed with great circumspection in explaining passages of Scripture which appear to teach the contrary, *and admit that we did not understand them* ... But as for myself, I shall not believe that there are such proofs until they are shown to me.[31]

What Bellarmine was saying was that, given sufficient proof, he and others would be obliged to change their position on the matter; but that Galileo had not provided such proof.[32] Consequently, the matter was at a standstill for everyone but Galileo and other forward-looking intellectuals like himself.

There was also the issue of Sacred Scripture. Some opponents of Galileo said that his "new science" was contrary to Bible passages such as Psalm 93—"And he has made the world firm, not to be moved." This scriptural passage and others like it are clearly prayers of praise and thanksgiving to God for having made the earth *stable*, which is of course a precondition for human life and therefore a great blessing for man—as we see when that stability is disrupted by earthquakes. But Galileo's opponents interpreted them as declaring with divine authority that the earth is the center of the universe, an idea that completely missed the meaning of the passage. It seemed to these opponents that to agree with Galileo would be to say that God's Word is in error.

Galileo's response to these opponents was brilliant, but also unprecedented. He began to lay out principles of biblical interpretation that would allow him to reconcile his heliocentrism with belief in the divine inspiration of Sacred Scripture. History would vindicate Galileo's understanding of Sacred Scripture, but only long after his death. (We have applied those principles already to the first creation account in Genesis.)

On top of insufficient proof and a seeming threat to the truth of Sacred Scripture, Galileo also committed a very serious mistake, a matter of poor judgment, not of poor science. In his criticism of the reigning philosophical/scientific system of the day, which was based on the thought of the Greek philosopher Aristotle, Galileo represented the Aristotelian thinkers of his day through a literary persona he created to represent their views—an unenlightened idiot named Simplicio. In one fell swoop, Galileo had antagonized a large number of university professors and Church leaders who were committed to the Aristotelian approach. He had also alienated his most powerful supporter—Pope Urban VIII.[33]

The lack of sufficient proof from Galileo, the desire to safeguard the truth of Sacred Scripture, and the personal insult to many thinkers in the Church created enough momentum to incite Church authorities to force him to recant his position. The commission of cardinals that condemned Galileo acted with the authorization of the pope and on his behalf, so their condemnation was an official act. But they did not declare geocentrism to be an unchangeable doctrine of the Church— and they could not have, even if they wanted to, since a mere commission of cardinals does not have that level of authority in the Church. And, more importantly, the Church is prevented by the Holy Spirit from teaching any error definitively. The condemnation of Galileo was a disciplinary act, not the settling of a question of dogma.

In retrospect, it was these cardinals, not Galileo, who committed the biggest mistake in the whole sad affair. Not recognizing the liberty that Catholic Tradition had always given to science, they condemned a scientific theory as a theological error.

THE REST OF THE STORY

Just as many are not aware that Galileo had not proven his heliocentrism adequately, there are also many who do not know the whole story of what happened after his condemnation in 1633. Three of the ten cardinals who judged Galileo refused to sign the verdict. He was

Copernicus

GALILEO HAD ANTAGONIZED A LARGE NUMBER OF UNIVERSITY PROFESSORS AND CHURCH LEADERS WHO WERE COMMITTED TO THE ARISTOTELIAN APPROACH. HE HAD ALSO ALIENATED HIS MOST POWERFUL SUPPORTER— POPE URBAN VIII.[3]

Aristotle Latin Text

A Crayon Sketch of Galileo

IN 1984, POPE JOHN PAUL II
APPOINTED A COMMISSION TO
REEXAMINE THE GALILEO CASE. IT
EXPLICITLY ACKNOWLEDGED THAT
"CHURCH OFFICIALS HAD ERRED IN
CONDEMNING GALILEO."

Galileo on trial before the Holy Office of the Inquisition in 1633

placed under house arrest, yet had a servant and "every convenience," according to his friend who observed his arrest. The pope personally saw to his comfort. And he was allowed to continue scientific research as long as he did not defend heliocentrism (also called "Copernicanism"). In fact, it was during his house arrest that he published his greatest contribution to science, namely his book on mechanics and gravity.

Not until 1687, when Newton published his Laws of Motion and his Law of Gravity, did scientists have the theoretical tools they needed to resolve the dispute between heliocentrism and geocentrism. However, it was not until the discovery in 1728 of the phenomenon called "the aberration of light" that there was direct experimental evidence of the truth of the heliocentric theory. Not long after, in 1757, Pope Benedict XIV, at the urging of the great Jesuit astronomer Roger Boscovich, removed Copernicus's book from the *Index of Prohibited Books* (a list of books that Catholics were forbidden to read without special permission). In 1822, Galileo's book defending Copernicanism was also removed from the Index. No one was ever condemned by the Church for a scientific position again. In 1984, Pope John Paul II appointed a commission to reexamine the Galileo case. It explicitly acknowledged that "church officials had erred in condemning Galileo."[34]

The last chapter was written in 1992 by Pope John Paul II himself. Referring to Galileo as the "inspired founder" of experimental science, he spoke directly to the issue of his condemnation, and actually called Galileo a *better theologian* than the cardinals who condemned him. In John Paul II's own words:

> Galileo, a sincere believer, showed himself to be more perceptive… than the theologians who opposed him. "If Scripture cannot err," he wrote to Benedetto Castelli, "certain of its commentators can and do so in many ways."[35]

What was the error of Galileo's opponents? The pope goes on to say that they failed to recognize what was obvious to Galileo himself: "…the Bible does not concern itself with the details of the physical world… which is the competence [i.e., the proper domain] of human experience and reasoning."[36] Galileo had not contradicted the Bible in his correct description of the physical world, because the Bible, as God's Revelation, is not about such details. (Here we should note that Pope John Paul II is not separating faith and science—he goes on to note that God's Revelation and the natural sciences do have important "points of contact,"[37] ones which we shall explore in future chapters.) Pope John Paul II apparently was not satisfied with praising Galileo with words alone—in 1994, the Vatican issued a postage stamp in Galileo's honor.

The Pope concluded his address by recognizing the irony involved in the Galileo case, showing that both sides of the controversy were dealing with a very limited view of the universe. For example, Galileo had asserted that the sun was the center of the universe, and not simply of the solar system, a fact we now know to be false:

> And since the cosmos, as it was then known, was contained within the solar system alone, this reference point could only be situated in the earth or in the sun. Today... neither of these two reference points has the importance they once had.[38]

SUMMARY

The Galileo event, it turns out, was a sad misunderstanding, an exception to the rule of the Church's long history of openness to the natural sciences and their ability to enlighten us with a better and truer understanding of the physical universe as time goes on. The rest of the Church's history is full of examples that show this openness.

But it is also true that today, as at the time of Galileo, theology and science are often undertaken in isolation from each other. Our next chapter will discuss how to bring them together again. The key to mastering that challenge is as simple as reading a book. But it does involve learning to read the biggest book of all.

Supplementary Reading

Patroness or Presecutor?
The Catholic Church and Scientific Discovery

"SCIENTIFIC FREEDOM: THE EXAMPLE OF NICHOLAS OF CUSA"

*(excerpted from Pierre Duhem, "The Church and Freedom of Thought" in Stanley Jaki,
Scientist and Catholic: An Essay on Pierre Duhem [Front Royal: Christendom, 1991], pp. 268–269)*

The earth, declared [Nicholas of Cusa,] the future bishop of Brixen, is not the vilest among the celestial bodies, and the men, animals, and plants that inhabit it are not inferior in nobility to those who inhabit the Sun and other planets.

Our philosopher recognized, at any rate, that we cannot know much about the beings that inhabit other planets. "We suspect," he says, "that the inhabitants of the Sun are more sunlike, more enlightened, illuminated, and intellectual. We suppose them to be more spiritual than those that are on the Moon who are more lunelike [moonlike]. Finally, on the earth, they are more material and gross...."

"These opinions are suggested to us in view of the influence of the Sun which is of igneous [i.e., a fiery] nature, by the influence of the Moon which is both aqueous [i.e., watery] and aerial, and by the earth's more material heaviness."

When for the first time, in Western Christianity, one hears speaking of the plurality of inhabited worlds, one sees the idea proposed by a theologian who had, a few years earlier, taken the floor in an ecumenical Council. He, who in a book soon to become famous, tried to guess the characters of the inhabitants of the Sun and the Moon, was to be honored by the confidence of the popes who succeeded one another in the chair of Peter. The highest ecclesiastical dignitaries were reserved for him.

Can one wish a more manifest proof of the extreme liberty which the Catholic Church, on the decline of the Middle Ages, left for the meditations of philosophers and for the tentatives of the physicists [i.e., the speculations of scientists]?

Supplementary Reading

"A SAINT DOES SCIENCE: THE EXAMPLE OF BLESSED NICHOLAS STENO"

(excerpted from Thomas E. Woods,
How the Catholic Church Built Western Civilization
[Washington D.C.: Regnery, 2005], pp. 96–98)

Standard textbooks very often do give Roger Bacon and Saint Albert the Great, and to a lesser extent Robert Grosseteste, their proper due. Other Catholic names in science, however, remain in undeserved obscurity. **Father Nicholas Steno** (1638–1686), for example, a Lutheran convert who later became a Catholic priest, has been credited with "set[ting] down most of the principles of modern geology," and has sometimes been called the father of stratigraphy (the study of the strata, or layers, of the earth). Born in Denmark, Father Steno lived and traveled throughout Europe over the course of his life, serving for a time as court physician to the grand duke of Tuscany. Yet despite his excellent reputation and creative work in medicine, he secured his scientific reputation in the study of fossils and the earth's strata.

His work began in an unlikely context: the dissection of the head of an enormous shark that a French fishing boat encountered in 1666. Weighing in at 2,800 pounds, the shark was the largest that most people had ever seen. Steno, who was known for his great skill as a dissector, was called upon to perform the dissection.

For our purposes, it suffices to concentrate on Steno's fascination with the shark's teeth. They bore a strange resemblance to so-called tongue stones, or *glossopetrae*, whose origins had been mysterious and obscure since ancient times. These stones, which the Maltese dug up from under the earth, were said to possess curative powers. Countless theories were proposed to account for them. In the sixteenth century, Guillaume Rondelet had suggested that they might

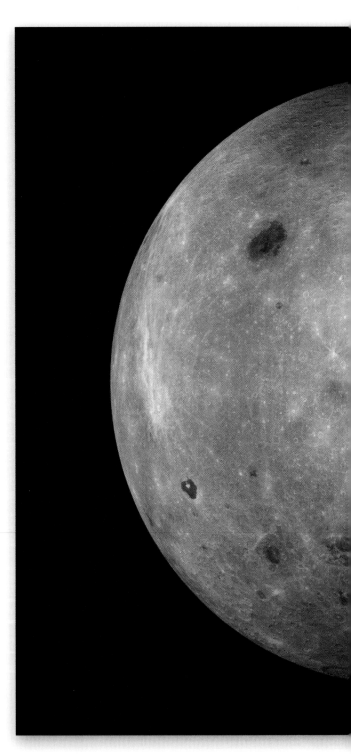

Supplementary Reading

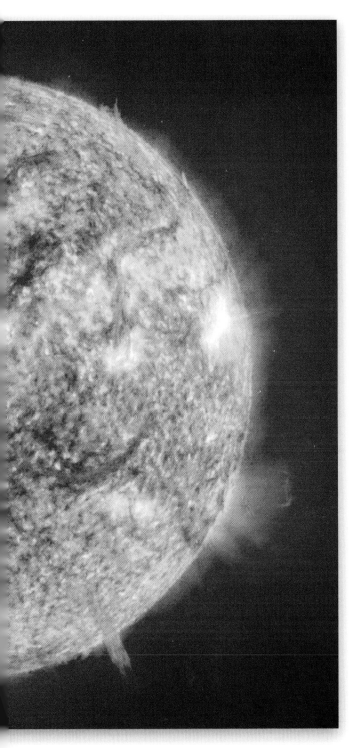

be shark teeth, but few were impressed with the idea. Now Steno had the chance to compare the objects side by side, and found the resemblance clear.

This was a significant moment in the history of science, since it pointed to a much larger and more significant issue than shark teeth and mysterious stones: the presence of shells and marine fossils embedded in rocks, far from the sea. The question of the glossopetrae, now almost certainly shark teeth, raised the broader question of the origin of fossils in general, and how they had come to exist in the state in which they were found. Why were these things being found inside rocks? Spontaneous generation was but one of the numerous explanations that had been proposed in the past.

Such explanations did not impress Steno, who found them scientifically dubious as well as offensive to his idea of God, who would not act in a manner so random and purposeless. He concluded for a number of reasons that the existing theories of fossils could not be reconciled with the facts as they were known. He threw himself into study of the question, devoting the next two years to writing and compiling what would be his influential work, *De solido intra solidum naturaliter contento dissertationis prodromus* ("Preliminary Discourse to a Dissertation on a Solid Body Naturally Contained Within a Solid").

This was no easy task, for Steno was essentially striking out into uncharted territory. There was no existing science of geology to which he could refer for methodology or first principles. The speculations in which he engaged, dealing with events and processes that had occurred in the distant past, ruled out direct observation as a way of verifying some of his conclusions.

Nevertheless, he pressed ahead boldly. Rocks, fossils, and geological strata, Steno was certain, told a story about the history of the earth, and geological study could illuminate that history. This was a new and

Supplementary Reading

revolutionary idea. Previous writers had assumed, with Aristotle, that the earth's past was fundamentally unintelligible. "Steno," writes his most recent biographer, "was the first to assert that the world's history might be recoverable from the rocks and to take it upon himself to unravel that history."

As the years passed, Father Steno would be held up as a model of sanctity and scholarship. In 1722, his great-nephew, Jacob Winslow, wrote a biography of Steno that appeared in the section on prospective saints in a book called *Lives of the Saints for Each Day of the Year*. Winslow, a convert from Lutheranism to Catholicism, attributed his conversion to the intercession of Father Steno himself. In 1938, a group of Danish admirers looked to Pope Pius XI to have Father Steno declared a saint. Fifty years later, Pope John Paul II beatified Father Steno, praising his sanctity and his science.

3. "THE GREATNESS OF GALILEO, CATHOLIC AND SCIENTIST"

(excerpted from Antonino Zichichi, "Galileo, Divine Man" in The Session Commemorating the 400th Anniversary of the Founding of the Pontifical Academy of the Sciences (1603–2003). Internet. Available from http://www.vatican.va/roman_curia/ pontifical_academies/acdscien/acta17 _anniversary/ part2.pdf; accessed April 17, 2006)

In history books in the millenniums to come, Galileo Galilei will be celebrated for his true role as

Supplementary Reading

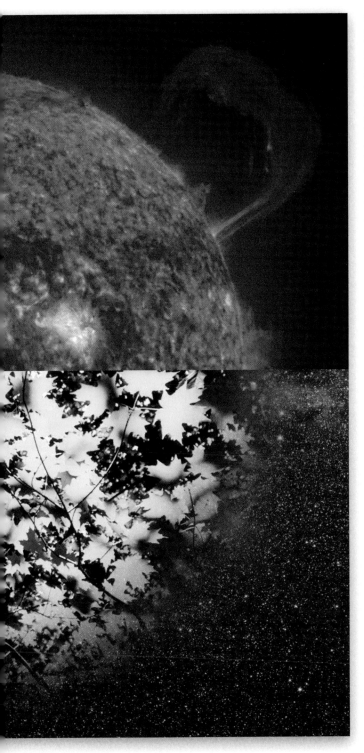

the father of science, the one who paved the way for humanity to understand how the world we live in is made. His work was founded on *intellectual humility, rigor,* and *reproducibility*. Most of what [Galileo's predecessors] had understood about the nature of the world, before Galileo managed to open the Book of Nature, proved to be completely wrong…

His greatness lies not only in his astronomical discoveries, extraordinary though these are. Just one would have been enough, and he made lots. Galilei's truly unique greatness lies in the fact that he was the first man to discover the first, fundamental signs of the Creator carved into "vulgar" matter—stone, string, wood.

If curiosity was all it took to discover science, our Stone Age ancestors would have done so. They were extremely curious. If logical rigor was all it took, the Greeks would have discovered it. **Galilei was motivated by an act of Faith in the Creator of the world. The Creator of whom he wanted to discover the imprints, these being the Fundamental Laws which govern the world.…**

Let me close with a quotation by Galilei, dated 1613. This is important for those who claim that Galilei changed his devotion to God after his discoveries.

Both Holy Scripture and Nature issue from the word of God: the first because it was dictated by the Holy Spirit, the Spirit of God, and the second because it is the most faithful agent of divine order.

…How could anyone but a holy man utter such words?

Study Guide

Faith and Science:
At the Crossroads of Nature and Spirit

VOCABULARY

Define the following terms:

1. Lateran IV
2. *Ex nihilo*
3. Stephen Tempier
4. John Buridan
5. Vatican I
6. Pius XI
7. Vatican II
8. Autonomy
9. Academy of Lynxes
10. Federico Cesi
11. Pontifical Academy of the Sciences
12. Robert Grosseteste
13. Roger Bacon
14. St. Albert the Great
15. Nicholas Oresme
16. Nicolaus Copernicus
17. Christoph Scheiner
18. Niccolo Zucchi
19. Francesco Grimaldi
20. Marin Mersenne
21. Bl. Nicholas Steno
22. Lazzaro Spallanzani
23. Pietro Secchi
24. Gregor Mendel
25. Georges Lemaître
26. John Paul II
27. Galileo Galilei
28. Geocentrism
29. Heliocentrism

STUDY QUESTIONS

1. Historically, does the Church have a positive relationship with science? Explain.
2. How did the Lateran IV teaching that God created the universe *ex nihilo* help to give birth to modern science?
3. How did the Lateran IV teaching that the universe had a first moment in time help to give birth to modern science?
4. How did Tempier's condemnation of the idea that God had to create the world exactly as it is help to give birth to modern science?
5. What rule of thumb did Vatican I offer to the relationship between faith and science?
6. How did Vatican II foster the sciences?
7. What is the significance of the Pontifical Academy of the Sciences?
8. What does the history of priest-scientists throughout the ages reveal about the Church's attitude toward science?

Study Guide

9. What is "the Galileo Affair"? Why is it a blemish on the Church's relationship with science?

10. What issues led to Galileo's condemnation?

11. What was the theological error committed by the cardinals who condemned Galileo? Has the Church continued this error? Explain.

PRACTICAL EXERCISES

1. The Church continues to be the subject of prejudice when it comes to her relationship to science and scientists. Create a list of steps by which a high school student can help dispel popular misconceptions about the Church.

2. Stephen Hawking, the great modern physicist and author of *A Brief History of Time*, once joked that he was afraid that his work on the origins of the universe might get him dragged before the Inquisition like Galileo. If Hawking asked you whether or not he should fear this fate, what would you say to dispel his "fear"?

3. The Church teaches that the sciences have a legitimate autonomy. Suppose a friend told you that scientists should never contradict the Bible. How would you answer him or her?

Endnotes

1. *WordReference.Com English Dictionary*. Internet. Available from http://www.wordreference.com/definition/patron; accessed April 11, 2007.
2. Cf. CCC 101–104.
3. DS 800, as quoted in CCC 327.
4. On the teaching that the universe was created out of nothing, see 2 Mc 7:28; on the idea of the universe being created in time, see the great words which begin the Book of Genesis (Gn 1:1) and the Gospel of St. John (Jn 1): "In the beginning . . ."
5. Paul Haffner, *Creation and Scientific Creativity: A Study in the Thought of S.L. Jaki* (Front Royal: Christendom Press, 1991), 41.
6. Ibid., 41.
7. Ibid., 60.
8. Idem., *Mystery of Creation*, 160.
9. *Dei Filius*, 1: DS 3002; cf. CCC 293.
10. *Dei Filius*, 5–6: DS 3017.
11. *Gaudium et spes*, 36.
12. *Gaudium et spes*, 59.

13. Marcelo Sorondo, *The Pontifical Academy of Sciences: A Historical Profile*, The Pontifical Academy of Sciences Extra Series 16 (Vatican City: 2003), 8.
14. Ibid., 8.
15. Ibid. 1–2. Cf. Pontifical Academy of Sciences, *Statutes* of 1976, art. 2, §1.
16. Ibid., 4–5.
17. Ibid., 18.
18. *(Author's note: This section was contributed in its entirety by Stephen M. Barr and Dermott Mullan)*
19. Pierre Duhem, "The Church and Freedom of Thought" in Stanley Jaki, *Scientist and Catholic: An Essay on Pierre Duhem* (Front Royal: Christendom, 1991), 268.
20. Barr, *Modern Physics*, 10.
21. Address to the Pontifical Academy of Sciences, 11/10/1979, 1.
22. George Weigel, *Witness to Hope: The Biography of John Paul II* (New York: HarperCollins, 2001), 100–101.
23. Ibid., 211.
24. This title is taken from Michael Sherwin, "Reconciling Old Lovers: John Paul II on Science

and Faith." Internet. Available from http://www.catholic.net/RCC/Periodicals/Dossier/0708-96/article4.html; accessed April 11, 2007.
25. Barbour, 9.
26. Ibid., 15.
27. Weigel, 629.
28. Barr, *Modern Physics*, 5–6.
29. Barbour, 14.
30. St. Augustine, *De actis cum Felice Manichaeo*, I.10 (P.L. 42.525).
31. Robert Bellarmine, *Letter to Foscarini*, as quoted in Barr, *Modern Physics*, 8.
32. Barr, *Modern Physics*, 8.
33. Barbour, 15.
34. Idem.
35. John Paul II, "Lessons of the Galileo Case," *Origins* 22, no. 22 (1992), 372.
36. Ibid., 373.
37. Idem.
38. Idem.

Chapter Five

A, B, C, Infinity: Learning to Read the Story of the Universe

A. Galileo and the Two Books

In Chapter Four we learned about Galileo Galilei and his pioneering approach to science. But we should also recognize that many of his insights were not merely scientific. Galileo did not just understand science, he also understood how to interpret scientific discoveries in relation to the great interconnected dramas of human history and Divine Providence, God's governance of the universe. He saw that the universe was like a book which could be read at different levels; he also realized that these levels supported and enriched each other.[1]

The Father of Modern Science was convinced that the details of the universe uncovered by science were only understood when one confronts deeper questions than those of science, questions of meaning and value. For Galileo, to read the Book of Nature meant to collect facts about it for the sake of a deeper understanding of the ultimate meaning of reality, to understand *nature* in terms of *spirit* (see Chapter One). To accomplish this requires another book: the Bible. According to Galileo, the Book of Nature and the Book of Scripture have the same author:

> If I ask who created the Sun, the Moon, the Earth, the stars, their positions and movements, I think the response will be that they are the *work* of God; and asking who dictated the Holy Scriptures, I know the answer will be the Holy Spirit, that is likewise of God. The world, therefore, is the work and the Scriptures are the *word* of the same God.[2]

Galileo's idea of the universe as a book gives us a fantastic analogy for our investigation of the relationship between faith and science. One can approach a book at many levels. Its words and the way they

"REASON... IS FINITE. IT MUST PROCEED THROUGH A MULTIPLICITY OF SEPARATE BRANCHES OF KNOWLEDGE... PHILOSOPHY AND THEOLOGY ARE, AS SCIENCES, LIMITED ATTEMPTS WHICH CAN REPRESENT THE COMPLEX UNITY OF TRUTH ONLY IN DIVERSITY, THAT IS, WITHIN AN OPEN SYSTEM OF COMPLEMENTARY ITEMS OF KNOWLEDGE."

(JOHN PAUL II TO TEACHERS AND UNIVERSITY STUDENTS IN COLOGNE CATHEDRAL, NOVEMBER 15, 1980)

are used are one level. Its storyline and plots are another. Ultimately, its themes and the values and truths they reveal form its deepest level.

Each "reading level"[3] of a great book has fascinating details, and each level must be grasped, at least basically, for its deeper levels to be understood. The key is to see the harmony between all of the levels, and how they enrich and reveal each other. This is how we must look at the universe—its details help us understand its deepest structure and history, which helps us to grasp its meaning.

To understand this better, let us start by looking at a certain set of books almost everyone is already familiar with.

BOOK LEARNING: THE "MAGIC" OF READING THE UNIVERSE

For many years, elementary and high-school teachers have complained that their students do not read as well or as often as they should. The major difficulty and challenge was helping students to see reading as more than an assignment—as something better and greater than book-learning. Real reading is not book-learning; it is "learning a book"—becoming familiar with the details of a story for the sake of encountering its deepest levels. When this occurs, the reader comes to love the book's characters and to learn their lessons—and this, every great English teacher knows, is the "magic" that transforms a student from a non-reader into a reader-for-life.

Coincidentally, it was magic that turned out to be the answer—the magic of *Harry Potter*, J.K. Rowling's series of adventure stories about a young wizard hero and his friends. Rowling's books have sold millions of copies, and the enthusiasm over the books has astounded reading professionals, who watched with amazement as children flocked to bookstores to buy the latest installment in the series. *Harry Potter* has turned millions of children, teenagers, and adults into "readers-for-life."

And in doing so, the *Harry Potter* series has some great lessons to teach about rediscovering faith on the frontiers of science, about reading the book of the universe.

A LESSON FROM HOGWARTS

For those who have read any of the Harry Potter books, it is not hard to understand their great popularity. They are filled with amazing details about a mysterious world in which every detail of our own world is present—teachers, school, sports, politics, crime, even plants and animals. And yet these familiar details have become amazing and fascinating through the presence of magical characteristics that they do not possess in our own world. Teachers teach spells and potions, school is a magical fortress filled with secrets and marvels, and athletics involves Quidditch, which is nothing less than high-flying broomstick mania. Every detail of the real world has been taken up and transformed through the amazing mind of J.K. Rowling, the genius behind *Harry Potter*.

These details make the stories intensely interesting and exciting. Yet they are just the surface of the *Harry Potter* saga.

As one reads on, and reads more deeply, the real themes and values shine through—the drama of good versus evil, the nature of love and friendship, and the question of what really matters in life. Even the magical details become less of a motivation to keep reading, although they never cease to be fascinating. They become a backdrop to the real story, which is about finding happiness and real meaning in life in a world threatened by terrifying evil and filled with beauty and danger, joy and tragedy.

The Potter stories could not happen without the magical details, and the magic is somehow mysteriously at the heart of the deepest meaning of the story. But the story cannot be reduced to spells and potions—ultimately, the Harry Potter saga is about the nature of love and happiness, about what it means to live.

Each new addition in the *Harry Potter* series succeeded in bringing these ongoing themes to a new and more intense level. In the final book, Rowling revealed her incredible creative power by creating a beautiful and fulfilling ending to the story—an ending that brought to completion all of the questions and loose ends that had emerged, and revealed the meaning behind all of the struggles of Harry and his friends, even those who died in their battle against evil.

Because Rowling had the basic plot in mind from the very beginning of the series, she was able to create a great ending for the *Harry Potter* saga—an ending that revealed a union with the story's beginning. In keeping with the mystery-adventure style she adopted, it was revealed in the final book that the end of the story was given in the beginning in a hidden way. All of the storylines and themes which developed out of the original book returned and were fulfilled in the end.

At this point, the readers of this book may be wondering whether its purpose has been switched from science to fiction! Actually, in keeping with the adventures of *Harry Potter,* this section has a secret message for you. If you reread the last several paragraphs and replace a few words, you will have the entire message of this chapter, given here in the beginning:

- Take out every reference to "magic" and "magical details," and substitute "science" and "scientific details";

- Take out every reference to the author and J.K. Rowling, and substitute "the Trinity" or "God";

- Take out every reference to the Harry Potter saga and the story, and substitute "history and the universe";

- Take out every reference to "Harry Potter" and "his friends," and substitute "humanity."

Here is what you get:

History and the universe are filled with amazing scientific details. These scientific details make history and the universe intensely interesting and exciting. Yet they are just the surface of history and of the universe.

As one reads on, and reads more deeply, the real themes and values shine through—the drama of good versus evil, the nature of love and friendship, and the question of what really matters in life. Even the scientific details become less of a motivation to keep reading, although they never cease to be fascinating. They become a backdrop to history and the universe, which are ultimately about finding happiness and real meaning in life in a world threatened by terrifying evil and filled with beauty and danger, joy and tragedy.

History and the universe could not happen without the scientific details, and scientific details are somehow mysteriously at the heart of the deepest meaning of history and the universe. But understanding history and the universe cannot be reduced to science—ultimately, they are about the nature of love and happiness, about what it means to live.

THE UNIVERSE HAS AN AUTHOR; IT HAS A PURPOSE, A BEGINNING AND AN END. AND IT HAS GREAT LESSONS TO TEACH US WHEN WE GO DEEP INTO ITS DETAILS AND THROUGH THEM, TO ITS MEANING.

History and the universe are an ongoing work of the Trinity, and each new addition has succeeded in bringing these ongoing themes to a new and more intense level. God gives every indication that he has the creative power to create a fulfilling ending to the story—an ending that will bring to completion all of the questions and loose ends that have emerged, and reveal the meaning behind all of the struggles of humanity, even of those humans who have died in their battle against evil.

God has had the basic plot in mind since he began history and the universe, so he will create a great ending for the saga of humanity—an ending that reveals a union with the beginning. In keeping with the mystery-adventure style the Trinity has adopted, readers will realize that the end of the story was given in the beginning in a hidden way, and that all of the storylines and themes which developed out of the origins of history and the universe will return and be fulfilled in the end.

Here we see how similar the universe is to a book—it has an Author; it has a purpose, a beginning and an end. And it has great lessons to teach us when we go deep into its details and through them, to its meaning.

There are also some very important differences between *Harry Potter* and the universe. For one thing, J.K. Rowling has never published a guide for how to read her story. Readers are left to pick through it and decide which details are the really important ones and how to best interpret them. But the Author of the universe has not left us guessing about such things. He has given us a guide to reading the universe at all of its levels, a guide indicating which of the many details are the most important at getting the whole story—Sacred Scripture is the word of God about the universe and ultimately, about himself. It is indispensable for really understanding history and the universe.

Also, while the saga of *Harry Potter* is completely dependent on Rowling, as history and the universe are upon God, Rowling is not part of her story. Yet the Author of the universe has not created a story that does not involve him. In fact, the climax of history is the moment when he enters the universe, when God becomes man in Jesus Christ. And the fulfillment of history will be when he returns in glory. Unlike the story of Harry Potter, the book of the universe is an unfinished one—for humanity, the last drama has yet to occur.

The final difference is also significant—the characters in the Harry Potter series do not have the ability to read their own story. In fact, they only think, feel, and act in imagination—when the story is not being written or read or at least thought about, they do not exist as anything but ink on a page.

But the amazing characters in our story—human beings—do have the ability to read their own story. We can both participate in the drama of the universe, but can also read that drama through reflection. We are in the story but not entirely of the story—we can both live it and know it.

So without further ado, let us learn to read the book of the universe, starting with an example of how *not* to read it: by using science as our only guide—the folly of *science without wisdom*.

THE AUTHOR OF THE UNIVERSE HAS NOT CREATED A STORY THAT DOES NOT INVOLVE HIM. IN FACT, THE CLIMAX OF HISTORY IS THE MOMENT WHEN HE ENTERS THE UNIVERSE, WHEN GOD BECOMES MAN IN JESUS CHRIST.

B. "Science without Wisdom"[4]

As we saw in our consideration of scientism in Chapter Two, it is possible to approach the book of the universe as if only science can put us in touch with its deepest meaning. Dr. Anthony Rizzi is one of a number of scientists who have pointed out the danger of approaching the world from an exclusively scientific point-of-view. He gives an excellent example of what happens when one approaches the book of the universe in a *scientistic* way—the myth of the "nothingness" of the atom and of human beings:

> We are taught that an atom is composed of electrons and a nucleus. The electron is point-like and most of the mass of the atom is in the nucleus of the atom. If the nucleus of the atom were such that it was the size of a basketball, the "edge" of the atom would be two *miles* away. It is thus said and believed that

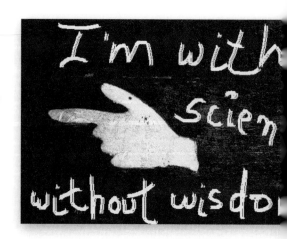

the atom is filled with mostly space. The inference is then drawn that since we are made of atoms, we are mostly nothing.[5]

If the atom is mostly space, and a human being is made of atoms, then a human being is mostly space—a vast nothingness. "Mostly nothing" seems to be a valid conclusion about human beings based on what science has revealed about the proportions of the atom—until we move past the details given by science and begin to look at the bigger picture. After noting that the typical human being contains 10^{28} atoms, Rizzi demonstrates the insufficiency of a purely scientific approach to the book of the universe:

> Science never poses the question: is man one thing or is he 10^{28} things? He cannot be in the same way and at the same time both 1 and 10^{28}, because 1 does not equal 10^{28}. In short, one must understand how the philosophical fact that you are one, that you are not a multiplicity but an individual person, fits with the physics fact that you are 10^{28} atoms.[6]

Here is where the falsehood is revealed: The very same scientist who would tell us that the atom—considered purely from the proportion of its parts—is mostly nothing, and that a human being, made up of atoms, is also mostly nothing, would finally have to conclude that a human being is 10^{28} things, and not one human being!!! But pure common sense and experience are enough to know that the atomic details cannot be the whole picture. In some way, the human being remains one human being while containing (without destroying) 10^{28} atoms.[7] Rizzi draws a very important conclusion from this observation:

> Here we begin to see reality itself is *multi-layered*. Reality is not a song with one voice, *univocal*, but a song with multiple voices that can make up chords. Reality is not homogeneous [exactly uniform in every way] but heterog eneous [containing diversity].[8]

"Science alone" (i.e., scientism) as an approach to reality is nothing more than "science without wisdom." Reality requires more than science to be understood; the book of the universe cannot be fully appreciated through a mere analysis of its details. We must go beyond science in order to appreciate the significance that science holds for grasping the deeper meaning of the universe.

WE MUST GO BEYOND SCIENCE IN ORDER TO APPRECIATE THE SIGNIFICANCE THAT SCIENCE HOLDS FOR GRASPING THE DEEPER MEANING OF THE UNIVERSE.

C. Learning the Levels

What are the different levels at which the book of the universe can and must be read in order to be understood? St. Thomas Aquinas (1225–1274), following Aristotle, made a very important distinction regarding the levels of reality and our approach to these levels.[9] Each one builds upon the other.

The lowest level is the level of the physical details of the universe. At this level, reading the book of the universe means looking at particular physical things and drawing conclusions about all other things *that are also physical*. For instance, through the study of a diseased organ a biologist can know the processes and functions of the disease that afflicts it. Then, he or she can apply that knowledge to the treatment of patients who exhibit that disease. We are able to know truths about all of them from the study of one or a few examples.

St. Thomas calls this level of reading the universe "*physica,*" or physics, although he uses this term to apply to all natural sciences and not simply the specialized science of physics as we know it today. In *physica* we are dealing only with material, changeable reality. We are looking at the physical realities which make up the universe; at things which are made of matter and so must be understood as such.[10]

IN *PHYSICA* WE ARE DEALING ONLY WITH MATERIAL, CHANGEABLE REALITY. WE ARE LOOKING AT THE PHYSICAL REALITIES WHICH MAKE UP THE UNIVERSE; AT THINGS WHICH ARE MADE OF MATTER AND SO MUST BE UNDERSTOOD AS SUCH.

The next level at which the universe can be read is that of *mathematica*, or mathematics. At this level, reading the book of the universe means approaching things from the perspective of their quantity. We know quantity only first by encountering it at the level of the physical. But we do not need the physical in order to understand quantity. We can discuss quantities in themselves, such as when we recognize that 2+2=4 without two sets of two oranges to combine and count.

In *mathematica*, we have pierced through to something that characterizes all physical things, and not just this or that kind of thing (such as an organ of the human body). We have taken a step up; we are at a level where the physical universe can be read in a very broad way, a way applicable to all physical things—in the words of the great Galileo, "mathematics is the alphabet with which God has written the universe." Yet even here we have still not reached the highest level.

The deepest level at which the universe can be read is at the level of realities which are not always physical and which, in some cases, are not physical at all. Of these things Aquinas says "either they never exist in matter … or they exist in matter in some instances but not in others." Thomas calls this level of knowing reality "divine science," and for an obvious reason: the highest non-physical reality we can know is the source of all reality, God. But this level of knowing also has another name, which in Greek literally means "beyond physics." This is the level of *metaphysica*, or "metaphysics."[11] We get to this level by first gaining some facility with the first two, which we can achieve through our education and ordinary experience.

THE DEEPEST LEVEL AT WHICH THE UNIVERSE CAN BE READ IS AT THE LEVEL OF REALITIES WHICH ARE NOT ALWAYS PHYSICAL AND WHICH, IN SOME CASES, ARE NOT PHYSICAL AT ALL, THE LEVEL ST. THOMAS AQUINAS CALLS "DIVINE SCIENCE" (BECAUSE IT DEALS WITH THE REALITY OF GOD) AND "METAPHYSICS" (BECAUSE IT GOES "BEYOND PHYSICS")

We will approach the primary object of metaphysics, i.e., God, in Part II of this text. But there are a number of other things revealed by metaphysics which are essential to reading the book of the universe, and we must first turn to these.

D. Metaphysics: Infinity Between and Beneath the Lines

THE GRAMMAR OF THE UNIVERSE

As we saw above, St. Thomas Aquinas identified metaphysics as a level of knowing wherein we comprehend objects which are physical in some instances but not in others. As we saw in Chapter One, the adjectives that metaphysicians use for something that is not physical but which truly exists are "spiritual" and "immaterial" (this last word means "not made of matter"). To be physical is to consist of stuff, to be extended in space, to have parts. To be spiritual and immaterial would be to exist but not be extended in space, to be partless. God, angels, and the human soul are examples of spiritual realities. As far as we know, human beings are the only "hybrid" beings in the universe that are physical and spiritual, body and spirit (the human spirit is also called the *soul*).

By looking at objects that are physical in some instances but not in others, we cross the bridge from *physica* and *mathematica* into *metaphysica*. Crossing this bridge between a purely physical reading of the book of the universe and the richer, deeper, spiritual levels of reality and meaning within it is to find the place where theology and science meet.

To go back to our analogy, metaphysics allows us to clearly see reality between and beneath the lines of the book of the universe, to see the reality of its Author and its own deepest dimensions. Through it we learn the grammar of the universe and all of its parts, a grammar that nature shares with spirit.

We need to be ready to learn some new terms, or at least redefine some terms we already know. Some of the traditional English terms that are used in metaphysics are also used to mean very different things in ordinary language. We will focus on two: *existence* and *causation*.

So as to make things very concrete, I have decided to take this opportunity to study my favorite metaphysical example—my dog, a beagle that my daughter named Lucy after Lucy Pevensie, her favorite character in C.S. Lewis' *The Chronicles of Narnia*. Let us allow Lucy to lead us across the bridge from *physica* to *metaphysica*.

Existence—the first and most basic thing about Lucy, the one thing she shares in common with the whole universe and everything in it, is obviously not her cuteness or even her dogness. It is her *existence*, her *being*—if Lucy did not exist she would not be a part of the universe at all.

*Lucy has being, but she **is not** being.* If Lucy was being itself, then she would have always existed, and everything that ever existed would have to share in, or participate in, Lucy! But there was a time not long ago when Lucy did not exist. Her existence is something that she *has*, not something she *is*. And she did not give existence to herself—existence comes to all things from without—it is like a gift.

Existence is the most fundamental reality of the universe, the primary thing studied in metaphysics. Even something I imagine, such as a *Patronus* (the guardian being which Harry Potter can summon for protection), has existence—the Patronus exists *as* something thought. All things, even thoughts, are connected by existence and share in it as a common characteristic in different ways.

But even in our own language, we see existence as more than a characteristic. It is not just something every existing thing *has*, it is also something every existing thing *does*. Lucy pants, jumps, and barks, but before all and above all, she *exists*. The Latin word *existere* is a verb, an action-word, that literally means "to stand forth"— in metaphysics, it means to stand forth from nothingness, from non-existence.

Think about this for a moment—*if you can say something true about existence, then you have said something true about every existing thing in a single statement.*

WE SEE EXISTENCE AS MORE THAN A CHARACTERISTIC. IT IS NOT JUST SOMETHING EVERY EXISTING THING *HAS*, IT IS ALSO SOMETHING EVERY EXISTING THING *DOES*.

You have made it this far through our discussion of existence, and so you may be asking, "What is existence in itself? A being is something that has being, but what is Being? Where do all beings get their existence from?" To be Being Itself is to exist necessarily, and to be the source of being for all things, to not simply exist, but to be the very act of existing without further qualification. It is "the infinite fullness of pure unlimited existence, and the one ultimate Source of all being."[12] It would be, in fact it is, God. As St. Thomas Aquinas would say, God is the act of being subsisting in itself.

An important metaphysical principle for understanding the relationship between faith and science is to note that, above and beyond any other consideration, the most basic relationship between God and the universe is that God is the Giver of the gift of existence to all things. God is not simply perfect. He makes all things, and all the perfections of those things, *real* by sharing with them from his own unlimited existence.

Right away we can see that existence is something not limited to physical realities. All physical things exist, but existing is not necessarily tied to physical reality. It transcends *physica*. With one short leap, Lucy has taken us way past science.

Causation—Lucy has been the reason for a number of changes at my house since she came to live with us three years ago. Nearly all of my children's plastic toys bear her teeth marks. She has also been

responsible for holes all over my backyard. In these and many other cases, Lucy has caused real changes in the things and people around her. In classic metaphysical terms, Lucy is the *cause* of many things (some good, others not so good).

Understanding the nature of cause and effect is a major part of understanding the book of the universe. An *efficient cause* is that which contributes in a real way to the being of another by its action. Science continuously explores the cause-effect relationships which make up the material universe. But causal relationships bear some important characteristics which transcend the purely material universe studied by science.

We should start by noting that not only is causality important to science, but to the very ability to think about anything at all. The great foundation for all thought about anything is the Principle of Sufficient Reason: that every being has the sufficient reason for its existence either in itself or in another thing.[13] Here is a question one can and should pose about every thing in existence: does the existence of this thing explain itself, or does it have its explanation in a different thing? The way that this is related to causality is that any being that does not have its sufficient reason in itself requires an efficient cause. To deny this would lead you into a situation of utter absurdity; in the words of W. Norris Clarke, "if nothing at all is required for something new to come into existence, then anything can happen at any time with no explanation needed or able to be provided." This is the very opposite of our experience of the world.[14]

The existence of Lucy, for instance, is not self-explanatory. For one thing, Lucy had beagle parents that explain how she first came to be. For another, Lucy requires many conditions to be in place for her to exist at any moment, such as a stable environmental temperature and a healthy diet. When one wants to explain Lucy, one must make reference to many other things that are not Lucy that in their own way cause Lucy to be.

Is it possible for a being to be self-explanatory, requiring no cause for its existence? To answer, we must first rule out the possibility of a being causing itself. A *self-caused being* is an impossibility, because such a being would have to preexist or be outside itself in order to cause itself—an utter absurdity. But what about an *uncaused* being, a being that has its existence not from another but by its very nature? Such a being would have to be the source of existence and the ultimate cause of all other beings, to exist necessarily. Here we land right back with God as "the infinite fullness of pure unlimited existence, and the one ultimate source of all being." God is the Uncaused (not the Self-Caused) Cause of all else that exists.

Another characteristic of causality becomes clear when we think about intelligent causes such as human beings. Humans, because they are endowed with reason, are capable of understanding cause-effect

AN IMPORTANT METAPHYSICAL PRINCIPLE FOR UNDERSTANDING THE RELATIONSHIP BETWEEN FAITH AND SCIENCE IS TO NOTE THAT, ABOVE AND BEYOND ANY OTHER CONSIDERATION, THE MOST BASIC RELATIONSHIP BETWEEN GOD AND THE UNIVERSE IS THAT GOD IS THE GIVER OF THE GIFT OF EXISTENCE TO ALL THINGS.

relationships in themselves. Therefore, a human being is able to string causes together, to cause not some immediate effect only, but also to bring about a "domino effect" involving many cause-effect relationships that are all intended to bring about a final desired effect. Humans are also capable of consciously employing chance in an intelligent way when they act as causes of things. For instance, a fisherman uses a net that covers a wide area in the hopes that by chance one or many fish might be in that area.

These cases reveal that it is possible for an intelligent being to be the first cause in a whole chain of causes, and also to include other causes within its own causality. Therefore, it is possible to distinguish between *primary causality* and *secondary causality*. Primary causality is when an intelligent agent employs other causes to bring about a desired effect—secondary causes are those other causes.

In the case of God, we can say that God's causality is the greatest realization of primary causality; in fact, God is the only being that can be called Primary Cause without any further qualification. God creates the universe and sustains it in existence. But he does so not by replacing secondary causes, but by governing true secondary causes with perfect unlimited intelligence. God's use of natural causes, including "chance," as we shall see in Chapter Six and Chapter Eight, reveals his power, intelligence, and skill in an even greater way than if he directly caused all things.

We must consider one more aspect of causality. To cause something is to make an effect come to be. But causing does not necessarily involve a change in the causing being (the *agent*) itself. Material beings always change while they change other things; for example, Lucy expends energy when she chews up toy light sabers. But being a cause does not necessarily involve being changed; it involves changing something else. A perfect cause would never be diminished or altered by causing other things. God is unchanging, but yet out of his perfect fullness he is able to be the primary cause of the universe and every thing in it.

GOD IS THE ONLY BEING THAT CAN BE CALLED PRIMARY CAUSE WITHOUT ANY FURTHER QUALIFICATION. PRIMARY CAUSALITY IS WHEN AN INTELLIGENT AGENT EMPLOYS OTHER CAUSES TO BRING ABOUT A DESIRED EFFECT— SECONDARY CAUSES ARE THOSE OTHER CAUSES.

LUCY AND INFINITY: THE TRULY MAGICAL UNIVERSE

We are beginning to see in living color the point that Dr. Anthony Rizzi pointed out earlier—that reality is not exactly uniform in every way, but contains diversity. Our brief romp with a beagle has brought us, through ordinary observation and logic, to conclusions about the universe that reach beyond the physical and even bring us to the reality of God himself, who is Perfect Being and Primary Cause of all things. The ordinary things that we observe on a daily basis, the stuff of science that is ever examined and investigated, are the details that point beyond themselves to a wider, fully dimensional universe, one that is physical and spiritual.

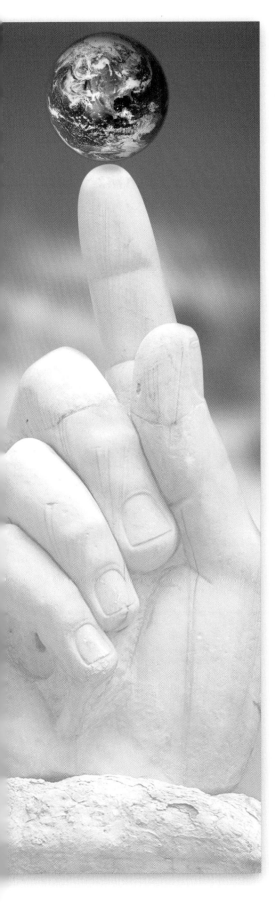

Earlier, I observed that the excitement of Harry Potter's world is that it is filled with amazing details in which every detail of our own world has become fascinating through the presence of magical characteristics that in reality they do not possess. Metaphysics shows us that we too often sell our own world short. The Author of the book of the universe created a reality that only seems ordinary when we do not look at it closely enough. Physicality and spirituality, the gift of existence, the spiraling interaction of causes, all in their varied combinations, show us a truly awesome universe.

METAPHYSICS: THE KEY TO A FRIENDLY REUNION BETWEEN FAITH AND SCIENCE

In this section, we have learned the "grammar" of the book of the universe. In doing so, we crossed a crucial bridge that joins science and faith, at least potentially, if not actually. By looking at existence and causality we grasped concepts that apply to the object of science—that is, the material universe. But we also saw that they are not limited to the material universe; they show ways in which the material elements of the universe are like the spiritual elements revealed by God. Existence and causality show us how the whole universe, both material and spiritual, is both like and unlike God.

Learning grammar is usually not the fun part of reading. Generally, we learn grammar so that we can read, not because we want to know it in itself. Metaphysicians are like grammarians, a special breed that enjoys the study of these things for their own sake. Without them, reading the universe would be difficult if not impossible. But with our new metaphysical knowledge, we are poised to engage in the real adventure of this text—to look directly at scientific findings in the light of faith and to see how theology, when done on the cutting edge of science, reveals the credibility of the Christian Faith, even while the Christian Faith affirms science.

One of the great tragedies of our own day and age is that few have bothered to learn this grammar. Slowly over the course of centuries, the worlds of theology and science have drifted apart, each reading only its own "book" and forgetting how to read the masterpiece of the other. Scientists like Fr. Stanley Jaki, Stephen M. Barr, Peter E. Hodgson, Paul Davies, Ian Barbour, Rev. John C. Polkinghorne, Fr. Michal Heller, Kenneth R. Miller, Francis S. Collins, and Owen Gingerich have done much to revive the relationship.

As noted earlier Pope John Paul II, even before he became pope, played a significant role in fostering this dialogue. Let us look at four principles that guided Pope John Paul II in his efforts to renew the dialogue between science and faith.

E. Reading the Book of the Universe with Pope John Paul II

STEP ONE: DISTINGUISHING IN ORDER TO UNITE

As we have already seen, the Pope's vindication of Galileo was directly related to his commitment to the Catholic teaching that science and faith represent two distinct orders of knowledge. John Paul II would repeat the teaching of Vatican I and Vatican II many times, using his own words:

> Both religion and science must preserve their own autonomy and their distinctiveness. *Religion is not founded on science nor is science an extension of religion* [emphasis added]. Each should possess its own principles, its pattern of procedures, its diversities of interpretation and its own conclusions.... While each can and should support the other as distinct dimensions of a common human culture, neither ought to assume that it forms a necessary premise for the other.[15]

In the Galileo case, some believers had tried to impose on scientific knowledge a limit that did not fit it.[16] In modern times, it is more often the case that scientists will try to overreach their own findings and make the whole world fit into purely physical boundaries. To both errors, John Paul II was outspoken on the fact that *real unity preserves legitimate differences.*

STEP TWO: RECOGNIZING THE BLESSINGS OF UNITY

Separationists like Stephen Gould might wonder why the pope would bother with trying to unite the distinct kinds of knowledge given by science and faith. But John Paul II saw that the two really need each other to be complete.

In the first place, the pope saw that faith can actually help a scientist be more scientific, and that science can help a believer deepen his understanding of the Christian Faith. As he put it, "Science can purify religion from error and superstition; religion can purify science from idolatry and false absolutes. Each can draw the other into a wider world, a world in which both can flourish."[17] Without science, a believer will be missing a lot of the sharp detail of God's creation, and can fall into the trap of arriving at mistaken conclusions about how God acts. Without faith, a scientist will make errors about the ultimate meaning of the world they study, and will fall prey to the error of "overscientizing" reality. In either case, real wisdom will be

lost. Einstein expressed a similar view when he said: "Science without religion is lame; religion without science is blind."

One real danger for science separated from faith is that it will develop technologies from its findings that are destructive. Evils such as global nuclear arms proliferation and human cloning are prime examples of science making itself absolute, and of humanity falling victim to what science, devoid of value and meaning, creates.

STEP THREE: THE LOVE OF WISDOM: FINDING THE MISSING LINK BETWEEN SCIENCE AND FAITH

Many religious thinkers, even Church leaders, have regarded the sciences as good but have warned scientists to avoid trying to explore larger questions than those the scientific method can answer. But according to John Paul II, scientists are highly qualified to approach the ultimate questions, and in fact, should attempt to grapple with them—as long as they realize that something more than science is needed to answer them. As we have already seen, this "something more," which can shed light on the greater questions of the value and meaning of the world which science investigates, is metaphysics and, more broadly, philosophy in general.

Philosophy, which means "love of wisdom," takes a broader approach than science, and uses common experience and logic to investigate questions such as "Why does the world exist? What is the meaning of the world and of human life? What things should human beings do, and what should they avoid?" It is through philosophy, John Paul II insisted, that the desired unity between science and faith can come about, and through which the dialogue between science and the Church occurs.[18]

Philosophy is also where the autonomy of science ends. Science is based on the idea that real truth exists, and that human beings were created to find it. Therefore, it must submit its findings to a process of integration, without alteration, into a unified worldview that does not make its findings the be-all and end-all of human knowledge. That is, scientists must avoid materialism, reductionism, and scientism, which are all false views of reality, and begin to see science as one part of a total approach to truth.[19]

STEP FOUR: MAN, THE KEY TO THE UNITY BETWEEN SCIENCE AND FAITH

Pope John Paul II recognized the human person as the key to unity between faith and science. The human person can be studied scientifically, and much insight has come from the scientific understanding of the nature of the human body, including the brain. But the human ability to do science itself shows that man is more than a body, that he *transcends* (a word which literally means "climbs over") the world which he observes in scientific discovery:

> ...the adventure of science has made us discover and experience with new vividness the immensity and transcendence of man's spirit, capable of penetrating the abysses of the universe, of delving into its laws, of tracing its history, rising to a level incomparably higher than the other creatures that surround him.[20]

Science's findings concerning the human body prove that science is necessary for understanding man; but man's ability to do science shows that more than science is necessary for the whole truth about humanity to be known.

In summary, the study of man is a place where science and philosophy meet. It is also the place where the Church has much to offer—in particular, the truth which God has revealed about himself as the Creator of all things and humanity as his image.

THE "DISPASSIONATE SEARCH" FOR "MARVELOUS MYSTERIES"

John Paul II's reverence for science and his excitement about the possibility of unity between science and faith can be summed up in a single paragraph, one which he wrote to the Jesuit priest/scientist who until recently served as the Director of the Vatican Observatory:

> Our knowledge of each other can lead us to be more authentically ourselves. No one can read the history of the past century and not realize that crisis is upon... both [the Church and science]. The uses of science have on more than one occasion proven massively destructive, and the reflections on religion have too often been sterile. We need each other to be what we must be, what we are called to be.[21]

Science, which John Paul II saw must be a "dispassionate search" (another way of saying "calmly objective search") that does not give way to making conclusions before investigation,[22] has revealed "marvelous mysteries" about the universe.[23] Our response to these should be wonder, awe, and openness to answers about the universe which science cannot give. In this way, science and religion serve each other; like spouses, they make each other complete.

F. Looking Forward: Faith and the Frontiers of Science

We have come to the end of the first part of our journey, a part entitled "A Friendly Reunion: The Relationship between Natural Science and Supernatural Faith." With an eye towards a reunion between science

Song of the Angels

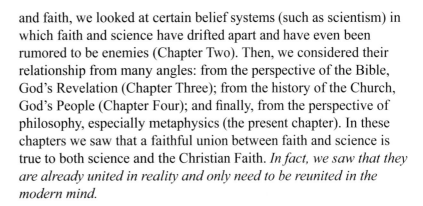

and faith, we looked at certain belief systems (such as scientism) in which faith and science have drifted apart and have even been rumored to be enemies (Chapter Two). Then, we considered their relationship from many angles: from the perspective of the Bible, God's Revelation (Chapter Three); from the history of the Church, God's People (Chapter Four); and finally, from the perspective of philosophy, especially metaphysics (the present chapter). In these chapters we saw that a faithful union between faith and science is true to both science and the Christian Faith. *In fact, we saw that they are already united in reality and only need to be reunited in the modern mind.*

The next two parts of the text deal directly with science in the light of the two principal subjects in the Christian Faith, which we earlier defined as the truth God has revealed in Sacred Scripture, Sacred Tradition, and the teaching of the Church. God's Revelation concerns two things directly: himself and humanity. It deals with all other things in relation to these two subjects. Therefore, we will follow God's lead and do the same.

Part II of this text, entitled "God and Science: The Credibility of the Creator" contains three chapters on God. In Chapter Six, we will investigate whether or not science has disproved God's existence or simply helped us understand the reality of God more clearly. In Chapter Seven, we will examine some marvelous discoveries by modern science that point to the existence of God. Chapter Eight will be entirely devoted to the special and controversial question of biological evolution and its relation to God.

In Part III of this text, entitled "In His Image: Human Personhood and Modern Science," humanity itself will take the center stage.

In both parts we will rely on what we have established so far, especially in this chapter. By the end, we will see that John Paul II's claim that philosophy is absolutely necessary for the dialogue between science and faith is true. By introducing metaphysics, we will be able to approach all the levels of the universe and even God in the harmony that exists between Creator and creation.

THE SEARCH FOR ANSWERS ABOUT THE UNIVERSE WILL BE SEEN TO OFFER CLUES ABOUT THE UNIVERSE'S MAKER. AND THE CHRISTIAN FAITH WILL ALSO TAKE ON A GREATER CLARITY, IN THAT OUR DEEPER UNDERSTANDING OF THE UNIVERSE WILL ALSO HELP US TO UNDERSTAND GOD'S TRUTH MORE FULLY. IT WOULD NOT BE INCORRECT TO SAY THAT MOTHER NATURE WILL TEACH US ABOUT FATHER GOD, AND THAT FATHER GOD WILL SHED LIGHT ON MOTHER NATURE.

Scientific research will take on a new meaning; the search for answers about the universe will be seen to offer clues about the universe's Maker. And the Christian Faith will also take on a greater clarity, in that our deeper understanding of the universe will also help us to understand God's Truth more fully. It would not be incorrect to say that Mother Nature will teach us about Father God, and that Father God will shed light on Mother Nature. Then, as believing thinkers and thinking believers, we will be better able to embrace both.

Supplementary Reading

Patroness or Persecutor?
The Catholic Church and Scientific Discovery

1. "GALILEO ON READING THE BOOK OF NATURE"

(excerpted from Antonino Zichichi, "Galileo, Divine Man" in The Session Commemorating the 400th Anniversary of the Founding of the Pontifical Academy of the Sciences (1603–2003). Internet. Available from http://www.vatican.va/roman_curia/pontifical_academies/ acdscien/acta17 _anniversary/ part2.pdf; accessed April 17, 2006.)

Galileo on Divine Power and Authorship of the Universe

"We do not seek that which God could have made, but that which he made. But I ask you: if God could have made the world infinite or not: if he could and did not, making it finite, as it is de facto, he did not exercise his power more in making it so, than if he had made it as large as a pea."
(Galileo Galilei, *Opere*, VII, 565)

"…God could have made the birds fly with bones of heavy gold, with veins full of living silver, with flesh heavier than lead and with small, heavy wings, and in doing so he would have demonstrated his power even further; he could have made fish heavier than lead, that is 12 or more times heavier than water: but he made the first of bones, flesh, and the lightest of feathers, and the second as light as water, to teach us that he enjoys simplicity and easiness…."
(Galileo Galilei, *Opere*, VII, 566)

**Galileo on Using Caution
in Reading the Bible and the Universe**

"Take note, theologians, that in your desire to make propositions concerning the movement or fixity of the [Sun] and the Earth a matter of faith, you expose yourselves to the risk of having eventually to condemn for heresy those who assert that the Earth is fixed and that it is the [Sun] that moves; eventually, I say, at such a time as it might be sensibly or necessarily demonstrated that the Earth moves and the Sun stands still."
(Galileo Galilei, *Opere*, VII, 541)

Supplementary Reading

EFFIGIES D. THOMÆ AQVINATIS

**Galileo: The Book of the Universe
is Written in Mathematical Language**

"…this grand book (the universe) which is always open in front of our eyes, but which cannot be understood if first one has not learnt to understand the language, and read the alphabet in which it is written. It is written in the language of mathematics, and its characters are triangles, circles, and other geometric figures, without which it would be humanly impossible to understand a word of it; without which one wanders vainly in a dark labyrinth."
(Galileo Galilei, *Opere*, VI, 232)

2. "ST. THOMAS AQUINAS ON STUDYING THE LEVELS OF REALITY"

(excerpted from St. Thomas Aquinas, In Boeth. De Trin. 5.1 resp., in Mary T. Clark, An Aquinas Reader [New York: Fordham, 2000], p. 30).

…The speculative sciences are differentiated according to their degree of separation from matter and motion.

Now, there are some objects of speculation that depend on matter for their being, for they can exist only in matter. And these are subdivided. Some depend on matter both for their being and for their being understood, as do those things whose definition contains sensible matter and which, as a consequence, cannot be understood without sensible matter. For example, it is necessary to include flesh and bones in the definition of man. It is things of these sort that **physics** or **natural science** studies. On the other hand, there are some things that, although dependent upon matter for their being do not depend on it for their being understood, because sensible matter is not included in their definitions. This is the case with lines and numbers—the kind of objects with which **mathematics** deals. There are still other objects of speculative knowledge that do not depend upon matter for their being, because they can exist without matter; either they never exist in matter, as in the case of God and the angels, or they exist in matter in some instances and not in others… The science that treats of all these is… **divine science**, which is so called because its principle object is God. By another name it is called **metaphysics**; that is to say, *beyond physics*, because it ought to be learned by us after physics, for we have to proceed from sensible things to those that are non-sensible. It is also called **first philosophy**, inasmuch as all the other sciences, receiving their principles from it, come after it.…

Supplementary Reading

3. "SCIENCE AND METAPHYSICS: AVOIDING MISUNDERSTANDINGS OF DIVINE CAUSALITY"

(excerpted from Christoph Cardinal Schönborn, "In the Beginning God Created…" Internet. Available from http://stephanscom.at/edw/katechesen/articles/2005/12/02/a9719/; accessed April 2, 2007.) This has been reproduced as part of Chance or Purpose? Creation, Evolution, and a Rational Faith, trans. Henry Taylor, ed. Hubert Philip Weber (San Francisco: Ignatius Press, 2007), p. 27.

The first and most usual misunderstanding is that God is seen as the first cause. He is indeed the first cause of all causes but he is not as it were at the beginning of a long chain of causes, like a pool player who hits a ball which rolls and hits another ball which in turn hits yet another—as if God were just the first cause in a long series of causes.

…We believe in a creator, not in one cause among others, one which occasionally intervenes when the limits of all other causes have been reached. God does not intervene like a mother who intervenes when her children fight but who otherwise lets them play with each other. Of course there are wonderful interventions of God, as we will see later. God is sovereign in relation to his creation and he can heal a cancer with his sovereign creative power. This is what we call a miracle. But at present we are talking about the act of creating the world, and this is not just the first push in a long chain of causes but is rather the more fundamental thing of **sovereignly conferring** being. "God spoke and it came to be." All that exists owes its being to this call, to this word, to this creative act of God. He created everything, heaven and earth, and there is nothing that was not created by him. He created everything in heaven and on earth, the visible and the invisible (for we believe that there are also invisible creatures, namely the angels). Everything is created reality. This is the first and most important affirmation to be made…. But before going further, let us raise the following question: is this affirmation

a pure article of faith, or can each human being understand it with his reason? The *Catechism answers* (286): "Human intelligence is surely already capable of finding a response to the question of origins. The existence of God the Creator can be known with certainty through his works, by the light of human reason,[24] even if this knowledge is often obscured and disfigured by error. This is why faith comes to confirm and enlighten reason in the correct understanding of this truth."

Supplementary Reading

4. "SCIENCE AND METAPHYSICS, PART II: GOD'S CAUSALITY INVOLVES NO CHANGE IN GOD"

(excerpted from Christoph Cardinal Schönborn, "In the Beginning God Created…" Internet. Available from http://stephanscom.at/edw/katechesen/articles/2005/12/02/a9719/; accessed April 2, 2007.) This has been reproduced as part of Chance or Purpose? Creation, Evolution, and a Rational Faith, trans. Henry Taylor, ed. Hubert Philip Weber (San Francisco: Ignatius Press, 2007)

…[F]rom the side of God the act of creating involves "no movement." Why? All making and producing and acting that we observe in the world is a moving or changing of something that already exists. A carpenter makes a table out of wood, he changes the wood, he forms it, giving a new shape to some pre-given material.

Someone at home takes a bunch of ingredients and makes a wonderful meal out of them, shaping pre-given elements into something new. But it is not something absolutely new, it is not a real creating, it is only a shaping. Things are changed so that they become edible. It is the same way with the artist, with the technician, even with intellectually creative people. Even my best ideas are not absolute novelties. They always presuppose that others have already done some thinking and that I have already done some thinking.…

Now we see what is decisively different about the creative act of God: **it is without movement.** It does not change that which already exists. It does not form some pre-given material… Thus St. Theophilus of Antioch, writing around the year 180, says: "If God had drawn the world out of some pre-existing stuff, what would have been so special about that? If you give to a human worker some material, he makes out of it whatever he wants. But the power of God shows itself in the fact that he starts from nothing to make anything he wants." This does not mean that "nothing" is something out of which he produces things, but that God's creative act is a sovereign act of bringing into being. We can also say: it is a pure act of "calling into being." God spoke and it came to be. That is what is so wonderful and so unique about the biblical belief in creation.

Study Guide

Faith and Science:
At the Crossroads of Nature and Spirit

VOCABULARY

Define the following terms:

1. The Two Books
2. "Science without Wisdom"
3. Matter (physical reality)
4. Physica
5. Mathematica
6. Metaphysica
7. Existence

8. *Existere*
9. Efficient Cause
10. Principle of Sufficient Reason
11. Primary Causality
12. Primary Cause
13. Secondary Causality

STUDY QUESTIONS

1. How is the universe like a book with different "reading levels"?
2. Compare the *Harry Potter* series with the drama of history and the universe. How are they alike? How are they different?
3. Give an example of "science without wisdom."
4. What are the three elements of St. Thomas Aquinas' multi-leveled approach to the Book of the Universe?
5. How does metaphysics give us the "grammar of the universe" at its richest, deepest level?
6. What are the characteristics of existence?
7. What is the difference between "being" and "Being"?
8. Describe God as uncaused cause.
9. How is "cause and effect" absolutely essential to the very ability to think about anything at all?
10. Is change within an agent essential to its being an agent? Explain.
11. Is metaphysics compatible with science? How about with faith?
12. Why is metaphysics the key to a faithful reunion of science and faith?
13. What principles did Pope John Paul II develop for a healthy relationship between faith and science?

Study Guide

PRACTICAL EXERCISES

1. Think of a novel which you have been assigned to read in English class in the past 2–3 years. On the basis of your reading, as well as teacher instruction and other resources offered to help you understand the book, reflect on the "book-learning" approach (in which the deeper meaning of the story is missed) to "learning a book," a deeper reading of the story. Then, answer the following questions:

    a. Is the story interesting if only the details of the story are noticed?

    b. Does one even understand the details when they are studied as if they were the only element of the story?

    c. Are there values and meanings which are central to the story but could also be central to another story without the same details?

    d. Summarize the novel according to its levels: details, characters, and themes.

2. Jacques Maritain, the famous twentieth century Catholic philosopher, believed that the relationship between essence (what a thing is) and existence (that a thing is) is a reality that requires a special "intuition of being," an inner silence that allows us to "listen to" the mystery of existence whispered by all things.

    Find a quiet space, preferably outside, and spend five minutes silently attentive to the things around you. When you find yourself focused on something, consider first what it is, and then consider the fact of its existence. Finally, consider how existence unites all things.

    After you are done, answer this question: Did I have an intuition of being?

Endnotes

1. Barbour, Religion and Science, 15.
2. Antonino Zichichi, "Galileo, Divine Man" in *The Session Commemorating the 400th Anniversary of the Founding of the Pontifical Academy of Sciences (1603–2003)*. Internet. Available from http://www.vatican.va/roman_curia/ pontifical_academies/acdscien/acta17_anniversary/ part2.pdf; accessed April 17, 2006.
3. John F. Haught, *Deeper than Darwin: The Prospect for Religion in the Age of Evolution* (Cambridge: Westview, 2003), 14–15. My use of the book analogy is different than Haught's, but his development of the analogy originally inspired this chapter.
4. The title of this section is from Chapter 1 of Anthony Rizzi, *The Science Before Science: A Guide to Thinking in the 21st Century* (Baton Rouge: IAP Press, 2004), 1.

5. Ibid., 2.
6. Ibid., 23.
7. Idem.
8. Ibid., 23–24.
9. St. Thomas Aquinas, *In Boeth. De Trin.* 5.3, resp.
10. Ibid., 5.1, *resp.*
11. Ibid., 5.1, *resp.*
12. Clarke, 87.
13. Ibid., 21.
14. Ibid., 21.
15. John Paul II, "Letter to the Reverend George V. Coyne, S.J., Director of the Vatican Observatory" (June 1, 1988).
16. Sherwin, "Reconciling Old Lovers."
17. John Paul II, "Letter to the Reverend George V. Coyne, S.J" (June 1, 1988).

18. Sherwin, "Reconciling Old Lovers."
19. Ibid.
20. John Paul II, "Address to a group of scientists gathered to honor the centenary of the birth of Albert Einstein" (September 28, 1979).
21. John Paul II, "Letter to Reverend George V. Coyne, S.J" (June 1, 1988).
22. Idem., "Address to the Pontifical Academy of Sciences" (November 8, 2004), 2.
23. Idem., "Address to International Conference on Space Research" (January 11, 1997), 4.
24. Cf. Vatican Council I, can. 2 §1: DS 3026.

Part Two

GOD AND SCIENCE:
THE CREDIBILITY OF THE CREATOR

Chapter Six

The Biggest Question: Has Science Disproved God?

A. God: Forgettable or Just Forgotten?

In early nineteenth century France, the question of God made an interesting appearance in an encounter between a scientist and a powerful ruler. The scientist, *Pierre-Simon Laplace* (1749–1827), was one of the greatest mathematicians and scientists of his day. When he presented a ground-breaking work on astronomy and celestial mechanics to his emperor, Napoleon Bonaparte, the emperor attempted to shock his favorite scientist with an observation: "Monsieur Laplace, they tell me you have written this large book on the system of the universe, and have never even mentioned its Creator." Laplace's response was quick and honest: "Sire," he said bluntly, "I had no need of that hypothesis."

To many atheists, this encounter marks the moment in which science broke though the ignorance of religious belief. But it was nothing of the sort. Laplace was not an atheist, and he died a faithful Catholic. He simply meant to point out that much about the universe can be understood without invoking God's miraculous intervention, a principle that is biblical and is supported by the teaching of the Church (see Chapters Three and Four).

Within a century after Laplace's death, an idea emerged that he would have found shocking and unfounded; the idea that *everything* about the universe can be understood, in fact *must* be understood, without any reference to God. Somehow, the idea of God as an unnecessary hypothesis for explaining specific natural phenomena mutated into *scientific atheism,* the conviction that science has revealed that God does not exist. It is a popular position among scientists today, as we

...THE UNIVERSE CAN BE UNDERSTOOD ON ITS OWN TERMS, A PRINCIPLE THAT IS BIBLICAL AND IS SUPPORTED BY THE TEACHING OF THE CHURCH.

SCIENTIFIC ATHEISM, WHICH REJECTS THE CHRISTIAN FAITH, IS A KIND OF FAITH ITSELF; NOT IN GOD, BUT IN AN UNPROVABLE ASSERTION.

saw in our encounter with materialism, reductionism, and scientism in Chapter Two. It poses the very first question to which we must turn in Part II of our attempt to find faith on the frontiers of science: has science made God an "unnecessary hypothesis" entirely? Has science disproved God?

SCIENTIFIC ATHEISM AS BLIND FAITH

How does one respond to scientific atheism? The first response is a scientific one, and it is rather obvious. We first mentioned it back in Chapter Two—*scientific atheism is a belief system, not a scientifically proven fact.* No scientific evidence has ever proven that God does not exist.

There is an important irony here. Scientific atheism, which rejects the Christian Faith, is a kind of faith itself; not in God, but in an unprovable assertion. Even more, scientific atheism is a blind faith— it is an approach to the world which creates a kind of "forbidden zone" for human thought. To be a scientific atheist, you have to hold unproven ideas and never hold any ideas which contradict them. In the words of Stephen Barr, the scientific atheist "will not allow himself to contemplate the possibility that anything whatever might exist that is not completely describable by physics. That is simply a forbidden thought." [1]

We have stumbled upon an important difference between scientific atheism and the Christian Faith. Because the Christian Faith teaches that the world was created by God in and through the *Logos,* who is divine rationality "in person," Christians believe that the world is thoroughly knowable, that we can understand it through rational investigation. Therefore, nothing is unthinkable, at least in the sense of investigating possibilities. But for the scientific atheist, like all materialists, there are many things which must never be thought about—God, the soul, Heaven, Hell, angels, demons, and any other immaterial realities are examples of "forbidden thoughts."[2]

SCIENTIFIC ATHEISM IS THE CONVICTION THAT SCIENCE HAS REVEALED THAT GOD DOES NOT EXIST.

While believers accept certain truths as dogmas because they are revealed by God, the scientific atheist holds his position on an unprovable speculation. In this way, scientific atheism is much more confining than religious faith. The ultimate principle of religious faith is a positive one—there **is** a God. But scientific atheism is based on a negation, a denial—there is *nothing* (i.e., "no thing") that is not material. The scientific atheist does not acknowledge anything that is beyond explanation in terms of matter and mathematics: "What cannot be explained by [scientific atheism] is eliminated from consideration. . . The materialist lives in a very small world, intellectually speaking."[3]

So scientific atheism is certainly not broad-minded. But before we disqualify it, let us be thorough and start by assuming what some of its adherents assume—that the world has always existed. Many scientific atheists have been attracted to the idea that nature has no temporal starting-point, that it has always "been there." They recognize that it is absurd to hold that the universe simply pops out of nothing with no cause to explain it. And since they also hold that there is no God to cause the universe, they conclude that our universe is a perpetually existing one, which stretches back infinitely with no beginning. If their assumption is correct, is it still reasonable to argue that God exists and that He created the universe?

SCIENTIFIC ATHEISM AND THE PERPETUAL UNIVERSE IDEA

What if the universe just stretched back infinitely, such that there was never a starting point to it, or a first moment?

It is an incredible question, one that we usually never even attempt to imagine. But the question of "beginning, or no beginning" has been asked about the universe many times throughout the history of Western Civilization. Thinkers as great as the Greek philosopher Aristotle have held that the universe, the total system of existing things, has always existed in some form or another. As we saw in Chapter Four, it is part of Divine Revelation that the world was created with a beginning; that is, that it was created in time, freely, by God. But the possibility that the world has no beginning has had a long life-span in the history of ideas.

When the scientific revolution, which began in Europe in the sixteenth century, began to blossom in the nineteenth century, the idea of the perpetual existence of the universe became a cherished belief among many scientists. As they used scientific methods to delve deeper and deeper into the secrets of the physical universe, it seemed to many of them that the universe was a perfectly interlocking system; a machine which had operated endlessly, without a first moment. Twin theories—*the law of the conservation of mass* and *the law of the conservation of energy*—seemed to support this view. The law of the conservation of mass states that when matter undergoes changes (for example, in chemical reactions) the total amount of mass in the universe does not change. The law of the conservation of energy states that energy cannot be created or destroyed, but only converted from one form to another. These principles seemed to imply that matter and energy must have always existed, which, if true, would also imply that the universe had always existed.[4]

It is not hard to see how the twin principles of conservation would lead minds to consider the perpetual universe possibility and even to assert that it was the most probable possibility. But many scientists also assumed that an ever-existing universe also meant that the idea of a Creator was to be entirely set aside. If there was no beginning, then why bother with the idea of an all-powerful Creator who gave the universe its start?

IT SEEMED TO MANY 19TH CENTURY SCIENTISTS THAT THE UNIVERSE WAS A PERFECTLY INTERLOCKING SYSTEM; A MACHINE WHICH HAD OPERATED ENDLESSLY, WITHOUT A FIRST MOMENT.

B. *God and the Limits of a Perpetual Universe*

ST. THOMAS BELIEVED, AS A MATTER OF FAITH, THAT THE UNIVERSE DID HAVE A BEGINNING, BUT HE WAS WILLING TO CONSIDER THE IDEA OF AN ETERNAL UNIVERSE FROM A PURELY PHILOSOPHICAL POINT OF VIEW. HIS CONCLUSION WAS THAT REASON BY ITSELF COULD NOT SETTLE THE QUESTION OF WHETHER THE UNIVERSE HAD A BEGINNING OR NOT.

We will leave the discussion of whether the universe did in fact have a beginning until the next chapter. For now, let us suppose "for the sake of argument" that it did not and see where that leaves us. Many people might think that the statement "the universe never had a beginning" is an atheistic one in itself. To say that something is without a beginning seems to be saying it is uncaused; and if the universe is uncaused, then it has no Creator and no need to acknowledge God. But if the universe did not have a beginning, does that also mean that the universe is uncaused? The answer is "no"—at least, according to St. Thomas Aquinas (1224–1274), not only one of the greatest theologians in the history of the Church but generally acknowledged as one of the great philosophers of history.

St. Thomas' attitude shows how our faith never stops us from thinking critically about all of the possibilities, even ones that contradict our faith. For even though he believed, as a matter of faith, that the universe did have a beginning, he was willing to consider the idea of an eternal universe from a purely philosophical point of view. His conclusion was that reason by itself could not settle the question of whether the universe had a beginning or not. We only know that the universe had a beginning, he said, because God revealed to us that it does. On the other hand, St. Thomas Aquinas believed that human reason by itself, i.e., without the aid of Divine Revelation, *could* prove that the universe has a Creator. Obviously, then, for him the universe must have a Creator *whether or not it had a beginning.* In other words, "having a beginning" and "being created" are not the same thing.

First, St. Thomas observed that the universe could have always existed because it was caused to do so by God; that is, it could have always been because God caused it to always be. If so, it could have gone on forever and ever without a first moment, but God would still be the explanation (i.e., the sufficient reason) for its existence. As an analogy, think about a play or a book. A book has a beginning and an end. But the reason we say the book has an *author* has to do with the fact that *it exists at all.* Even if it had a beginning and no end, or an end and no beginning, it would need an author. Anything that exists, but might not have existed, has to have its existence explained. There must be a cause or explanation of its existence. That is why if there is a book, there must be an author.

In the same way, we might entertain the possibility that the universe may or may not have a beginning, just as we might entertain the possibility that it may or may not have an end. But the reason we say that God creates it has to do with the fact that it exists at all. Even if the universe had no beginning and no end, or an end and no beginning, it still requires a Creator.

Let us now investigate the incredible argument by which St. Thomas proved the existence of God, regardless of whether the universe had a first moment or not.

A METAPHYSICAL MOMENT

We learned in our last chapter that, in order to read the book of the universe on all its levels, physical and spiritual, we need to rely on a branch of philosophy called metaphysics. Our escape from the confining mindset of scientific atheism brings us to a metaphysical moment, one that starts with a basic observation: none of the beings in our experience (e.g., ourselves, plants, planets, atoms, molecules, animals, etc.) are self-sufficient. All of them need certain conditions to be in place before they can actually exist.[5] In our last chapter, we discussed this with regard to the Principle of Sufficient Reason.

As we look around us, we see that beings depend upon other beings outside of themselves in order to exist. For example, beings depend upon things that came before them. This is especially obvious in the case of animals, which have parents who generated them. The parents are causes of their offspring's existence. St. Thomas Aquinas called such causes, which produce effects in such a way that those effects can continue to exist even after their causes themselves have ceased to exist, *"non-simultaneously acting causes."* But this kind of causality is not what St. Thomas was focusing on to construct his argument for a Creator.

There is a second kind of dependency in which a cause keeps a thing existing in the present moment. You needed to have parents to come into existence, but you do not need them to exist right at this moment—your parents are not holding you in existence as we speak. But there is another kind of causing, in which the effect would cease to exist should the cause cease to exist or stop its causing activity. St. Thomas Aquinas called such things *"simultaneous causes"* or *"simultaneously acting causes."* For example, the earth is causing its "gravitational field" to exist *right now*. The existence of the earth is a *present condition* for the existence of its gravitational field—the earth is the simultaneous cause of its gravity. A gravitational field is an example of something that depends on another thing, distinct from itself, in order to exist, in such a way that this dependence is simultaneous with the ongoing existence of that distinct thing.[6]

Apply the same idea to yourself—you are a being that relies on other beings as conditions for your existence. Air, temperature within a certain range, cosmic forces, such as the stability of the proton, and the existence of the water molecule—without any one of these, you would not exist, at least not bodily. They exist, therefore you can exist—they are simultaneously acting causes of your existence. And they each have simultaneously acting causes that make it possible for them to exist—for instance, the existence of the water molecule

NONE OF THE BEINGS IN OUR EXPERIENCE ARE SELF-SUFFICIENT. ALL OF THEM NEED CERTAIN CONDITIONS TO BE IN PLACE BEFORE THEY CAN ACTUALLY EXIST.

St. Thomas Aquinas

FOR THE QUEST FOR KNOWLEDGE TO MAKE SENSE, THERE HAS TO BE AT LEAST ONE THING THAT CURRENTLY EXISTS WHICH DOES NOT DEPEND ON ANOTHER THING FOR ITS EXISTENCE, A BEING THAT IS TOTALLY *UNCONDITIONED* IN ITS EXISTENCE. THIS BEING HAS TO BE THE ONGOING REASON OF THE WHOLE CHAIN, THE THING THAT ALL OTHER THINGS DEPEND ON FOR THEIR EXISTENCES

known

unknown

relies on the stability of the proton, which makes the atomic elements (such as hydrogen and oxygen) capable of existing.

Now let us apply this analysis to all of reality: can all beings be conditioned, dependent on the ongoing existence of others, for their existence? The answer is "no." Think about it—for A to exist, B must exist, for B to exist, C must exist, and so on. But this chain of simultaneously acting causes cannot be an unending one, because then the whole chain would never get to a being which makes A (or B, or C, etc.) capable of existing, a being which "grounds" the chain. Nor can it just go around in a circle: A depending on B, B on C, and C on A, because A cannot be making other things exist while also depending on those very things for its own existence. In either scenario, there would be no ultimate reason for the whole chain of causes, and, if this were the case, there would be no reason, no intelligibility, in any part of the chain.

Yet, scientific investigation depends on the possibility of asking a question and finding a reasonable answer. For the quest for knowledge to make sense, there has to be at least one thing that currently exists which does not depend on another thing for its existence, a being that is totally *unconditioned* in its existence. This being has to be the ongoing reason of the whole chain, the thing that all other things depend on for their existences, the condition for all other beings. It has to be self-sufficient, self-explanatory, and uncaused.[7] In short, for any conditioned thing to exist *right now,* there has to be a God, who is "to all things the cause of being"[8]

In summary, the preserving power which holds all things in being, right here and right now, "can ultimately only be something that is not in turn held in being by something else."[9] Our investigation of what we can obse rve through our common human experience leads us to God, if we patiently and intelligently pay attention to the way the cosmos works.

And we would be led right to him even if the universe was ever-existing. Even if the great chain of *non-simultaneously* acting causes stretched back infinitely, "a father being a cause of a son and another person the cause of that father, so on, endlessly,"[10] there must be a beginning to the chain of *simultaneously* acting causes which make anything exist in the present moment. God stands at the beginning of that chain—all things ultimately depend on his existence for their own existence at every moment, no matter how many moments there have been or will be.

C. Simply Divine:
God, the Cause of all Causes

The examination of any and every being in our experience leads us through a great chain of simultaneously existing things to the One Source of all being, a Source that is self-sufficient for its own existence. We have traveled the chain of beings all the way back to God himself. As we ponder this marvel, can we describe him more specifically—that is, can we say what his characteristics are? For guidance, let us rely on the insights of the metaphysician W. Norris Clarke, who can help us understand some important conclusions about God, the Source of all being.

GOD IS INFINITE IN PERFECTION

We began our attempt to escape scientific atheism by looking at all the beings in our experience. In each case, be it an asteroid or an omelet, what we see is a *finite* being—a being with limits. Finiteness, contingency and "being conditioned" are three ways of saying the same thing—because I do not have all powers and perfections, I must rely on other existing things for my own existence. Therefore, a self-sufficient Being would have to be *infinite, non-contingent and unconditioned*—it would have to possess all powers and perfections in an unlimited way in order to be able to sustain in existence any and all other things.

And this must be true of all powers and perfections we see in the universe. Goodness, beauty, truth—all of these perfections are God's in an unlimited way, such that he can share them with his creatures. In fact, God is these perfections—for example, God is not simply good, he is Goodness. God cannot share what he does not have; any perfection in the universe is perfectly, infinitely, God's first. It is only ours by participation.

GOD IS SINGULAR:
THERE IS ONLY ONE GOD

To be infinite means to be unlimited. But if two different infinite, self-sufficient beings existed, neither would actually be infinite; each one would be limited by its difference from the other.

Think of it this way: we distinguish things from each other by their limits—I distinguish my house from your house because my house is made of brick and yours is made of wood, or by the difference in their color, size or location. If our houses were exactly the same in every way, including location, we would have to admit that there was only one house, not two.

THE GREAT CHAIN OF SIMULTANEOUSLY EXISTING THINGS LEADS US TO THE ONE SOURCE OF ALL BEING, A SOURCE THAT IS SELF-SUFFICIENT FOR ITS OWN EXISTENCE.

IF GOD IS THE INFINITE SOURCE OF EXISTENCE AND OF ALL POWERS AND PERFECTIONS, THIS MEANS THAT HE IS *UNCHANGING*, NOT BOUND BY TIME—PAST, PRESENT, AND FUTURE.

But herein lies the problem—if there were two infinitely perfect beings, they would be absolutely identical and indistinguishable. Each would have all powers and perfections in an indistinguishable way. So there really could not be two self-sufficient beings—hence there can logically be only one God.

But what about the Trinity? Christians do not believe that there are three Gods. We believe that there is one Divine Being, one God, in three Divine Persons—Father, Son, and Holy Spirit, who possess one Divine Being perfectly and totally.

ETERNAL WITH A CAPITAL "E"

Some people have used the word "eternal" to mean ever-existing. If the universe is eternal in this ever-existing sense, it would still be teeming with the changes of the beings within it—it would be ever-existing, but also ever-changing. But if God is the infinite Source of existence and of all powers and perfections, this means that he is *unchanging,* not bound by time. He does not ever gain or lose perfections; even when he acts, he does not change, "since he is above and outside the whole order of time and change." This is the metaphysical definition of the word "eternal."

Joseph Cardinal Ratzinger, now Pope Benedict XVI, once described God's eternity as a circle within which time carries onward like a line.[11] That means that God's reality is a perfect NOW—God is not hurried from past to future, rushing through a continuously passing present, as we are. Rather, when we encounter him in prayer, or in an experience of natural beauty or human love, we touch a perfect fullness that never passes away.

GOD IS SIMPLE

Because God is self-sufficient, he is not composed of different "component principles." If God were like us, a composition of many parts, then like us something would have had to put his parts together. Instead, God is perfectly uncomposed; he is "one simple identical perfection of the pure fullness of existence."[12]

We use many terms to describe God's infinite perfection; we say that God is just, good, merciful, loving, wise, etc. But this is not because there is any real division of qualities in God. It is we that are limited in our ability to express the reality of God. None of our terms can fully express it. His fullness, simple and uncomposed, can only be expressed by us as we see it incompletely and from different points-of-view.[13]

GOD IS ALL-POWERFUL (OMNIPOTENT) AND ALL-KNOWING (OMNISCIENT): GOD, THE CAUSE OF CAUSES

If God is the source of all powers and perfections, then there is no limit to his own power. And if he is the source of all things, then he knows all things perfectly. But here is an amazing logical consequence of God's simplicity: his power and his knowing cannot be separate. God not only acts through his intelligence—*his acting and his knowing are one and the same.*

God knows all things perfectly, but not by learning about them. Learning is a passing from ignorance to knowledge, and that involves limitation in two ways. First, ignorance is itself a limitation of knowledge. And, second, passing from one state to another takes time, which means being limited by time. Since God is not limited, he does not acquire knowledge by "learning." We know things because they are there to be known. God does not know all things because they are there; rather, all things are there because he creatively knows them and wills them, giving being to them.

Imagine an artist who wants to paint a beautiful landscape. He first must look at it and come to know its characteristics. But in the case of the Perfect Artist, God, knowing the landscape, and willing it, *makes* the landscape in all its beauty. He is the ultimate source of all that it is (omnipotent) and the unrestricted act of knowing all that is (omniscient).

We need to consider God's knowing and power more closely, because by doing so we will get a glimpse of one of the most important metaphysical points in the relationship between faith and science. We have already focused on God as the cause of existence, as necessary for the great chain of all beings. But this fact entails another: God is the cause of all causes. God causes not only the existence of all things but even their ability, their power, to cause other things. Therefore, God is not a substitute cause for things, filling in to do this or that function in the natural order. Instead, God enables things to act according to their natures but, nonetheless, to bring about the effects he intends. God's creative power is intelligent: he creates an ordered universe of natural causes, which possess regularity and intelligibility.

In a recent statement, the Catholic International Theological Commission put it this way: "In freely willing to create and conserve the universe, God wills to activate and to sustain in act all those secondary causes whose activity contributes to the unfolding of the natural order he intends to produce."[14]

So God is the cause of all things in a primary way, but not in a way that removes or cancels out the activity of his creatures. From an

immediate perspective, on the ground-level that we see all around us, there are happenings that are fully explainable by the interactions among creatures that bring about things in their own way, according to their own natures.[15] At this level, God truly is an "unnecessary hypothesis," as Laplace noted to Napoleon. But this does not change the fact that, ultimately, on a level our minds can only dimly see, God's *Providence* is the ultimate explanation. *Divine Providence* is "God's all-wise, all-loving, and all-encompassing guidance of nature, history," and even the course of our own lives.[16]

To scientific atheism, it all appears accidental, a random process. But with God there can be no accidents, in the sense of unguided events. He even writes straight with crooked lines, bringing good out of evil. And in doing so, "God's action does not displace or supplant the activity of creaturely causes…"[17] He allows his creatures to be as he makes them to be, and that includes their own ability to act. Let us look at this on a small human scale and on a grand cosmic scale to make sure we understand it.

A young man's car breaks down. While waiting for a tow truck in a nearby coffee shop, he meets the woman whom he eventually marries. God was not the immediate cause of his car breaking down. A creaturely cause (a leaky gasket or a dead alternator) is the immediate cause. But God is the cause of all causes, *"behind" each cause as the sustaining Source of its existence and its power.* Twenty years and six children later, the man can truly tell his wife, "thank God my car broke down that day." In fact, he can and should thank God directly for this gift, which seemed at the time to leave him completely out of luck.

Let us look at a bigger example. Science has made us aware of the fact that the dominant life forms on our planet were once the dinosaurs, which roamed the Earth up to 65 million years ago. But scientific evidence points to a catastrophic event in their history—it is probable that the dinosaurs were made extinct by the collision of a large asteroids with planet Earth in the area of what is now the Yucatan peninsula.

This is fully explainable on the level of natural causes: by the nature of asteroids, the nature of dinosaurs, the nature of earth, and the nature of gravity. Put them all together, and you have ash blown into the atmosphere from an explosion that so radically changed the Earth's climate that the dinosaurs could not survive. But this is not the whole story: the asteroid collision brought about changes that allowed mammals to flourish. In the words of Frances Collins: "We probably wouldn't be here if that asteroid had not hit Mexico."[18] We should thank God for that asteroid.

God is, therefore, the ultimate explanation of the history of the universe. But that history does not cease to be the universe's own history—God makes it possible and guides it, but his creatures have a real role to play in it. He causes them, including their ability to cause other things. Therefore, the drama of the universe is both God's and his creatures.

GOD OF THE GAPS?

Some believers, impressed by God's creative omnipotence and omniscience, have not entirely grasped the point about God as the "Cause of all causes." Instead, they search the wonders of nature for some sign that shows God intervening directly in the natural course of things to bring about natural effects. This approach is often called the *God of the Gaps.*

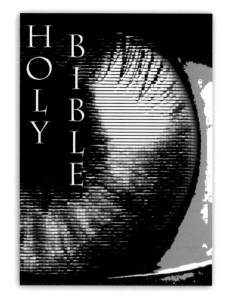

In this approach, some phenomenon not yet explained by science is held up as proving that God has intervened in the world in an extraordinary way. If there is no natural explanation, the argument goes, then the explanation must be supernatural. Or to be more precise, God is not working through secondary causes, but is acting directly to produce the phenomenon.

People who advance arguments of this type are claiming that something miraculous has happened or is happening in a regular and predictable way in a natural phenomenon. However, that is very different from the miraculous as we find it recorded in Sacred Scripture. There, God does indeed intervene directly in the natural course of things, but in a way that is *singular*—that is, miracles do not happen over and over again, so that when the same conditions exist the same miracle always occurs. Jesus' raising of Lazarus from the dead (Jn 11) is a prime example of a true miracle—Jesus does something which reverses nature in a way that can only be supernatural. However, although he does perform other resurrection miracles, including his own Resurrection, he does not do so in a predictable, repeatable way in the ordinary course of things. We will talk more about miracles in the concluding chapter of this text.

SOME BELIEVERS SEARCH THE WONDERS OF NATURE FOR SOME SIGN THAT SHOWS GOD INTERVENING DIRECTLY IN THE NATURAL COURSE OF THINGS TO BRING ABOUT NATURAL EFFECTS. THIS APPROACH IS OFTEN CALLED THE *GOD OF THE GAPS.*

Doubting Thomas

The problems with the God of the Gaps approach are much the same as the problems with concordism that we examined in Chapter Three. The first is that it is a misunderstanding of what reason tells us about how God creates, sustains, and guides the universe in its natural circumstances: contrary to the God of the Gaps approach, God acts by enabling, not by displacing or supplanting, natural causes.

The second problem is of a practical nature. In numerous cases in the past, science reached the point where it could explain phenomena that had been thought unexplainable except by God's direct intervention. One example would be the ancient attribution of lightning and thunder to the direct activity of God—we now know that God brings about thunder and lightning through secondary causes. When science "catches up" with the phenomenon in question, it can scandalize believers and give the impression that God has been explained away by science, and that God is irrelevant.

But as we have seen, God has created a world full of wondrously regular causes of which he is the ultimate explanation. Believers can have recourse to God to *explain* all things, but not as the immediate cause of all things. *As a general rule, God operates through natural causes.*

GOD IS NOT A WHAT, BUT A WHO: GOD IS PERSONAL

One of the perfections that exist in the visible universe created and sustained by God is the one that is possessed only by human beings—the quality of being "a center of intelligent, free, responsible, loving action." This is the quality of being a *person,* a *who,* and not simply a *what.* But as we have already seen, God must himself have this perfection without limit if he is the ultimate source of it, the one who communicates it and sustains it in all finite beings who have it, such as ourselves. This means that God is infinitely intelligent, wise, free, and loving, that his eternal decision to share being with us is a decision that is personal. God's creating is an act done by Persons (the Trinity) for persons (humanity).[19] God loves us into existence.

GOD IS CREATOR

It is obvious that, if God is the infinite Source of all the perfections of all limited things, including and especially their existence, then God is Creator of all things. But let us be sure we understand exactly the far-reaching and amazing nature of God's status as Creator. Since God is perfect and unchanging, his motive for creating all things could not be self-serving—since he has all perfections infinitely, creating cannot have offered God any good that he does not already possess. He already enjoys all goodness in himself, so the only reason for creating, or any other action, must be to share, to communicate, his goodness to creatures. "God enjoys himself, and he wants us to join him"—this is the whole meaning and purpose of the universe.[20]

D. Beauty and Being: Converts from Scientific Atheism

In the same century in which many scientists dismissed the existence of God, one scientific atheist found God in the foothills of the Caucasus Mountains:

GOD HAS CREATED A WORLD FULL OF WONDROUSLY REGULAR CAUSES OF WHICH HE IS THE ULTIMATE EXPLANATION. BELIEVERS CAN HAVE RECOURSE TO GOD TO *EXPLAIN* ALL THINGS, BUT NOT AS THE IMMEDIATE CAUSE OF ALL THINGS. *AS A GENERAL RULE, GOD OPERATES THROUGH NATURAL CAUSES.*

THE RISEN CHRIST
MICHELANGELO (1521)

I was 23 years old, but for almost ten years the faith had been ripped out of my soul; after passing through crises and doubts a religious emptiness took possession of it.... Suddenly the following event occurred.... The evening was approaching... we were driving through the southern prairie, bathed in the spicy aroma of honey, grass and hay, [the land] shining in the mild light of the setting sun. Off in the distance the first of the Caucasus Mountains was already blue. I saw these mountains for the first time. I gazed eagerly on them and drank in the air and the light, listening to the revelation of nature. My soul had for a long time now been used to seeing in nature nothing but a *dead desert* covered by a veil of beauty, worn by nature like a mask that deceives. Suddenly my soul was filled with joy and trembled with excitement at the thought: *what if there were...* what if there were no desert, no mask, no death, what if there were instead the mild love of the Father, all this beauty being his veil, his love... Was that possible? Didn't I know from my years of study that God does not exist? Could there be any doubt about this? Could I acknowledge these new thoughts in myself without feeling ashamed on account of my cowardice, without feeling panic in the presence of "science" and its court of justice? O you Caucasian mountains, I saw your ice glistening from one sea to the other, I saw your snow reddened by the morning sun, your peaks reaching up into the sky, and my soul melted in ecstasy. The first day of creation shone before my eyes. There was no life and no death, just an eternal and unchangeable Now. An unexpected feeling arose in me and surged up: the feeling of victory over death.[21]

Sophia (Divine Wisdom)

This young man was Sergei Bulgakov (1871–1944), who became one of the greatest philosophers and theologians in Russia. At that moment, he saw the beauty of the world and realized that it did not need to exist, that it was totally and entirely dependent on God. And in addition, it was beautiful. It did not have to be, but it was. And in this beauty, Bulgakov saw "God's veil," barely concealing a loving Creator.

Fr. Sergei Nikolaevich Bulgakov

Bulgakov lived in a different time, and he admittedly had a religious upbringing that made his atheism extremely painful for him. But Francis Collins, the former director of the Human Genome Project and current director of the National Institutes of Health, recounts a remarkably similar story even after growing up in a non-religious American family. He embraced atheism while studying physics, discounting religion as anti-scientific, "an outmoded superstition." Even after encountering faith in a hospital patient, he was sure that investigating the religions of the world would show him to be right. It did not, and Collins began to believe in God, although only in a general way. Finally, his search became an encounter with created beauty, and then with a Person:

On a beautiful fall day, as I was hiking in the Cascade Mountains during my first trip west of the Mississippi, the majesty and beauty of God's creation overwhelmed my resistance. As I rounded a corner and saw a beautiful and unexpected frozen waterfall, hundreds of feet high, I knew the search was over. The next morning, I knelt in the dewy grass as the sun rose and surrendered to Jesus Christ.[22]

In his book *The Language of God,* Collins tells the whole story of his journey and the incredible lessons which modern science can show those who doubt God's existence.

Why did the beauty of creation have such an impact on these two men? Perhaps the lavish abundance of beauty, so overwhelming and so unnecessary, showed them something of the personality of God. Christoph Cardinal Schönborn, marveling at the beauty of creation, compares God to Mozart :

All of [Mozart's] works are "contingent," they could as well have not come into being (which would have been very unfortunate for mankind). Most of them came to be for particular purposes, in response to commissions and orders. But many just came from the creativity of genius, including those which were commissioned. Purpose and beauty do not break apart here. A work of art may have a purpose, but it is more than its purpose.[23]

In encountering the world, we find it overflowing with "non-purposeful beauty." "This beauty, free of all practical purpose, these splendid patterns that … have no usefulness but are simply a manifestation of beauty, 'selflessly' pouring themselves out: we understand their *meaning* only when we see creation in terms of its goal of praising the creator."[24] This is the common experience of Bulgakov and Collins, both scientific atheists who became believers. The "unnecessary beauty" of creation compelled them to believe in the existence of Laplace's "unnecessary hypothesis," an all-loving Creator.

WHY DID THE BEAUTY OF CREATION HAVE SUCH AN IMPACT ON SERGEI BULGAKOV AND FRANCIS COLLINS? PERHAPS THE LAVISH ABUNDANCE OF BEAUTY, SO OVERWHELMING AND SO UNNECESSARY, SHOWED THEM SOMETHING OF THE PERSONALITY OF GOD.

E. The Divine Playwright

Our pursuit of God, his existence and his infinite perfection, has brought us almost as far as natural reasoning can go. But before we conclude this chapter, let us visit an idea with which we ended Part I—the universe and its history as a book. In that chapter, we looked at the multi-leveled drama of the book of the universe; now we turn to think about God, its Divine Author.

Within any book, there are many cause and effect relationships that bring about a whole host of events. The great fantasy trilogy, The

Lord of the Rings, is about an epic adventure caused by an event that happened before the story—the making of the "magic" ring. The accidental finding of the ring by a hobbit named Bilbo Baggins is one cause among many of the battles, struggles, and victories of the characters which make up the story being told. But the story itself is caused, at a different level altogether, by the author, J.R.R. Tolkien.

Tolkien has absolute dominion over his story as a story—he is the cause of all the other causes we meet in it, including Bilbo. The story as a whole and all its details depend upon Tolkien. He is the one who makes a great story out of all of its parts and characters. Yet he does so by allowing the whole story to unfold according to its own time and its own inner logic, a logic created by Tolkien. So, on the one hand, the story unfolds according to this inner logic; on the other, Tolkien has a universal dominion over the characters, plot, and storyline of his work.

What makes Tolkien one of the great authors of English literature is that his characters have a real freedom which he gives them and allows them to exercise. We can love and admire those characters, even mourn them when they die, because they have their own greatness. The fact that the story has an author does not make it any less of a great story. In fact, the greatness of the author as an author is what accounts for the greatness of the story and the characters he or she creates in it.

What is true of a human author and his or her story is a dim analogy, but a helpful one, for the relationship of God to his creation, the universe. As Creator, God is not determined by the timeline of the story; rather everything in it depends on him. And yet, because God is infinitely greater than even the greatest of human authors, his creatures have *real* freedom, *real* independence. Not one of the natural causes investigated by science is God "inserting" himself in the story, filling in the gaps. Rather, the whole story *depends* on God *as* the one who gives it its basic pattern, its laws, and its very existence, and who thus directs the whole to a good end.

SHAKESPEARE IN HEAVEN

It would be difficult to say more about our Divine Author on the basis of metaphysics alone. But we have more than metaphysics to go on—our Divine Author has revealed himself within his story. If we transfer our idea of authorship to another kind of creative writing, such as a play or a movie script, then we can complete our comparison—God, the great playwright, has, in sovereign freedom, stepped on to the stage of his play as one of the characters.[25] Imagination can help us glimpse the big picture, the world stage.

Imagine a playwright sitting at his writing desk, setting out his masterpiece. Yet, as he writes, the play itself emerges

WHAT MAKES TOLKIEN ONE OF THE GREAT AUTHORS OF ENGLISH LITERATURE IS THAT HIS CHARACTERS HAVE A REAL FREEDOM WHICH HE GIVES THEM AND ALLOWS THEM TO EXERCISE.

IMAGINE A PLAYWRIGHT SITTING AT HIS WRITING DESK, SETTING OUT HIS MASTERPIECE. YET AS HE WRITES, THE PLAY ITSELF EMERGES SIMULTANEOUSLY—SET, SCENERY, BACKDROP SEEM TO FLOW FROM HIS PEN MUCH LIKE INK COMES FROM YOURS OR MINE. WE WATCH AND WAIT FOR THE ACTION TO BEGIN.

William Shakespeare

simultaneously—set, scenery, backdrop seem to flow from his pen much like ink comes from yours or mine. We watch and wait for the action to begin.

In time, a character emerges from the pen and begins to speak and act. Yet, something strange happens—the character does not follow the script. In fact, the first character turns against the script, and begins to speak and act in contradiction to it. As the other characters come forward, the whole pattern of the play as it was meant to be performed is thrown off; from this point forward, chaos begins to enter as the participants in the drama begin to drown each other out or cut each other off.

Others emerge and do the same. Still others come and play their part some of the time and not others. Only a few follow the playwright's pattern faithfully, and many do not even know the part they should play. Quickly there are dozens of anti-plots, almost as many as there are characters.

Throughout, we turn and watch the playwright and are amazed. He does not cease writing; he does not cease bringing new characters on the stage. From the look of patient determination on his face, it seems that the show must go on, even though it seems to be fatally disrupted and contrary to his intention. He continues to spin out new characters and new aspects of the plot. He also never ceases to offer direction to the confused players that ramble about the stage.

Slowly, a new plot emerges from his mind—the plot by which the broken plot is to be repaired. The drama of the play becomes a battle of plots, and from the very beginning every anti-plot seems to have the upper-hand over this new one. His new plot starts weak and becomes weaker. In fact, as we watch it seems to die out, the faithful characters falling by the wayside, their performances broken, their voices silenced.

It is at this moment that we look back to the playwright, certain that he is finished. But when we look to his writing desk we are startled to find that he is not there. Turning back to the absurd, noisy ramblings and meaningless action on the stage, we are stunned into silence as we notice him in a new locale—among the actors, carrying the dialogue!

His words are clear, his performance flawless. As he meets the other characters, he shows by word and action his complete dedication to the play, and a complete comprehension of each of their own parts in it. Quickly he becomes the center of the drama, and just as quickly the carriers of the many anti-plots join up against him—to silence his voice and to banish him from the stage for good. He, like many of his faithful players, is cast aside and flung from the scene.

The author has now become the victim of his own broken play. He now carries the same fate as his rebellious characters—he is swallowed up in the discord, his final words drowned out by their jeering. The anti-plots have become united, not in the author's intention, but rather in the overthrow of the one plot they were all created to play.

All seem to pause to acknowledge his departure. We pause as well and look back to the writing desk. There, across the manuscript, we see these words written in the margin of every page—*"When I am cast aside, I take the play forward."*

We turn back, and see the playwright turned performer re-emerge and speak a single line. And instantly, the play is transformed, as we realize that by re-entering the play, the playwright has turned all of the anti-plots into a preparation for a new act. *All of their absurd ad-libbing, their posturing, and their fighting for center stage had been accommodated by the script!!!*

It is as if, within the play itself, a whole new play has begun. Now the playwright's role permits no substitution. Now his script is unavoidable. While this new play goes on within the old one, the characters of the old play begin to throw off their anti-plots, to be drawn into the new act. Many still fiercely battle against this new drama, but every attempt to weaken it only makes it stronger. Over time we realize that the playwright has done it—in allowing the freedom of his characters, he has found a way to complete the masterpiece. The show had to move toward its completion before it could be seen that in its disruption it became even greater thanks to the marvelous mind that created it.

At an unexpected moment, the drama comes together around the playwright turned performer. Both acts end simultaneously, with the new act giving a perfect end to both. All the wild imaginings and random actions, all the anti-plots find a place in the One True Plot, the plot which died and rose to a new life.

We take one last glance at the writing desk to see it melt away, to be replaced by our normal surroundings. We see the sun, or the walls of our room, we look across at a friend or a loved one. The theater and the stage expand into the vast, ever-expanding universe that we inhabit. The numbers of characters multiply into the billions of men and women who inhabit it with us. But as we go forward we are left with great questions—which part do I play? And which plot am I following?

THE DRAMA COMES TOGETHER
AROUND THE PLAYWRIGHT TURNED
PERFORMER. BOTH ACTS END
SIMULTANEOUSLY, WITH THE NEW ACT
GIVING A PERFECT END TO BOTH. ALL
THE WILD IMAGININGS AND RANDOM
ACTIONS, ALL THE ANTI-PLOTS FIND A
PLACE IN THE ONE TRUE PLOT,
THE PLOT WHICH DIED AND ROSE TO
A NEW LIFE.

F. Conclusion

As we conclude this chapter with the drama of the Creator, we can see that scientific atheism has actually helped us to continue our journey to rediscover faith on the frontiers of science. By challenging us with the possibility of a perpetually existing universe, our consideration of scientific atheism led us to a deeper understanding of who and what God is and how he creates and acts within his creation.

Now we can turn our attention to an unexpected twist in the plot of modern science. The achievements of Laplace and his fellow nineteenth century scientists, for all their brilliance, would ultimately be surpassed by the amazing discoveries made by the great scientists of the twentieth century. The conclusion of the drama of scientific atheism is that science itself has surpassed and corrected the findings that some believed made atheism inevitable. The advance of science has now made the credibility of the Creator an issue that, far from being irrelevant, has actually come to the forefront of science itself.

Supplementary Reading

The Biggest Question: Has Science Disproved God?

1. "GOD'S CREATIVE ACT: AN ACT IN ETERNITY, NOT IN TIME"

(excerpted from Christoph Cardinal Schönborn, "In the Beginning God Created…" Internet. Available from http://stephanscom.at/edw/katechesen/articles/2005/12/02/a9719/; accessed April 2, 2007.) This has been reproduced as part of Chance or Purpose? Creation, Evolution, and a Rational Faith, trans. Henry Taylor, ed. Hubert Philip Weber (San Francisco: Ignatius Press, 2007), pp. 46–47.

The doctrine of creation says that God did not create in time, at some point on a time line. His creative act is not a temporal act. I know that this is hard to understand. All that we experience is experienced on the time line of yesterday, today, tomorrow. The creative act of God is not the first act in a long stretch of time, it is not once done and then over with, as if God has, as it were, done his job and can now put his hands in his pockets.

No, "in the beginning God created…" This beginning is always in God's eternity. For us creatures it is a temporal beginning. Once I began to be… For God there is no temporal beginning. Once the universe began to be 14 billion years ago, but God's creative act is not in time, He rather creates time. He is eternal. And his act of creating is not accomplished in this or that moment, but he calls the world into being and holds it in being. **Creation takes place now, in the now of God.**

In the Letter to the Hebrews we read: "He upholds all things by the word of his power" (Heb 1:3). This is why we have to say that if God would let go of us and of creation even for a second, we would fall back into the nothingness from which we came and from which he called us. I grant you that this is not easy to grasp. It requires us to try to transcend our temporal and spatial ways of thinking. Then we enter into a wonderfully coherent view of the world.

Supplementary Reading

2. "FREEDOM AND DIVINE CAUSALITY: GOD'S FREEDOM IS THE SOURCE OF OUR FREEDOM"

(excerpted from Christoph Cardinal Schönborn, "In the Beginning God Created…" Internet. Available from http://stephanscom.at/edw/katechesen/articles/2005/12/02/a9719/; accessed April 2, 2007.) This has been reproduced as part of Chance or Purpose? Creation, Evolution, and a Rational Faith, trans. Henry Taylor, ed. Hubert Philip Weber (San Francisco: Ignatius Press, 2007), p. 47–48.

God creates in absolute freedom—nothing forces him to it, nothing requires it of him. He does not act out of need, as we do. We are always in need of something that we lack, like food or sleep, because [we] want to realize something, to realize ourselves. God does not have to realize himself. By creating he does not complete his being. Creation is not a part of him nor are we a part of him, but we are freely set in being by him, freely created. This means that we are willed by him.

This has immense consequences for our understanding of our world and our ourselves. Since God has created in sovereign freedom, he has given his creatures real independence of being. Creatures are themselves, they really have their own being, their own power of acting, the gift of their autonomy. This reaches all the way to the freedom of human beings, to the fact that God has created freedom, which is the greatest marvel of all in creation.

Before we look at the consequences of this, let us distinguish the Christian position from three other… accounts of the relation between God and the world. a) There is the emanationist account according to which the world is an emanation of God, a "piece" of him that is of lesser value, an inferior form of God; b) [there is the] pantheistic account [which] sees everything in God as God. God is in everything but in such a way that everything is God, even the trees and the animals; c) [there is the] monistic account [which] says that there is only one substance or being and that is God; all else either does not exist or is God. All three of these accounts, which even today have many defenders…, commit this one fundamental mistake: they keep God from being God and they keep creatures, which are only "parts" of God, from having any being of their own. These three accounts seems to be very "devout" and so they are always deceiving people. They seem to exalt the creature, raising it to a divine level, but the truth is the very opposite.…

Supplementary Reading

I said that creation has a real being of its own as a result of the fact that God creates in sovereign freedom without having any compulsion or urge to create, that he gives creatures their being and power of acting as a gift. If creatures were an "emanation" of the divine being, then they would not be independent in being, they would not have their own being and reality. It is just because we are created by God in complete freedom that we can really "be ourselves."

3. "ONGOING CREATION AND THE DIVINE GIFT OF BEING"

(excerpted from Christoph Cardinal Schönborn, "He Upholds the Universe By His Word and Power" Internet. Available from http://stephanscom.at/edw/katechesenarticles/2006/02/15/a10185/; accessed April 2, 2007.) This has been reproduced as part of Chance or Purpose? Creation, Evolution, and a Rational Faith, trans. Henry Taylor, ed. Hubert Philip Weber (San Francisco: Ignatius Press, 2007), p. 79–80.

One thing we know with certainty, with philosophical, rational certainty: all that we observe in material beings once did not exist. The sun came to be, so did the moon, the earth, and life in all its forms, including man and reaching down to you and me. Material things that once were not, will one day pass away. What once came to be does not exist through itself. It is unstable in its existence, it can and it will pass away. And so it is meaningful and necessary to ask: what holds all of this in being? We have to try to answer this question.

Can we enter into this thought? Nothing that exists as matter exists "necessarily" but could as

Supplementary Reading

well not exist. The sun could have not come to be. The same holds for me. I am because I came to be. Philosophy calls this the contingency, the non-necessity of being. What then keeps us in being, why do we exist? Why do we not fall back into nothing? Psalm 104 answers: "When thou hidest thy face, they are dismayed; when thou takest away their breath, they die and return to their dust" (verse 29). Philosophy and theology call this preservation in being the continuing or ongoing creation. God holds in being everything that is. Without this support the contingent world would not be. The power of holding everything in being cannot be in turn a material power. It cannot be a material energy, cannot be a measurable reality, otherwise it too would have to be held in being by something, and this in turn by something else, and so on ad infinitum. This why the Jesuit philosopher Rainer Koltermann says: "The preserving power can ultimately only be something that is not in turn held in being by something else." It cannot be a power that has come to be, a finite and limited power, a measurable energy; it can only be a power that does not draw its power from another source. It must be an absolute power, beyond all time, infinite. "These characteristics are essential for God." (Koltermann, Grundzuege der modernen Naturphilosophie. Ein kritischer Gesamtentwurf [Frankfurt, 1994], 134.)

It is this power that we call the *creatio continua,* the ongoing creation. This is what "holds the world together from within." If God were to "let go" of creation, it would [revert] back into the nothingness from which it came. It does not exist through itself, it is held in being.

Study Guide

The Biggest Question: Has Science Disproved God?

VOCABULARY

Define the following terms:

1. Pierre-Simon Laplace
2. Scientific Atheism
3. Perpetual Universe (Idea)
4. St. Thomas Aquinas
5. Non-simultaneously Acting Causes
6. Simultaneously Acting Causes
7. Unconditioned
8. Finite
9. Divine Infinity
10. Divine Singularity
11. Eternal
12. Divine Simplicity
13. Omnipotence
14. Omniscience
15. Divine Providence
16. Secondary Causes
17. God of the Gaps (Idea)
18. Miracle
19. Person

STUDY QUESTIONS

1. Why is scientific atheism inseparably tied to the notion of a perpetual universe?
2. Is scientific atheism a kind of faith? If so, how is it different from the Christian Act of Faith?
3. Does scientific atheism create a "forbidden zone" for human reason? If so, explain.
4. Why did the discovery of the laws of the conservation of matter and energy lead many nineteenth century scientists to assert that the universe had no beginning?
5. Is the perpetual universe idea a necessarily atheistic idea? If not, how can it be reconciled with belief in God?
6. Explain why there must be an uncaused, unconditioned Cause for the universe to exist at the present moment.
7. Why must God, the uncaused Cause, be infinite?
8. Why must there be only one God, i.e., only one uncaused Cause? Does this contradict the Christian dogma of the Trinity? Why or why not?
9. Why must God, the uncaused Cause, be eternal?
10. Why must God, the uncaused Cause, be perfectly simple? Why must we still use many different terms to describe him?
11. Why must God, the uncaused Cause, be omnipotent and omniscient?
12. What does it mean to call God "the Cause of causes"?
13. Does the existence of secondary causes exclude Divine Providence as an explanation for events? Why or why not?

Study Guide

14. How does the "God of the gaps" approach to science involve a misunderstanding of God as the Cause of all causes?

15. Why must God be personal?

16. What are the characteristics of God as Creator?

17. Why is beauty such a powerful antidote to scientific atheism?

18. How does Tolkien's trilogy, *The Lord of the Rings*, give us a glimpse into God's relationship to the universe as the Cause of all causes?

PRACTICAL EXERCISES

1. A friend reveals to you that he does not believe in God. Explain to your friend why it is reasonable to believe in God's existence.

2. Recently, a group of scientists have developed a position called Intelligent Design Theory ("ID" or "DT") regarding the origins of living things. According to these thinkers, certain living things have an "irreducible complexity" that makes them inexplicable by natural causes. They conclude that these biological phenomena must have had a purposeful Intelligent Designer, although not necessarily God. Review the section on the "God of the Gaps" above. Is ID (DT) a "God of the Gaps" position? Defend your answer.

3. A friend tells you that, even if God exists, there is no way that he can be guiding history and the universe because science has revealed them to have other causes to explain events within them. Using the notions of God as Cause of causes and Divine Author, refute this position.

Endnotes

1. Barr, *Modern Physics*, 15.
2. Ibid., 15–17.
3. Ibid., 17.
4. These two principles are now recognized by scientists to be the same principle.
5. Clarke, 216.
6. Barr, *Modern Physics*, 258–259.
7. Clarke, 216.
8. Barr, *Modern Physics*, 261.
9. Koltermann, *Grundzuege der modernen Naturphilosophie. Ein kritischer Gesamtentwurf* (Frankfurt, 1994), 134, as quoted by Christoph Cardinal Schönborn, "He upholds the universe by his word and power." Internet. Available from http://www.stephanscom.at/edw/katechesen/articles/2006/02/15/a10185/; accessed April 11, 2007.
10. Barr, *Modern Physics*, 259; cf. St. Thomas Aquinas, *Summa contra Gentiles*, II.38 ad 5.
11. Clarke, 236.
12. Ibid., 231.
13. Ibid., 237.
14. International Theological Commission, "Communion and Stewardship: Human Persons Created in the Image of God," 68. (Hereafter referred to as "ITC.")
15. ITC, 69.
16. "Providence," in Gerald O'Collins and Edward G. Farrugia, *A Concise Dictionary of Theology*, rev. (New York: Paulist Press, 2000), 216.
17. ITC, 68.
18. Francis S. Collins, *The Language of God: A Scientists Presents Evidence for Belief* (New York: Free Press, 2006), 95–96.
19. Clarke, 238–239.
20. Ibid., 238.
21. As quoted in Christoph Cardinal Schönborn, "He upholds the universe by his word and power." This has been reproduced as part of *Chance or Purpose? Creation, Evolution, and a Rational Faith*, trans. Henry Taylor, ed. Hubert Philip Weber (San Francisco: Ignatius Press, 2007), p. 85.
22. Collins, 225.
23. Christoph Cardinal Schönborn, "He upholds the universe by his word and power." This has been reproduced as part of *Chance or Purpose? Creation, Evolution, and a Rational Faith*, trans. Henry Taylor, ed. Hubert Philip Weber (San Francisco: Ignatius Press, 2007), p. 85.
24. Idem., "He created each thing according to his kind." Internet. Available from http://stephanscom.at/ edw/katechesen/articles/2006/01/24/a10066; accessed April 11, 2007.
25. The Swiss theologian Hans Urs von Balthasar (1905–1988) devoted the central part of his trilogy to this analogy, composing a five volume *Theo-Drama: Theological Dramatic Theory* (San Francisco, Ignatius Press: 1988–98); trans. Graham Harrison.

Chapter Seven

The Twist in the Tale: Modern Science *versus* Scientific Atheism

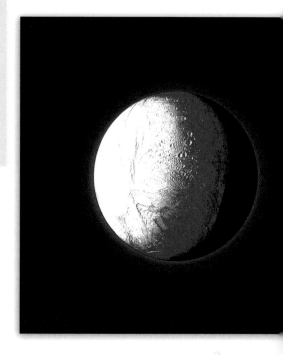

A. Marvels Beyond All Expectations

In 1919, the eyes of the world were focused on France. The battles of World War I were over, and representatives of the great powers had converged upon the palace of Versailles, once the home of the French monarchy. They were negotiating the end of the war that had ravaged Europe and killed 13.5 million people. It was a moment of great hope and incalculable importance for humanity. But during the negotiations, another momentous event was taking place, though little noticed—two expeditions of astronomers were making their way to Sobral, Brazil, and the west African island of Principe in order to view a total solar eclipse that was to occur on May 29.

These scientists were not so interested in the eclipse itself. Rather, they wanted to look at a cluster of stars which were positioned very near the sun; only during an eclipse, when the sun's intense radiance is blocked out by the moon, would these stars "come out" and be observable. Nor were they really interested in these particular stars, which form a cluster called the Hyades. They were testing a new theory of gravity, which predicted that gravity attracts light as well as ordinary matter. Their goal was to see if the light from these stars would be deflected slightly as it passed close by the sun on its way to the earth. They would be able to detect this deflection by observing if the positions of these stars in the sky appeared to be slightly shifted from their actual position. If they did appear out of place, this would confirm the bold new gravitational theory, a possibility so revolutionary that it would be well worth their efforts and travel.

Any new theory of gravity was bold, since the old one—proposed by none other than Isaac Newton, the greatest physicist the world

ANY NEW THEORY OF GRAVITY WAS BOLD, SINCE THE OLD ONE—PROPOSED BY NONE OTHER THAN ISAAC NEWTON, THE GREATEST PHYSICIST THE WORLD HAD KNOWN— HAD PASSED EVERY EXPERIMENTAL TEST FOR 232 YEARS.

IN THIS CHAPTER, WE WILL LOOK AT THREE "TWISTS" IN THE TALE OF SCIENTIFIC DISCOVERY THAT HAVE OCCURRED SINCE EINSTEIN'S GREAT BREAKTHROUGHS. IN EACH CASE, WE WILL SEE THAT THEY HAVE IMPORTANT EVIDENCE TO OFFER FOR THE CREDIBILITY OF THE CHRISTIAN FAITH. EVEN MORE, THEY HAVE HELPED TO DEEPEN OUR UNDERSTANDING OF GOD'S CREATION AND HIS REVELATION.

had known—had passed every experimental test for 232 years. The scientists set up their observation sites, gathered their data, and returned to Europe. On November 6, at a special meeting in London of the Royal Society, one of the oldest and most prestigious scientific bodies in the world, they reported their findings. The next day, the *Times of London* ran the following headline:

Revolution in Science
New Theory of the Universe
Newtonian Ideas Overthrown

Within hours, the news raced around the world. The scientist who had proposed the new theory—the so-called *General Theory of Relativity*—became a household name. Indeed, his name, Albert Einstein, is probably better known than that of any other scientist who has ever lived. And rightly so, for his theoretical breakthroughs opened a whole new era in the history of science, and would allow other scientists to uncover some of the greatest mysteries of the universe, including many of the mysteries of the universe's origin.

This new scientific era, today almost 100 years old, would be full of surprises. From the time of Copernicus up until the end of the nineteenth century, the trend of scientific discoveries had seemed to some people to be leading away from the traditional religious conception of the universe. Indeed, throughout the nineteenth century atheism became more common among scientists and intellectuals generally, partly because of what they thought science was saying (and partly for other reasons). But in the twentieth century, science began saying things that were totally unanticipated; there was one "twist in the plot" after another. Many people came to see that the old "scientific atheism" was based on outdated scientific ideas. In this chapter, we will look at three "twists" in the tale of scientific discovery that have occurred since Einstein's great breakthroughs. In each case, we will see that they have important evidence to offer for the credibility of the Christian Faith. Even more, they have helped to deepen our understanding of God's creation and his Revelation.

The first of these plot twists has to do with one of the implications of Einstein's theory of gravity that he himself found hard to accept, and indeed resisted for years. This implication would hit the scientific community like an explosion—literally.

B. Starting Things Off With a Bang

In our study of scientific atheism, we noted that scientific atheists often assert that the universe has always existed. They mistakenly believe that a perpetual universe would also be an uncaused universe;

i.e., that such a universe would have no source outside itself. In the last chapter, we saw that this jump was philosophically unjustified. Even a perpetual universe would be "contingent" and therefore need an ultimate cause. But the Christian Faith tells us more than this. It says not only that the universe has a cause, but that it had an actual beginning in time, an actual first moment at which it appeared out of nothing, thanks to God's will and power. The Book of Genesis begins with the words, "In the beginning...", as does the Gospel of St. John in its own retelling of the creation account. The Church, in her doctrinal pronouncements, has also spoken of the universe being created by God *"ab initio temporis,"* "from the beginning of time."[1] So it seemed to many that if the scientific evidence that pointed to the universe's perpetual existence had not disproved God's existence, at the very least it had weakened the authority of the Bible and the Catholic Church.

Among the many who believed in a perpetually existing universe was the great Albert Einstein. Though by his own account, he was "religious" in some sense, and often spoke of God, his conception of God and God's relation to the world made it hard for Einstein to accept the idea of a first moment, a temporal beginning to the universe. The great irony is that it was his own General Theory of Relativity that played a key role in bringing back the idea of a Beginning. To understand why, we must look more closely at the theory that made him famous and the equations he used to demonstrate it.

EINSTEIN'S EQUATIONS

In Einstein's theory of gravity, things attract each other by warping the space (actually the space *and time*) near them. The way matter warps space and time is described by a set of equations, now called "Einstein's Equations." These remain among the fundamental equations of theoretical physics in our own day.

The logic that led Einstein to these equations back in 1916 left a certain ambiguity. There was a "term" that could be included in the equations or left out; it did not seem to make much difference either way. Today this term is called the "cosmological constant." Einstein thought the theory would be simpler and more elegant without this term, so he originally decided to leave it out. However, Einstein quickly noticed something that disturbed him. His equations could only describe a universe that was expanding or contracting, not a stable universe that could exist for infinite time into the past and future. He therefore put the cosmological constant back into the equations, thinking that it would allow the theory to describe a stable eternal universe. (Later, the physicist Arthur Eddington showed that, even with the cosmological constant, the expansion or contraction of the universe was an unavoidable fact.)

THE CHURCH TEACHES NOT ONLY THAT THE UNIVERSE HAS A CAUSE, BUT THAT IT ALSO HAD A BEGINNING IN TIME, AN ACTUAL FIRST MOMENT AT WHICH IT APPEARED OUT OF NOTHING, THANKS TO GOD'S WILL AND POWER.

EINSTEIN'S EQUATIONS COULD ONLY DESCRIBE A UNIVERSE THAT WAS EXPANDING OR CONTRACTING, NOT A STABLE UNIVERSE THAT COULD EXIST FOR INFINITE TIME INTO THE PAST AND FUTURE.

Alexander Friedmann

Georges Lemaître

Had Einstein believed what his theory was telling him, instead of running away from it, he could have *predicted* both the expansion of the universe and "the Big Bang," which were discovered by astronomers years later. His philosophical belief in an eternal universe made him miss the most important implication of his own theory. He later reproached himself severely for this blindness, as he saw it, and called it the biggest blunder of his life.[2]

HUBBLE AND HIS TELESCOPE

The scene now switches from Europe to America. The last name of *Edwin Powell Hubble* is known to many Americans from the famous Hubble Space Telescope. But he did not invent this telescope. It was named in his honor because of a great discovery he made in the 1920's using another telescope, one located at the Mt. Wilson Observatory in California.

On the basis of a hypothesis of an earlier astronomer, Hubble peered into space to investigate what Einstein had denied, namely, that other galaxies were moving away from our own. His observations showed that this expansion really was occurring, and at incredibly high speeds. The expansion was so massive and so fast that some other galaxies were actually millions of light-years away.[3]

Even before Hubble's findings, mathematics and physics had begun to take Einstein's insights in the very direction that he himself considered too revolutionary—toward a universe that is expanding from a beginning. Two thinkers independently discovered that Einstein's Equations of gravity can describe such a universe: one was a Russian mathematician named Alexander Friedmann, the other was a Belgian physicist and Catholic priest named *Georges Lemaître*. As we saw in Chapter Four, it was Lemaître who saw the significance of Hubble's discovery and related it to his own theoretical work with Einstein's equations. In 1927, Lemaître proposed that the universe has been expanding for billions of years, and had started out very small. If that were so, then all of the matter in the universe must originally have been concentrated in a super-dense mass, which Lemaître called "the primeval atom." It was the explosion of this atom, said Lemaître, that had led to the expansion of the universe that Hubble would observe in 1929. Thus was the *"Big Bang Theory"* born.[4] Friedmann and Lemaître are given joint credit as the founders of this theory. Not long after Hubble's results were announced and Lemaître proposed his theory, Einstein admitted that the evidence seemed to support what he once thought to be absurd—that we live in a dynamic, expanding universe that had a first moment, a beginning in time. He revealed his change of mind in 1933 in a way that displayed his great humility and character; after listening to a lecture in which Fr. Lemaître explained his ideas on the beginnings of the universe, Einstein stood up and applauded enthusiastically.

The Big Bang Theory in its standard form says something much more profound and strange than the fact that stars and galaxies and matter had a beginning. It says that *space and time themselves* had a beginning. This is an important point, so it needs to be explained at some length. What Hubble saw was simply that the distance between galaxies was increasing. The obvious interpretation of that is that galaxies are moving *through space* away from each other. But what is actually going on, according to Einstein's theory, as Lemaître understood, is that the space between the galaxies is *stretching.* Space itself is like a stretchable fabric. So, the amount of space is actually growing. If you followed this process backwards in time, you would find that space itself was smaller in the past. And if you followed it far enough back, you would find that the amount of space would go to zero at the very moment of the Big Bang. Space would shrink to nothing. If you could run the film of the universe's history backwards, the entire universe—the matter *and the space*—would seem to "wink out" altogether at the Big Bang. So before the Big Bang there was no space at all.

It gets even stranger: since Einstein's theory says that space and time are part of one fabric called "spacetime," accordingly, *there was no time* either before the Big Bang. In fact, it is meaningless (in the standard Big Bang Theory) even to say "before the Big Bang." There is no such thing as "before," since "before" implies a time previous to the Big Bang, and there was no time previous to the Big Bang. Strange as it may seem, the Big Bang was "a day without a yesterday."

This is a mind-boggling idea, and even graduate students of physics have a hard time coming to grips with it. But one person understood it very well 1,600 years ago—St. Augustine. St. Augustine's autobiography, *The Confessions,* contains a very famous discussion of the nature of time. It is so profound that physicists who work in the field called "quantum cosmology" frequently quote from it.[5] Even the eminent twentieth century philosopher and mathematician Bertrand Russell (an atheist and no friend of religion) once praised St. Augustine for his "admirable relativistic theory of time."

St. Augustine

St. Augustine was trying to answer the taunts of pagans. The pagans mocked the Jewish and Christian belief that God created the world a finite time ago (they believed the universe was perpetual) by asking, "What was God doing for all that time before he created the world? Why did he wait for an infinite time doing nothing before he got around to creating the world?" St. Augustine gave his answer in the form of a long prayer: "You [O Lord] created time, and no time could pass by before you created it. But if there was no time 'before' you created heaven and earth, why do they ask what you did 'then'? There was no 'then,' where there was no time."[6] This is the same answer that a modern physicist would give: there was no "then" before the Big Bang as it is understood in Einstein's Theory

Front row: Arthur Eddington and Hendrik Lorentz; back row: Albert Einstein, Paul Ehrenfest and Willem de Sitter at the Leiden Observatory, circa September 1923.

IN 1959, TWO-THIRDS OF AMERICAN ASTRONOMERS AND PHYSICISTS STILL BELIEVED, CONTRARY TO THE IMPLICATIONS OF EINSTEIN'S THEORY, THAT THE UNIVERSE HAD NO BEGINNING. IT IS GENERALLY ADMITTED THAT THE SCIENTIFIC COMMUNITY WAS SLOW IN ACCEPTING THE BIG BANG THEORY IN PART BECAUSE OF A WIDESPREAD PREJUDICE IN FAVOR OF AN ETERNAL UNIVERSE.

of General Relativity. The idea of time in physics before Einstein was the same as the ancient pagans' idea of time. The idea of time in the standard Big Bang Theory is St. Augustine's idea of time, the Christian idea of time.

To sum up: when we talk about "the beginning," we really mean not just the beginning of the universe, but the beginning of time. As the Fourth Lateran Council in 1215 and the First Vatican Council in 1870 taught, God created the universe "from the beginning of time" (*"ab initio temporis"*).

THE END OF THE DEBATE

Einstein was not alone in being made uncomfortable by the idea of a beginning. Arthur Eddington, himself a renowned physicist who had been on one of the 1919 expeditions that proved Einstein's theory, responded to Lemaître's theory by declaring, "The notion of a beginning is repugnant to me ... I simply do not believe that the present order of things started off with a bang." An eminent scientist named Walter Nernst even wrote that the foundation of science itself would be undermined by denying that the universe and time had always existed. In fact, the idea of an ever-existing universe persisted for many years after Hubble's discovery that the universe is expanding. In 1959, two-thirds of American astronomers and physicists still believed, contrary to the implications of Einstein's theory, that the universe had no beginning. It is generally admitted that the scientific community was slow in accepting the Big Bang Theory in part because of a widespread prejudice in favor of a universe with no beginning. This prejudice was one reason (although not the only one) that a new hypothesis emerged that explained the expansion of the universe without the universe having a beginning. This so-called Steady State Theory eventually fell by the wayside as the evidence against it and in favor of the Big Bang Theory accumulated.[7]

It is a strange story how the Big Bang Theory ended up being confirmed. In 1948, two students realized that the Big Bang, if it had occurred, must have been unimaginably hot, because of the enormous squeezing of the matter—one second after the Big Bang, the temperature of the universe would have been ten *billion* degrees centigrade. This had an interesting consequence: the universe just after the Big Bang would have been filled with intense radiation, much of it in the form of light, and a residue of that radiation would remain even now in the form of microwaves, filling the universe in a faint "afterglow" of the Big Bang.

Curiously, this idea was ignored. Almost two decades would pass before anyone would follow it up. When finally someone had the idea of looking for this radiation, they were too late—someone else had already discovered it accidentally. The two scientists who found it, *Arno Penzias and Robert Wilson,* did not use a telescope, but a radio detector. Stephen Barr described their process of discovery:

> They found a noise, or static, that seemed to come equally from all directions in the sky. At first they thought that it was a problem with the device itself, or some local interference—they even considered the possibility that heat given off by bird droppings inside the antenna was responsible. Eventually, however... the true significance of what they were seeing was realized. They were hearing a whisper from the Big Bang.[8]

Robert Jastrow, astrophysicist

Since then, several other pieces of evidence have confirmed their discovery, and very few now dispute the theory of the "hot Big Bang." Calculations made by scientists suggest that the event, apparently the first moment of our universe, happened almost 14 billion years ago. Physicists agree that all of the stars and galaxies that we observe were once packed into an almost "infinitely dense,... point of pure energy."[9]

GOING OUT WITH A BANG: MODERN SCIENCE VERSUS MATERIALISM

The discovery of the Big Bang was a revolution in science. But the revolution involved a battle not over science, but over the materialistic assumptions of many in the scientific community. The significance of the Big Bang has been compellingly described by the astrophysicist Robert Jastrow:

> For the [modern materialist] scientist... the story ends like a bad dream. He has scaled the mountains of ignorance; he is about to conquer the highest peak; as he pulls himself over the final rock, he is greeted by a band of theologians who have been sitting there for centuries.[10]

Jastrow's point is that the Big Bang was more than just a glimpse into the origins of the universe. It also represented a major crack in the materialist worldview. For it suggests that the physical universe does not contain its own explanation entirely within itself. Materialism tends to reduce the explanation of things to merely giving an account of how they arose from whatever existed beforehand. They explain what happens today by what happened yesterday. But what if there were a "day with no yesterday," as the Big Bang Theory suggests? The Big Bang forces upon us deeper questions about the mystery of the universe, questions such as why the universe exists at all, and why it is the way it is.[11]

THEOLOGY ON THE CUTTING EDGE: THE BIG BANG AND FAITH

Elsewhere in his book, Robert Jastrow makes another provocative declaration:

> Now we see how the astronomical evidence leads to a biblical view of the origin of the world. The details differ, but the essential elements in the astronomical and biblical accounts are the same; the chain of events leading to man commenced suddenly and sharply at a definite moment in time, in a flash of light and energy.[12]

Does the Big Bang prove, in a scientific way, the existence of God and the divinely inspired truth of the Bible? The answer is no. Pope John Paul II once cautioned that we should not be too hasty in our use of the Big Bang Theory in this way.[13] Theoretical physicists explore other scenarios besides the standard Big Bang Theory. In some of these scenarios the Big Bang was not the beginning of time, space, and matter, but merely the beginning of a particular phase of the history of the universe. However, while there is a possibility that the Big Bang was not the beginning of the universe, there exist theoretical-physics arguments that suggest—even if they do not absolutely prove—that the universe had a beginning at *some* point. The weight of scientific theory and experiment at the present moment seems to lean strongly toward the conclusion that there was a Beginning.

Most Catholic theologians and philosophers would say that the existence of a first moment in time cannot be absolutely proven scientifically, because it is impossible to see past something that is supposed to be the first moment to verify that it is truly first. In the words of Fr. Paul Haffner, a priest and physicist, the beginning of the universe "is like a safe with a combination-lock and the combination is locked inside the safe."[14] The words "In the beginning..." will always remain to some extent a matter of faith, because of the limitations of science, and the difficulty of "proving a negative."

So why is the Big Bang Theory important for rediscovering faith on the frontiers of science? Three reasons stand out.

First, the Big Bang Theory is important because it suggests that more than science is needed to explain the universe. As John Paul II observed, the problem of the universe's beginning requires "[the kind of] human knowledge which rises above physics and astrophysics and is called *metaphysics*."[15] When one runs up against the very limits of time and space, one has to confront the Cause that transcends time and space.

Second, the Big Bang Theory shows that the idea of a "Beginning" can be made sense of scientifically, something that was not at all clear before Einstein's theory. It shows that it is not absurd to think about an act of power and creativity that is not the mere unfolding of a process *within* the realm of matter, space, and time, but actually brings matter, space, and time into existence out of nothing.

Third, the Big Bang Theory shows us that time—like space and matter—is not a necessary feature of existence, but merely a feature of the physical universe. Therefore, where there is no universe, there is also no time. Or put in theological terms, time itself is something created, so that it only exists as a result of creation. This supports the traditional concept, clearly formulated by St. Augustine, of God's "timelessness." God, transcending the universe, also transcends time. *Time,* the measurement of change, does not apply to God who, being perfect, never changes. The Big Bang, as potentially the first moment in time, draws the mind to marvel with St. Augustine at the eternal mystery of God who is outside of time.

The Big Bang has brought us to the cutting edge of science and its relationship to faith. Now we can move to the next plot twist, which emerged when scientists began to theorize about the kind of events that must have happened *after* the Bang.

C. Curious Coincidences: The Setting of the Stage

The Big Bang Theory of Friedmann and Lemaître sent physics in a new direction. It is the foundation on which all of modern cosmology is built. (Cosmology is the study of the cosmos as a whole and how it develops.) At the same time, enormous strides were being made by "particle physicists" in understanding the basic forces of nature, the subatomic particles of which matter is made, and the mathematical laws that govern them. Scientists could begin to address such fundamental questions as how matter originated and how it got formed into galaxies and stars. Strange and surprising answers awaited them. And many of these answers had something in common—they seemed to reveal a universe that had been fine-tuned for the possibility and existence of life, including human beings.

These surprising discoveries are commonly referred to as *anthropic coincidences.* The word "anthropic" comes from the Greek word *anthropos,* which means "human being." An anthropic coincidence is defined as a feature of the universe that is exactly what is needed for the existence of life, but yet seemingly could have been otherwise.[16] Had such features been otherwise, *human beings would not exist.* Let us look at two examples of anthropic coincidences.

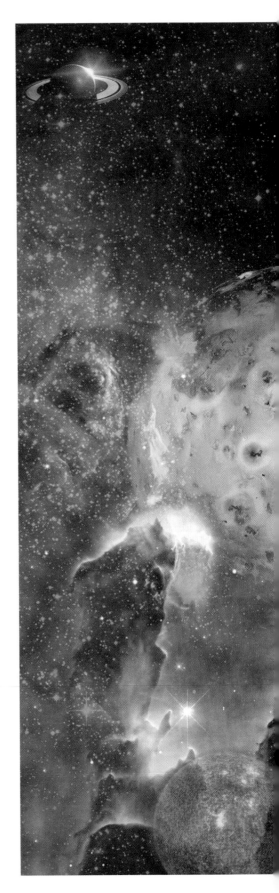

GRAVITY AND THE BIG BANG

As cosmologists studied the mathematics of the Big Bang, a remarkable feature of the universe's first moments came to light. Scientists had understood since the time of Isaac Newton that all massive objects are attracted to each other by gravity. So, as all of the matter in the universe flew apart at fantastic speeds just after the colossal explosion of the Big Bang, the attraction of gravity was trying to pull it back together. There was therefore a competition between the outward impetus from the explosion and the inward force of gravity. This competition had to be very precisely balanced, otherwise one of two disasters would have happened. Had the gravitational attraction been too strong, it would have quickly halted and then reversed the expansion, and the matter would have come crashing back together while the universe was still very tiny. On the other hand, had the gravity been too weak, the matter would have spread out much too quickly and stars and galaxies would not have been able to form. We would either have had no universe, or one that would not support life. As Harvard astrophysicist Owen Gingerich puts it, "The balance between the energy of expansion [i.e., the force of the explosion] and the braking power of gravitation had to be extraordinarily exact…"[17]

Why so exact? The reason is that near the time of the Big Bang both the outward speed of expansion and the inward pull of gravity were vastly greater than they are now. (The outward speed was much greater back then because gravity has had 10 billion years since then to slow it down. The gravitational pull was much greater because all the matter was much more densely packed.) So great was the gravitational pull in the moments after the Big Bang, that if it had not been in precise balance, it would have recollapsed the universe in a tiny fraction of a second.

How exact was the balance? One way to measure it is by the temperature of the explosion. Imagine that you could have set the temperature of the Big Bang as you set the temperature of your oven. The dials on most ovens have markings every 25 degrees, and so if you are careful you can set the temperature to within a few degrees. For baking a soufflé, that is quite good enough. An oven whose temperature could be set to within a hundredth of a degree, say, would be much more sophisticated—you might find such a thing in a research laboratory, but not in a kitchen. But for the Big Bang to happen in such a way that life as we know it could result, the "dial" had to be set, not to an accuracy of a hundredth of a degree, or a millionth, or even a billionth, but to *thirty decimal places,* that is to 0 .000000000000000000000000000001 of a degree. Otherwise, this soufflé—this universe that was able to bring forth living things—would have been ruined. The balance necessary for our universe was so exact that it is unbelievably improbable. And yet exactly what needed to happen *did* happen.

MOVE OVER, SKYWALKER: THE STRONG NUCLEAR FORCE IS WITH US

A second anthropic coincidence has to do with the origins of the building blocks of life—the formation of atoms. As scientists analyzed the process of the Big Bang and the events that followed it, much attention was focused on the structure and formation of atoms and atomic elements—hydrogen, carbon, oxygen, etc. According to modern theory, none of the atomic elements existed at the very beginning of the universe. A few were constituted shortly after the Big Bang. All of the others were either formed within stars as they burned or in post-Big Bang explosions of stars called *supernovas.* These supernova explosions also served to spew the elements made inside stars out into space, where they could form into new stars, planets, and living things. Scientists emphasize that everything we see around us, and we ourselves, are quite literally made of stardust.[18]

The process of the formation of atomic elements began with the formation of the nuclei of these elements, each of which is made up of one or many neutrons and protons. The simplest and earliest nucleus was that of the simplest form of hydrogen (hydrogen 1), which has a single proton as its nucleus. Then pairs of particles fused to make a two-particle nucleus—hydrogen 2. (This element is also called *deuterium,* from the Greek word *deuteros,* which means "second," because it is the second kind of nucleus.) The process of "fusion," by which smaller nuclei combine to make larger ones, continued until all of the elements were made. These fusion processes release energy, and are what power the sun and other stars—and thus they are the energy source, ultimately, for life on earth.

What interests us is the attractive force that causes protons and neutrons to stick together to form nuclei. It is called the *strong nuclear force.* Scientists discovered that the strength of this force is also fine-tuned in such a way as to make life possible. If it were only a few percent weaker, protons and neutrons could not stick together; if it were only a few percent stronger, the fusion processes in stars would be able to happen in a completely different way that would allow them to burn hundreds of times faster than they do. In the first case, the building blocks of life would never have formed; in the second, the sun (and other stars) would have burned out so quickly that there would not have been time for living organisms to evolve.[19] This force in us seems to be *for us.*

SCIENTISTS EMPHASIZE THAT EVERYTHING WE SEE AROUND US, AND WE OURSELVES, ARE QUITE LITERALLY MADE OF STARDUST.

THE STRENGTH OF THE FORCE THAT CAUSES PROTONS AND NEUTRONS TO STICK TOGETHER— THE STRONG NUCLEAR FORCE— IS ALSO FINE-TUNED IN SUCH A WAY AS TO MAKE LIFE POSSIBLE.

THE FAMOUS ASTROPHYSICST FRED HOYLE, AN ATHEIST, REMARKED THAT THE UNIVERSE LOOKS LIKE A "PUT-UP JOB," I.E., SOMETHING CAREFULLY ARRANGED. THE WELL-KNOWN PHILOSOPHER ANTONY FLEW, WHO HAD SPENT MOST OF HIS LIFE ARGUING FOR ATHEISM, CONVERTED TO BELIEF IN GOD, PRIMARILY BECAUSE OF THE ANTHROPIC COINCIDENCES. SOME ATHEIST SCIENTISTS HAVE ALSO BEEN LED TO BELIEF IN GOD.

ANTHROPIC COINCIDENCES AND GOD THE CREATOR

We have looked at two examples of anthropic coincidences, but physicists and cosmologists have discussed many more. These coincidences have to do with strengths, ranges, and characteristics of the basic forces of nature; the masses, electric charges, and other properties of the particles that exist; the properties of space and time (for example, that time has an "arrow," and that space has three dimensions); and various other features of the laws of physics and the structure of the universe. Numerous factors have to balance just right and be in just the correct relationships to each other. To explain most of the anthropic coincidences would require lengthy technical discussions that would be beyond a book like this. Fortunately, many books and articles have come out in recent years that explain them in a way accessible to non-scientists.[20]

Could all these anthropic coincidences really *just* be coincidences? Most people who have looked into the matter find that impossible to believe. Let us go back to the oven analogy—except now let us imagine the laws of physics are like a device with a large number of switches, knobs, and dials that control various features of the universe. One switch would turn on and off the force of electromagnetism; a dial would set the strength of that force, another dial would control the mass of the electron, and so forth. If all those switches and dials have to be set to just the right positions—some of them to fantastic accuracy—in order for life to appear, and we indeed find them set that way, is that not pretty strong evidence for a Creator who had the intention of creating a world with life in it? So it has seemed to many people, even many who did not start off believing in God. The famous astrophysicst Fred Hoyle, an atheist, remarked that the universe looks like a "put-up job," i.e., something carefully arranged. The well-known philosopher Antony Flew, who had spent most of his life arguing for atheism, converted to belief in God, primarily because of the anthropic coincidences. He is not alone among thinkers who have been led to belief in God by the anthropic coincidences, which have had a similar impact on many scientists.

If you are still unsure, consider this quote from Roger Penrose, a famous English mathematical physicist and Oxford scholar. He is describing the size of the number that represents the odds *against* the emergence of human life:

> This is an extraordinary figure. One could not possibly even write the number down in full in the ordinary... notation: it would be 1 followed by 10^{123} successive 0's. *Even if we were to write a 0 on each separate proton and on each separate neutron in the entire universe*—and we could throw in all the other particles for good measure—we should fall far short of writing down the figure needed.

Do the anthropic coincidences "scientifically prove" the existence of God? That would be saying too much. As in the case of the Big Bang Theory, we must be cautious and not try to prove too much from scientific discoveries. After all, they may come to be seen in a different light after future scientific discoveries. In fact, some people have already proposed a way to explain some of the anthropic coincidences without invoking God. It is called the "multiverse" hypothesis.

The multiverse idea can be explained with the same control-panel analogy we used before. Suppose that all those "switches" and "dials" are not set to the same positions everywhere in the universe, but vary randomly from place to place. For example, the strength of the strong nuclear force might be different here and in parts of the universe very far away. (They would have to be *very* far away indeed, since there is conclusive evidence that in all the places we can see with telescopes the "dial settings" are the same as here.) If so, in most places in the universe the dial settings would be wrong for life; but—if the universe were big enough—there might be some places where the dial settings were just right for life to be possible. In other words, if you buy enough lottery tickets, one is bound to be the "lucky ticket." The multiverse idea is interesting, but it is not yet a testable scientific theory, and it is hard to see at present how it could ever become one. But even if it turned out to be true, it would not really get rid of the "anthropic" argument for God. The point is that a "multiverse"—i.e., a universe some of whose "switches" and "dials" were set differently in different places—is a very strange kind of a universe, and probably could not arise unless some *other* "switches" and "dials" were set to special values. The lesson of the anthropic coincidences is that a universe that can give rise to life probably has to be very special indeed.

The seeming fact that the universe had to be extremely precise, fine-tuned "just so" for human beings to exist, seems suspiciously like a plan. The anthropic coincidences leave one which the overwhelming impression that, contrary to scientific atheism, the universe's fine-tuning was built in by a "Fine-Tuner"—God the Creator, who made the universe for the sake of humanity.

D. Beauty Beyond Description: Symmetry, Modern Physics, and the Argument from Design

Scientific atheists see the world as being governed not by a personal God, but by blind and impersonal forces, mechanisms,

THE SCIENTIFIC ATHEIST DOES NOT DENY THAT THERE ARE ELEGANT PATTERNS, HARMONIOUS STRUCTURES, BEAUTIFUL FORMS, AND REMARKABLE EXAMPLES OF ORDER TO BE FOUND IN NATURE.

Johannes Kepler

MODERN SCIENCE HAS DISCOVERED THAT THE VERY LAWS OF PHYSICS *THEMSELVES* EXHIBIT PATTERNS EVEN MORE ELEGANT, STRUCTURES EVEN MORE HARMONIOUS, FORMS EVEN MORE BEAUTIFUL, AND ORDER FAR MORE REMARKABLE THAN THOSE WHICH THEY WERE INVOKED TO EXPLAIN.

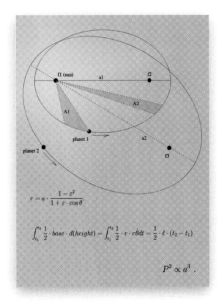

and processes. Everything, they believe, can be explained by a combination of mathematical laws and pure chance. An ordinary person might point to some beautiful natural phenomenon—a gemstone, a rainbow, an aurora borealis, the harmonious movements of the planets—and say, "Here, clearly, is evidence of the divine Artist at work." The scientific atheist, while not denying the beauty of these things, would answer, "We do not need to invoke any Artist, because we know exactly how these things arise. We understand the forces and principles that cause those gemstones and rainbows to form; and we know that those forces and principles are purely natural." The scientific atheist does not deny that there are elegant patterns, harmonious structures, beautiful forms, and remarkable examples of order to be found in nature. He thinks, however, that they can all be explained, ultimately, by the laws of physics.

This is where the next plot twist came in. Modern science has discovered that the very laws of physics *themselves* exhibit patterns even more elegant, structures even more harmonious, forms even more beautiful, and order far more remarkable than those which they were invoked to explain. It turned out that, in discovering the laws of physics, scientists did not "explain away" the beauty and order that was visible in nature, but instead uncovered a beauty within the depths of nature much greater than that which is visible on its surface.

Let us look at one example. Consider the harmonious movements of the planets. These were known even to the ancients. In fact, ancient people were deeply impressed by the orderliness that they saw in the heavens. At the beginning of the seventeenth century, Johannes Kepler unlocked the secrets of these movements and published his three great Laws of Planetary Motion. (One of these was that the planets went around the sun in elliptical orbits, with the sun at the "focus" of the ellipse. The second was that in its course around the sun a planet always "sweeps out equal areas in equal times." The third was a precise algebraic relationship between the times it takes planets to orbit the sun and their distances from the sun.) Kepler himself saw these as magnificent examples of divine artistry. He exclaimed in his great treatise entitled *Harmonices mundi* (The Harmonies of the World), "I thank thee, Lord God our Creator, that thou allowest me to see the beauty in thy work of creation."

More than eighty years later, Isaac Newton discovered his Universal Laws of Motion and the Law of Gravitation. These explained all three of the laws of Kepler, and much else about the movements of the heavenly bodies. In fact, it was Laplace who showed in his great work *Mécanique céleste* (Celestial Mechanics) that Newton's laws could account with great exactness for all of the complex movements of the various bodies of the solar system. And it was this success that led him to tell Napoleon, referring to God, "I have no need of that hypothesis." But, in fact, the laws of Newton were far more majestic and mathematically elegant than even the laws that Kepler had discovered and which had made Kepler cry out in praise of his Creator.

And that is only the beginning of the story. For, as we have seen, more than two centuries later Einstein found that Newton's laws did not exhaust the richness of the phenomena of gravity. He showed that Newton's law of gravity was just an approximation to a much more beautiful and profound theory of gravity, in which gravity was caused by the curvature of a four-dimensional space-time manifold, and in which that curvature was described by the sophisticated set of tensor equations now known as Einstein's Equations. And evidence has begun to emerge in recent decades that Einstein's theory is itself but a piece of some even deeper and more remarkable mathematical structure. This newer theory (which is still untested) is so mathematically rich that one of the leading theorists, Ed Witten, proclaimed its "wonder, incredible consistency, remarkable elegance, and beauty."

This is the third twist in the plot: the deeper into nature that science has penetrated, the *more* beauty it has uncovered. That is why as the twentieth century unfolded, fundamental physicists began to be guided more and more in their search for deeper laws by the criterion of beauty. Stephen Barr describes how one of the greatest discoveries of twentieth century physics, the Dirac Equation, was found:

> The physicist Paul Dirac was seeking an equation to describe electrons in a way that would be consistent with the principles of relativity theory. In this search he was guided primarily by mathematical beauty: "A great deal of my work is just playing with equations and seeing what they give," he said. In this case, as he was playing with some equations he found something "pretty." "[It] was a pretty mathematical result. I was quite excited over it. It seemed that it must be [of] some importance." *Notice that it was the "prettiness" of the mathematics that convinced him he was on the right track* [emphasis added]. Soon after, he found the great equation...[21]

In fact, Dirac famously remarked that it was more important to have "beauty in one's equations" than to have them fit the experiment. Werner Heisenberg, one of the founders of quantum mechanics, also stressed the importance of the criterion of beauty in physics. He wrote, "In exact science, no less than in the arts, beauty is the most important source of illumination and clarity."

Some people have argued that the beauty referred to by physicists like Dirac is purely a subjective judgment, one based on personal taste. Maybe scientists come to think that their theories are beautiful just because they discovered them, that is, out of some kind of vanity. But there is a powerful argument against this: they did not see the beauty *after* they discovered the theories, it is the beauty

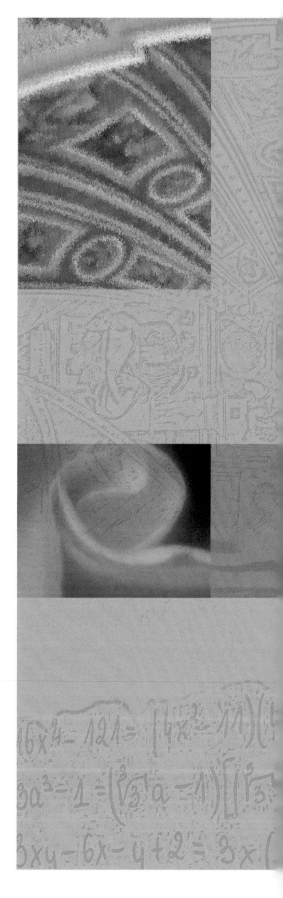

that often *led* them to the theories, as we see in the case of Dirac's discovery. In fact, this has happened many times accidentally. Again and again throughout history, mathematicians have come up with mathematical ideas and developed branches of mathematics purely for the sake of their "mathematical beauty" without ever dreaming that they had any relevance to the physical world, only to have it discovered much later that these parts of mathematics were needed to express fundamental laws of physics. For example, the idea of "complex numbers" was invented and thoroughly investigated by the early 1800s, at which time they seemed to have no relevance to physical reality at all. But in the 1920s it was discovered that they were needed to write the equations of quantum mechanics. In 1852, a kind of number called quaternion was invented by the mathematician William Rowan Hamilton. Quaternions seemed to be a very elegant, but scientifically useless, piece of mathematics, until it was found that quaternions were needed to describe the way electrons and similar particles "spin," as well as other properties of subatomic particles. These and many other examples reveal that the beauty found in the laws of physics, the artistic perfection of their design, is so perfect that it seems to be accessible in some cases simply though mathematical creativity!

Hermann Weyl, one of the great mathematicians of the twentieth century, who also played a leading role in theoretical physics, said in a lecture in 1931,

> Many people think that modern science is far removed from God. I find on the contrary, that it is much more difficult today for the knowing person to approach God from history, from the spiritual side of the world, and from morals; for there we encounter the suffering and evil in the world, which it is difficult to bring into harmony with an all-merciful and all-mighty God. In this domain we have evidently not yet succeeded in raising the veil with which our human nature covers the essence of things. But in our knowledge of physical nature we have penetrated so far that we can obtain a vision of the flawless harmony which is in conformity with sublime reason.[22]

What Hermann Weyl is saying here, and what Kepler was saying in his book *Harmonices Mundi,* is that the beauty, harmony, and order in the world are a sign of its creation by a Mind, by "sublime reason." This is a very ancient argument for the existence of God, sometimes called the "Argument from Design." It can be found in Sacred Scripture, especially in Proverbs 8:22–31, Jeremiah 33:25–26, and Wisdom 11:20.[23] We saw it clearly presupposed in Genesis 1, where God's designing intelligence and awesome power is described as bringing the world and its creatures into existence— even the shape of the story reveals God's design. It is also found in many places in the writings of early Christians. For example, at the beginning of the third century AD, Minucius Felix wrote,

> If upon entering a home you saw that everything there was well-tended, neat, and decorative, you would believe that some master was in charge of it, and that he was himself much superior to those good things. So too in the home of this world, when you see providence, order, and law in the heavens and on earth, believe that there is a Lord and Author of the universe, more beautiful than the stars themselves and the various parts of the whole world.[24]

Anglican theologian William Paley

As found in Sacred Scripture and in early Christian writings, the argument is primarily based on the fact that the universe as a whole is orderly, lawful, harmonious, and beautiful.

In the eighteenth and early nineteenth centuries, however, some theologians and philosophers began to make the argument in a narrower and more questionable way. They pointed to specific *things*—especially living things—as evidence that God had directly *intervened* in nature in a supernatural way to produce them. The argument was that these things were too complex to have been the products of mere chance or of merely natural processes. The Anglican theologian William Paley gave one of the most famous examples of such reasoning. (Often, when people think of "the Argument from Design, they have Paley's ideas in mind.) The trouble with some of these eighteenth century versions of the argument is that they pit "design" *against* "nature" and "law"—they assume that nature is chaotic and that, when we find complex and beautiful things in it, they stand out as proof that a Designer exists. Yet this is not what Minucius Felix meant in his quote above, which points to nature itself as designed and lawful. It was precisely this natural "order and law in the heavens and on earth" that pointed to God.

This narrowing and distorting of the emphasis of the "Argument from Design" by Paley had very unfortunate consequences, which we shall see in more detail in the next chapter on God and evolution. When Charles Darwin showed how the structures of living things might be explained naturally (just as Laplace and others had shown that structures found in the inanimate world, such as the solar system, could be), it led some people to think that the Design Argument for God's existence had been refuted.

The only thing that had been refuted (perhaps) was Paley's version of the design argument. But the irony is that twentieth century discoveries in physics and cosmology have actually given splendid examples of the older and deeper version of the design argument. For they have shown that the "order and law in the heavens and on earth" is much more profound and impressive than anyone had ever imagined. Indeed, as Hermann Weyl said, the laws of physics give us "a vision of the flawless harmony which is in conformity with sublime reason."

WE SEE, HOWEVER, THAT THE DISCOVERIES IN PHYSICS AND COSMOLOGY HAVE ACTUALLY STRENGTHENED THE OLDER AND DEEPER VERSION OF THE DESIGN ARGUMENT. FOR THEY HAVE SHOWN THAT THE "ORDER AND LAW IN THE HEAVENS AND ON EARTH" IS MUCH MORE PROFOUND AND IMPRESSIVE THAN ANYONE HAD EVER IMAGINED.

The physicist Stephen Barr uses a single term to sum up this great beauty uncovered by twentieth century physics—symmetry, a word that means "equal measure" in Greek. All order that we see, including the beautiful complexity of living creatures, comes from and is founded on the greater order of the universe's fundamental symmetry, the *symmetry* of the laws of nature.[25] In his words, "we do not live in a universe with a great deal of order. We live in a universe whose order is *perfect,* or nearly so..." Here is his version of the Argument from Design, based on the latest and the best science:

> ...if the universe is orderly and highly structured simply by the luck of the draw, then it is a miracle that miracles do not happen all the time... of a thousand naturally formed gemstones, one would not expect to find any that were without numerous small flaws, parts that did not fit the crystal pattern perfectly... Yet scientists have studied the universe with instruments of astonishing precision; and while they quite often find anomalous behavior that does not fit the laws of nature as they think them to be, it has always turned out that these anomalies could be accounted for by some more beautiful law. The universe does not appear more and more flawed the more closely one looks at it... *its fundamental patterns appear more and more wonderfully perfect the more closely they are examined.*[26]

As we continue, we will frequently reencounter the concept of symmetry, which is very helpful for seeing how science and faith, nature and spirit, creation and redemption fit each other with "equal measure." Symmetry and beauty are crucial to rediscovering faith on the frontiers of science.

E. The End of Scientific Atheism? The Curious Case of Antony Flew

Antony Flew

As we end our consideration of the many twists in the tale of modern science, "plot twists" in which modern science has pointed away from scientific atheism and toward the existence of God, there is no better way to conclude than with a story about the greatest atheist of twentieth century philosophy: Professor Antony Flew.

Antony Flew can rightly be called the grandfather of contemporary atheism. In 1953, as a doctoral student at Oxford, he published a paper entitled "Theology and Falsification," in which he developed an extremely intelligent argument against God's existence. So powerful was his argument that he became known as the leading atheistic thinker in the world for a half-century.

And then, fifty-one years later, at a debate in New York City in 2004, he made an astonishing announcement. Flew had changed his mind; he had come to believe in the existence of God! Three years later, in 2007, he published a book about his new position, entitled *There is a God: How the World's Most Notorious Atheist Changed His Mind.*

What caused Flew, the most convincing atheist of his day, to be convinced that God exists? Here is his explanation:

> I now believe that the universe was brought into existence by an infinite Intelligence. I believe that this universe's intricate laws manifest what scientists have called the Mind of God. I believe that life and reproduction originate in a divine Source.
>
> Why do I believe this, given that I expounded and defended atheism for more than half a century? The short answer is this: *this is the world picture... that has emerged from modern science* [emphasis added].[27]

Modern science, including the discoveries that we have considered in this chapter, caused Flew to abandon the opinion that made him famous. In a powerful parable, he sends a message about the close-mindedness and short-sightedness of what he calls "dogmatic atheism":

> Imagine that a satellite phone is washed ashore on a remote island inhabited by a tribe that has never had contact with modern civilization. The natives play with the numbers on the dial pad and hear different voices upon hitting certain sequences. They assume first that it's the device that makes these noises. Some of the cleverer natives, the scientists of the tribe, assemble an exact replica and hit the numbers again. They hear the voices again. The conclusion seems obvious to them. This particular combination of crystals and metals and chemicals produces what seems like human voices, and this means that the voices are simply properties of this device.
>
> But the tribal sage summons the scientists for a discussion. He has thought long and hard on the matter and has reached the following conclusion: the voices coming through the instrument must be coming from people like themselves, people who are living and conscious although speaking in another language. Instead of assuming that the voices are simply properties of the handset, they should investigate the possibility that through some mysterious communication network they are 'in touch' with other humans. Perhaps further study along these lines could lead to a greater understanding of the world beyond their island. But the scientists simply laugh at the sage...

The scientists of the tribe fail to consider all of the possible implications of their discovery, and so they laugh at the truth! Flew concludes by saying:

In this parable we see how easy it is to let preconceived theories shape the way we view evidence instead of letting the evidence shape our theories.... And in this, it seems to me, lies the peculiar danger, the endemic evil, of dogmatic atheism...

...I therefore put to my former fellow-atheists the simple central question: 'What would have to occur or to have occurred to constitute for you a reason to at least consider the existence of a superior Mind?[28]

Flew's surprising change of mind about God, a change based upon the "compelling and irrefutable" vision of reality offered by modern science, shows where the evidence of modern science points—to the existence of a divine Creator.

F. Conclusion: The Unfolding of the Plot

As we ended the last chapter, we returned to an earlier analogy— that the universe (including history) is an amazing book by an amazing Author. In this chapter we have seen how the journey of two small bands of scientists at the end of World War I was the beginning of a twist in the human part of the tale that no one without the eyes of faith could have anticipated. In the twentieth century, modern science found its way out of the straightjacket of scientific atheism prepared for it by brilliant yet short-sighted thinkers of the nineteenth century. It began to ask the ultimate questions about the universe, up to and including "why is there a universe at all?" And in one scientific finding after another, the answer "because of an all-powerful God, who made it for the sake of humanity" reemerged as a reasonable and credible answer.

In summary, what twentieth century physics has revealed is the credibility of the Christian Faith—its believability on the basis of natural reason.

But physics is not the only science in which the existence of God and the truth of the Christian Faith has seemed in danger of being swept away by the currents of progress. This is even more true of biology. The greatest controversy in the relationship between faith and science centers around the theory of biological evolution. For 140 years, American society has been the site of a great culture war, fought in print, from pulpits, in legal courts and even in politics regarding the compatibility of evolution and the Christian Faith, a war that still rages today. Is evolution the final nail in the coffin of Christian belief? Or is evolution simply one more example of God's intelligence, love, and power, the "disguised friend of faith," as Christian theologian and biochemist Arthur Peacocke once called it? In the next chapter, we will address this crucial issue.

Supplementary Reading

THE TWIST IN THE TALE: MODERN SCIENCE *VERSUS* SCIENTIFIC ATHEISM

1. "THE BIG BANG AND THE EXISTENCE OF GOD"

(excerpted from Christoph Cardinal Schönborn, "In the Beginning God Created…" Internet. Available from http://stephanscom.at/edw/katechesen/articles/2005/12/02/a9719/; accessed April 2, 2007.)

The scientific theory of the beginning of the universe that is now generally recognized is the theory of the Big Bang. Seventy-five years ago the American astronomer, Edwin Hubble, discovered that our universe is expanding at an unimaginable speed, the speed of light. In the meantime it has come to be assumed that the universe is expanding even faster.

It must, therefore, have once begun to expand at the big bang from a highly concentrated and compact point of beginning. It began explosively to expand. This theory is supported by observations and especially those concerning the "background radiation" in the universe, which is taken to be a kind of fallout from the Big Bang…

There is first of all the quite simple question: where did the universe expand to? Did it expand into space? But there is no space "outside" of the universe, beyond the gigantic dimensions of the cosmos, which is 14 billion light-years in extent, as is generally assumed (light travels 186,000 miles per second)…. Our galaxy alone, the Milky Way, is 100,000 light years across. Who can imagine such a thing? Well, beyond these gigantic dimensions of the cosmos there is no space. I recently read… that the space in which we live "emerged with the Big Bang and has been expanding ever since." There is no space outside of the universe.

The question of time is no less puzzling. For the Big Bang means that the universe had one beginning and moves towards an end. We are strongly tempted to ask what there was before the beginning. The answer can only be: just as there is space only because of the expansion of the universe—there is space wherever it expands—so it is with time. There is no time before time; it comes about with the Big Bang, just like space does. There is time only with the cosmos and within the cosmos.

Supplementary Reading

In recent decades the natural sciences have tried to approach this origin of the universe. Steven Weinberg, a Nobel Prize laureate in physics, wrote in 1977 a famous book called The First Three Minutes, which dealt with the first three minutes of the universe. It is fascinating to learn what the science of today says about the decisive first moments after the Big Bang. Everything that developed later, the galaxies, stars, planets, [and] life on our earth, all of it was decided in the very first moments....

Do we have here the point at which we should insert our belief in a Creator? Do we introduce him as it were at the limit reached by science? Does the Creator begin to act beyond this threshold? Let us be careful! We must not be too quick to assume that God produced the Big Bang [directly], as if in the smallest fraction of the very first second we come up against the wall behind which we find the Creator, or reach the point where only the Creator can explain what happened.

2. "MASS FIVE: AN EXAMPLE OF AN ANTHROPIC COINCIDENCE"

(excerpted from Owen Gingerich, God's Universe [Cambridge, MA: Harvard University Press, 2006], pp. 52–56).

[O]ur universe does seem singularly congenial as a home for intelligent life. L.J. Henderson's *Fitness of the Environment* extolled the remarkable life-enhancing properties of water, as well as pointing out the unique properties of the carbon atom, including the fact that carbon can bond with itself in a vastly larger number of combinations than any other atom. It is this wonderful property that makes complex organic chemistry possible.

Of course, these unique properties would have been of little avail in fostering life, had it not been for the substantial abundance of oxygen and carbon.... Curiously enough, neither oxygen nor carbon emerged in the first three minutes of the Big Bang. At first glance, this might be labeled God's Goof.... In the first minute of the Big Bang, ...there was no stable mass five, so at that point the fusion process stopped, well short of the twelve needed for carbon or the sixteen for oxygen....

But far from being a design flaw in our universe, the absence of mass five seems essential to our existence. The lack of a stable mass five means that the element-building in the stars takes place as a two-step process: first, hydrogen is converted into helium in the hot nuclear cauldrons at the cores of stars; and then, once helium is abundant, it is built up into heavier atoms, in a second process.... This second process requires a much

Supplementary Reading

higher temperature in the stellar interiors, one that is not reached until much of the hydrogen fuel has been exhausted—in the case of a star like the sun, only after about ten billion years. This guarantees a long, steady lifetime for sunlike stars. It is of course this tedious process that provides the stable solar environment in which the [sequences of life] can work themselves out.

If mass five were not absent, that could not happen. Suppose that mass five were stable. Then, in the opening minutes of the universe, characterized by the overwhelming abundance of protons (each with a mass of one unit), atom-building could have taken place as mass increased by steps of one, right up the nuclear ladder toward iron. This would have left no special abundance of carbon (mass twelve) or oxygen (mass sixteen), two essential building blocks of life....

What at first glance appeared to be God's mistake turns out to be one of the Creator's most ingenious triumphs.

3. "ORDER COMES FROM DEEPER, GREATER ORDER: NATURAL SYMMETRY AND GOD'S DESIGN"

(excerpted from Stephen M. Barr, Modern Physics and Ancient Faith [Notre Dame: University of Notre Dame Press, 2006], pp. 78–79).

[T]here are many things in nature that seem to bear out [the atheistic view that order can spring from disorder]. Indeed, the whole history of the cosmos seems to tell the same tale. Gravitation made the chaotically swirling gas and dust that filled the universe after the Big Bang condense into stars and planets. The same forces made those stars and planets settle into orderly arrangements like our solar system. On the surfaces of

Supplementary Reading

planets, chemicals clumped together under the influence of electromagnetic forces into smaller and then larger molecules, until at last molecules that could replicate themselves appeared, and biology began. This is the grand picture: order spontaneously from chaos. And presiding over the whole drama, the atheist tells us, is not some intelligence, but blind physical forces and mathematical necessity.

While this history of the cosmos is undoubtedly correct, the lessons the atheist draws from it are based on a superficial view of science. It is a view that really leaves out a major part of what science has taught us about the world, perhaps the most important part.

The overlooked point is this: when examined carefully, scientific accounts of natural processes are never really about order emerging from mere chaos, or form emerging from mere formlessness. On the contrary, they are always about the unfolding of an order that was already implicit in the nature of things, although often in a secret or hidden way. When we see situations that appear haphazard, or things that appear [to be] automatically or spontaneously "arranging themselves" into orderly patterns, what we find in every case is that what appeared to be… haphazard actually had a great deal of order already built into it…. Order has to be built in for order to come out.

…[I]n every case where science explains order, it does so… by appealing to a greater, more impressive, and more comprehensive underlying orderliness. And that is why, ultimately, scientific explanations do not allow us to escape from the Design Argument: for when the scientist has done his job there is not less order to explain but more. The universe looks far more orderly to us now than it did to the ancients who appealed to that order as proof of God's existence.

Study Guide

Faith and Science:
At the Crossroads of Nature and Spirit

VOCABULARY

Define the following terms:

1. Einstein's Equations

2. Cosmological Constant

3. *Ab Initio Temporis*

4. Edwin Powell Hubble

5. Big Bang Theory

6. Penzias and Wilson

7. Time

8. Cosmology

9. Anthropic Coincidences

10. *Anthropos*

11. Supernovas (atom formation)

12. Deuterium

13. Strong Nuclear Force

14. Multiverse Hypothesis

15. Johannes Kepler (*Harmonices mundi*)

16. Paul Dirac (Dirac Equation)

17. William Rowan Hamilton

18. The Argument from Design

19. Minucius Felix

20. Symmetry

STUDY QUESTIONS

1. What major changes occurred in science in the twentieth century? Why are they significant for the relationship between faith and science?
2. How is the idea of a perpetual universe an obstacle to belief in the authority of Scripture and the Church?
3. How did the Big Bang Theory originate?
4. Describe the major features of the Big Bang Theory regarding space and time.
5. Describe St. Augustine's explanation of time as it relates to the Big Bang Theory.
6. How was the Big Bang Theory finally confirmed?
7. Why did it take so long for the Big Bang Theory to gain acceptance? What does this reveal about the blind faith inherent in materialism and scientific atheism?
8. Why is the Big Bang Theory a major crack in the materialist worldview?
9. Does the Big Bang Theory prove that the universe had a first moment in time? Why or why not?
10. Does the Big Bang Theory prove the existence of God? Why or why not?
11. List three ways in which the Big Bang Theory is important for rediscovering faith on the frontiers of science.
12. In what new direction did the Big Bang Theory send physics?
13. Why is the role of gravity in the Big Bang considered an anthropic coincidence?
14. Why is the strong nuclear force considered an anthropic coincidence?
15. Using the device analogy, explain why it is unlikely that the anthropic coincidences are really just coincidences.
16. Do the anthropic coincidences scientifically prove the existence of God? Why or why not?

Study Guide

17. How do scientific atheists explain the phenomena of beauty in the universe?
18. What has modern science revealed about beauty in the universe? What does this fact imply?
19. Describe the processes of discovery in science and mathematics regarding beauty in the universe. Why does this process reinforce that the discovery of beauty is not simply a matter of purely personal taste?
20. What mistake was made in the eighteenth and nineteenth centuries by philosophers and theologians (e.g., William Paley) regarding the Argument from Design? What did this mistake fail to recognize?
21. Where does the beauty that we see around us come from, according to modern physics?
22. Restate the Argument from Design, using a) the notion of symmetry and b) the discovery of beauty and order in the laws governing the universe.

PRACTICAL EXERCISES

1. Rampant materialism created blinders for the scientific community that kept many from accepting the Big Bang. What other natural truths about the universe might be inaccessible to materialists? (Note: list only philosophical and scientific truths.)

2. Reread Genesis 1:1–2. How does the "formless void" compare to the idea of an infinitely dense, super-concentrated atom (Lemaître)? In your opinion, are Genesis 1:1–2 and the Big Bang Theory compatible?

3. Imagine a scenario in which a person won a multi-million dollar mega-lottery more than once. Should law enforcement officials begin to investigate? Does this give any insight into the importance of anthropic coincidences for the relationship between faith and science?

Endnotes

1. Lateran Council IV (1215): DS 800; Vatican Council I (1869–1870): DS 3002.
2. George Gamow, *My World Line* (English: Viking, 1970), 44. There are many historical ironies in this story. Theorists since Einstein's day have considered that Einstein's equations make more sense *with* the cosmological constant. And the term may indeed be needed to explain a discovery made in 1998. So even some of Einstein's blunders were pretty smart.
3. Barr, *Modern Physics*, 38–39.
4. Ibid., 43.
5. Steven Weinberg, *Reviews of Modern Physics* 61 (1989): 15, n.15.
6. St. Augustine, *Confessions*, XI.13, as quoted by Barr, *Modern Physics*, 48.
7. Barr, *Modern Physics*, 44–45.
8. Ibid., 46.
9. Collins, 64–65.
10. Robert Jastrow, *God and the Astronomers* (New York: W.W. Norton, 1992): 207.
11. Barr, *Modern Physics*, 35.
12. Jastrow, 14.
13. John Paul II, "Letter to the Rev. George V. Coyne, S.J." (June 1, 1988).
14. Paul Haffner, *Mystery of Creation*, 170.
15. John Paul II, "Discourse to the Pontifical Academy of the Sciences" (October 3, 1981), as quoted by Ibid., 170.
16. Ibid., 25. I have modified Barr's definition slightly for clarification.
17. Owen Gingerich, *God's Universe* (Cambridge: Harvard University Press, 2006), 49.
18. Barr, *Modern Physics*, 119.
19. Ibid., 119–121.
20. Collins, *The Language of God*, 74.
21. Barr, 23.
22. Herman Weyl, *The Open World: Three Lectures on the Metaphysical Implications of Science* (New Haven: Yale University Press, 1986), 28–29.
23. Barr, 66–67.
24. Minucius Felix, *Octavius* 18.4 as quoted in Barr, *Modern Physics*, 68–69.
25. Barr, *Modern Physics*, 80–81.
26. Ibid., 108.
27. Antony Flew, with Roy Abraham Varghese, *There is a God: How the World's Most Notorious Atheist Changed His Mind* (New York: HarperCollins, 2007), 88.
28. Ibid., 85–88.

Chapter Eight

Going "Deeper than Darwin"[1]: Faith and the Origins of Living Things

A. Strange Signs and Deceptive Discoveries

In Chapter Five, we learned how remarkably similar reading and appreciating a good book is to understanding the universe. We learned that to do either we must go beyond the details to the deeper levels of meaning, values, and truth to which they point. We also noted that, just as in the case of reading a book, it is possible to get so caught up in the scientific, physical details of the universe, that one narrows the universe down to these details. Our fascinating universe then ceases to be seen for what it truly is, and comes to be seen only as a blind and random mishap rather than as the creation of our loving God and Father.

As we move beyond the details of physics and chemistry and begin to explore the origins of the living things that flourish on our amazing planet, let us continue to apply the analogy between reading books and reading the universe. In particular, let us consider another story which, like *Harry Potter*, can aid us in understanding theology on the cutting edge of science, a story about a place which, like Hogwarts, has been made very famous through a recent movie — a story about Narnia.

The Silver Chair is the fourth book of the seven *Chronicles of Narnia*, C.S. Lewis' series about a world which has mysterious connections to our own. In the story, an English schoolgirl named Jill enters Narnia and is given a challenging quest—to rescue a prince who is being held captive by a magical and wicked enemy. To fulfill her quest she

THE FACT THAT SIGNS OF GOD'S CREATIVE ACTIVITY DO NOT APPEAR AS THEY WERE EXPECTED TO APPEAR PRIOR TO THE DISCOVERY OF EVOLUTION HAS CREATED A CHALLENGE FOR MANY.

must recognize four signs which she will find in her adventure. Once each sign is encountered, she and her companions must faithfully perform certain actions. As she stands on a mountain, looking down into Narnia, she is warned by Aslan, the loving creator and redeemer of Narnia, that the signs will not always be as obvious as they might seem. She is made to recite them, over and over, before she begins her quest. Then, once they are memorized, Aslan gives her the following counsel:

Here… I have spoken to you clearly: I will not often do so down in Narnia. Here on the mountain, the air is clear and your mind is clear; as you drop down into Narnia, the air will thicken. Take great care that it does not confuse your mind.

Aslan completes his counsel with a warning:

And the Signs which you have learned here will not look at all as you expect them to look, when you meet them there. That is why it is so important to know them by heart and to pay no attention to appearances. **Remember the Signs and believe the Signs**[2].

Jill begins her quest looking for the Signs, but never with the care and attention they deserve. In fact, she and her friends either overlook or misinterpret the first three, and each time the quest suffers and almost fails. Only after repeated misadventures caused by misinterpretations of the Signs do Jill and her friends learn how to see them for what they are and not for what they expect them to be.

Jill and her companions learn, through costly mistakes, to keep their eyes and their minds open. Slowly but surely they learn to detect and understand the Signs, even while they overcome the hardships and dangers their mistakes bring upon them. When they reach the final Sign, their learning experiences make it possible for them to finally overcome their obstacles and succeed at their attempt to rescue the captive prince.

The Silver Chair has an important moral for us and for everyone who wishes to understand the relationship between faith and science when it comes to the scientific consensus that all living things came into existence through a process of biological evolution. In a real sense, scientists and believers today are very much like Jill and her companions. We have been given very clear indications by God in Sacred Scripture and Catholic doctrine that he is the Creator of all things, including living things. Those living things, he tells us, are his creatures, willed by him and created by him. And yet, as in Jill's case, the fact that the signs of God's creative activity do not appear as they were expected to appear prior to the discovery of evolution has created a challenge. We remember the Signs, but do we still believe them? Or have we disbelieved or become confused because they now appear to us in ways that are different than we expected? To answer these questions, we must first look more closely at biological evolution.

B. Darwin's Theory of Evolution

For centuries, it was believed by many people that all of the different kinds of living things in the world were brought into being by *"special creation."* That is, it was thought that the first plants and animals of each kind were directly formed by God from inorganic (i.e., nonliving) matter by extraordinary acts of divine intervention. For example, the idea was that if one could trace back through the ancestry of cats, eventually one would come to the first group of cats, who had no ancestors, but were directly made by God. The reason many people believed this was not because they preferred supernatural explanations to natural ones. They believed it, quite simply, because no good natural explanation had been discovered. No one had ever come up with a plausible explanation of how things as intricate as plants and animals could have arisen by natural processes.

This made for a seemingly powerful argument for the existence of God. What else, it was asked, except a direct intervention by God could explain the complexity and brilliant beauty of all these living creatures? This kind of argument was easy to understand. And so, as we saw at the end of the last chapter, some theologians in the eighteenth and nineteenth centuries began to lean very heavily on this biological version of the Argument from Design. This turned out to be a mistake, because not long afterwards someone finally did come along with a brilliant idea for explaining how the various kinds of living things could have arisen naturally. That someone was Charles Darwin.

In 1859, Darwin published a book entitled *On the Origin of Species*, one of the epoch-making works in the history of science. Darwin proposed that all living species in the world descended from a small number of common ancestors, possibly even only one, which lived a long time ago. In other words, originally there was perhaps just one type of living thing, which gradually evolved over great stretches of time into the many forms of life we see today. Therefore, all the extremely diverse forms of life, including trees, fish, bacteria, frogs, and even higher mammals like deer and apes, are related to each other in a vast and very ancient tree of life. In a later book, *The Descent of Man*, Darwin proposed that humanity itself was a branch of this tree.[3]

This is the idea of the *evolution of species*, or just *evolution* for short. (Some people distinguish *macroevolution*, the emergence of new species from older ones, from *microevolution*, the minor incremental changes which occur within a species.[4]) The idea of evolution was not completely new. What was new was Darwin's theory of *how* and *why* this evolution happened, i.e., the natural mechanisms he proposed for explaining evolution.

One clue that led Darwin to his theory was the methods used by plant and animal breeders. Breeders take advantage of naturally

ALL THE EXTREMELY DIVERSE FORMS OF LIFE ARE RELATED TO EACH OTHER IN A VAST AND VERY ANCIENT TREE OF LIFE.

FOR CENTURIES, IT WAS ASKED
WHAT ELSE EXCEPT A DIRECT
INTERVENTION BY GOD COULD
EXPLAIN THE COMPLEXITY AND
BRILLIANT BEAUTY OF ALL THESE
LIVING CREATURES?

occurring variations among members of a species. Even in the same litter of puppies, for example, there are variations in size, color, and behavioral traits. In each generation, the breeder selects those animals or plants that possess the traits that he wants, and he allows only those to reproduce. Since traits tend to get passed on, gradually over many generations a new "breed" appears. In this way, for instance, domestic breeds of cattle and dogs were produced that were strikingly different from the wild varieties from which they originally descended. The effectiveness of breeding is obvious when one compares poodles and dachshunds to wolves.

There are two elements in this process: *naturally occurring variation* within a species and *selection*. What Darwin realized was that selection does not require the artificial conditions of a farm or laboratory or the decisions of a plant or animal breeder. It can happen naturally (although more slowly) in the wild; hence the name of the mechanism he proposed for evolution: *natural selection.*

Darwin pointed out that in the wild some variations would make members of a species better adapted to the challenges and opportunities of their environment. The organisms that inherited such advantageous variations would tend to thrive and have more offspring than other members of the same species. Thus, the advantageous variations would spread through the population as generations passed; while, on the other hand, disadvantageous variations would tend to die out, since their inheritors would be at a disadvantage and leave fewer offspring on average. The accumulation of small changes over many generations could produce, he argued, new kinds of plants and animals. Some species would change more rapidly than others. Some would divide into two or more species. And some would die out altogether.[5] In every case it would depend on the complicated interactions of natural variation and environment. Ultimately, the world as we know it now, a world teeming with a multiplicity of species, would be the result. Natural selection, then, is "a process by which organisms better fitted to their environment [leave] more progeny with their characteristics to the next generation than less well adapted organisms."[6] The theory that species originated by an evolutionary process driven by natural selection acting on natural variation is called "Darwinian evolution" or "Darwinism."

Darwin's theory raised questions that could not be answered in his day. For example, why did not interbreeding among members of the same species blend their characteristics and over time eliminate all the "variations"? (For example, why did the plants with red flowers and the ones with white flowers in the same species not interbreed to produce eventually only pink flowers?) Another problem was that evolution required advantageous variations to get passed on with little or no change to the next generation, so that they would not be lost. But there also had to be something which *did* cause changes from one generation to the next, or else there would not be any way for "variations" to arise in the first place. Questions such as these could not be answered until Gregor Mendel, an Augustinian monk, discovered the basic principles of heredity and thus inaugurated the science of genetics. In the first several decades of the twentieth century, the ideas of Darwinian evolution and the ideas originated by Mendel were combined into a more rigorous theory of evolution called "neo-Darwinism." This "neo-Darwinian synthesis" is the basis of the modern understanding of the origin of species and is accepted by virtually all biologists today. According to the modern neo-Darwinian theory of evolution, the "variations" on which natural selection acts are *genetic variations* that arise by chance, for example, through mutations—or, as it is often put, "random genetic variation." (Those little words "random" and "chance" have led to much misunderstanding and needless trouble, as we shall see.)

While many religious people accepted Darwin's theory of evolution, there were also many who did not. Indeed, there are many Christians today who bitterly oppose the ideas of Darwinian evolution. As we have seen, some of them think it is contrary to the teaching of the Book of Genesis. Others have theological or philosophical objections to it. (We shall look at some of these objections and the answers to them more closely in this chapter.) On the other side, many scientific atheists have interpreted Darwinian evolution in reductionist and materialist ways. They have argued that Darwinian evolution has unavoidable atheistic implications, and have used it as the basis of a militant anti-religious ideology, sometimes called "evolutionism." (One could call this ideology "atheist Darwinism," "reductionist Darwinism," or "materialist Darwinism".)

Evolution has frequently been used to attack religion ever since Darwin's day; and this has frightened many religious believers into thinking that evolution is indeed incompatible with Christianity. Their counterattacks against evolution have been used by atheists as evidence that Christians are opposed to science. In other words, religious opponents of evolution and evolutionist opponents of religion have tended to feed off each other and to provoke each other to more and more extreme positions. Ironically, as we will see, they have something important in common—they suffer from the same misunderstandings of the Christian Faith.

THE CATHOLIC CHURCH AND EVOLUTION

Where has the Catholic Church historically stood on the question of evolution? The "short answer" is that the Church has never condemned either the idea of evolution or the Darwinian theory of it, and Catholics have always been free either to accept or reject it. For example, the 1907 version of the famous *Catholic Encyclopedia*,

Gregor Mendel

GREGOR MENDEL, AN AUGUSTINIAN MONK, DISCOVERED THE BASIC PRINCIPLES OF HEREDITY AND THUS INAUGURATED THE SCIENCE OF GENETICS.

Charles Darwin

THE BASIC IDEAS OF EVOLUTION
AND NATURAL SELECTION
ARE, THEOLOGICALLY, NOT
CONTROVERSIAL FOR CATHOLICS
AND NEVER HAVE BEEN.

in its article "Catholics and Evolution," summarized the theory of evolution as it stood at that time, and then said, "This is the gist of the theory of evolution as a scientific hypothesis. It is in perfect agreement with the Christian conception of the universe." A very popular book was published in the 1920s called *The Question Box*, which explained Catholic beliefs in a question and answer format. It was written by a priest and carried an *imprimatur* and *nihil obstat*, which are formal acknowledgments by the Church that a book contains nothing contrary to Catholic doctrine. In answer to the question "May a Catholic believe in evolution?", the book said, "As the Church has made no pronouncement upon evolution, Catholics are perfectly free to accept evolution, either as a scientific hypothesis or as a philosophical speculation." This has consistently been the attitude of the Church from the time of Darwin, down to our own day.

That is the "short answer." The "long answer" requires that we make some distinctions. The first distinction is between "evolution" and "evolutionism," i.e., between the actual *science* of evolution and the radically reductionist and materialist *philosophy* or *ideology* that some people base on it. Unfortunately, since Darwin himself was influenced by reductionist and materialist ideas, especially later in life, and since several leading evolutionary biologists have promoted such views in their own writings, some people find it hard to see the difference between the actual science and the "spin" that atheists put on it. In spite of that, we must always be careful, along with the Catholic Church herself, to make that distinction. Occasionally one will hear Catholic theologians criticize "Darwinism;" however, in those cases, they are usually using the term to mean atheistic evolutionism, not the scientific theory of evolution. Unfortunately, the use of the same term by different people to mean different things has caused many misunderstandings.

A second distinction must be made between the various parts of the theory of evolution. There are three: a) the idea that species of plants and animals evolved from other, earlier species; b) the Darwinian or neo-Darwinian mechanism of evolution (i.e., natural selection); and c) the idea that humanity itself is the product of evolution.

The Church and her theologians have never seen any objection, difficulty, or problem, from the point of view of Catholic doctrine, with the first two aspects. The basic ideas of evolution and natural selection are, theologically, not controversial for Catholics and never have been. However, the third aspect, the evolution of the human race, does raise significant theological and philosophical questions, for it touches on deep questions about the nature of human beings. These questions require more extended treatment, and so we will postpone a full discussion of them to a later chapter. For now, we will just briefly summarize the history of the Church's thinking on this aspect of evolution.

First, it should be noted that there was no official Catholic teaching at all on evolution for almost a hundred years after Darwin published his theory. The first official statement by the Church that touched on evolutionary questions was the encyclical letter *Humani generis*, of Pope Pius XII, written in 1950. So, from 1859 to 1950, one has to talk about the opinions of theologians, rather than explicit Church doctrine. From the beginning, Catholic theology emphasized that man is both physical and spiritual, and that the spiritual is not "reducible" to matter. One cannot, therefore, ever hope to completely explain a human being just from the point of view of physics, chemistry, or biology. We are biological organisms, to be sure, but we are also much more than that.

The Church and her theologians, as well as many philosophers, have always insisted that the human "spiritual soul," not being merely physical, cannot possibly arise as the result of physical processes alone. Even in procreation, the spiritual soul of the child is not produced by a simple rearrangement of atoms, as happens when sperm and egg combine. In the same way, the spiritual souls of the first human beings were not the result of a merely biological process. In other words, *the human spiritual soul did not evolve*. That leaves the question of whether the *human body* evolved. From the time of Darwin, Catholic theologians saw this as an "open question," about which no definite conclusion could be drawn from Catholic doctrine.

At first, most Catholic theologians were skeptical of the idea that the human body had evolved from lower organisms. As time went on, however, and scientific evidence accumulated, this skepticism slowly faded.

In 1950, Pope Pius XII taught in *Humani generis* that the evolution of the human spiritual soul was incompatible with Catholic doctrine, but that the evolution of the human body was an allowable scientific hypothesis. He was just "making official" what the thinking of the Church had been all along. In Chapter Eleven we will see that Pope John Paul II significantly developed Pius XII's teachings, and that Pope Benedict XVI has even declared that the theory of evolution is a true enrichment of human knowledge.

So, when it comes to evolution as a matter of biology, Catholics have never had a quarrel with it. That is why there was never an attempt to prevent evolution from being taught in Catholic schools. There was never a Catholic equivalent of the famous Scopes Trial, in which a science teacher was brought to trial for teaching about evolution.

THE EVIDENCE FOR EVOLUTION

What is the evidence for evolution? It comes from many directions. One source of evidence is the *fossil record*—the remains of long-dead organisms found by digging deep into the layers of rock and sediment under the Earth's surface. As we saw in an earlier chapter, Bl. Nicholas Steno showed that the deeper layers of sedimentary rock were deposited earlier, so that the fossil record gives us a "timeline" for the

THE FIRST OFFICIAL STATEMENT BY THE CHURCH THAT TOUCHED ON EVOLUTIONARY QUESTIONS WAS THE ENCYCLICAL LETTER *HUMANI GENERIS*, OF POPE PIUS XII, WRITTEN IN 1950.

ONE SOURCE OF EVIDENCE FOR EVOLUTION IS THE FOSSIL RECORD.

Pope Pius XII

appearance of various kinds of plants and animals on earth. A second source is *comparative anatomy*, which studies the similarities and differences of different species. A third is *biogeography*, which studies the geographical distribution of different plants and animals over time. A fourth, which has undergone the most explosive growth over the last thirty years, is *genetics*. *Genes* are the blueprints for the construction of living bodies through the assembly of protein molecules, the "workhorses of life's processes," which are necessary for all the processes of physical life.[7] By comparing the "gene sequences" of different species, biologists can see deep relationships between them that are not apparent just by studying the creatures themselves. Furthermore, because scientists know something about how fast genetic mutations take place, they are able to work out genetic "timelines"; these coincide with timelines established from fossil records. There is now a huge amount of interlocking and mutually supporting evidence that confirms that all living things on earth, including human beings, are indeed related to each other in a giant tree of life.

This is a good place to say something about the word "theory." In everyday speech the words "theory" and "fact" are sometimes used in contrast to each other: a theory is something uncertain and not yet proved, while a fact is something well-established. From this, some people argue that the "theory of evolution," since it is still called a theory, is not yet regarded as well-established. However, this is based on a misunderstanding of the way scientists use the word "theory." In science, a precise and coherent set of ideas for explaining some set of phenomena is called "a theory" of those phenomena. After it is generally accepted, it is often referred to as "*the* theory" of those phenomena. So, "the theory of relativity," "the BCS theory of superconductivity," and "the Big Bang Theory" are all regarded by scientists as very solidly established. The same is true of the theory of evolution.

Darwin's book, *On the Origin of Species*, was and remains a "great work in the history of ideas," in the words of Christoph Cardinal Schönborn. Here is Schönborn's description of the accomplishment of this great English biologist:

> …with an astounding gift for observation, enormous diligence, and mental prowess, [Darwin] succeeded in producing one of… history's most influential works. He could already see in advance that his research would create many areas of endeavor. Today one can truly say that the "evolution" paradigm has become, so to speak, a "master key," extending itself within many fields of knowledge.[8]

Biological evolution has become the accepted model for explaining the diversity of the world's living creatures among contemporary scientists, and is a crucial stop on our journey to find faith on the cutting edge of science. Let us now consider Darwin's evolutionary hypothesis in relation to the truth that God is the Creator and Sustainer of all living things.

C. *Misunderstandings and Misinterpretations of Evolution by Believers*

There are many people who have no trouble accepting the idea of evolution or Darwin's theory of natural selection, but find it hard to accept the idea that we human beings are the product of evolution. The evolution of human beings does indeed raise special questions, because of our spiritual nature. That is why we are going to postpone discussion of human evolution until a later chapter. However, there are many people who see an incompatibility between Christianity and Darwin's theory *even as an account of the origin of plants and animals*. We shall explore the reasons for that now. We will see that there are two basic reasons. The first involves misunderstandings of Christian theology—misunderstandings sadly shared even by many Christians. The second involves reductionist and materialist interpretations of Darwin's theory.

The most obvious theological mistake concerns the way the Book of Genesis should be understood. We have already seen in Chapter Three why it is an error to read Genesis as if it were a science textbook. It is wrong to read it that way because that is not how it was intended either by its human authors or by its divine Author. As Pope Leo XIII said in his 1893 encyclical *Providentissimus Deus*: "The sacred writers did not intend to teach men . . . the essential nature of the things of the visible universe." Nevertheless, many non-Catholic Christians do read the Book of Genesis in this "literalistic" way, and that is one of the primary reasons why they reject evolution. We will come back yet again to the Book of Genesis to discuss how it should be read. In doing so, we will see that there is nothing in it that is contrary to evolution.

The other theological mistakes are more subtle. There are three important ones which we shall discuss: (1) That chance is incompatible with Divine Providence; (2) That natural selection is incompatible with Divine Design and Purpose; and (3) That natural explanations eliminate the possibility of the creative activity of God in the universe.

CHANCE VERSUS PROVIDENCE

Chance plays an important role in Darwinian theory. *Chance* is the intersection of two or more lines of causality that are independent of each other, in a way that is accidental and unintended by the agents involved.[9] As we saw, species evolve because of "genetic variations" and the effects of "natural selection." Biologists explain genetic variations as "random" occurrences, or as a matter of chance. Those genetic variations produce variations in the organisms themselves and affect

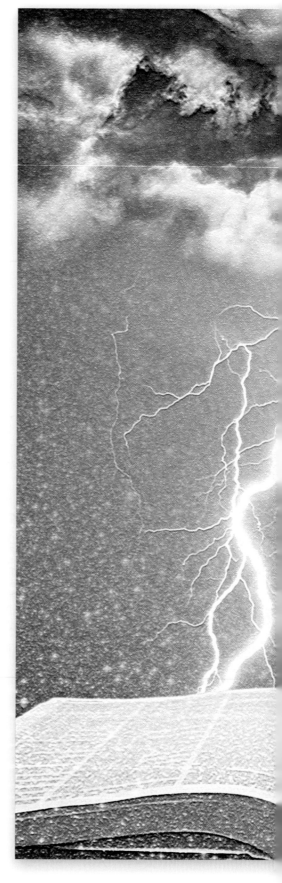

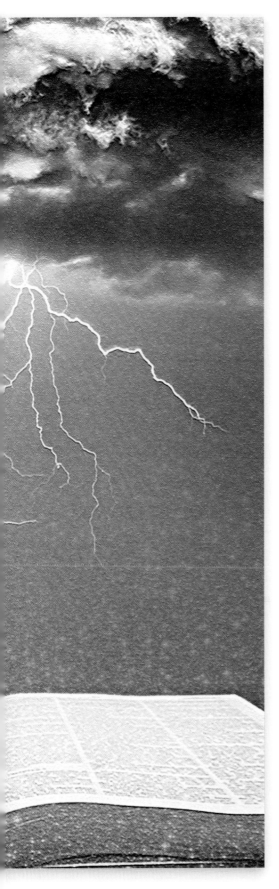

the way they interact with their environments. Those environments, being very complicated, also involve chance in many ways. This is why the process of evolution is often presented as a blind, blundering, trial-and-error process. *And, on the level of natural causes, that is not an incorrect way to think about it.* The question arises whether this somehow contradicts the teaching that an all-knowing God is governing the universe and that all things in it are part of a "divine plan," which is called divine Providence. In other words, if we agree with evolutionary biologists that "chance" plays a large role in evolution and that genetic mutations are "random," are we denying the doctrine of God's governance of all creatures?

The simplest way to answer this is to quote St. Thomas Aquinas. In his long treatise *Summa contra Gentiles*, there is a chapter (Book 3, chapter 74) with the title "That divine Providence does not exclude fortune and chance," in which the great theologian argues exactly that. St. Augustine writes in his book, *The City of God*, that no one can in this life "escape being tossed about by chance and accident."[10] Scripture itself speaks of the role of chance in the world. In a very famous passage, the Book of Ecclesiastes says, "I returned and saw under the sun, that the race is not to the swift, nor the battle to the strong, neither yet bread to the wise, nor yet riches to men of understanding, nor yet favor to men of skill, but time and chance happens to them all" (Eccl 9:11).

Of course, all these texts were written many centuries before Darwin's theory came along. But that is precisely the point: it did not take Darwin's theory to show people that many things in this world depend on chance. Anyone who reads history knows it. Indeed, anyone who has lived knows it. So really, Darwinism does not raise any new theological question here. It is the same question that St. Thomas Aquinas analyzed in his treatise more than seven hundred years ago. Nevertheless, new or not, it is an important question. What is the answer?

The first step is to recognize that chance is to some extent in the eye of the beholder. If someone deals a poker hand from a deck of cards, it is a matter of chance which cards will turn up. One might even calculate the "odds" of getting certain hands. But to someone who knows exactly the order of cards in the deck, the outcome of the deal is not at all uncertain or a matter of chance. He knows exactly what hand will be dealt. So what is chance for one person need not be chance for another. For God, who knows everything, nothing is a matter of chance. That is why the Book of Proverbs says, "The lot is cast into the lap, but the decision is wholly from the Lord" (Prv 16:33).

The eminent biologist Francis S. Collins deals directly with the chance element in evolution in his book *The Language of God*. He poses the question: "How could God take such chances? If evolution is random, how could he really be in charge, and how could he be certain of an outcome that included intelligent beings at all?" He answers in this way:

The solution is actually readily at hand, once one ceases to apply human limitations to God. If God is outside of nature, then he is outside of space and time. In that context, God could in the moment of creation of the universe also know every detail of the future. That could include the formation of the stars, planets, and galaxies, all of the chemistry, physics, geology, and biology that led to the formation of life on earth, and the evolution of humans, right to the moment of your reading this book—and beyond. In that context, evolution could appear to us to be driven by chance, but from God's perspective the outcome would be entirely specified. Thus God could be completely and intimately involved in the creation of all species, while from our perspective, limited as it is by the tyranny of linear time, this would appear a random and undirected process.[11]

In summary, accepting the presence of chance or random events in evolution, as well as in human life, is not a denial of God's Providence. Even in the "accidental" elements involved in life, God is still the Lord of history and the universe.

NATURAL SELECTION VERSUS DESIGN AND PURPOSE

Before Darwin, when people assumed that each type of plant and animal had been directly crafted by the hand of God through "special creation," it was easier to say that living things, including ourselves, were "designed." Moreover, since God presumably had a reason for making each creature and for making it exactly the way it is, one could also say that each living thing had a "purpose." Darwin's theory seemed to undercut that way of thinking. Rather than being crafted directly by the hand of God, species were crafted by the blind and impersonal forces of random genetic mutations and natural selection. Both design and purpose seemed to go out the window.

Perhaps the first thing to be said is that even if this were true in biology, it is not true in physics, as we saw in the last chapter. The laws of physics themselves have a magnificent structure and harmony that point to a Designer. And the anthropic coincidences suggest that the universe itself has a purpose: its laws seem "fine-tuned" to allow life. But let us return to the issues raised by evolution.

The fact that a process makes use of chance or randomness in no way implies that it was not designed or that it has no purpose. To help us understand this point, the philosopher Dennis Bonnette invites us to envision a roulette game.[12] The game of roulette depends on it being impossible for the players to predict exactly where the ball will land on any given spin of the roulette wheel. But this is not because the process, which involves chance, is without plan or purpose. In fact, everything is carefully orchestrated. The ball is given a round

Dennis Bonnette

THE FACT THAT THE SIGNS OF GOD'S CREATIVE ACTIVITY DO NOT APPEAR AS THEY WERE EXPECTED TO APPEAR PRIOR TO THE DISCOVERY OF EVOLUTION HAS CREATED A CHALLENGE FOR MANY.

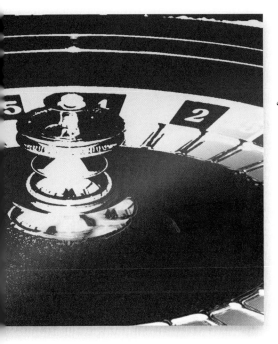

shape to allow it to bounce around the table. The wheel is carefully crafted so as to facilitate the bouncing of the ball at the beginning of the spin when the speed of the turning of the wheel is strongest, and to facilitate the landing of the ball in a numbered slot when the speed slows to a certain point. The whole set-up is designed to operate in a precise way, in accordance with the laws of physics. Not only would a physicist be able to explain in general terms how the roulette wheel functions, but he also would be able to tell you exactly where a particular ball would land if he were given the exact force of the spin, the exact dimensions of the ball, the diameter and shape of the wheel, etc.

We see, then, a situation that involves at the same time chance and also design and purpose, and where in fact chance is involved in both the purpose and the design. The *purpose* is that of a certain kind of game. That game cannot be played unless *chance* is a part of it. (It is a "game of chance.") In order for the roulette wheel to produce the required "chance" or "random" events, it has to be *designed* in a certain way.

We know of many examples in ordinary life where people design and bring about outcomes through the use of chance. For example, a hunter who uses birdshot while hunting incorporates chance (the spreading out of the shot when fired from his gun) in an attempt to bring about an intended effect (the hitting of a major organ in the bird, causing its death).

There are a countless number of similar examples in nature, where nature accomplishes its purpose by "playing the odds." Many insects produce large numbers of larvae, because most will be eaten by fish, birds, or other predators. Whether a particular larva gets eaten is a matter of chance, and the chances of its survival are very small. However, the small chance of survival of the individual larvae is compensated for by their large numbers. And the large numbers of larvae are not an accident. That is part of the "survival strategy" (an unconscious one, to be sure) of the species. The same thing happens with the seeds of plants. In human procreation, the chances of a single sperm fertilizing an egg are extremely small, and for that reason many sperm are produced. In each of these examples, there is an evident "natural purpose," namely reproduction. Now, if nature can so arrange things that many sperm are sent in search of an egg, in order that one of them might "win through" and produce an offspring, why should not God arrange that many genetic mutations occur in nature, so that a few of them might "win through" to make a new and interesting species? In fact, that is exactly what happens, and it is not clear why we should see "purpose" in one case and not in the other.

Sometimes, then, chance or randomness does not reflect a lack of order, design, or guiding purpose, but is a part of a larger overarching order, design, and purpose. Unfortunately, many people have jumped from the mere fact that chance plays an important role in the world—which, of course, everyone has always known—to the idea that the world is entirely a matter of chance, that there is no ultimate meaning or purpose to anything, and that the universe is "unguided" and "unplanned."

Let us ask, then, why God might have decided to create a world in which "chance" plays a role in his plan. Many reasons suggest themselves. Professor Michael Tkacz of Gonzaga University notes, "One of the reasons Thomas Aquinas thought it was necessary to acknowledge the chance element in nature is that it is the way that novelty is introduced into nature."[13] Think again of human procreation. Because we reproduce sexually, so that genes from two people are combined to produce each offspring, there is a constant "reshuffling" of the genetic deck. This means that new and interesting individuals are constantly being produced. No two people are exactly alike. So the chance that is built into the system of human procreation has the effect of drawing forth ever new possibilities and thus helping to realize the rich possibilities of the human species. In the same way, the system of evolution is constantly producing new kinds of creatures, thus realizing the wonderful possibilities of the material world.

Tkacz cites the following passage from St. Thomas in which the same point is made in somewhat technical philosophical language: "Nothing prevents the generation of something to be in itself designed when referred to one cause and, nevertheless, accidental and chance when referred to another cause.... This is because it [is God's] intention that all forms which are in the potentiality of matter be [realized]."[14] This conception of chance and contingency drawing forth novel forms is certainly consistent with the role of chance in neo-Darwinian evolutionary theory.

Another reason emerges if we ask ourselves what a world without chance would be like. It would be a world in which everything would happen in simple and predictable ways. One of the reasons that "chance" events arise, is that the world is a complicated place in which many things are going on that have nothing directly to do with each other. For example, my life follows a certain pattern, and your life follows a certain pattern. But my life and yours are only loosely connected with each other. So, when these two patterns intersect—for example, if I run into you on the street—it appears as a "chance event." It is not an event that could have been predicted by just knowing the pattern of my activities. In order for there to be no chance events, everything would have to be closely related to everything else in a highly organized way. That is, the world would have to have just a *single pattern*. That would translate into a world in which there would be nothing surprising in nature and in which we could not choose to impose our own patterns on things. It would be a world without freedom. It would be a completely regimented world in which we could not have any meaningful activity of our own. Our God is consistent—he made the world for the sake of free human beings, and so he made a world that supports freedom—an evolving world.

NATURE VERSUS GOD

St. Francis of Assisi

Some people who attack evolution do so because it is *naturalistic*. Naturalism in its extreme form says that *only* natural explanations are valid. In other words, it denies any supernatural reality, which is wrong. But some people who oppose extreme naturalism go too far in the other direction. They think any attempt to find natural explanations is an attack on God. They think that the more we can explain "naturally" the less there is for God to do. For example, if it is said that an insect species arose by the natural processes of evolution, such people see this as a rival explanation to saying that God is the Creator of the world and everything in it. They imagine that we must then subtract the insect from the list of things that God created.

In other words, such people see nature and God as being in competition with each other. The more nature does, the less God is doing. As we explained in Chapters Five and Six, this mistake is based on a failure to understand the fundamentally important notions of primary and secondary causes. If we say that a character in a play kills another character to get revenge, that does not take anything away from the author of the play as an explanation of the events in the play. In fact, the more we understand what the characters are doing on their own terms, at the level of cause and effect *within* the play, the *more* we understand the mind of the playwright, and the more we know what *he* was up to in writing the play. The primary cause (the author) creates his story *through* the actions of the secondary causes (the characters). That is why it would obviously make no sense to ask, "Do Beatrice and Benedick get engaged because they love each other, or do they get engaged because that is what Shakespeare wrote?" The answer is "*Both*." And, in fact, the first is only true because the second is true. In the same way, it is simply incorrect to ask, "Does this insect species exist because it evolved, or because God created the universe that way?" Again, the answer is "*Both*."

Of course, God can act directly without making use of secondary causes. He could create an insect species from thin air, rather than have it evolve by natural processes. However, God's use of natural causes, including "chance," reveals his power, intelligence, and skill in an even greater way than if he directly caused all things, as philosopher Marie George explains:

> [T]he use of intermediary [i.e., secondary] causes does not indicate a God who is less intelligent and powerful than one who would make things directly, but one who is more intelligent and powerful. Getting non-intelligent beings to participate in the production of the world is more difficult than doing everything oneself—one has to design the instruments (the elements) themselves in such a way as to allow them to share in this task. Another way of putting it is that just as forming students so well that they are not only knowledgeable, but also capable

of teaching others shows greater ability than only making them knowledgeable, so too *making things not only to be, but to be causes shows greater power* [emphasis added]. [Moreover, that] some of the intermediary causes [are] chance causes does not immediately discredit the intelligence of the designer, since chance can be put at the service of intelligence.[15]

The Catholic Encyclopedia article on evolution written in 1907 put it this way:

> If God produced the universe by a single creative act of his will, then its natural development by laws implanted in it by its Creator is to the greater glory of his divine power and wisdom.
> …St. Thomas says, "the potency of the cause is greater the more remote the effects to which it extends"; and Suárez [says], "God does not interfere directly with the natural order where secondary causes suffice to produce the intended effect."[16]

The Church has always taught that there is a natural order that comes from God, and the *greater* the powers and potentialities that God has implanted in nature, the *more* it shows forth his power and greatness.

We have now discussed some of the more serious philosophical errors that lead some people to see a conflict between Christianity and evolution conceived of as a natural process, involving chance, by which the species of plants and animals came into being. But the fault does not lie only with the misunderstandings of believers. As we noted, many people (including probably Darwin himself) saw evolution in crudely reductionist and materialist terms, leading to atheistic misinterpretations of the theory.

D. Atheistic Misunderstandings and Misinterpretations of Evolution

The atheistic misinterpretations of the theory of evolution are in many ways even simpler than the misinterpretations by believers. There are three important ones: (1) Evolution as Survival of the Fittest; (2) The Omission of Beauty; and (3) Evolution as Ideology.

EVOLUTION AS SURVIVAL OF THE FITTEST

The trend toward an atheistic misinterpretation of evolution can be traced back to Darwin himself, whether or not he fully embraced such an interpretation. Part of the problem is the language that Darwin used.

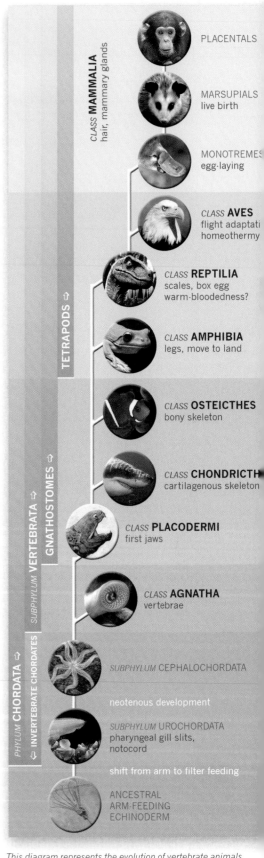

This diagram represents the evolution of vertebrate animals.

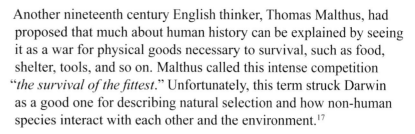

THE TREND TOWARD AN ATHEISTIC MISINTERPRETATION OF EVOLUTION CAN BE TRACED BACK TO DARWIN HIMSELF, WHETHER OR NOT HE FULLY EMBRACED SUCH AN INTERPRETATION.

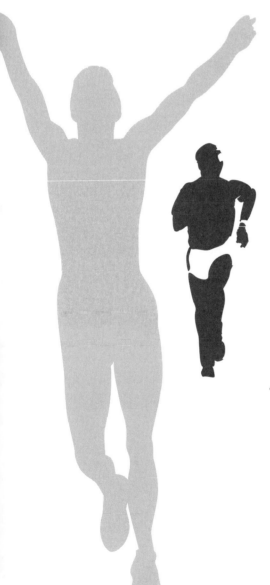

Another nineteenth century English thinker, Thomas Malthus, had proposed that much about human history can be explained by seeing it as a war for physical goods necessary to survival, such as food, shelter, tools, and so on. Malthus called this intense competition *"the survival of the fittest."* Unfortunately, this term struck Darwin as a good one for describing natural selection and how non-human species interact with each other and the environment.[17]

Darwin's use of the term clouded the understanding of many who would follow him. He did not mean that it is the most intelligent, or the strongest, or (in the case of humans) the most moral that survive to produce the next generations, but rather it is the organisms most fit for reproducing. "Fit," in *survival of the fittest* as Darwin used it, means to be a successful reproducer. It also means "fitting into" one's surroundings—meshing with one's environment.[18]

This use of a misleading term, when combined with the idea that the universe is unguided and without purpose, infected (and still infects) much evolutionary thinking. It made the whole universe seem intrinsically violent and aggressive, a universe of "blind pitiless indifference" as one contemporary evolutionary biologist refers to it.[19] But this is actually not the heart of Darwin's hypothesis. In fact, the survival of the fittest as the survival of the most violent is so out of step with the evolutionary hypothesis that one biologist has suggested that the term natural selection should be replaced by a new term, *natural breeding*, to make clear that producing offspring, not destroying opponents, is the driving force of evolution.[20]

Darwin's decision to label the evolutionary process as a matter of war rather than of reproduction would have grave repercussions. It would make it more difficult for some people to believe in a loving Creator. How could a loving God create a process that was at its very heart based on violence? But in truth, Darwin's process was about something very compatible with love—physical generation, the production of offspring, and (in the case of higher animals) the raising of and caring for those offspring. Yes, there is death involved in the process, but death itself is often a sacrifice for the sake of new life, and sacrifice is at the heart of real love. In the words of our Lord, "Unless a grain of wheat falls into the earth and dies, it remains just a single grain; but if it dies, it bears much fruit" (Jn 12:24).

A weakness that many people have is that once they have found the explanation of something, they think it is the explanation of everything. They begin to think that one key fits all locks. People in every profession have this weakness to some degree. Psychologists tend to look for psychological explanations; economists for economic explanations; political theorists look at things politically; and so on. Some evolutionary biologists have come to believe that every aspect of reality has a Darwinian explanation. Even Darwin, unfortunately, suffered from such a one-sided view.

Darwin's theory of natural selection is a stroke of genius. But it does not work as a total explanation of the whole world of living creatures and everything about it.

THE OMISSION OF BEAUTY

Darwin saw that the evolutionary process would involve an upward movement, from plants, to animals, and finally to man. But the increasing complexity of life over time is not only a matter of improvements in the ability to survive and breed. In fact, the world of living creatures is full of beauty that has no practical relevance to survival and breeding. The beauty of lilies, the fragrance of lilacs, the brilliance of bird plumage, the haunting melodies of birdsong, the grace of the antelope, the colors of fall foliage, the elegant shapes of seashells— the living world is bursting with what might be called surplus beauty, extravagant beauty, utterly unnecessary beauty: far more beauty than strictly necessary for sexual selection.

Darwinian biology's mechanistic approach to evolution is not wrong; it is merely too narrow. One has to look beyond it to develop a grander perspective on the process, one that includes more than survival. This allows one to see in the beauty of the living creatures of the world something like artistic genius.

As we saw in Chapter Six, Cardinal Schönborn explains the limitations of the mechanistic viewpoint by comparing God's creation to the symphonies of Mozart, the great Austrian composer. He asks, "Would it not be a good thing to consider the theory of evolution in the light of the creative power of Mozart?" Here is his answer:

> [Many of Mozart's symphonies] come from the creativity of genius.... Purpose and beauty do not break apart here. A work of art may have a purpose, but it is more than its purpose ... [I] deological evolutionism, hard nosed materialism that it is, strikes me by comparison as dismal and unimaginative.[21]

Darwin was looking in the right place, but not nearly with the right scope. Gazing narrowly at the means-end survival aspect of evolution, he overlooked—or at least did not grasp the significance of—the artistry and beauty of living creatures, one of the most compelling pieces of evidence that they are created by a loving God.

EVOLUTION AS IDEOLOGY

Darwin's contribution to modern science is immense. But no less significant has been the destructive misinterpretations to which his theory led. Some have inflated his scientific theory into an *ideology*, i.e., an all-embracing worldview which tends to explain everything in terms of a few principles like chance and survival. This is what is called "evolutionism." Unlike the theories of other great scientists,

THE ARTISTRY AND BEAUTY OF LIVING CREATURES IS ONE OF THE MOST COMPELLING PIECES OF EVIDENCE THAT THEY ARE CREATED BY GOD.

"EVOLUTIONISM" IS UNABLE TO HELP US ANSWER, OR EVEN ASK, THE DEEPER, GREATER QUESTIONS ABOUT HISTORY AND THE UNIVERSE.

his theory has come to be known as an "-ism." One does not talk about Newtonism, Einsteinism, or Heisenbergism, but one does talk about *Darwinism*. This is a symptom of a deeper confusion in people's minds between science and philosophy. Some people use the word "Darwinism" just to refer to the actual scientific theory (evolution), while others use it to mean the reductionist philosophy or ideology (evolutionism). Evolutionism is a poor substitute for sound natural philosophy and sound metaphysics. It is unable to bridge the gap between the visible and invisible worlds, unable to help us answer, or even ask, the deeper, greater questions about history and the universe.

The ideology of evolutionism has the following characteristics:

- the denial of the existence of God, or at least of his activity in the world;
- the assertion that only physical things and the natural world exist, and so the denial of spiritual or supernatural realities;
- the claim of being able to explain all of reality in terms of physical laws and chance;
- the claim that the existence of the universe itself and its laws have no explanation;
- the assertion that the universe is ultimately meaningless and without purpose;
- the reduction of human beings to purely physical organisms, like the lower animals which have no free will or intellect, so that man is seen as *entirely* the product of biological evolution.

THE TRUTH OF THE CHRISTIAN FAITH IS CERTAIN BEYOND AND BEFORE ALL OTHER TRUTHS AND IS THE VERY CERTAINTY ON WHICH OUR LIFE IS BASED.

It is obvious that these ideas go far beyond anything that science is able to say.

Is there any way to rescue Darwin's true and fruitful scientific insights from atheist ideologies? Can we cut the cancer of ideology away from the healthy tissue of evolutionary biology? The answer is yes, but only if we open our eyes and widen our view and allow ourselves to read the signs of God's creative activity. Let us return to Sacred Scripture to reencounter God's Revelation of this activity and its purpose.

E. Remembering the Signs: The Book of Genesis and the Theory of Evolution

Darwin, a member of the Church of England and originally a believing Christian, forgot a crucial fact about the Christian Faith—that its truth is certain beyond and before all other truths and is the very certainty on which our life is based. Rather than holding fast to God's Word given to us in Sacred Scripture and Sacred Tradition as transmitted by the Church, Darwin allowed his faith to falter because the signs of God's loving, creative activity did not appear as he expected. He exchanged the Christian Faith for a watery, ambiguous idea of God as a deistic First Cause, and all because of an appearance, not because of reality.

In our own quest to rediscover faith on the frontiers of science, let us look at the signs given us in Sacred Scripture. But unlike Darwin, let us approach Scripture and science with the eyes of faith.

THE WORLD IS TO BE CREATED BY THE WORD OF GOD'S COMMAND AND THE SPIRIT OF GOD'S PRESENCE, NURTURED BY THE VISION OF THE FATHER.

THE WORD OF GOD AND THE SPIRIT OF GOD (GN 1: 1–3)

"In the beginning, when God created the heavens and the earth… the spirit of God swept over the waters. Then God spoke…"

How does God bring about his creation? Many atheists and even many Christians seem able to envision only one way in which the production of living creatures could be the work of God—by sudden creation, like Geppetto building Pinocchio on his woodworking table.[22] Confronted with the evidence that living creatures did not arise in that way, some turn against religion and some turn against the scientific evidence. But when we turn to Sacred Scripture, we find that it offers us a much more subtle account of creation.

The beginning of the First Creation Account gives us the first clue in our quest to rescue Darwin's biology from his flawed philosophy. It declares that the whole act of creation happens through the powerful presence of God's Spirit, later to be revealed as the Holy Spirit, the third Person of the Blessed Trinity. Before God speaks any command, the Spirit of God is ready to act. Therefore, when God the Father speaks and brings about his creatures, all three Divine Persons, including God's Word (the Son) and God's Breath (the Holy Spirit)—are active. In creation, the Trinity is present— the world is to be "created by the Word of God's command and the Spirit of God's presence, nurtured by the vision of God the Father."[23]

The rest of Sacred Scripture makes clear that the presence of God's Word and God's Spirit brings freedom to his creatures, empowering them and allowing them to bring about God's purposes. As Jesus Christ, the Word made flesh, tells us, becoming his disciples and following his commands makes us free: "If you live according to my teaching, you will be my disciples. Then you will know the truth and the truth will *set you* free"(Jn 8: 31–32). And St. Paul fills out the message, adding that "where the Spirit of the Lord is, there

WHERE THE SPIRIT OF THE LORD IS, THERE IS *FREEDOM*.

St. Francis Xavier

is *freedom*" (2 Cor 3:17). The closeness and guidance of God does not rob free creatures of their freedom, of their ability to act. Indeed, it gives all creatures, living and non-living, the capacity to fulfill the purposes for which God made them.

From this perspective, we can see that Darwin's theory of evolution does not necessarily imply an absent God. Instead, it reveals creation to be "a total act shared by God and creature."[24] In the words of biologist Darrel Falk,

> Just as God built freedom into the nation of Israel, and just as God [builds] freedom into our lives today, so freedom may well be a central component of God's biological world as well. This is not to say that God does not play a supervisory role in creation in a manner resembling the role God plays in my life and yours. But there is no… Scriptural reason to assume that the biological world was created one species at a time by the God of the universe "pushing creation buttons" each time he wanted a new species. He does not do that in the daily affairs of my life (for which I am grateful), and there is no reason, Scriptural or otherwise, to assume that he does that in the biological world either. God's Spirit guides the progression of life. His presence is never far from creation, just as it is never far from the events of my life. Nonetheless, God respects my freedom and (I suspect) values freedom in the rest of creation as well.[25]

Falk uses the word "freedom" in this passage, but when referring to the freedom of the "biological world" he does not mean it in the sense of free will, which only humans have. Instead he is using the word to describe the reality of secondary causality: God grants every created nature the ability to have its own proper way of moving and its own proper effect on the surrounding world.

St. James

The idea that God's command and presence makes his creatures capable of acting to the utmost of their potential sheds light on many aspects of the history of life. It raises a number of questions, including the question, "Just exactly how does God 'command,' or communicate his will, to his living non-rational creatures?" Catholic theology has long recognized that God's will for his creatures is largely communicated to them in their specific natures, i.e., in the specific kinds of creatures He created them to be. In short, God commands his creatures by making them a certain way.

This perspective is well-illustrated by the rather recent discovery of RNA, DNA, and the genetic codes present in all living things. RNA and DNA offer compelling evidence of God "commanding" his living creatures by "writing" an intelligent code into their very cells.

Modern science has revealed that the presence of RNA and/or DNA in living things acts as the blueprint for their biological structures and characteristic activities. In the development of any living being, the formation of each and every cell is subject to the transmission of a code—the genetic code. The genetic code in DNA is duplicated and then copied from DNA to RNA. Then the code is conveyed to the amino acids which are assembled into proteins.

What is often overlooked is the fact that *the genetic code is an intelligent code*, in which information is coordinated in a way much like human writing, substituting the pen, paper, and alphabet with amino acids, proteins and DNA. According to Antony Flew, the notorious twentieth century atheist-turned-theist, the origins of the genetic code, which is nothing less than "a system of coded chemistry", cannot be explained without reference to an intelligent source.[26] Language-like structure, "coded chemistry," cannot be explained without reference to intelligence. Meaningful information does not emerge spontaneously from collections of mindless molecules. Flew quotes Nobel Prize-winning physiologist George Wald, who recommends that we assume that "mind… has always existed as the matrix, the source and condition of physical reality… It is mind that has composed a physical universe that breeds life, and so eventually evolves creatures that can know and create: science-, art- and technology-making creatures."[27] In the words of Francis Collins, the former director of the Human Genome Project, the genetic code is "the language of God," a set of intelligent commands from the Creator. Without the genetic code, evolution would be impossible.

God does not only command his creation, he is also present to it. God's presence to his creation, which we call Divine Providence, is nothing less than his guidance of history and the universe in a way in which he, as Primary Cause, uses secondary causes to bring about his intentions. It is interesting to think about *abiogenesis*— the formation of the first living thing(s)—from this perspective. The word *abiogenesis* literally means the genesis of life from nonliving things. Most scientists think that a convergence of natural causes somehow resulted in the first living cell (or cells) from which all living species eventually evolved, though how this happened is not yet understood.

Scientists have known since the 1950s that certain kinds of non-living molecules can spontaneously combine, under the right conditions, to produce important "biological building blocks" that are required for living cells, such as amino acids.[28] This discovery encouraged the hope that abiogenesis would soon be understood . However, it has turned out to be a much harder problem than people thought.[29]

Many even hypothesize that life had to emerge elsewhere in the universe and travel to Earth inside comets or asteroids in order to allow enough time for this process to occur naturally. Earth itself has only been hospitable to life for 3.8 billion years, and the first evidence of cellular life on Earth is found in rocks almost exactly

GENETIC CODE IS "THE LANGUAGE OF GOD," A SET OF INTELLIGENT COMMANDS FROM THE CREATOR.

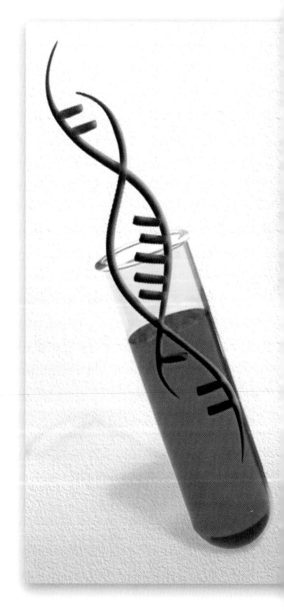

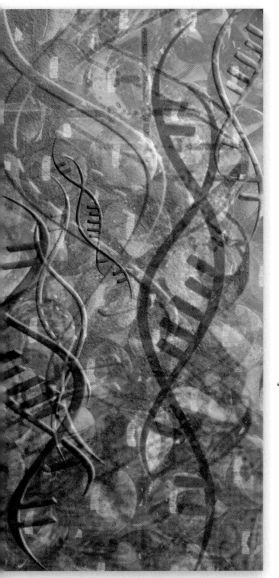

that old, allowing almost no time for life to emerge by chance on this planet. Some people conclude from this that the formation of the first living thing on earth was an event, or sequence of events, of extremely low probability. Of course, scientists may someday find a mechanism that shows the probabilities to be much higher than they now appear. But let us suppose that they do not.

The near impossibility of abiogenesis ceases to be a problem if we keep in mind what Scripture reveals, namely that God's loving presence to his creation guides, but does not replace, natural causes. Even extremely small chances that are effectively zero can work out through Divine Providence.[30] God, who not only provides to, and for, all things their power of existence but also their ability to act as true causes,[31] can predetermine that a "vanishingly small" possibility such as life emerging naturally from non-living matter *will* happen— not through a miracle, but through the natural potential he gave to his creation to bring about life.

Faith in Divine Providence, therefore, gives a perspective on abiogenesis that some Darwinians overlook. Rather than dismissing God, the theory of evolution puts God's care and creative presence into the spotlight. In the words of metaphysician Dennis Bonnette, "God's omnipotent creative design can overcome mathematician's probabilities... Despite all contrary odds, if God so eternally chooses, life's totally natural Earthly origination is possible."[32]

EXCLUDED POSSIBILITIES: EVOLUTIONARY BIOLOGY AS THE GREAT "AMEN"

The presence of the Trinity to creation, making it capable of His purposes for it, gives us the framework for understanding the compatibility of the scientific theory of evolution and the Christian, biblical doctrine of creation. The first great account of creation in Sacred Scripture also offers us a second hint. There we learn that the various living species are intended by God to be real causes, *co-creating* with him because of the power he gives them to act. In the Book of Genesis, God *speaks*, but it is his creation that *acts*.

So, on the third day of creation, God does not act; he commands the Earth to act by saying, "Let the Earth put forth vegetation" (Gn 1:11). On the fifth day, God does not act; he commands the water to act, saying "Let the waters bring forth swarms of living creatures." On the sixth day, God does not act; he commands the Earth to act again, saying, "Let the Earth produce living creatures according to their kinds." What we see, therefore, is God working *through* his creation. Thanks to his commands, the world is active in the production of living creatures, in which environment (water, earth) is an active agent. In the Genesis account, water and earth

DESPITE ALL CONTRARY ODDS, IF GOD SO ETERNALLY CHOOSES, LIFE'S TOTALLY NATURAL EARTHLY ORIGINATION IS POSSIBLE.

produce living creatures, leaving room for Darwin's idea that the environment provides the context and the stimulating force for the production of changes in living creatures and the proliferation of numerous species. Such a scenario does not imply the absence of God; it reveals a world actively responding to God's command and God's active presence.

God creates by commanding the world. The world acts in creation by unfolding the potential with which God suffuses it. What is produced is a *co-creation*, in which creatures , even "the most elementary particles of matter," participate in God's power and purpose. God makes creatures co-creators "by giving them the laws, the powers and the capacity for acting on their own."[33]

Is there a word that can summarize this relationship between God and creatures in the act of co-creation? Yes, and it reveals a remarkable connection. God's "Let there be" in creation corresponds to the "Let it be" pronounced by believers whenever they pray. In Hebrew, the word for "let it be" is *amen*. As the *Catechism of the Catholic Church* teaches, "*Amen* expresses solidity, trustworthiness, faithfulness…" It goes on to declare that amen "may express both God's faithfulness towards us and our trust in him."[34] The word "amen" expresses both God's faithfulness to creatures and the response of creatures to God.

The "amen," the "let it be," of believers and all creatures is the expression of their willingness and openness to participate in God's plan. Genesis 1 reveals that even unconscious matter and non-rational living creatures display an "amen" in their acting according to their laws, powers, and capacity for action.

But this ability to participate in God's plan can only come to creatures through the power and presence of God, that is through the command of God's Word and the presence of God's Spirit. Only when God says his own "Amen" ("Let there be") can creatures respond with the "amen" of their participation in God's plan. The greatness of the biblical account of creation is that, long before Darwin, it sees the both/and of an originating, empowering, "Amen" of God and the responding, empowered, participating "amen" of the universe, its elements and each level of creaturely existence.

Some scientific atheists have seen the long length of the universe's existence without life as a sign that there is no divine craftsman behind it. When we remember the signs, we can see that this long period is something very different and much more amazing—it is a long chorus of response, a growing sustained and magnificent "amen" offered by the universe in response to God's powerful Word and omnipresent Spirit. The billions and billions of years simply reveal that it takes finite creatures a very long time to pronounce their "amen," while God's "Amen" is perfect and eternal, taking no time at all.

IN HEBREW, THE WORD FOR "LET IT BE" IS *AMEN*. "AMEN" EXPRESSES BOTH GOD'S FAITHFULNESS TO CREATURES AND THE RESPONSE OF CREATURES TO GOD.

F. Believing the Signs: The Christian Faith and the Origins of Living Things

EVOLUTION AND THE EXAMPLE OF GREAT BELIEVERS

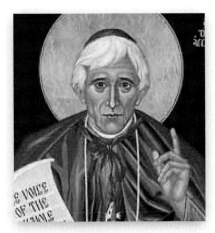

St. Augustine

St. Thomas Aquinas

Bl. John Henry Newman

Darwin deserves credit for being a pioneer of the scientific theory of evolution as we know it today. But long before Darwin, as well as after him, many Christian thinkers have understood the creation of living things as being the result not of "special creation" but of the unfolding of natural potentialities that God has implanted in matter, i.e., by God's acting through secondary causes that co-operate with and bring to completion his plan of creation.

St. Augustine (AD 354–430), the greatest theologian of the early Church, is a great example of a believer who actually believed that a special act of creation was unlikely. He held that all things were produced by God in a single instant, taking the form of "spiritual seeds" that unfolded over time into the actual bodily existence of living creatures.[35]

Augustine's reason for this theory is simple—he believed that God miraculously intervening, over and over again, to bring about the vast multiplicity of living creatures actually took away from divine perfection as reflected in creation. If God needed to constantly intervene in his creation, making each living creature through a direct act, than it would reveal an imperfection in God's initial creative action. It would seem as if God forgot to create everything or was incapable of creating a universe that could fulfill his purposes for it through the potential with which he endowed it. Many consider St. Augustine to be the real father of the *idea* of evolution, as distinct from the scientific theory.

St. Thomas Aquinas (AD 1225–1274), the greatest theologian of the Middle Ages, agreed. He acknowledged that, on the surface, the notion of special (successive) creation seemed to be more in accord with what the Book of Genesis says. But he concluded that St. Augustine's explanation was more in accord with reason and was preferable as an explanation of the literal meaning of Genesis.[36]

In modern times, great and influential Catholic thinkers such as *Bl. John Henry Newman* and G.K. Chesterton have been able to see the signs of God's creative activity in the evolutionary hypothesis. Newman believed that God lets his creative action develop through secondary causes. God imparted, said Newman, "certain laws to matter millions of ages ago, which have surely and precisely worked out … those effects which he … proposed." He concluded that "Mr. Darwin's theory need not be atheistical, be it true or not; it may simply be suggesting a large idea of divine prescience [i.e., foreknowledge] and skill."[37]

One important example of a believing scientist who embraced the notion of an evolutionary origin for living creatures is *Theodosius Dobzhansky*, who was hailed by the late Stephen Jay Gould as one of the greatest evolutionists of his generation. Dobzhansky is famous for declaring that "nothing in biology makes sense except in the light of evolution." He saw nothing in the evolutionary hypothesis to be contrary to creation as it is portrayed in the Bible: "Does the evolutionary doctrine clash with religious faith? It does not. It is a blunder to mistake the Holy Scriptures for elementary textbooks of astronomy, geology, biology, and anthropology. Only if symbols are construed to mean what they are not intended to mean can there arise imaginary, insoluble [unsolvable] conflicts."[38]

Theodosius Dobzhansky

Perhaps the most important example of such an approach is to be found in the writings of *Pope John Paul II*. In his letter to Fr. George Coyne, Director of the Vatican Observatory, he revealed his desire that Catholics think seriously about the Christian Faith and evolutionary biology as harmonious and mutually complementary. And in an address to the Pontifical Academy of Sciences in 1996 the pope declared that: "The theory of natural evolution, understood in a sense which does not exclude divine causality, is not in principle opposed to the truth about the creation of the visible world, as presented in the book of Genesis."[39] We will discuss John Paul's position on evolution in more detail in Chapter Eleven.

SOME OF THE GREATEST MINDS OF CHURCH HISTORY HAVE BELIEVED THE SIGNS OF GOD'S CREATIVE ACTIVITY IN THE LIGHT OF AN EVOLUTIONARY VIEW OF THE UNIVERSE.

As we can see, some of the greatest minds of Church history have believed the signs of God's creative activity in the light of an evolutionary view of the universe. While not proving evolutionary biology to be true, the convergence of so many great minds in favor of such an approach as harmonious with the Christian Faith is an important indication that agreeing with Darwin's science does not mean agreeing with philosophical misinterpretations of it.

BELIEVING THE SIGNS: THE CHURCH AND THE WORLD

The fact that many great believers have favored something like the evolutionary theory is compelling evidence that Darwin's biology does not require Darwin's philosophy. But perhaps an even more compelling example of the harmony between faith and evolutionary biology is the symmetry it reveals between the first creation and the New Creation, between the order of nature brought about through God's creative activity and the order of grace and the supernatural brought about through our redemption in Jesus Christ.

The Church teaches that these two orders of reality are distinct but not opposed to each other. The created world is good. Therefore, when it is redeemed by the Son of God, the Word made flesh, the created world is revealed to be a preparation for a New Creation which elevates, heals, and fulfills the physical universe.

The Church also teaches that the first creation was brought about for the sake of the second creation. In the first creation, God brought the natural world into existence. In the New Creation, he brings about the Church as the beginning and the "initial budding forth" of the Kingdom of God.[40] Therefore, we should expect symmetry between the universe and the Church—in some mysterious way, they have a corresponding pattern. Evolution may be key to seeing that symmetry.

For example, in each creation there is a long period of preparation. Before the first human being ("Adam") could emerge, eons had to pass, in which slowly the way was prepared for him, by the formation of the elements, of the sun and earth, of the first living thing; and then stage after stage of evolutionary development had to occur. So too, the coming of Christ, the "second Adam," required that a "way be prepared for him." From the calling of Abraham, Isaac, and Jacob, and the forming of the Jewish people, many centuries had to pass, and stage after stage of the unfolding of God's Revelation, before "in the fullness of time" Christ appeared. And Christ's Body, the Church, continues to undergo growth as members are added to it, and it achieves "full stature." In both cases, what appeared to be chance, the small and unforeseen events that had momentous consequences, the "randomness" of history, played a role in the unfolding of the divine plan.

Each creation, the first and the second, involves an environment that is essential to its development. In the first creation, the elements such as earth and water constitute the stuff out of which life emerges. In the New Creation, natural elements are supernaturalized in the sacraments and in the Liturgy, which is the Church's participation in the worship Jesus Christ offers to the Father in the Spirit. And in interaction with this supernatural environment, supernatural life emerges in all those who believe.

Each creation also begins with a single form of life. The world of living creatures begins with one organism that, containing all future life within itself, diffused that life to all of its offspring and descendents. In the Church, the one man, Jesus Christ, contains all of eternal life in himself and diffuses that life to all who believe and are reborn in him.

Each creation involves a progress from simpler forms to more complex forms. In evolution, matter becomes simple, single-celled organisms which ultimately evolve into more complex forms of life. In the New Creation, the Church progresses to a deeper and deeper understanding of God's truth, to more diverse forms of the Christian life, including within itself an ever-increasing variety of human races, languages, peoples, and cultures.

But the New Creation also seems to develop in a contrasting way to the first creation, though maintaining the symmetry that exists between the two creations. It is almost as if the first creation is the mirror-image of the second:

In the first creation, the one form of life becomes many; in the New Creation, the many forms of human life become one in the one Body of Christ.

In the first creation, simplicity yields to a diversity which divides the species. In the second creation, the divided are reunited while retaining their diversity.

In the first creation, the few are sent out to separate and become many. In the second creation, the few (the apostles and first disciples) are sent out to unite the many into one.

In the first creation, the one organism possessing life succeeds in passing on that life by surviving. But in the second creation, the One who bears the fullness of eternal life succeeds in passing that life along by dying.

Evolution, therefore, reveals symmetry between the world and the Church, the first creation and the New Creation. It reveals the Church to be the fulfillment of the natural world, and helps to explain the ancient Christian declaration that "the world was created for the sake of the Church."[41]

G. Looking Forward — The Missing Amen

In summary it is safe to say that, on the basis of philosophy, the example of great Christians, and our own theological investigation, faith can be found on the frontiers of evolutionary biology. The signs encountered by Darwin can be fully understood only when approached with the eyes of faith.

Earlier, we noted that evolution is best understood as the "amen" of creatures responding to the "Amen" of God. But as we imagined that chorus of creatures participating in God's creative activity, we might have noticed a unique set of voices.

No one of the many living and non-living creatures we encounter on the cutting edge of science can say "amen" to God in the way God says "Amen" to creation, except one. Only one of the creatures able

EVOLUTION REVEALS SYMMETRY BETWEEN THE WORLD AND THE CHURCH, THE FIRST CREATION AND THE NEW CREATION.

to be studied by science can say "amen" to God with intelligence, freedom, and love. The "amen" of creation would be missing its most perfect expression without the one creature that can sum up the "amen" offered by creation to God in the same "melody" with which God says it to the universe. Our journey to the frontiers of science now brings us to the question of the human person, the greatest of the creatures which fill the physical universe.

In Part III of this text, entitled "In His Image: Human Personhood and Modern Science," humanity itself will take the center stage. Chapter Nine will consider the whole truth about the human person as revealed by God in Scripture and in Church Teaching. In that chapter, human personhood will be defined, as well as the nature of man as the image of God.

Chapter Ten will consider the claims of some scientists that humanity does not have a unique status in the universe, that is, that human beings are not significantly different from the other animals. Human behavior and human aptitudes will be examined to show why this claim is incorrect.

Finally, we will return to biological evolution as it concerns human beings, looking at what science tells us about the origins of humanity in the light of faith, in Chapter Eleven.

Supplementary Reading

Going "Deeper than Darwin":
Faith and the Origins of Living Things

1. "CREATION AND EVOLUTION"

(excerpted from Christoph Cardinal Schönborn, "Creation and Evolution: To the Debate as it Stands." Internet. Available from http://stephanscom.at/edw/katechesen/articles/2005/10/14/a9347/; accessed April 2, 2007.)

I see no difficulty in joining belief in the Creator with the theory of evolution, but under the prerequisite that the borders of scientific theory are maintained… When science adheres to its own method, it cannot come into conflict with faith…

In 1985, a symposium took place in Rome under the title "Christian Faith and the Theory of Evolution." I had the privilege of taking part in it and contributed a paper. Then Cardinal Ratzinger, now Pope Benedict XVI, presided, and, at its conclusion, Pope John Paul II received us in an audience. There he said:

Rightly comprehended, faith in creation or a correctly understood teaching of evolution does not create obstacles: Evolution in fact presupposes creation; creation situates itself in the light of evolution as an event which extends itself through time—as a continual creation—in which God becomes visible to the eyes of the believer as "creator of heaven and earth."

But Pope John Paul II then added the thought that for the creation, faith and the theory of evolution to be correctly understood, the mediation of reason is necessary, along with, he insisted, philosophy and reflection… For me the question that has emerged from this debate is not primarily one of faith vs. knowledge but rather one of reason. The acceptance of purposefulness, of "design," is entirely based on reason, even if the method of the modern natural sciences may require the bracketing of the question of design. Yet my common sense cannot be shut out by the scientific method. Reason tells me that plan and order, meaning and goal exist, that a time-piece does not come into being by accident, even less so the living organism that is a plant, an animal, or, above all, man.

I am thankful for the immense work of the natural sciences. Their furthering of our knowledge boggles the mind. They do not restrict faith in the creation; they strengthen me in my belief in the Creator and in how wisely and wonderfully he has made all things.

Supplementary Reading

2. "EVOLUTION ACHIEVES GOD'S DESIGN: A CREATION TEEMING WITH NOVEL FORMS OF LIFE"

(excerpted from Christoph Cardinal Schönborn, "He Created Each Thing According to Its Kind" Internet. Available from http://stephanscom.at/edw/katechesen/articles/2006/01/24/a10066; accessed April 2, 2007.)

We find in the world a tremendous multiplicity: of human beings, of creatures, of stars, of beings on our planet, of living beings, whether plants or animals. The basic message of the first page of the Bible is this: *this multiplicity is good, it is willed by God, it comes from the will of the Creator*. This is a familiar teaching for biblically trained ears, but it is not a familiar teaching in the history of human thought. We have only to look a little into this history in order to discover two basic directions of thought that arrive at entirely different results. In the intellectual history of mankind it has always been necessary to deal with the indisputable fact of multiplicity. Why does

there exist a multiplicity? If we are not to rest satisfied with the obvious observation that there is in fact a multiplicity, then we have to go deeper and ask where the many things come from. One intellectual tradition says that the many is a sign of some kind of "mishap," some "primordial mishap." Originally there was unity, the One. This unity was broken by the "primordial mishap" and so there came about the multiplicity of beings. The One poured over into the many and was dissolved.... For this tradition multiplicity is a sign of falling away, of decline and decay, and the farther we depart from unity, the weaker and the more multitudinous the world becomes.... Multiplicity is the expression of a decadent and negative state of affairs, which really ought not to exist. This is why in this tradition the task is always to take back the multiplicity and to return to unity; the many have to be gathered together again so as to be reduced to unity....

The biblical view shows a multiplicity which is neither a mishap nor an accident, but rather the expression of the nature and will of God. St. Thomas Aquinas, the great doctor of creation, asks himself in one place whether the multiplicity and variety of things in the world derives from God. He discusses the doctrine of accident that was held by the atomists and materialists in the ancient world, and he says in opposition to it that multiplicity corresponds to the inmost intention of the Creator, that God wanted a world full of variety. Whereas the atomist Democritus said that multiplicity is the result of the accidental play of matter, St. Thomas says that God intended just such a creation.

For he brought things into being in order that his goodness might be communicated to creatures, and be represented by them; and because his goodness could not be adequately represented by one creature alone, he produced many and diverse creatures, that what was wanting to one in the representation of the divine goodness might be supplied by another. For goodness, which in God is simple and uniform, in creatures is manifold and divided (St. Thomas Aquinas, *Summa Theologica*, I, 47, 1).

In other words, no one creature suffices to reflect God. It takes the whole fullness to make manifest God's abundance. The multitude of creatures is the many-sided expression of God's goodness.... There is no such thing as a negative creature.

Supplementary Reading

3. "DISCOVERING THE TRUE HARMONY BETWEEN THE CHRISTIAN FAITH AND EVOLUTIONARY SCIENCE"

(excerpted from Christoph Cardinal Schönborn, Chance or Purpose? Creation, Evolution and a Rational Faith *[San Francisco: Ignatius Press, 2007], pp. 165–175).*

Where, then, is the answer to be found? I would like to put forward a theory about this, which may be illustrated by a metaphor that I found in a book by Joachim Illies: the image of two ladders, Darwin's ladder and Jacob's ladder. This image is meant to symbolize the ascending movement of evolution and the movement of the Creator Spirit coming down from God. These are two movements in two different directions, which offer something like an overall view only when both are seen together....

The correct path to follow is not to choose between the "Darwinian story" and "creationism," as people like to suggest, but a coexistence of "Darwin's ladder" and "Jacob's ladder." There is a great deal to support the view that life has developed through a long process, a gradual ascent from the most simple beginnings up to the complexity of man. It is marvelous to penetrate ever more deeply into the common building blocks of life and thereby into the way that all life is related. It is not only unnecessary, however, but contrary to reason, to view this grandiose path of life up to man as being an exclusively random process....

The alternative to a merely random process is not complete determinism, but the "limitation" of the creatures' own autonomous activity and of the divine creative Spirit, which sustains this activity and makes it possible. In the beginning was the Word, not random chance. Chance, in the sense of something unplanned happening, does exist, but it is not the great creative principle that ideological Darwinism would like to make of it....

Gratitude and wonder, adoration and praise remain with us and grow. "O Lord my God, thou art very great!" (Ps 104: 1). This wonder in our hearts must never die away.... The "Darwinian ladder" has made available to us— thanks also to genetics—a marvelous insight into the way life has ascended, the way it has come into existence and has been shaped and developed. The "Jacob's ladder" that connects this ascending and descending movement of life with heaven, with the activity of the living God, of his [Word] and his creative Spirit, cannot replace the labors of research in "climbing" up the "Darwinian ladder." It does not tell us how the Creator made his works, how he has sustained them and guided their development. However, it does tell us with absolute certainty, more certainly than any scientific theories that it is his Word, Christ, the Logos, through whom and toward whom everything has been created; and that his Spirit, who was moving over the face of the waters at the very beginning (Gn 1: 2), and who is love, is moving in all created things and gives them meaning and purpose. *Logos* and *agape*, reason and love, are the material from which the world was made, of which it consists, and with which it is being perfected. It is well worth living in this conviction—and dying in it. For what kind of an evolution would it be if resurrection and eternal life were not its ultimate goal?

Study Guide

Going "Deeper than Darwin": Faith and the Origins of Living Things

VOCABULARY

Define the following terms:

1. Special Creation
2. Charles Darwin
3. On the Origin of Species
4. The Descent of Man
5. Macroevolution
6. Microevolution
7. Natural Selection
8. Darwinism
9. Neo-Darwinism
10. Evolutionism
11. Pius XII (*Humani generis*)
12. Fossil Record
13. Comparative Anatomy
14. Biogeography
15. Genetics
16. Genes
17. Theory
18. Leo XIII (*Providentissimus Deus*)
19. Chance
20. Providence
21. Naturalism
22. Survival of the Fittest (Malthus)
23. Survival of the Fittest (Darwin)
24. Natural Breeding
25. Ideology
26. Abiogenesis
27. Amen
28. St. Augustine (theory of creation)
29. St. Thomas Aquinas (theory of creation)
30. Bl. John Henry Newman (creation and evolution)
31. Theodosius Dobzhansky (creation and evolution)
32. John Paul II (creation and evolution)

STUDY QUESTIONS

1. What lesson does C.S. Lewis' The Silver Chair have for those approaching the issue of biological evolution in the light of faith?
2. Why was the lack of evidence regarding the origins of life seen as a powerful argument for God's existence, prior to Darwin?
3. How did Darwin discover the mechanism for evolution?
4. What did genetics contribute to Darwin's theory of evolution?
5. Explain the difference between Darwinism, neo-Darwinism, and evolutionism.
6. Where has the Catholic Church historically stood on the question of evolution?
7. Where does the Church stand now on the theory of evolution?

Study Guide

8. Where does the Church stand on the idea that humanity is the product of evolution?

9. From what scientific sources does the evidence for evolution come?

10. Is the reality of chance in the universe and in evolution a denial of divine Providence? Explain.

11. Does the fact that a process makes use of chance necessarily imply that it is not designed or that it is without purpose? Explain.

12. Give an example in which a person designs and brings about an outcome through the use of chance. How does this apply to the question of God in relation to evolution?

13. According to Thomas Aquinas, why did God introduce the element of chance into nature?

14. What would a world without chance be like?

15. Are God and nature in competition with each other? Explain.

16. Using the analogy of a playwright, explain how God is like an author with regard to secondary causes in evolution.

17. How does God's use of natural causes and chance reveal his power, intelligence, and skill in an even greater way than if he directly caused all things?

18. Why is the understanding of evolution as a violent survival of the fittest an atheistic misinterpretation of evolution?

19. Why is the omission of beauty an atheistic misinterpretation of evolution?

20. List the characteristics of the ideology of evolutionism.

21. Who, according to the Christian Faith, are the two great principles through whom God created living things? What attribute characterizes the effects of these two principles among human beings, according to the Bible?

22. From the answer to (11), what conclusion can be drawn about the role of creaturely causes in the origins and development of living creatures?

23. How does the abiogenesis hypothesis lend credence to the biblical viewpoint that God willed his creation and guides it according to his plan?

24. How does the creation account in Genesis 1 reveal that the idea of evolution is not incompatible with divine creation and design in the origin and development of living things?

25. Explain the significance of the biblical word "Amen" to the issue of the compatibility of biological evolution and the Christian Faith.

26. How does the biblical word "Amen" reveal the origin and development of living species to be both God's work and the work of God's creatures?

27. Explain the potential symmetry between an evolutionary view of the origin and development of living things and the redemption in Christ of all things.

28. Might evolution be the key for understanding the mystery of symmetry between the natural universe and man's supernatural destiny, between the old creation and the New Creation? If so, give some examples.

29. Why is man the only creature in the visible universe that can give God an "amen" that is the same as God's "Amen" to creation?

Study Guide

PRACTICAL EXERCISES

1. Imagine the mindset of a scientific creationist. Why might such a person reject evolution as incompatible with the Christian Faith? What elements of this chapter might help a scientific creationist to rethink his or her position?

2. Think of a situation in which a person plans an outcome for another person (or persons) using a combination of design and chance. How is this like the idea of evolution when considered in the light of faith?

3. Imagine that you have a time machine, and that you travel back in time and become a friend of the young Charles Darwin. How might you explain to him the difference between God as First Cause (understood in a deistic sense) and the Christian notion of God as Uncaused Cause? How might your explanation impact his thinking about the universe?

Endnotes

1. The title of this chapter is inspired by John Haught, *Deeper than Darwin: The Prospect for Religion in the Age of Evolution* (Boulder: Westview Press, 2003).
2. C.S. Lewis, *The Silver Chair*: Book 4 in *The Chronicles of Narnia* series (New York: Scholastic, 1987), 21.
3. Collins, 96-97.
4. Ibid., 131-132. Macroevolution is also called *interspecies transformism* by other authors.
5. Paulinus Forsthoefel, *Religious Faith Meets Modern Science* (New York: Alba House, 1994), 67-70.
6. Ibid., 142.
7. Darrel Falk, *Coming to Peace with Science: Bridging the Worlds Between Faith and Biology* (Downers Grove: Intervarsity Press, 2004), 171.
8. Christoph Schönborn, "Creation and Evolution: To the Debate as It Stands." Internet. Available from http://stephanscom.at/edw/ katechesen/ articles/2005/10/14/a9347/; accessed April 12, 2007.
9. Clarke, 207-209.
10. St. Augustine, *City of God*, 19,4.
11. Collins, 205.
12. Dennis Bonnette, *Origin of the Human Species*, 2nd ed. (Ypsilanti, Mich.: Sapientia Press, 2003), 55.
13. Michael Tkacz, "A Designer Universe: Chance, Design, and Cosmic Order," a presentation given at the "Physics and the God of Abraham" Conference,

Gonzaga University, April 2004, 8. Internet. Available from http://www.gonzagafaithreason.org/files/pdfs/ A-Designer-Universe.pdf; accessed July 15, 2007.
14. Ibid., 7. Cf. St. Thomas Aquinas, *In Aristotelis Metaphysicorum*, XII.1403.
15. Marie I. George, "On Attempts to Salvage Paley's Argument from Design," in *Science, Philosophy, Theology*, ed. John O'Callaghan (South Bend, Indiana: St. Augustine's Press, 2002).
16. E. Wasmann, "Evolution," in *The Catholic Encyclopedia*, Vol. V (New York: The Gilmary Society, 1909), 654. Francisco Suárez (1548-1617) was a Jesuit theologian and philosopher.
17. Forsthoefel, 68-69.
18. Joan Roughgarden, *Evolution and Christian Faith: Reflections of an Evolutionary Biologist* (Washington: Island Press, 2006), 37.
19. Richard Dawkins, *River Out of Eden* (New York: Basic Books, 1995), 133.
20. Roughgarden, 37.
21. Christoph Schönborn, "He Upholds the Universe by His Word and Power." Internet. Available from http://stephanscom.at/edw/ katechesen/ articles/2006/02/15/a10185/; accessed April 12, 2007.
22. Falk, 101.
23. Ibid., 92.

24. Leo Cardinal Scheffczyck, as quoted in Schönborn, "He Upholds the Universe."
25. Falk, 102-103.
26. Flow, 127.
27. Ibid., 131-132.
28. Collins, 90-91.
29. Bernard Lovell, *In the Center of Immensities* (New York: Harper and Row, 1978), 63.
30. Bonnette, 117-118.
31. Schönborn, "He Upholds the Universe"
32. Bonnette, 120.
33. Ibid.
34. CCC 1062.
35. St. Augustine, *De Genesi ad litteram*, VI.18.
36. St. Thomas Aquinas, *In II Sent.* 12.3.1, as quoted in Barr, *Modern Physics*, 6.
37. Peter E. Hodgson, *Science and Belief in the Nuclear Age* (Naples, Fla.: Sapientia Press, 2005), 54.
38. T. Dobzhansky, "Nothing in Biology Makes Sense Except in the Light of Evolution," *American Biology Teacher* 35 (1973): 125-129.
39. John Paul II, "Address to the Pontifical Academy of Sciences" (October 22, 1996), 4.
40. *Lumen gentium* 5.
41. *The Shepherd of Hermas*, Visio II.4.2.

Chapter Nine

In His Image:
The Human Person from
the Divine Perspective

ONLY THE HUMAN PERSON IS CAPABLE OF SAYING "LET IT BE," *AMEN*, TO GOD WITH THE SAME FREEDOM AND LOVE WITH WHICH GOD SAYS, "LET THERE BE," AMEN, TO CREATURES. *THE GREAT AMEN IS OURSELVES.*

A. Looking Back: The "Amen" is Ourselves

As we ended the last chapter we made a crucial transition—from lower creatures to the human person. We noted that only one creature is capable of saying "let it be," *Amen*, to God in the same way that God says, "let there be," *Amen*, to creatures. All creatures participate in God's act of creation as secondary causes, but only one kind of visible creature can offer itself intelligently, freely, and lovingly to this great co-creating partnership. That creature is the human person. *The Great Amen is ourselves.*

The *Catechism of the Catholic Church* proclaims this fact of the unique and central role of humanity in God's plan of creation and Redemption. It begins by quoting the first creation account: "God created man in his own image, in the image of God he created him, male and female he created them" (Gn 1:27). Man is this image because "of all visible creatures only man is 'able to know and love his creator.' He is 'the only creature on earth that God has willed for its own sake,' and he alone is called to share, by knowledge and love, in God's own life."[1]

In order to understand the human person in the light of the Christian Faith and modern science, we must first grasp the meaning of these words. Only then can we ask whether modern science has anything to say regarding this exalted view of being human. So, we will consider the Second Creation Account (Gn 2), which gives a beautiful glimpse into humanity's greatness, after asking what it means to be an image.

AN IMAGE DOES NOT SIMPLY REVEAL SOME PARTIAL FACT CONCERNING THE THING IT REPRESENTS; AN IMAGE EXPRESSES THE THING IT IMAGES DIRECTLY, SUCH AS IN A SELF-PORTRAIT.

B. The Forming of the Image: Genesis 2, Reason, and Freedom

THE ABC'S OF IMAGING GOD

The great theme of the Christian Faith regarding the human person is that all human beings are created in the image of God. But what does it mean to be an *image*?

St. Thomas Aquinas developed an excellent way of understanding the uniqueness of an image: by contrasting *images* with *vestiges*. Some things that are made are simply vestiges (traces) of their maker, as when an archaeologist finds stone tools made by early humans. Some information about the maker can be gathered through such vestiges, such as that the maker had opposable thumbs, or that he or she was an intelligent creature. According to St. Thomas, vestiges of the Trinity can be found in all creatures.[2]

But an image does not simply reveal some partial fact concerning the thing it represents; an image expresses the thing it images directly, such as in a self-portrait. As St. Thomas Aquinas says, "An image represents a thing in a better defined manner according to all its parts and the arrangement of its parts."[3] In other words, an image is a precise representation of something. An image, unlike a vestige, is an image because of its likeness to what it resembles. An image has its own explanation only in the thing it represents; to understand an image, you must first understand what it is an image of.

To get back to our main subject, we must ask this question: how does man achieve the state of being the image of God? He first does so not by his own efforts, but through God's generosity to humanity. The Second Creation Account gives us a glimpse of how God lovingly bestows his image on us.

THE SECOND CREATION ACCOUNT: THE BREATH OF LIFE

The First Creation Account (Gn 1) has already pointed us in the direction of humanity's uniqueness, telling us that man and woman are created in God's image. Using poetic, figurative language, Genesis 2 beautifully describes the creation of the image of God, which is humanity.

First, God fashions man from the dust of the earth; second, God also breathes into man's nostrils "a breath of life" (Gn 2:7). Man is not yet fully human until the second step. Without it, man remains without the life God intends for him.

IN GENESIS 2, MAN IS NOT FULLY HUMAN UNTIL GOD BREATHES "A BREATH OF LIFE" INTO HIS NOSTRILS.

What is this mysterious breath which God bestows upon humanity? The Book of Wisdom gives us a helpful explanation, and shows that this gift of God applies not only to the first humans, but to all: "[God] inspired them with an active soul and breathed a living spirit into them" (Wis 15:11). Since God is purely spiritual, then it is clear that his breathing into man's nostrils symbolizes God giving to humanity a level of existing and acting that is spiritual as well. The spiritual principle in man is the *human soul*.

Man cannot resemble God unless he is spiritual, since God is pure Spirit. But the image of God in humanity is much more specific. The Bible and the Christian Faith tell us that God is Truth. We have already seen that God is the unlimited, infinite source of all perfections in creation, including the orderliness and knowability of all things. Another way of saying this is to say that God is Absolute Truth, the source of the truth of all things. This is what Jesus means when he refers to himself as "the Light of the world": he is God himself, the perfect source of the truth of all things.

The Bible also tells us that God is Love—"He who does not love does not know God; for God is Love" (1 Jn 4:8). *Love* in the fully personal sense of the term refers to giving one's self completely for the good of another. As the *Catechism* explains, "God's very being is love. By sending his only Son and the Spirit of Love in the fullness of time, God has revealed his innermost secret: God himself is an eternal exchange of love, Father, Son and Holy Spirit."[4] God's "family structure" is the perfect expression of the meaning of the word "love" in its purest sense.

If "God's very being is Truth and Love,"[5] then being God's image must somehow involve these two attributes too. Man cannot be the image of God who is Truth and Love unless man participates in truth and love in some way. He does so in his possession of two qualities which human beings alone among the animals have—reason and free will. *Reason*, which is the ability to know truth, and *will*, which is the ability to love and to determine yourself and your actions, are the twin foundations of man's imaging of God. These powers constitute human freedom and are the roots of human dignity.

In summary: God is Truth and Love, and the human person is in his image because he can know truth and he can love freely. Understanding these two human attributes reveals the image of God within every one of us.

> REASON, WHICH IS THE ABILITY TO KNOW TRUTH, AND *WILL*, WHICH IS THE ABILITY TO LOVE AND TO DETERMINE ONE'S SELF THROUGH ONE'S FREE ACTIONS, ARE THE TWIN FOUNDATIONS OF MAN'S IMAGING OF GOD.

RATIONALITY: THE FIRST FOUNDATION OF IMAGING GOD

Of all visible creatures, only man is able to know truth and to pursue truth, a capacity called *reason*. What does this capacity entail? Christoph Cardinal Schönborn offers us one key aspect of human reason—man has a *capacity for objectivity*. The capacity for

> HUMAN RATIONALITY, THEREFORE, INVOLVES THE ABILITY TO TRANSCEND THE SENSES AND TO UNDERSTAND THE MEANING OF UNIVERSALS SUCH AS CIRCULARITY, A CONCEPT WITH AN INFINITE SCOPE.

A HUMAN BEING, UNLIKE A DOG, CAN GO BEYOND THE SENSES AND GRASP THE INNER WORKINGS OF THINGS, SUCH AS A STEAM ENGINE.

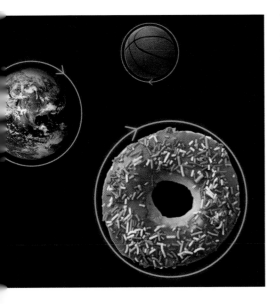

objectivity is man's "ability to go beyond his immediate interests and needs and to perceive himself and others as the beings they are in their own right."[6] He continues:

> I do not just feel, I can also examine my feelings, approach them "objectively," interpret them. I am not completely immersed in my world, I can look at it, can change it, compare it with other things, and can stand over against it with a critical spirit. I can think about it as well as myself.[7]

This objectivity is also the power to transcend mere appearances and get at how things are in themselves.

Philosopher Dennis Bonnette gives us one way of seeing the uniqueness of reason by contrasting it with the way lower animals know things. He invites us to imagine a dog, an uneducated aborigine, and a civilized person all observing a train pulling into a station every day for many days. All three see the train, and recognize the train even if different cars, engines, or cabooses are used from day to day. The common visual image makes it possible for all three to recognize the train.

But there the similarities cease. The dog, which does not possess reason, would perceive the similarities between each experience and would act according to its instincts (running, hiding, growling, etc.). The uneducated aborigine would not know the engine's nature, but would be searching for an answer to the "why" of the train. He might make mistakes about the nature of the train, expecting some kind of magic to make it move or even imagining that it is an animal instead of a machine. But the civilized person would understand something of the essence of the train—"the inner workings of [causes] producing steam whose expansion drives pistons to move wheels."

In time, with some explanation, the aborigine would come to the civilized person's understanding of the train, whereas the dog would continue to "bark uselessly." The difference between the dog and the two men is that the dog's perception is only *sensory* (i.e., on the level of the senses), while the aborigine's perception, like the civilized person's, is both sensory and rational.[8]

Human rationality, therefore, involves the ability to transcend the senses and to understand the meaning of *abstract concepts*. Abstract concepts are those that philosophers call *universals*—ideas which do not refer to this or that object but to all possible objects of a certain kind. Some examples of abstract concepts are "justice," "visibility," and "beauty."[9]

For instance, consider one such abstract concept—*circularity*. It applies to all circles and circular objects "of any size, position, and orientation." In fact, circularity is not a physical object, although it can be correctly attributed to all physical objects which are circular. Its universality has an "unlimited reach" to all possible circular things: it is infinite in scope.[10]

Another element of human reason is that it involves the ability to judge the truth and falsehood of propositions (i.e., statements proposed to be true). For instance, we can think about "2 + 2 = 4" and come to the conclusion that it is a correct or true mathematical equation. A computer can also distinguish between true and false propositions, but only when a human with understanding builds it and programs it to carry out such steps in an automatic way. But unlike a computer, we can reason correctly about true or false propositions even when we have not been programmed to do so, that is, even when we have never been given a precise set of instructions telling us exactly what to do.[11]

Even more fascinating is that human beings can not only judge truth and falsehood, but they are also capable of certitude that some truths are necessarily true. For instance, take the mathematical equation "1 ≠ 0." Once we understand the concepts involved, namely "1," "0," and "inequality," and the idea "1 ≠ 0" is grasped, we also can see with certainty the impossibility that "1 = 0." To paraphrase Stephen Barr, humans can know with certainty that necessary truths like 1 ≠ 0 are "true here and now, true a billion years ago and true a billion years hence, true in galaxies too remote to be seen with a telescope, even true in any other possible universe." To be human, therefore, is to know truth in itself and even to recognize the utter necessity of some truths. Indeed, we can even know that some truths remain true in an infinite number of cases, such as "$a \times b = b \times a$, for all numbers a and b."[12]

THE AMAZING INDESTRUCTIBLE SOUL

The amazing fact of the human capacity to know truth is clearly essential to human uniqueness and dignity. But it reveals something even more astounding: that the soul is *immaterial* and therefore *immortal*.

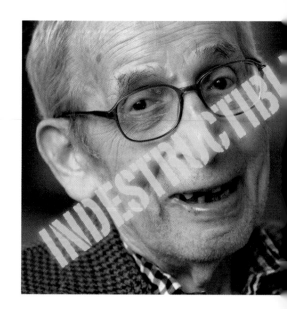

BECAUSE THE HUMAN SOUL IS NOT MADE UP OF MATTER, IT CANNOT BE PHYSICALLY DESTROYED.

Think of it this way. If the human ability to know truth is such that we can get beyond how things appear to the bodily senses and know them as they really are, and can know things (like circularity and beauty) in the abstract, independent of their concrete existence in the physical world, and can know that some truths are true in all cases, even in infinite cases, then our ability to know truth trancends the capacity of any merely physical thing, including the brain. This shows that the human faculty of reason is not made up of matter. Although it may rely upon the senses and upon matter in various ways, human reason *in itself* is something intrinsically spiritual, and reveals that the human soul is intrinsically spiritual.

But if the human soul is spiritual, and thus not made up of matter, it cannot be physically destroyed. To destroy something is to divide it into separate parts, to break it up. But only something that is material can be divided or decomposed.[13] Reason uncovers what is also revealed by God—namely that the soul is immortal, that "it does not perish when it separates from the body at death."[14]

Now let us investigate a second power that is foundational to human beings as the image of God and that stems from human reason: free will.

FREE WILL: IMAGING GOD WHO IS LOVE

Man's capacity for knowing truth, as we have seen, means that humans can know things in themselves, in their *essences*. But because of this ability, human beings are also capable of knowing things in relationship to *goodness*. Goodness refers to that which contributes to the perfection of a being. For example, in a plant or animal health is "a good," and in a rational being knowledge and friendship are "goods." We can also say that food is good for an animal because it contributes to its having the good of health; and a book may be good for a human being because it contributes to his or her having the good of knowledge. The goodness of some goal we seek or some action we perform refers to its ability to meet some need we have or to actualize some potential that we possess. For instance, we can comprehend that going to the mall can meet the need we have for a new pair of shoes or a new jacket. We can also comprehend that going to the mall allows us to see a funny movie and actualize our capacity for laughter. In both cases we use our ability to know things as they are in themselves and in their relation to goodness, to consider actions we may perform, and then perform them or avoid performing them based on rational deliberation.[15]

This ability to act or not to act on the basis of reason is called *freedom*, "the power, rooted in reason and will, to act or not to act, to do this or that, and so to perform deliberate actions on one's own responsibility."[16] Based on reason, human beings are capable of consciously choosing or avoiding this or that action. Unlike the other animals, which are moved by appetites and instincts, humans are capable of directing their appetites and instincts through reason. Animals are moved by appetites and instincts, but humans can move themselves. This freedom includes the "possibility of *choosing between good and evil*, and thus of growing in perfection or of failing and sinning."[17] It is by our wills that we enact freedom, and our free wills are in turn grounded in our reason, our ability to know the truth.

Consequently, human beings are capable of love. There are many dimensions or levels to love. The first is one we share with the animals—the inclination to act due to being attracted by a good. In

BECAUSE HUMAN BEINGS ARE CAPABLE OF REASON, THEY ARE CAPABLE OF FREEDOM; BECAUSE HUMAN BEINGS ARE CAPABLE OF FREEDOM, THEY ARE CAPABLE OF LOVE.

human beings this attraction "causes a desire for the absent good and the hope of attaining it; [it] finds completion in the pleasure and joy of the good possessed."[18] In the fully human sense, love is the free choice to will the true good of another.[19] Humans are capable of knowing the true good of another person and of freely choosing to act for the sake of that good. In this way human beings can love in the way that God loves, not just for the good someone brings me, but for the sake of their own good. We see, then, that fully human love is not a mere "feeling" or emotion; it is an act of the will. To love someone is to will what is good for that person—and in the case of proper self-love it is willing what is genuinely good for oneself, i.e., what helps to perfect oneself.

The greatest kind of love is *charity*: the "virtue by which we love God above all things for his own sake, and our neighbor as ourselves for the love of God."[20]

As mentioned above, animals are capable of something like love; they are attracted to goodness as well. *But this attraction is one that possesses the animal and is not possessed by it.* Humans on the other hand, are made capable, by reason and will, of *self-possession*. Therefore, they are capable of making themselves into a gift for others, including God.

In summary, reason and freedom are the twin foundations of man's imaging of God. Man knows truth, and so he images God who is truth and light. Man can also move himself freely to seek the good of others, and so images God who is perfect love and a perfect communion of love. These two faculties together are the spiritual pillars on which human uniqueness and our imaging of God are based.

C. An Image in Three Dimensions: Substance, Sex, and Subjectivity

We have gone a long way toward understanding why human beings, out of all the visible creatures on the planet, can alone be called the image of God. Now that we have seen the foundations of this unique status, we must turn to consider the specific ways in which reason and freedom are realized.

To be a human being is to be able to know and love, but human knowledge and human love are expressed in very particular ways. What makes human love different from angelic love and divine love is that human love is twofold: 1) humans love in their unique status as a union of body and soul; and 2) human love is expressed in the equality and diversity of masculinity and femininity.

THERE ARE LEVELS TO HUMAN LOVE THAT RANGE FROM THE ATTRACTION TO GOOD THINGS THAT WE SHARE WITH THE ANIMALS TO THE SELFLESS LOVE OF GOD AND NEIGHBOR CALLED CHARITY, MADE POSSIBLE BY SUPERNATURAL GRACE.

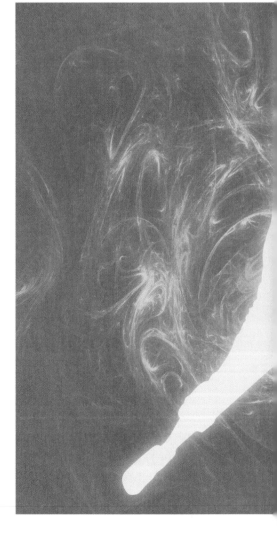

IN KNOWING AND LOVING, HUMANITY IS LIKE GOD; IN THE SPECIFIC WAYS WE LOVE (AS A UNION OF BODY AND SOUL AND AS MALE AND FEMALE), HUMANITY IS UNIQUE.

Because of our status as spiritual creatures, human beings love as persons, something that, unlike bodies and sexuality, we do share in common with angels and with God. To summarize, then: in our body/soul unity (substance), our masculinity and femininity (sex) and in our personhood (subjectivity), human beings know and love as God's image. Let's consider each of these in this order.

"BODY AND SOUL BUT TRULY ONE"[21]

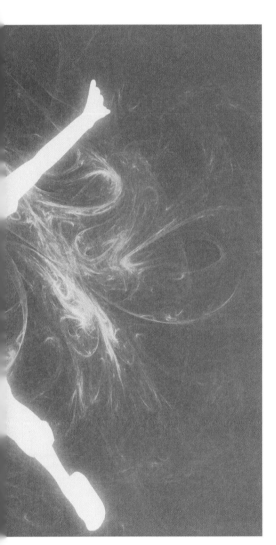

It is clearly true that something of man is immaterial; that is why humans can exercise the faculty of reason, as we saw above. But as we also saw in the Second Creation Account, the Lord God made man from dust. In other words, the human person is a being that is both bodily and spiritual simultaneously.[22] To be human is to be a hybrid, a creature that has one foot in the world of non-rational animals and another in the world of angels, although he is neither.

But, although it is mysterious and almost unfathomable, man is not two things. He is one, a single substance made up of two distinct elements. Those elements are a material body and an immaterial soul. The union of these two, body and soul, forms a single human nature.[23]

This fact means that bodiliness is essential to being human. The Christian Faith rejects all forms of *dualism* (i.e., theories that assert that body and soul are separate and only accidentally linked). This is what is meant by the Church teaching that the intellectual (rational) soul is the form of the human body, a teaching first declared at the *Council of Vienne* in 1311–1312 (and later at Lateran Council V in 1513).[24]

The body is so essential to being human that even our spiritual powers of reason and freedom are dependent in some way on our bodiliness. The Christian Faith affirms what neuroscience has clearly demonstrated: that the brain is necessary for most, if not all, acts of reason and will, at least in this life.[25] But the Christian Faith also declares what is attested to by our own experience and philosophical reflection, that the brain is not sufficient by itself for acts of reason and will.

Because of the close dependence of body and spirit, man is the image of God in a bodily way as well as a spiritual one.[26] Our imaging of God bleeds over from our souls to our bodies, thanks to the intimate unity between them.

The fact that human beings are a union of physical body and spiritual soul means that the biological production of human beings through sexual intercourse, *procreation*, involves God in a very special way. A bodily process cannot of itself produce a spiritual soul, nor can a perishable body produce an immortal reality. The Church therefore teaches that every human soul is created immediately by God.[27]

Each soul is made by God new and unique, and *always*. When the material that makes up the human body is organized sufficiently for human life, God does not fail to infuse the soul.[28] This is true even when human life is created in ways contradictory to God's plan and to human dignity; even a human created through cloning would have an immortal soul.

Why did God create humanity as a hybrid of body and spirit? Perhaps it is because of his love for unity. God, as we know, is three divine persons who are so intimately united that their real distinction does not diminish the perfect unity of the divine nature. God's creation then should also be a unity in some way. But in order for there to be such a unity, a creature that possesses both body and spirit was necessary to unite the physical universe with the realm of spirit. Humanity is the link between the world of atoms and the world of angels.

So man, the image of God, is a unity of body and soul that brings about the unity which God intended for the entire realms of matter and spirit. But he also intended another unity within humanity itself: the unity of man and woman.

MAN AND WOMAN: "A UNITY IN TWO"[29]

In the words of the *Catechism of the Catholic Church*, "God created man and woman *together* and willed each *for* the other."[30] Therefore, the difference between man and woman and their relationship are essential elements in their imaging of God.[31]

We have already noted that, due to the union of body and soul, bodiliness has a part to play in man's acts of reason and will. Therefore, it is necessary to also declare that man's spiritual acts are also touched by maleness and femaleness, masculinity and femininity: "Each [sex] possesses a way of being in the world, to see, to think, to feel, to engage in mutual exchange with other persons who are also defined by their sexual identity."[32] "Sexuality affects all aspects of the human person in the unity of body and soul."[33]

In their imaging of God, man and woman are *equal*, *different*, and *complementary*. First, the Christian Faith teaches that man and woman are equally created in God's image. Both have reason and freedom, and neither has a superiority to the other. Second, it also affirms that man and woman are different—each exercises reason and freedom in a way "proper and [unique] to their sexual identity."[34]

But the third characteristic is just as crucial: "man and woman were made 'for each other'"; that is, they are *reciprocal* (mutually supportive) and *complementary* (mutually enriching and completing). In marriage, they become "one flesh" and have the potential of uniting "their bodies and spirits in an attitude of total openness and self giving." When they do so, "they form a new image of God," who is a

WHY DID GOD CREATE HUMANITY AS A HYBRID OF BODY AND SPIRIT? PERHAPS IT IS BECAUSE OF HIS LOVE FOR UNITY. GOD, AS WE KNOW, IS THREE DIVINE PERSONS WHO ARE SO INTIMATELY UNITED THAT THEIR REAL DISTINCTION COINCIDES WITH THE UNITY OF THE DIVINE NATURE.

perfect communion among persons. The image of God which is found in each and every human person is fulfilled in a special way in this union of man and woman.[35]

The surprising and exciting fact is that a new image of the Trinity is formed when man and woman, in their marital sexual union, give themselves in an act in which each person becomes a gift offered to the other. This idea, which is at the heart of the teaching of Sacred Scripture and the Church regarding the Sacrament of Matrimony, was given a profound new expression by Pope John Paul II in his series of addresses entitled the "Theology of the Body."[36] The structure of the human body, he tells us, reveals that we were created to offer ourselves sexually, in a complete and unbreakable unity of love, to a member of the opposite sex in marriage. Sex is a unique way in which humanity images God—in reason, in freedom, bodily, and as male and female. It should also be noted that God calls some individuals to a life of celibacy in imitation of Christ, in which they make a gift of their human sexuality to God. Celibacy is the objectively superior form of the Christian life because it is a more perfect imitation of Christ than even marriage.

PERSONHOOD AND COMMUNION

The spiritual powers of reason and free will, made manifest and expressed visibly in the human body united to the human soul and gloriously revealed in marital love, point to the fact that man is the image of God because man, out of all the visible creatures on this planet, is a *personal being*, a subject (one who possesses himself or herself) and not simply an object. With human beings the visible world takes a major leap—human beings are visible creatures that are *persons* and not simply *members of a species*.

A *person* is a being capable of knowledge and love; a human person is a person who, due to knowledge and love, exists bodily in the world as a relational and social being.[37] Because a human person can know and freely determine himself or herself, he or she has a level of uniqueness that is much more radical than simply being an individual member of a species. An individual is a unique *what*, but a *person* is also a *who*, with a unique *personality*.

Because of this self-possession, which reveals a deep interior life, the human person is capable of having the closest contacts with the whole world, especially with other persons. That contact begins on the natural bodily level, through the senses, but also blossoms into an interpersonal contact, a contact that is interior as well as exterior.[38] Because of reason and will, human persons are capable of *communion*—a commitment of self to others in an essentially giving way. Personhood is the basis of the human ability to form *communities*, such as families, friendships, local, state, and national societies, teams, and the Church, which is the Body of Christ.[39]

Because a human being is a person, he is the subject of special rights. No good, even if it seems to be that of society as a whole, is sufficient grounds for the violation of man's body or soul. Pope John Paul II said that when it comes to persons, one rule applies. Positively expressed, that rule is the obligation to love: "Thou shalt love!" Negatively, that rule is expressed as a prohibition: "Thou shalt not use!"[40] The message is clear: a *person is not an object to be exploited but a subject to be loved*. Only by loving others, and never using them in an exploitative fashion, can we respect the absolute integrity and dignity of human beings.

The highest form of communion that human persons can have is their relationship with God, expressed and realized especially in receiving the Sacrament of the Eucharist, which we appropriately call Holy Communion, because in it Christ gives himself to us—Body, Blood, Soul, and Divinity—and we give ourselves to him in return.

In the Trinity, there is a perfect communion of persons who share a single divine life. In human communities, even though humans have been wounded by sin, the human race reveals the image of God once again. Personhood and community are the final dimensions of the image of God that is humanity.

SIN: THE IMAGE DISTORTED BUT NOT DESTROYED

The beautiful truth about the human person in the light of faith and reason also has a shadow-side: the reality of sin. Freedom, which enables humans to choose goodness, love, and communion, also enables them to fail at freedom, to freely disobey God, and to pursue aims contrary to the purposes for which he created them. Sin is the failure to pursue God's invitation to communion with him and other human persons.[41]

Sadly, sin impairs and disfigures the image of God in man; however, it cannot entirely destroy it. Salvation is the restoration of God's image in humanity by the Son, who Scripture reveals to be the perfect image of the Father (Col 1:15). In the Incarnation, the Son takes on a human nature in order to restore that nature to its original glory. St. Athanasius paints a beautiful picture of this process:

> ...when [the image] has been defaced by stains, he who the portrait is in likeness of must come once more to enable the portrait to be renewed.... In the same way also the most holy Son of the Father, being the image of the Father, came to our regions to renew man once made in his likeness....[42]

Even the worst sinner is an image of God, however disfigured. In Christ, through the mercy of God, that image can be renewed.

ONLY BY LOVING OTHERS, AND NEVER USING THEM IN AN EXPLOITATIVE FASHION, CAN WE RESPECT THE INTEGRITY AND DIGNITY OF HUMAN BEINGS, WHO ARE PERSONS AND NOT SIMPLY THINGS

D. Conclusion:
The Human Person,
Stewardship, and Science

As the image of God, human beings share the world with other creatures but are distinguished from them by reason, free will, and love. Therefore they have a special relationship with the rest of visible creation; only human beings are capable of enjoying the privilege of sharing God's own governance of the universe. In fact, this vocation is given by God himself. In the First Creation Account we read that God blessed the man and woman, saying "Be fertile and multiply; fill the Earth and subdue it" (Gn 1:28). Man does not replace God but does act as his steward of the universe and its goods. *Stewardship* is a participation in the ownership of something of which primary ownership belongs to another.[43]

In stewardship over creation, man rules over it much as someone might act as master of someone else's household, such as the servants in the story Jesus tells of the man who gives his servants money to invest and then to return to him with interest (Lk 19:12–27). Man is master of creation, but not in a way in which he can abuse the world. In fact, his dominion over the world involves a responsibility and service which he owes to God.[44]

Science and technology are both ways in which man exercises his dominion and stewardship of creation. The fact that human beings can know the world and its creatures so thoroughly through scientific investigation reveals the fundamental difference and dignity of humanity with regard to the rest of visible creation. Human beings are the only creatures in the visible world that approach the world scientifically; when they do so, they reveal that to be human is to be more than an animal or a mere biological machine.

In the next chapter, we will see that this fact has come under significant attack by some scientists, who claim that man is fundamentally no different than any of the other visible creatures of the world. They argue that we are just animals, and as such are nothing but highly sophisticated machines. Our minds, they say, are nothing but the workings of a computer called the brain. They challenge us with a crucial question: is man truly a divine mystery, a person in God's image? Or is man merely matter, nothing more than an advanced mammal or a biological computer?

These questions must be answered in our quest to rediscover faith on the frontiers of science.

WE ARE MASTERS OF GOD'S CREATION, BUT NOT IN A WAY IN WHICH WE CAN ABUSE THE WORLD; OUR DOMINION INVOLVES A RESPONSIBILITY AND SERVICE WHICH WE OWE TO GOD

Supplementary Reading

In His Image:
The Human Person from the Divine Perspective

1. "HUMAN BEINGS ARE THE CROWN OF CREATION: THE WITNESS OF FAITH AND REASON"

(excerpted from Christoph Cardinal Schönborn,
"What is Man that Thou are Mindful of Him? Is Man Really the "Crown of Creation"?" Internet.
Available from http://stephanscom.at/edw/katechesen/articles/2006/07/17/a11155; accessed April 2, 2007.)

What the Bible says about man has been richly elaborated by the Christian tradition and before that by the Jewish tradition. Thus we read in the "Letter to Diognetus" from the early second century: "God loved men. *For their sake he made the cosmos* and subjected everything on earth to them. To them alone he gave understanding and speech, them alone he allowed to look up to heaven, them alone he formed in his image, to them alone he sent his Son. He promised them the kingdom of heaven and he will give it to those who love him."

We have here a very man-centered view of the world and a very God-centered view of man. Man is the center and summit of creation. Everything is made for his sake. Evidence of this is the observable bodily and spiritual superiority of man (language, reason, upright posture) as well as his special supernatural gifts (existing as God's image, as the goal of the incarnation of God, as called to eternal beatitude).

Christianity shares this conviction with Judaism. In the Talmud we find the beautiful simile: the world is created by God like a wedding chamber prepared by a father for his son. Having prepared everything, he led his son into the chamber....

At the dawn of the modern world a young genius, Giovanni Pico della Mirandola (1463–1494), celebrated the surpassing dignity and greatness of man and did so in the spirit of the Renaissance (which should be understood as something Christian). In one place in his *Oration on the Dignity of Man* he lets God speak to man, reminding man as follows of his unique position in the world:

Adam, we give you no fixed place to live, no form that is peculiar to you, nor any function that is yours alone. According to your desires and judgment, you will have and possess whatever place to live, whatever form, and whatever functions you yourself choose. All other things have a limited and fixed nature prescribed and bounded by our laws. You, with no limit or no bound, may choose for yourself the limits and bounds of your nature. We have placed you at the world's center so that you may survey everything else in the world. We have made you neither of heavenly nor of earthly stuff, neither mortal nor immortal, so that

Supplementary Reading

with free choice and dignity, you may fashion yourself into whatever form you choose. To you is granted the power of degrading yourself into the lower forms of life, the beasts, and to you is granted the power, contained in your intellect and judgment, to be reborn into the higher forms, the divine.

2. "HUMAN BEINGS ARE BOTH PART OF NATURE AND THE IMAGE OF GOD"

(excerpted from Christoph Cardinal Schönborn,
"What is Man that Thou are Mindful of Him? Is Man Really the "Crown of Creation"?" Internet.
Available from http://stephanscom.at/edw/katechesen/articles/2006/07/17/a11155; accessed April 2, 2007.)

[An opposing view] to the Judeo-Christian view is often put forth today: *man is a part of the whole*, that is the heart of the argument that has been used from ancient times until today. Immersed in the stream of life man is not different from the other creatures; there is in man no spiritual principle, no power, no special calling that sets him apart. He should be satisfied with this and should finally have the humility to give up his aspiration to be something more.

… [In this one-sided view] an essential aspect of the human phenomenon remains here unexpressed. It is true that everything on earth, matter and life and even man, is embedded in this gigantic event of the becoming of the cosmos as a whole. Whether we should call this process of becoming by the name of evolution, is another issue. But this much is certain: we owe our bodily existence to the becoming of the world, beginning with the elements that emerged in the process of the unfolding of the universe and extending to those conditions that have made life possible on our "gentle planet."

This state of being immersed in the stream of becoming is entirely compatible with the biblical view of man. It is a wonderful thing about our earthly existence that we human beings are really related to other creatures. We share with them the same laws of matter, the same basic elements of life. We occupy the same environment as all other living beings. We are together with them in the Noah's Ark that is our planet.

Just how deeply our bodily existence is woven into the history of the universe has been shown very vividly by Arnold Benz, professor of astrophysics in Zurich. The material elements that form our body emerged in mighty nuclear fusions in the stars:

Supplementary Reading

The carbon and oxygen in our bodies come from helium burning in some old star. Two silicon nuclei fused right before and during a supernova and became the iron in our blood. The calcium of our teeth formed during a supernova from oxygen and silicon. The fluoride with which we brush our teeth was produced in a rare neutrino interaction with neon. The iodine in our glands came about when neutrons were trapped in the collapse before a supernova. We are directly connected with the development of the stars and are ourselves a part of the history of the cosmos. (Benz, *Die Zukunft der Universums. Zufall, Chaos, Gott?* [Muenchen, 2001], p. 35.)

The astrophysicist Marco Bersanelli of the University of Milan adds: "We are literally 'children of the stars.'"

There is no shame in acknowledging this. There is no shame in being a part of the universe. The ancients liked to speak of man as a microcosm. This means that in him the whole of the universe is present and that he is present in it. It is fascinating to explore the links connecting man with what is smallest and what is greatest, with the infinitely small world of atoms and with the immeasurably vast world of galaxies.

…[O]n the one hand, man is tied into the whole of nature as a result of the fact that we are all creatures; on the other hand, man occupies a unique position as a result of the fact that he is made in the image of God.

3. "MAN IS THE STEWARD OF THE CREATED WORLD"

(excerpted from International Theological Commission, Communion and Stewardship: Human Persons Created in the Image of God. *Internet. Available from http://www.vatican.va/roman_curia/congregations/cfaith/cti_documents/rc_con_cfaith_doc_20040723_communion-stewardship_en.html; accessed April 2, 2007.)*

57. …Created in the image of God to share in the communion of Trinitarian love, human beings occupy a unique place in the universe according to the divine plan: they enjoy the privilege of sharing in the divine governance of visible creation. This privilege is granted to them by the Creator who allows the creature made in his image to participate in his work, in his project of love and salvation, indeed in his own lordship over the universe. Since man's place as ruler is in fact a participation in the divine governance of creation, we speak of it here as a form of stewardship.

58. According to *Gaudium et spes*: "Man was created in God's image and was commanded to conquer the earth and to rule the world in justice and holiness: he was to acknowledge God as maker of all things and relate himself and the totality of creation to him, so that through the dominion of all things by man the name of God would be majestic in all the earth" (34). This concept of man's rule or sovereignty plays an important role in Christian theology. God appoints man as his steward in the manner of the master in the Gospel parables (cf. Luke 19:12). The only creature willed expressly by God for his own sake occupies a unique place at the summit of visible creation (Gen. 1:26; 2:20; Ps 8:6–7, Wisdom 9:2–3).

Supplementary Reading

59. Christian theology uses both domestic and royal imagery to describe this special role. Employing royal imagery, it is said that human beings are called to rule in the sense of holding an ascendancy over the whole of visible creation, in the manner of a king. But the inner meaning of this kingship is, as Jesus reminds his disciples, one of service: only by willingly suffering as a sacrificial victim does Christ become the king of the universe, with the Cross as his throne. Employing domestic imagery, Christian theology speaks of man as the master of a household to whom God has confided care of all his goods (cf. Mt 24:45). Man can deploy all the resources of visible creation according to his ingenuity, and exercises this participated sovereignty over visible creation in and through science, technology and art.

60. Above himself and yet in the intimacy of his own conscience, man discovers the existence of a law which the tradition calls the "natural law." This law is of divine origin, and man's awareness of it is itself a participation in the divine law. It refers man to the true origins of the universe as well as to his own (*Veritatis splendor*, 20). This natural law drives the rational creature to search for the truth and the good in his sovereignty of the universe. Created in the image of God, man exercises this sovereignty over visible creation only in virtue of the privilege conferred upon him by God. He imitates the divine rule, but he cannot displace it. The Bible warns against the sin of this usurpation of the divine role. It is a grave moral failure for human beings to act as rulers of visible creation who separate themselves from the higher, divine law. They act in place of the master as stewards (cf. Mt 25:14 ff) who have the freedom they need to develop the gifts which have been confided to them and to do so with a certain bold inventiveness.

61. The steward must render an account of his stewardship, and the divine Master will judge his actions. The moral legitimacy and efficacy of the means employed by the steward provide the criteria for this judgment. Neither science nor technology are ends in themselves; what is technically possible is not necessarily also reasonable or ethical. Science and technology must be put in the service of the divine design for the whole of creation and for all creatures. This design gives meaning to the universe and to human enterprise as well. Human stewardship of the created world is precisely a stewardship exercised by way of participation in the divine rule and is always subject to it. Human beings exercise this stewardship by gaining scientific understanding of the universe, by caring responsibly for the natural world (including animals and the environment), and by guarding their own biological integrity.

Study Guide

In His Image:
The Human Person from the Divine Perspective

VOCABULARY

Define the following terms:

1. Image
2. Vestige
3. Soul (human)
4. Love (divine)
5. Reason
6. Freedom
7. Capacity for Objectivity
8. Sensory
9. Universals (abstract concepts)
10. Immaterial
11. Immortality of the Soul
12. Goodness
13. Love (human)
14. Charity
15. Self-Possession
16. Dualism
17. Council of Vienne
18. Person
19. Human Person
20. Communion
21. Stewardship

STUDY QUESTIONS

1. Why must man's imaging of God involve truth and love? How does it involve these two crucial elements?
2. What three abilities characterize rationality?
3. Explain why rationality also reveals the human soul to be immaterial and immortal.
4. Why is reason absolutely essential to free will?
5. Why is free will absolutely essential to love?
6. What elements of human knowing and loving are unique to humans? What elements do humans share in common with angels and with God?
7. Why is man appropriately called "a hybrid being"? What consequence does this have for human rationality?
8. Is the human body part of man's imaging of God? Why or why not?
9. What special role must God play in the sexual procreation of new human beings? What characterizes this divine action?

Study Guide

10. Why did God create man as a hybrid being, a unity of body and soul?

11. What three things characterize the relation between man and woman as willed by God?

12. Explain the one unique element of being a person that is true only of human persons.

13. What is the relationship between personhood and communion?

14. Explain the special rule of Pope John Paul II that applies to all persons, expressed both negatively and positively. Does this role have consequences for society? Explain.

15. How is sin related to man's imaging of God?

16. What is the nature of man's stewardship of the universe? How is it both a privilege and a responsibility?

17. How is science involved in the human stewardship of creation?

PRACTICAL EXERCISES

1. Imagine that you are an astronaut who discovers life on another planet. How would you be able to identify whether a life form is a creature in the image of God or just simply a creature of God? Make a list of behaviors that would reveal the life form to be rational, free, and personal.

2. Make two lists of human behaviors. The first list should only include characteristics of personhood. The second should only include human characteristics that humans share with animals.

3. John Paul II said "A person is not an object to be used, but a subject to be loved." Make a mental examination of the actions and words you observed in the past week on television. Which were actions and words of use? Which were actions and words of love?

Endnotes

1. CCC 356.
2. Aidan Nichols, *Disovering Aquinas* (Grand Rapids: Eerdmans, 2002), 75.
3. St. Thomas Aquinas, *In I Sent.* 3.3.1.
4. CCC 221.; cf. 1 Cor 2: 7–16; Eph 3: 9–12.
5. Ibid., 231.
6. Christoph Schönborn, "What is Man that Thou art Mindful of Him? Is Man Really the Crown of Creation?"
7. Ibid.
8. Bonnette, 101.
9. Barr, 191.
10. Ibid.
11. Ibid., 197–198.
12. Ibid., 199–204.
13. F.C. Copleston, *Aquinas* (Baltimore: Penguin, 1955), 161.
14. CCC 366; cf. Pius XII, *Humani generis*: DS 3896; Paul VI, CPG §8; Lateran Council V (1513): DS 1440.

15. Copleston, 179–180.
16. CCC 1731.
17. Ibid., 1732.
18. Ibid., 1765.
19. Cf. Ibid., 1765.
20. Ibid., 1822.
21. Cf. Ibid., 362–368.
22. Cf. Ibid., 362.
23. Cf. Ibid., 365.
24. Haffner, *Mystery of Creation*, 78.
25. Barr, 173.
26. ITC, 31.
27. Cf. CCC 366.
28. Haffner, *Mystery of Creation*, 74.
29. CCC 371.
30. Ibid. 371.
31. ITC, 33.
32. Ibid., 33.

33. CCC 2332.
34. ITC, 36.
35. Ibid., 38.
36. For an excellent introduction to John Paul II's Theology of the Body, see Brian Butler, Jason Evert, Mark Hunt, and Crystalina Evert, *Theology of the Body for Teens: Discovering God's Plan for Love and Life* (Ascension: 2004).
37. ITC, 40.
38. Karol Wojtyla, *Love and Responsibility* (San Francisco: Ignatius Press, 1993), 23.
39. ITC, 42–43.
40. Ibid., 40–43
41. Ibid., 44.
42. St. Athanasius, *On the Incarnation*, II.14.
43. ITC, 57.
44. Ibid., 58–59.

Chapter Ten

Image or Illusion? Scientific Challenges to Human Dignity and Personhood

BY VIRTUE OF HIS SOUL
AND SPIRITUAL POWERS OF
INTELLECT AND WILL, MAN IS
ENDOWED WITH FREEDOM,
AN OUTSTANDING MANIFESTATION
OF THE DIVINE IMAGE.

A. A Challenge to the Foundations of Human Dignity

Throughout the previous chapter we surveyed the twin pillars on which human dignity and uniqueness are founded: reason and free will. We can summarize the whole chapter with one sentence from the *Catechism of the Catholic Church*: "By virtue of his soul and spiritual powers of intellect and will, man is endowed with freedom, an outstanding manifestation of the divine image."[1] These powers allow human beings to transcend themselves, their sense appetites, instincts, desires, and even the entire universe in order to love other persons, especially God, and to know the goodness, beauty, and truth of things.[2]

But human transcendence is an unacceptable concept to some who, in an attempt to espouse a scientific approach to the world, have actually lapsed into scientism. Much of the conflict between science and faith has not been centered on the question of the existence of God, but on the question of the true dignity and uniqueness of humanity. In particular, reason and freedom have been vigorously questioned and even discarded by some thinkers.

According to these thinkers, "science has dethroned man." It has removed him from his centrality and primacy in the universe. In the words of the atheist mathematician and philosopher Bertrand Russell, science has revealed man to be "a curious accident in a backwater" of the universe.

Bertrand Russell

Stephen Barr has described the materialist view as follows:

"Science has dethroned man." Far from being the center of things, he is now seen to be a very peripheral figure indeed. Every great scientific revolution has further trivialized him and pushed him to the margins. Copernicus removed Earth from the center of the solar system. Modern astronomy has shown that the solar system itself is on the edge of a quite ordinary galaxy, which contains hundreds of billions of other stars. That galaxy is, in turn, one of billions and perhaps even an infinite number of galaxies. Earth is an insignificant speck in the vastness of space: its mass compared to all the matter in the observable universe is less than that of a raindrop compared to all the water in all the oceans of the world. All of recorded human history is a fleeting moment in the eons of cosmic time. Even on this cozy planet, which we think of as ours, we are latecomers. *Homo sapiens* have been around at most a few hundred thousand years, compared to the 4 billion years of life's history.[3]

Here are three areas in which the twin pillars of human dignity, reason and free will, have been called into question by modern scientism:

- *Man's difference from and superiority to the animals*—Studies in animal intelligence have revealed a surprising degree of mental sophistication in non-human animals, especially those which make and use tools.[4] In particular, chimpanzees and gorillas have been taught sign language and have been observed engaging in behaviors that look very much like lying, deception, joking, arguing, and correcting. This has led some to conclude that man is not qualitatively different from the other animals on our planet;[5]

- *Man's superiority to artificial intelligence*—Computers can receive input from the world, encode it, store it and retrieve it, analyze it, use it to make decisions, and then put those decisions into effect. This has led many neuroscientists and even philosophers to assert that the human mind is simply a computer, and that computers can do everything of which the human mind is capable;[6]

- *The reality of human freedom*—Science has uncovered the fact that the entire universe is subject to mathematical laws. As our knowledge has increased, so has the belief that humans themselves are determined by physical laws. For if the body is made up of matter, and matter is governed by unbreakable laws that totally determine its activities, then it seems clear that the body is itself determined by such laws, and all human behavior along with it.[7]

ACCORDING TO *SCIENTISM*, MAN IS NOTHING MORE THAN THE MOST ADVANCED FORM OF BIOLOGICAL LIFE, COMPLETELY DETERMINED BY THE LAWS OF CHEMISTRY, WHICH ARE IN TURN COMPLETELY DETERMINED BY THE LAWS OF PHYSICS.

According to scientism, these three areas of research reveal that man is nothing more than the most advanced form of biological life, completely determined by the laws of chemistry, which are in turn completely determined by the laws of physics. This reductionist notion of humanity underlies the recent startling proclamation of *Francis Crick*, who was a co-discoverer of the double helix formation of DNA. He calls his position the *Astonishing Hypothesis*:

> The Astonishing Hypothesis is that "You," your joys and your sorrows, your memories and your ambitions, your sense of identity and free will, are in fact nothing more than the behavior of a vast assembly of nerve cells and their associated molecules. As Lewis Carroll's Alice might have phrased it: "you are nothing but a pack of neurons."[8]

Has modern science revealed reason and free will to be illusions rather than the twin foundations of the divine image? Is a human being only "a machine for propagating DNA"?[9] Let us consider each of these issues in detail and confront the question of humanity and human nature on the frontiers of science.

B. Washoe, Kanzi, and Koko: Is Man Simply a Naked Ape?

For more than half a century, attempts have been made by scientists to teach chimpanzees and gorillas to use language. Some researchers have made remarkable claims regarding the intelligence of the primates involved in their studies. One of the most famous cases involved a chimpanzee named *Washoe*.

Two researchers taught Washoe American Sign Language (ASL), which was originally developed for use by deaf people. ASL involves a set of hand gestures that symbolize various concepts. By age seven, Washoe had developed the ability to sign 175 different words.[10] It has been claimed that Washoe taught another chimpanzee, Loulis, to sign as well.[11]

A twenty-eight year old pigmy chimpanzee named *Kanzi* points to symbols on a board or punches them on a keyboard to request games, treats, and activities (such as caveman movies like *Quest for Fire*, which he refers to as "Fire TV"). Kanzi has even created sharp chips out of flint by slamming them onto the floor, and then used them to cut through cords in order to obtain a key to a box which contained a treat.[12]

There are even animals who seem to engage in human activities of an unsavory kind, such as lying. A gorilla named *Koko*, who was taught to use American Sign Language over thirty years ago by psychologist Penny Patterson, seemed on one occasion to lie in order to shift the blame for knocking a sink off of its moorings, signing the words "Kate there bad" while pointing to the sink (Kate was the name of a female research assistant).[13]

DO GORILLAS OR CHIMPS HAVE A CAPACITY FOR REASON THAT IS NOT FUNDAMENTALLY DIFFERENT FROM THAT OF HUMANS?

THE FALSE APPEARANCE OF INTELLIGENCE IN ANIMALS COMING FROM HUMAN INFLUENCE, THE *CLEVER HANS EFFECT*, COMES ABOUT THROUGH VARIOUS TYPES OF HUMAN/ANIMAL INTERACTIONS, INCLUDING DELIBERATE TRAINING AND UNINTENTIONAL CUEING.

These studies and others, some including dolphins, sea lions and, in one case, an African gray parrot, have led some scientists to conclude that certain animals have all of the basic capacities for rationality that human beings possess. Are these scientists correct? Or have they been deceived by behaviors that only *resemble* human behaviors?

Is the intelligence level of gorillas or chimps really not fundamentally different from that of humans? If so, there are two possibilities. One is that apes have our capacities of intellect and will and are endowed with spiritual souls. The second is that we are deceived about our own powers and do not have spiritual souls ourselves. That is, we differ mentally from apes only in degree not in kind, and these differences are the result merely of greater brain capacity, not of any supposed spiritual element in us. If this is the case, then we are nothing more than "naked apes."

But we should consider another possibility—that the animal researchers merely imagined that they had seen evidence of animal rationality in Kanzi, Koko and the rest. In fact, closer inspection has revealed that it is not philosophers and theologians who have deceived themselves about human minds, but a few animal researchers who have deceived themselves about animal minds. To understand how they deceived themselves, we need to meet a horse named Hans.

THE CLEVER HANS EFFECT: A HORSE IS ONLY A HORSE, OF COURSE

A century ago, a German horse by the name of Clever Hans grabbed the attention of the European scientific community. This wonderful animal wowed people with his ability to solve basic math problems, expressing his answers by tapping his hoof. But a psychologist ultimately showed that Hans was actually responding to unintentional cues from his human handlers. For instance, Hans' keepers would visibly relax when the horse tapped the correct number of times, which would make Hans stop tapping. The psychologist ended the mystery of the calculating horse by blindfolding Hans, who then became unable to see the unintentional cues. Likewise, when a person who did not know the answers himself was chosen to ask Hans questions, Hans was unable to give the right responses. Hans's cleverness turned out to be a matter of keen senses, not rationality.

The false appearance of intelligence in animals coming from human influence upon those animals came to be called the *Clever Hans Effect*.[14] It comes about through various types of human/animal interactions, including deliberate training and unintentional cueing.

Just such an effect has been detected by examiners of the various ape studies we have described, most importantly by the psychologist *Herbert Terrace* and anthropologists *Thomas and Jean Sebeok.*

Terrace, who conducted his own experiments as well as analyses of the experiments of other scientists, insists that chimpanzees and other apes do not possess language ability like that of humans. What the use of language by animals like Washoe really involves is the stringing together of random sign language symbols with one sign language symbol that has a reward attached to it in the animal's memory. For instance, one study involved a chimp named Lana who learned to sign "please machine give apple." But the use of the first three symbols (please, machine and give) could be explained away as not having any real meaning to Lana other than that their use before "apple" involved obtaining an apple as reward.[15] In other words, Lana was doing what all dogs do when they sit on command in order to receive a treat.

Terrace also noted that the researchers involved failed to report data on the order of the signs used by the animal and also altered the data by deleting signs repeated over and over again. The researchers actually excluded numerous useless repetitions of one or more of the signs involved; this cleaning up made the apes' signing appear much more like human speech than it actually is.[16]

For their part, the Sebeoks concluded that most of the interpretations given by the researchers were guilty of the *anthropomorphic fallacy*, "the error of attributing human qualities to animals based upon the temptation to put one's self in the animal's place. This results in viewing its actions in terms of an intelligent human point-of-view, of what it would mean 'if I did that.'"[17] The result, especially when combined with the Clever Hans Effect, justifies being skeptical about all claims made about animals trained by humans. According to the Sebeoks, "Every experimental method is necessarily a human method and must… constitute a human influence on the animal."[18]

This is an important fact that is often overlooked—the activities displayed by Washoe, Kanzi, and other lab animals are never observed occurring spontaneously in animals in the wild who have not been subject to interaction with humans. While animals do communicate, no animals have ever created *language*, an invented system of signs used by agreement. Agreement means that the words chosen are done so on the basis of social convention and not natural inclination. Animals do use natural signs, such as a beaver slapping its tail on water as a sign of danger, but these come from the animal's instincts, not from social agreement.[19]

The ability to engage in language is a fantastic advantage for survival. The well known linguist *Noam Chomsky* points out the irony when he notes that, if animal researchers are correct, animals are capable of conventional language, a great survival advantage, but only use it when taught to do so by researchers![20]

WHILE ANIMALS DO COMMUNICATE, NO ANIMALS HAVE EVER CREATED *LANGUAGE,* AN INVENTED SYSTEM OF SIGNS CHOSEN ON THE BASIS OF SOCIAL CONVENTION RATHER THAN NATURAL INCLINATION.

Noam Chomsky

The insights of Terrace, the Sebeoks, and Chomsky only scratch the surface of the difference between Washoe and even the simplest human intelligence. A closer look at human rationality, delving even further than we have already, reveals a huge gap between animal intelligence and human reason.

THE HALLMARKS OF HUMAN RATIONALITY

What separates you and me from Washoe and the rest of the primate world? Over and above those qualities of human intelligence already explained in Chapter Nine, five additional human qualities reveal a radical, unbridgeable difference between animal intelligence and human reason: self-consciousness, awareness of time, appreciation of the beautiful, a sense of morality and responsibility, and the development of culture.[21] None of these qualities of intelligent activity can be detected among the other living species on our planet.

Self-consciousness:

Perhaps the greatest expression of the difference between animals and man was given by Walker Percy, the Louisiana novelist and Catholic philosopher. Considering the many scientists who have devoted themselves to proving that human intelligence is nothing more than an advanced form of animal intelligence, he observed that human beings are constantly trying to prove that they are no different from the rest of the animals, and by doing so prove their uniqueness beyond the shadow of a doubt, because no other species tries to prove that it is NOT unique![22]

Ironically, the very attempts at disproving human uniqueness testify most eloquently to it. For only man is capable of proving or disproving anything. And only human beings can ask questions about their own minds, because they, unlike other animals, are gifted with *self-consciousness*—the awareness of self and the ability for self-reflection.

"Only man knows that he knows"—only a human can think about himself, his origins, his destiny, his life, his behavior, his death, the possibility of life after death. An animal brain, which is purely material, is not capable of transcending itself in order to see itself.

Continuing his reflections, Walker Percy asked a penetrating question: "Why are these scientists so lonely?" (He was asking why it is so important to some scientists to prove that humans are not "alone on this earth" in being a truly rational species.) We cannot answer exactly why, but we can answer *how* they can have that kind of loneliness. It is only because they are self-aware; they have self-consciousness. Washoe, even with his ability to use sign language, does not.

Walker Percy

ONLY HUMAN BEINGS ARE GIFTED WITH SELF-CONSCIOUSNESS, THE AWARENESS OF SELF AND THE ABILITY FOR SELF-REFLECTION. AN ANIMAL BRAIN IS NOT CAPABLE OF TRANSCENDING ITSELF IN ORDER TO SEE ITSELF.

Awareness of time:

No chimpanzee has ever demonstrated any interest in history. None has ever created a calendar or a way of measuring time. Some animals can learn from past behaviors and modify them accordingly, such as higher mammals, which can be trained. Others prepare for future events, such as squirrels that store nuts for the winter and birds that migrate. But such activities are easily explained by instincts that arise through natural selection, not from reflection and planning.[23]

Animals perceive and associate successions of events, as when a dog is trained to go to its kennel by giving it a treat whenever it does so. But humans can grasp the essence of cause-effect relationships.[24] This is why we can think in terms of time and history. Once again, the human ability to transcend the material world allows human beings to approach it and think about it as something that changes and develops. Animals do not have the same awareness of time.

Appreciation of the beautiful:

Both animals and human beings are capable of tool use and tool making. But when archaeologists look for evidence of truly human activity in their digging, they have a sure method of detecting it—look not only for tools, but for tools that have been *artistically designed*.

For instance, stone tools found in layers of sediment dated to the African Middle Stone Age (about 50,000 years ago) show a distinct difference from those found in earlier layers. The tools are not just usable; they are symmetrical, bearing equal measure on all sides, and not just on the side used for cutting. In other words, they are designed to be visually pleasing—to be beautiful. And in this way there can be no doubt that they are human tools—tools that reveal rationality in their design.[25]

Once recognized, the *human aesthetic capacity*, the human desire for and appreciation of beauty, is a clear and unbridgeable difference between man and animals. While instinct and natural selection can easily explain the intricate nests created by some birds, neither instinct nor natural selection can explain the greatness of the works of Michelangelo, the invention of music, or even the appeal of Disney World.

What is beauty? It has been described as the coming together of three characteristics in a being or beings. The first characteristic is *unity*—in order to be beautiful, a thing must have a wholeness, a completeness. The ancients referred to this as *integrity*. Second, to be beautiful, a thing must have *harmony*, a "fitting together" of everything integral to it. In physical beings, this is called proportion or symmetry. The ancients referred to this quality as *consonance*. Finally, to be beautiful, a thing must have *splendor*. This splendor,

ALTHOUGH ANIMALS PERCEIVE AND ASSOCIATE SUCCESSIONS OF EVENTS, SUCH ACTIVITIES ARE EASILY EXPLAINED BY INSTINCTS THAT ARISE THROUGH NATURAL SELECTION, AND NOT FROM REFLECTION AND PLANNING.

THE HUMAN DESIRE FOR AND APPRECIATION OF BEAUTY IS A CLEAR AND UNBRIDGEABLE DIFFERENCE BETWEEN MAN AND ANIMALS.

which comes from harmony and integrity, is what evokes feelings of delight, wonder, awe, and respect from those who perceive it.[26]

Among animals, only humans seem to show any appreciation for these qualities of integrity, harmony, and splendor.

Sense of morality and responsibility:

Fr. Paulinus Forsthoefel, a geneticist and Jesuit priest, sums up this difference between human beings and animals as follows:

> [Humans] are deeply concerned with what is right and what is wrong in human behavior. As far as we can tell, no animal ever reflects on whether what it is about to do is morally right or wrong. It is programmed by its heredity and experience to do what benefits it and its species and to avoid what does not. Thus the great devotion of a mother fox for its young is truly amazing, but she cannot help acting so....
>
> But true moral judgments are impossible for animals because such judgments presuppose an awareness of ethical principles. To formulate such principles is beyond an animal's capabilities. Animals have not yet arrived at a "Ten Commandments for Animals." Further, for ethical principles to have any meaning, one must presuppose the freedom to act or not to act in accord with them. Animals act according to their drives, their instincts. What in humans would be conscious self-sacrificing behavior, like that of the worker bees gathering nectar for the nourishment of the larvae in the hive, is purely for them instinctive behavior.[27]

Development of culture:

Unlike other animals, human beings preserve their culture, add to it, and pass it along to future generations. *Culture* is the web of behavior patterns, symbols, achievements, art, ideas, and values found in any human society. It includes things as commonplace as cooking styles and recipes to others as exalted as architecture, art, and music.[28]

Animals can learn from each other, but this occurs through mimicry. Although animals that are trained by humans might be imitated by other animals, the effects of human influence (learned signs, etc.) do not survive to the next generation, and fade away once that influence is removed.

But human cultures have survived and flourished for thousands of years. A culture is held in common by its human members, even while it grows and changes under the influence of new members or by the encounter with other cultures.

We did mention earlier that one example may have been found of an animal teaching and deliberately passing on learned behavior—

the example of Washoe and Loulis. However, the same researcher who claimed that Washoe taught Loulis also conceded that Loulis mainly learned by imitation.[29]

In summary, the gap between spiritual human rationality and physical animal intelligence is much more than a matter of brain size or advanced brain structure. It is a difference in kind. Man is more than a naked ape, although we should keep in mind that humans are animals as well—we do depend on our bodies and especially our brains in order to think. But we can transform purely instinctive patterns and brain activity, which we share with animals, into something much more. We can also fail to do so and not rise above the level of behavior which we share with the animals.[30] Indeed, we can choose to become far more depraved than any other animal could ever become.

The above list of differences between humans and animals reveals that the activities of other animals do not demonstrate rationality. What about intelligence among creatures that do not live? We now turn to artificial intelligence and the intelligence of computers.

C. Artificial Intelligence: Is the Human Mind a Complex Computer?

WELCOME TO THE COMPUTER AGE: DEFINING COMPUTERS

The world that we live in has been vastly changed through progress in technology and above all, in computer technology. Computers have become more and more powerful over time, and have been made capable of vastly more efficient and complex activities. Anyone who has used computers for five years or more is already aware that this progress continues at a very rapid pace.

A question that has been around for as long as computers, but is taken with increasing seriousness, is whether computers will ultimately be capable of thought at the human level. The reverse question also arises: is the human mind nothing more than a "wet computer" or "a machine made out of meat"? According to the materialist/reductionist mindset, the human mind is nothing more than the brain, which, with its sophisticated neural circuitry, certainly has a great deal in common with computers.

THE GAP BETWEEN SPIRITUAL HUMAN RATIONALITY AND PHYSICAL ANIMAL INTELLIGENCE IS MUCH MORE THAN A MATTER OF BRAIN SIZE OR ADVANCED BRAIN STRUCTURE. IT IS A DIFFERENCE IN KIND.

In 1996, what seemed to some like a devastating answer was given to this question. On February 10th of that year, the reigning world champion of chess, Gary Kasparov, was defeated by the program "Deep Blue" running on an IBM computer. Due to its ability to calculate all possible combinations on the board for the next ten to fifteen moves, the computer played at championship strength. The defeated Kasparov said that with Deep Blue, "quantity had become quality."[31]

Did Kasparov's defeat reveal that computer technology, or artificial intelligence, will ultimately develop all the qualities that human intelligence is capable of such as self-consciousness, abstraction, certitude, etc.? To answer that question we must first define what a computer is.

A *computer* is a machine that manipulates numbers, usually two numbers, 0 and 1. The computer is made capable of this by a human engineer who either establishes two types of voltages or magnetizes one piece of material and not another. These two then represent the two digits 0 and 1. In this sense, it is not really two numbers but rather material markers that represent those numbers that the computer manipulates.

The computer is then programmed to manipulate those markers according to an *algorithm*, a sequence of steps which act like a recipe, to produce new strings of markers. In this way, computers are capable of carrying out some forms of reasoning that have been reduced to routine steps by a programmer.[32] Though numerals are symbols (they stand in for mathematical realities), this process drains the numerals that are eventually computed of their meaning— "what is left is form without specific content": "Computers... cannot have any understanding of the meanings of the symbols they manipulate. A computer does not know whether the symbols it is printing out refers to numbers or to Tom, Dick and Harry."[33]

Presented with this argument, most reasonable people would acknowledge that the difference between human intelligence and artificial intelligence is unbridgeable, because computers fail to understand what they compute. However, many materialists would not be so easily convinced of this; they would question what "understanding" means. How can "understanding" be measured scientifically (i.e., through brain probes or some other physical process)? All that can be measured is what the computer actually computes, what it prints out. Ultimately, then, for extreme reductionists, "understanding" is nothing but a matter of computation and observable results. They would hold that humans, like computers, exhibit nothing more than computing skills when they solve a problem. However, even if we forget about "understanding," and keep to matters of mere computation, are computers equal to the human mind?

COMPUTERS CANNOT HAVE UNDERSTANDING OF THE MEANINGS OF THE SYMBOLS THEY MANIPULATE.

The answer is no, according to some eminent mathematicians and philosophers. Computers are much faster than the human brain and can keep much more information in their memories than we can, but they are severely limited by the fact that they have to follow a set of rigid rules—their "program" or "algorithm." In a sense they are trapped by their own rules, and thus cannot rise above a certain level. The argument that shows this is based on a powerful and epoch-making theorem that was proved in 1931 by the mathematician *Kurt Gödel*.

MATHEMATICS "OUTSIDE THE BOX": KURT GÖDEL AND THE LUCAS-PENROSE ARGUMENT

Mathematics involves understanding ideas. But a lot of it can be reduced to mechanical computation. Think of the rules for doing long division or multiplying two large numbers that you learned in elementary school. You could teach people to follow those mechanical rules even if they had no idea what they were doing or what it meant. In fact, you can teach a computer to follow those rules. The same can be done with more advanced kinds of mathematics too. Mathematical statements can be expressed in strings of symbols called "formulas," and then those formulas can be manipulated using mechanical rules to get new formulas. For example, you might start with the formula $a = b$ and by applying the rules of algebra get the formula $a + 1 = b + 1$, or the formula $a^2 = b^2$. To the extent that "doing mathematics" can be reduced to following rules, it can be done by machines. The question then arises as to whether *all* mathematics can be done by machines. And, if not, are there kinds of mathematics that we humans can do but machines cannot do? To put it another way, could human mathematicians be put out of business by machines?

When a kind of mathematics is reduced to a system of symbols and formulas and rules for manipulating them, it is said to have been "formalized" or reduced to a "formal system." In 1931, the great mathematician Kurt Gödel proved that mathematics cannot be completely formalized, in his two incompleteness theorems. There is more to "doing mathematics" than blindly following rules; therefore, there is more to it than a machine can do.

Gödel started by asking what would happen if mathematics *could* be completely formalized. If that could be done, it would be possible to prove *any true mathematical formula* just by following the rules. What Gödel discovered was that this is impossible no matter how many rules are put into place. In fact, Gödel showed how to take any set of self-consistent mathematical rules and "beat the system," so to speak, by finding true formulas that cannot be proved just by

THERE IS MORE TO "DOING MATHEMATICS" THAN BLINDLY FOLLOWING RULES; THEREFORE, THERE IS MORE TO IT THAN A MACHINE CAN DO.

THE ABILITY TO UNDERSTAND AND TO GRASP ABSTRACT IDEAS GIVES THE HUMAN MIND THE POWER TO EXPLORE THE WORLD OF MATHEMATICAL TRUTHS BEYOND THE POWER OF A MERE COMPUTING MACHINE.

following those rules. The formula that he used to show how to find such formulas is called a "*Gödel formula*" in his honor. No matter how you try to reduce mathematics to following rules, there are always Gödel formulas that cannot be proved that way, but which are nevertheless true mathematical statements. And the remarkable fact is that not only are the Gödel formulas true, but *we human beings can prove that they are true*—in fact Gödel showed they are true. The reason we are able to show they are true is that we know how to think in ways that are not in the rulebook. We can "think outside the box."

This suggests that we are not just machines that follow rules. Indeed, Gödel himself was convinced that the human mind was more than just a machine. That materialist idea he called "a superstition of our time." However, Gödel did not try to use his famous theorem to prove anything about the human mind—at least he did not publish any such proof. The first person to do that was a philosopher at Oxford University named *John R. Lucas*, who published his argument in the 1960s. It attracted a lot of attention, but it did not convince many materialists, who thought his arguments were not rigorous enough to be convincing.

Lucas's argument was taken up again by an eminent mathematician named *Roger Penrose*, who defended it and tried to make it more rigorous in a book entitled *The Emperor's New Mind*, published in 1989. Again, many people tried to tear the argument down by showing that it had logical flaws. In 1994, Penrose replied to the arguments of his critics in a book called *Shadows of the Mind*. The debate continues to this day.

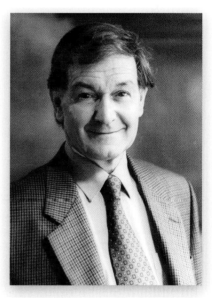

Roger Penrose

Penrose, unlike Gödel and Lucas, is not a religious believer. However, his experience as a mathematician has convinced him that the human mind's power to explore the world of mathematical truths lies far beyond the power of a mere computing machine. According to him, what gives the human mind that power is precisely its ability to *understand*, to grasp abstract ideas. A computer is trapped in its own rules. A human being, by contrast, can think about the rules themselves. He can understand why they have the structure they do and what their limitations are. He can use his mathematical insights to discover new rules that are consistent with the old ones, but go beyond them. He can discover new ways of proving things, rather than following the well-worn grooves of old mathematical ways of reasoning. A human being can think about any and all propositions, and can even reason about the process of reasoning. At this level even a human child can do more than the fastest, best designed computer.

A computer can use numbers, adding them and subtracting them. But a child can grasp the concept of *number*, a concept that embraces the entire series of numbers, which is infinite. The human mind does not simply compute, it *comprehends*, which literally means "holds together," a vast, even infinite multiplicity of things in a single, simple insight.[34]

Here we see the image of God once again—the human mind's ability to image God is revealed in its ability to understand things in a simple, undivided way. God is a simple and indivisible unity, an infinite act of understanding that grasps all of reality in a single thought. God is the Infinite Mind; man, by reflection, is the finite mind,[35] a reality which no computer, no machine however sophisticated, can begin to match. If Penrose and Lucas are right, then the incompleteness theorems of Kurt Gödel are telling us something that faith has known all along.

We have considered two major challenges to the superiority of man and of his imaging of God. The third is different. While the first two are related to reason, the last is related to free will.

D. Human Freedom and Modern Science

CAUSAL DETERMINISM: THE HUMAN WILL ON THE CUTTING EDGE

In Chapter Five, we were introduced to Pierre-Simon Laplace, the nineteenth century French scientist who said of God that "he had no need of that hypothesis" in understanding the solar system. Laplace is also famous for giving one of the clearest expressions of an idea called *physical determinism* or *causal determinism*. This is the idea that the universe operates only according to fixed laws that determine everything that happens within it.

According to physical determinism, if someone knew all of the laws of the universe as well as everything going on in the universe at some point in time, he could predict exactly all the events that would later happen in the universe. (Of course, he would have to have a mind of infinite power to do the calculations.) This is often called the "billiard ball" hypothesis because it makes the whole universe like an enormous pool table—as long as you know the data about the balls, you know exactly what will happen when this one hits that one, and when that one hits the next one, etc. Those who hold such an idea also place human beings on the great cosmic pool table. While we tend to consider ourselves as possessing freedom, determinism says that what we imagine to be free actions are actually entirely determined by the vast system of the universe.

OUR CHOICES ARE NOT FORCED BY PHYSICAL CAUSES, ALTHOUGH THEY CAN CERTAINLY BE INFLUENCED BY THEM.

Pierre-Simon Laplace

QUANTUM INDETERMINANCY

PROVIDES THE POSSIBILITY FOR

FREE WILL TO EXIST.

According to Laplace;

> We may regard the present state of the universe as the effect of its past and the cause of its future. For an intellect which at a certain moment would know all forces that set nature in motion—nothing would be uncertain and the future just like the past would be present before its eyes.[36]

This idea directly challenges a key element in man's imaging of God—human freedom. If determinism were correct, then the world would be "causally closed"—completely sealed off from anything other than physical causes that follow precise, inflexible laws. Human behavior would be totally determined, as would everything else in the material universe. And in fact, this seemed to be the case to many scientists up until the 1920's, when quantum theory, "the greatest and most profound revolution in the history of physics,"[37] blew the determinism of Laplace out of the water.

QUANTUM THEORY: THE PROBABLE VERSUS THE PREDICTABLE

Quantum theory developed out of the study of light and subatomic particles.[38] It is a theory that applies to matter at its tiniest levels, "the level of electrons, protons, neutrons, quarks," etc.[39] The details of quantum physics are extremely complex and difficult to explain. They were also extremely shocking to those who believed in a rigidly deterministic universe.

What quantum theory revealed was that, even if we had all of the information about a physical system at one time, we still could not predict its future behavior with certainty but only with a relative probability. *Quantum indeterminacy* refers to the fact that the nature of the universe is *probabilistic* (based on probabilities) versus *deterministic* (completely inflexible).[40]

Quantum indeterminacy does not prove free will, but it does provide the possibility for it. Free will is a spiritual faculty. In order for it to exist, it must have "room to operate"—that is, the world of matter, especially the human brain, must not be totally under the control of physical laws. For free will to exist, the laws of physics must have indeterminacy built into them. Quantum theory reveals that they do.[41]

Our choices are not forced by physical causes, although they can certainly be influenced by them. Once again the development of science reveals that the challenge of scientific materialism does not rule out the truth of the Christian Faith.

E. Conclusion: "Man Outweighs the Entire Work of Creation"

In a series of catechetical lectures, Christoph Cardinal Schönborn takes on some of the challenges to the unique dignity of the human person. He points out that our age is faced with a crucial question about humanity: is man still to be regarded as the "crown of creation," or has he sunk to the level of an insignificant speck on a "tiny satellite of a marginal star"? Schönborn answers the question by quoting a saying of the Jewish rabbis: "Man outweighs the entire work of creation":

- Yes, man exists on a speck, but an "inconceivably privileged" one that, as far as we know, is the only planet in the universe which supports life, including beings who can know the universe for what it is;

- Yes, man is a part of nature, sharing many qualities with the animals, but is also a creature that can examine that place, think about it, and exercise free will in shaping it and caring for it;

- Yes, man is directed by "instincts" and "drives," but only he can know this and come to understand it. Only he can know his moral obligation to raise himself above those instincts and drives and order them responsibly.[42]

In man, an animal body becomes the expression and visible manifestation of an immortal soul. In man, animal memory, sensory perception, and image apprehension, become comprehension, self-consciousness, and objectivity. In man, animal appetites and inclinations become the foundation of love and of "purpose-driven lives." Man is the transformation of the animal and material cosmos into a spiritualized nobility it would never be capable of otherwise. Man crowns creation by being the perfect expression of what creation can be.

But our picture of man and his uniqueness would be incomplete without consideration of perhaps the most controversial issue, involving human beings, on the cutting edge of faith and science— human evolution and the issue of the origins of humanity.

MAN IS THE TRANSFORMATION OF THE ANIMAL AND MATERIAL COSMOS INTO A SPIRITUALIZED NOBILITY IT WOULD NEVER BE CAPABLE OF OTHERWISE.

MAN CROWNS CREATION BY BEING THE PERFECT EXPRESSION OF WHAT CREATION CAN BE.

Supplementary Reading

Image or Illusion?
Scientific Challenges
to Human Dignity and Personhood

1. "CHALLENGES TO MAN'S SUPERIORITY AND DIGNITY"

(excerpted from Christoph Cardinal Schönborn, "What is Man that Thou are Mindful of Him? Is Man Really the "Crown of Creation"?" Internet. Available from http://stephanscom.at/edw/katechesen/articles/2006/07/17/a11155; accessed April 2, 2007.)

In the pastoral constitution, *Gaudium et spes*, Vatican II said, "Believers and unbelievers agree almost unanimously that all things on earth should be ordained to man as to their center and summit."

Is this position still tenable 40 years later? Is everything on earth really ordered to man?... To call man the crown of creation sounds for many like an arrogant excess of self-esteem. Today we read and hear that while *faith* raised man high above all other living beings, *science* has cast him down from his lofty pedestal.

It has become standard to speak of the three main ways in which science has given offense to man's sense of his worth. On this subject the well-known investigator of human behavior, Anton Festetics, has written:

The first offense came from Copernicus in Cracow (the earth is not the center of the universe), the second came from Darwin in London (we come from the animals) and the third came from Freud in Vienna (the analysis of our psyche). We were offended most of all by Darwin's blasphemy about our kinship with the primates, a fact which embarrasses us and angers us, since precisely the apes look so similar to us as to mimic us. (*Die Presse*, January 1, 2006, p. 30.)

235

Supplementary Reading

Just one more example that serves to strengthen man's sense of being offended by scientific progress: A few months ago scientists succeeded in decoding the genome of the chimpanzee; it is supposedly over ninety-eight percent identical with the human genome. "The crown of creation" has been shaken. It has strong competition.

Man as crown of creation has been challenged in three ways:

1) The earth has lost its central position in the world, it now exists somewhere on the edge of a galaxy of over a hundred billion stars and this galaxy exists on the edge of over one hundred billion galaxies in the universe.

2) Man comes from the animals. This need not be a problem for faith nor even for reason, as we shall see. What stirs up controversy is the supposition that man emerged in a gradual way from nature, that there is, as a result, no fundamental discontinuity between animal and man, no metaphysical difference between them. Man as a being endowed with spirit is thought to be nothing radically new in the vast world of life.

3) The soul of man has been cast down from its spiritual height and been debunked as the mask of unconscious drives. Man is determined not by spirit but by libido. Being thus dethroned in these three ways, the crown of creation is now rolling, as it were, in the dirt. If man remains here in the dirt, then science has definitively dethroned man. Is man a king or a slave? What is man? Psalm 8 prays:

> When I consider thy heavens, the work of thy fingers, the moon and the stars which thou has ordained: what is man that thou are mindful of him? and the son of man that thou visitest him? (vv. 4–5)

Is man a piece of nature or the crown of creation? Or is he both? Does he come from the animals, or is he a special creation of God, or is he both? Modern science has pushed him to the edge of the universe, reducing him to a tiny point on a tiny planet. Is he, on the contrary, the most essential goal of the gigantic event of the coming to be of our world?

Supplementary Reading

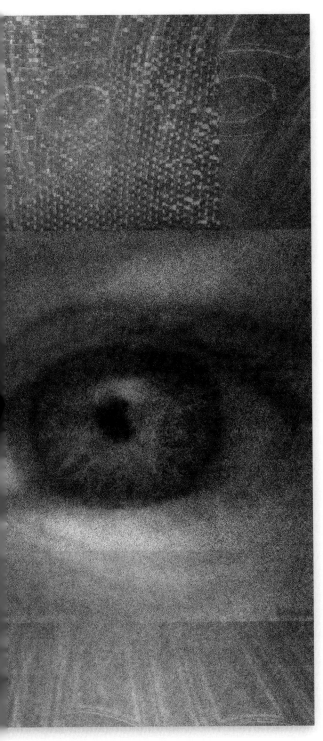

Or is he both? Is he humiliated as a result of realizing that he is lost in the universe, or is he exalted as a result of being the point in the universe, tiny as the point is, where the universe can become aware of itself and reflect on itself? The psalmist continues in his prayer of praise:

> For thou hast made him a little lower than the angels, and hast crowned him with glory and honor. Thou madest him to have dominion over the works of they hands: thou has put all things under his feet: all sheep and oxen, yea, and the beasts of the field; the fowl of the air, and the fish of the sea, and whatsover passeth through the paths of the seas. O Lord our Lord, how excellent is thy name in all the earth! (vv. 6–10)

2. "A PROOF OF THE HUMAN SOUL: BY MATERIALISTS!"

(excerpted from Christoph Cardinal Schönborn, "What is Man that Thou are Mindful of Him? Is Man Really the "Crown of Creation"?" Internet. Available from http://stephanscom.at/edw/katechesen/ articles/2006/07/17/a11155; accessed April 2, 2007.)

Materialism is intellectually untenable, it is in fact self-contradictory.... Let me clarify... by bringing in the beautiful example used by the Jewish philosopher Hans Jonas. In writing his great work, *The Ethics of Responsibility*, he realized that all talk of ethics and responsibility makes no sense if there is no spirit, no soul, no reason, no free will. Genes do not accept responsibility. They are not arraigned in court when they produce cancer cells. Neither are animals held accountable. Only human beings have responsibility because they can (normally) be held accountable for their deeds... Here is the example that Hans Jonas uses to refute materialism.

Around the year 1845 in Berlin a group of like-minded young physiologists was formed. They were disciples of the famous Johannes Mueller and wanted to transform physiology into an "exact" science. They met each week

Supplementary Reading

at the home of the physicist, Gustav Magnus. Two of them,

Ernst Bruecke and Emil du Bois-Reymond, solemnly swore "to uphold the truth that there are no other forces at work in an organism than the common physical-chemical forces." The young Helmholtz soon joined these two (who had met him in the home of Magnus) as a third taker of the oath. As each of the three rose to great fame and brilliant scientific success, they remained faithful to their youthful commitment. But what escaped them was the fact that the act of entering into this oath already violated the oath. In the act of swearing they entrusted the control over the functioning of their brains to something entirely non-physical, namely to their relation to truth; and yet by the content of their oath they denied this control in principle. To promise something, knowing that you can either do the thing promised or take the equally available option of not doing it: this is to grant that there is within the whole of reality a power that is different from the forces that are inherent in matter and at work in the interaction of inorganic bodies. (*Macht und Ohnmacht des Subjektivitaet*, Frankfurt, 1981, p. 13 ff.)

What follows from this? These three scholars were right to admit, for the purpose of their scientific research, only "physical-chemical forces." But they were wrong in assuming that this says *everything* there is to say about man. Their oath shows that there is the dimension of spirit, soul, reason, freedom, which cannot in turn be the product of the material conditions for spiritual activities.

But if the spiritual principle in man cannot derive from its material conditions, whence does it derive? Reason requires us to assume a spiritual principle in man that the philosophical traditions have usually called "soul." Only the *soul* makes man fully man. Though it cannot be scientifically "demonstrated," there could not be, without this spiritual principle that transcends matter, any such thing as science, which is after all a

Supplementary Reading

"spiritual function."

3. "GREAT THINGS IN SMALL PACKAGES: POPE BENEDICT XVI ON HUMAN GREATNESS AND HUMAN SMALLNESS"

(excerpted from God and The World: A Conversation with Peter Seewald [San Francisco: Ignatius Press, 2002], pp.118–121).

On Man's Greatness

...Man's greatness is quite undeniable. This little creature, which biologically is among the more deprived creatures, with diminished sensual sensibilities (here, too, we see greatness in what is inferior), has developed faculties that open up space to him. Man can look out into space with his human eye and turn again from outer space to gaze upon the tiniest details of his own life. Again, he has in this way penetrated into the chambers of the wellsprings of life itself, so that he can now attempt either to change it or, alternatively, to make good use of it and help its development.

I think that the greatness of man is more obvious to us nowadays than ever before.... Man, ...with all humanity, holds in his hands the entire sum of hidden human potential....

He is called to greatness, but his freedom can allow the contrary temptation, that of wanting to be great over against God and thus to become a kind of anti-God, to develop into a serious threat....

On Man's Smallness

...God took man, on this little speck of dust that is earth, so seriously that he came and lived here himself and has bound himself to this earth for all eternity.

That corresponds to the model of divine action that is known to us. God always takes up exactly what seems unimportant and shows himself to man in what seems like a speck of dust, or, as in Nazareth, in a little place that is next to nowhere. Thus God always corrects our standards of judgment. It shows that what is quantitatively immeasurable belongs to a quite different order of reality from the immeasurability of the heart, as Pascal has already remarked. What is quantitative has its own indisputable status, but it is also important to see this quantitative value, for instance the infinite size of the universe, in relative terms. One single understanding and loving heart has quite another immeasurable greatness. It corresponds to a quite different order from any quantitative entity, in all its great power, but it is no less great.

Study Guide

Image or Illusion?
Scientific Challenges
to Human Dignity and Personhood

VOCABULARY

Define the following terms:

1. Trancend
2. Bertrand Russell
3. Astonishing Hypothesis (Crick)
4. Washoe
5. Kanzi
6. Koko
7. Clever Hans Effect
8. Herbert Terrace
9. Thomas and Jean Sebeok
10. Anthropomorphic Fallacy
11. Language
12. Self-Consciousness
13. Beauty
14. Unity (integrity)
15. Harmony (consonance)
16. Splendor
17. Culture
18. Computer
19. Algorithm
20. Formal System
21. Kurt Gödel
22. Gödel Formula
23. John Lucas and Roger Penrose
24. Causal Determinism
25. Quantum Theory
26. Quantum Indeterminacy
27. Probabilistic

STUDY QUESTIONS

1. What are the basic claims of scientism regarding the human person?
2. What three attributes of man are challenged and/or denied by scientism?
3. How does the Clever Hans effect challenge the claim that animal intelligence and human intelligence are different only in degree and not in kind?
4. What flaw did Herbert Terrace reveal to be inherent in animal intelligence research?
5. What flaws did the Sebeoks locate in animal intelligence research?
6. What criticism did Noam Chomsky offer of claims of language ability in animals?
7. How does human self-consciousness reveal human rationality to be essentially different from and superior to animal intelligence?
8. How does human awareness of time reveal human rationality to be essentially different from and superior to animal intelligence?
9. How does the human appreciation of beauty reveal human rationality to be essentially different from and superior to animal intelligence?
10. How does the human sense of morality and responsibility reveal human rationality to be essentially different from and superior to animal intelligence?

Study Guide

11. How does the human phenomenon of culture reveal human rationality to be essentially different from and superior to animal intelligence?

12. How does the very nature of algorithms reveal artificial intelligence to be essentially inferior to human rationality?

13. How would a materialist respond to the claim that computers do not understand what they compute?

14. Explain how Gödel's Theorem, as explained by Lucas and Penrose, reveals a capacity in human rationality not possessed by any computer. What is this capacity?

15. How does Lucas and Penrose's use of Gödel's Theorem forcefully demonstrate that man is the image of God, if we understand God as "the unrestricted infinite act of understanding"?

16. How does quantum theory remove the obstacle of causal determinism to the recognition of human freedom?

PRACTICAL EXERCISES

1. Apply the anthropomorphic fallacy to your experience of your own pet (or any animal). Have you ever thought that your pet might have a human, spiritual form of intelligence? If so, how might your interaction with the animal have influenced its behavior?

2. Describe an experience of something beautiful, using the characteristics of beauty described in the text.

3. Man is defined by Aristotle as a "rational animal." What characteristics do we share with animals? How are those characteristics transformed by the "hallmarks of human rationality" described in this chapter?

Endnotes

1. CCC 1705; GS 17.
2. Barr, 168.
3. Ibid., 20.
4. Ibid., 170.
5. Bonnette, 74–75.
6. Barr, 171.
7. Ibid., 171–172.
8. Francis Crick, as quoted in John Haught, *Science and Religion: From Conflict to Conversation* (New York: Paulist, 1995), 72.
9. Barbour, 155.
10. Forsthoefel, 90.
11. Suzanne Chevalier-Skolnikoff, "Cuing and Ape-Signing. A Piagetian Analysis of Methods for Instructing Animals" in Thomas A. Sebeok and Robert Rosenthal, ed., *The Clever Hans Phenomenon: Communication with Horses, Whales, Apes and People* (New York: New York Academy of Sciences, 1981), 89–90.
12. Eugene Linden, "Can Animals Think?" *Time* (3/22/93).

13. Ibid.
14. Bonnette, 90.
15. Ibid., 86–87.
16. Ibid., 87–88.
17. Ibid., 75.
18. Thomas A. Sebeok and Jean Umiker-Sebeok, "Performing Animals: Secrets of the Trade" *Psychology Today* 13 (November 1979): 91.
19. Bonnette, 80–81.
20. Forsthoefel, 91.
21. Ibid., 29–95.
22. Walker Percy, *Lost in the Cosmos: The Last Self-Help Book* (New York: Farrar, Straus and Giroux, 1983), 254.
23. Forsthoefel, 92–93.
24. Bonnette, 98–99.
25. Ibid., 163–164.
26. Clarke, 298–302.
27. Forsthoefel, 94.
28. *New Catholic Encyclopedia*, second ed., s.v. "Culture" (Washington, D.C.: Thomson Gale, 2003).

29. Bonnette, 74.
30. Forsthoefel, 95.
31. Charles Krauthammer, "Deep Blue Funk: Kasparov Wrestles a Machine. Civilization Hangs in the Balance," *Time* (2/26/1996).
32. Barr, 207–209.
33. Ibid., 210.
34. Ibid., 221–224.
35. Ibid., 225.
36. Laplace, *A philosophical essay on probabilities*, §2.
37. Forsthoefel, 175–176.
38. Collins, *The Language of God*, 81.
39. C. John Collins, *Science and Faith: Friends or Foes?* (Wheaton: Crossway Books, 2003), 221.
40. Barr, 176.
41. Ibid., 179.
42. Schönborn, "What is Man that Thou art Mindful of Him?"

Chapter Eleven

The Emergence of the Image: Modern Science and the Origins of Humanity

A. "A Little Child(?) Shall Lead Them": The Dikika Baby and the Origins of Humanity

In December 2000, in a remote part of Africa north of the Ethiopian badlands along the Great Rift Valley, a team of scientists came face to face with an amazing glimpse into the past. While fossil hunting, they spotted a small skull peering down a slope. Years of painstaking excavation revealed other bones as well: a torso, a foot, a kneecap, and tiny finger bones. The skull even contained teeth, which further examination revealed to be baby teeth.

Ultimately, scientists identified the bones to be those of a baby, probably a female of about three years of age at the time of her death, the cause of which is still unknown. But the date of that death is just as important—using sophisticated methods of dating, scientists estimate the age of the bones to be 3.3 million years, making it the world's oldest fossil of its kind.[1]

This fossil, nicknamed the *Dikika Baby* after the place where it was found, has been hailed as a tremendously important find for understanding human origins. According to the majority of experts, the Dikika Baby is a member of *Australopithecus afarensis*,

AS WE ATTEMPT TO REDISCOVER FAITH ON THE FRONTIERS OF MODERN SCIENCE, THE DIKIKA BABY POINTS TO A KEY ISSUE: HOW CAN WE RELATE WHAT WE KNOW FROM FAITH TO WHAT WE KNOW FROM SCIENCE ABOUT HUMAN ORIGINS? HOW CAN ONE SAY THAT MAN IS MADE IN THE IMAGE OF GOD, AND ALSO THAT HE BEARS AN ANCESTRAL LINK TO PRIMATES SUCH AS CHIMPANZEES AND GORILLAS?

an evolutionary ancestor of all human beings. Scientists were astonished to find that the Dikika Baby had a lower body much like a human child's and an upper body and head with ape-like features, including shoulder blades that would be useful for climbing. These suggest a creature which could walk on two feet but also climb and spend time in trees.[2]

As we attempt to rediscover faith on the frontiers of modern science, the Dikika Baby points to a key issue: how can we relate what we know from faith to what we know from science about human origins? How can one say that man is made in the image of God, and also that he bears an ancestral link to primates such as chimpanzees and gorillas?

"The Lord does not look at the things man looks at. Man looks at the outward appearance, but the Lord looks at the heart" (1 Sm 16: 7). These words from the Old Testament remind us that appearances can be deceiving. Could the Dikika baby's discovery be a stepping stone, rather than a stumbling block, on the path to greater understanding of God and his divinely revealed truth? Perhaps this little primate, herself not human with a rational soul but almost certainly an animal ancestor of humans, may lead us to a deeper appreciation of God's magnificent wisdom, love, and power—a wisdom, love, and power which links the Dikika Baby to you and to me.

In order to make sense of the Dikika Baby, let us start with Divine Revelation as offered us in Sacred Scripture, Sacred Tradition, and in the teaching of the Church, and then consider the contributions of modern science. Following this, we will consider the ways the two might be related in a search for contact between them.

Our main question is this: can the scientific evidence regarding the evolution of the human species illuminate what God has revealed about the origins of humanity in Scripture and Church teaching? Approaching both with respect for the nature of each, in an attitude of faith seeking understanding, we can hope to obtain great insights into the emergence of the divine image which is the human person.

Let us begin by examining the Church's teaching on biological evolution itself, particularly as it relates to the origins of humanity.

B. Human Evolution in Catholic Teaching

The Christian Faith does not forbid or reject the possibility that human beings received their bodies from a long process of descent from animals, a divinely guided process that may well have begun with a single-celled organism billions of years prior to the appearance of humanity. Although we have seen openness to something like evolution in thinkers such as St. Augustine and St. Thomas Aquinas, evolution had to emerge as a scientific theory of human origins before the Church could teach about it directly.

Following its emergence and growing acceptance in the scientific community, the first reference to evolution in official Catholic teaching occurred in the teaching of *Pope Pius XII.* In his 1950 encyclical *Humani generis*, he declared that human evolution is not intrinsically opposed to God's Revelation:

> ...the teaching authority of the Church does not forbid that, in conformity with the present state of the human sciences and sacred theology, research and discussions, on the part of men experienced in both fields, take place with regard to the doctrine of evolution, insofar as it inquires into the origin of the human body as coming from pre-existent and living matter, for the Catholic Faith obliges us to hold that souls are immediately [i.e., directly] created by God.[3]

Pope Pius XII

The words "pre-existent and living matter" sound strange to ears not accustomed to philosophical and theological terminology, but actually they are easy to understand. *Pre-existent* refers to "prior to becoming human." *Living matter* means "already a living organism," i.e., an animal. In this teaching we can see, fifty years before her discovery, that the Dikika Baby's relation to humanity is by no means forbidden as a possibility by the Church. (*How* a living animal, even a higher primate, could suddenly become human is a matter that we will return to later in this chapter.)

In 1986, *Pope John Paul II* reaffirmed Pius XII's openness in an even more positive way. While Pius XII had not forbidden research and discussions regarding evolution, John Paul II went further by declaring that:

> There are no difficulties in explaining the origin of man in regard to the body by means of the theory of evolution. According to the hypothesis mentioned it is possible that the human body, following the order impressed by the Creator on the energies of life, could have gradually been prepared in the form of *antecedent living beings* [i.e., living beings that existed prior to humanity].[4]

ACCORDING TO JOHN PAUL II, THERE ARE NO DIFFICULTIES IN EXPLAINING THE ORIGIN OF MAN IN REGARD TO THE BODY BY MEANS OF THE THEORY OF EVOLUTION.

But again, following Sacred Scripture and the whole history of Church teaching, John Paul affirmed the truth about the human soul:

> The doctrine of faith affirms that man's spiritual soul is created directly by God ... the human soul, on which man's humanity definitively depends, cannot emerge from matter, since the soul is of a spiritual nature.[5]

The pope's 1986 statement contained the assertion that the evolutionary origin of the human body is a hypothesis, "only a probability not a scientific certainty." However, he would use much bolder language a

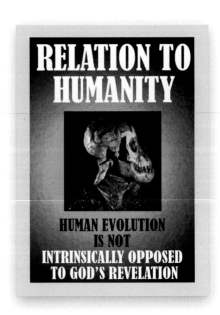

RELATION TO HUMANITY

HUMAN EVOLUTION IS NOT INTRINSICALLY OPPOSED TO GOD'S REVELATION

decade later. On October 22, 1996, the pope addressed the Pontifical Academy of Sciences regarding evolution. Looking back to Pius XII's statement in 1950, the pope declared that the increasing probability of biological evolution revealed through new findings "lead us toward recognition of evolution as more than a hypothesis."[6]

This increase in certainty about evolution was the result of "different scholarly disciplines" all converging in their discoveries on the conclusion that evolution is the truth about animal and human life. The strength of the evolutionary hypothesis had been bolstered by various researchers in different fields all discovering independently the same phenomena which point to the truth of evolution.[7]

The pope also noted that evolution is not a single theory; actually, when it comes to the question, "Why evolution?", there are many theories. Some of these are "materialist and reductionist theories" that are not compatible with the truth about God revealed in the Christian Faith.[8] The pope gives as examples theories which make man's spiritual reality nothing more than the product of physical forces or which describe the soul as epiphenomenal. *Epiphenomenalism* is the theory that spirit exists along with the body, is dependent upon matter, and ceases to exist when the body ceases to exist. These theories, and others, do not do justice to the truth about human beings as the image and likeness of God.[9]

At this point, the pope tells us something crucial for understanding the relationship between evolution and faith regarding human origins: "With man, we find ourselves facing a different *ontological* order—an *ontological* leap." "Ontological" refers to existence, and "ontological order" is another way of saying "level of existence." For example, animals are of a higher ontological order than plants. The pope is saying that the "leap" to rationality and spirituality that occurred at the origins of humanity puts us on a fundamentally higher level of existence than other animals. In other words, while man's origin did not involve a rupture in the physical animal world, it did involve a leap to a higher level, in which the animal world was brought up to a qualitatively better way of existing.

Evolutionary science cannot follow this leap because it is a "passage into the spiritual realm": "the sciences... describe and measure with ever greater precision, the many manifestations of life, and write them down along the time line. [But] [t]he moment of passage into the spiritual realm is not something that can be observed this way...."[10]

In fact, John Paul II explains exactly why man cannot simply be scientifically observed:

> [Man's] experience of metaphysical knowledge, of self-consciousness and self-awareness, of moral conscience, of liberty, or of *aesthetic and religious experience* [i.e., the experience of beauty and of God]—these must be analyzed

through philosophical reflection, while theology seeks to clarify the ultimate meaning of the Creator's designs.[11]

So, according to John Paul II, we cannot simply approach the evolutionary data, such as the fossil record and the human genetic code, and expect to understand man's origins entirely. We must apply philosophical and theological reasoning if we are to discern the whole truth about humanity, especially the reality of the human soul.

But the pope does not dismiss science's contribution. Through "experimental research," valuable signs of "specifically human life" can be detected.[12] Later, we will see that scientific investigations into the presence of tool-making and of burial rituals among certain of our prehistoric forebears qualify as examples of the "experimental research" to which the pope refers.

With John Paul II's 1996 address, we come to his last official teaching on the issue of evolution as it relates to human origins. Recently, *Pope Benedict XVI* reaffirmed John Paul II's teaching in a question-and-answer session with priests that was held in Italy on July 24, 2007. He specifically rejected the opinion of some in the United States and Germany that "whoever believes in the Creator cannot think about evolution and whoever affirms evolution must exclude God." Calling this position an absurdity, he remarked as follows:

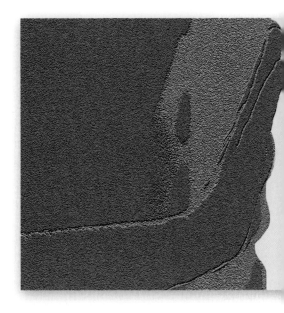

> …there is a great deal of scientific proof in favor of evolution, which appears as a reality that we must see and that enriches our knowledge of life and of being as such.

The pope also echoed John Paul II in regard to the insufficiency of a purely scientific view which leaves out philosophy and theology:

> But the doctrine of evolution does not answer everything and does not answer the great philosophical question: Where does everything come from? And how does everything take a path that ultimately leads to the person? It seems to me that it is very important that reason opens up even more, that it sees this information [about evolution], but that it also sees that this information is not enough to explain all of reality.[13]

Benedict XVI offered another comment on evolution at the dawn of his papacy, during his inaugural homily. He declared that "we are not some casual and meaningless product of evolution. Each of us is the result of a thought of God. Each of us is willed, each of us is loved, each of us is necessary."[14] His declaration must remain fresh in our minds when we turn to the scientific data regarding evolution and human origins. The process described by science can only be truly understood if we see it as not only a natural process, but also as an act of divine love. But first, let us look at the specific contributions of Divine Revelation to understanding human origins.

"WE ARE NOT SOME CASUAL AND MEANINGLESS PRODUCT OF EVOLUTION. EACH OF US IS THE RESULT OF A THOUGHT OF GOD. EACH OF US IS WILLED, EACH OF US IS LOVED, EACH OF US IS NECESSARY." (BENEDICT XVI, HOMILY, MASS FOR THE INAUGURATION OF HIS PONTIFICATE)

C. The Origins of Humanity According to Divine Revelation

THE CREATION ACCOUNT IN GENESIS 2–3

Our consideration of the origins of humanity according to Divine Revelation begins with Genesis 2–3. Genesis 2, as we have already seen, describes the creation of the first man and the first woman. Genesis 3, also known as the account of the Fall, narrates the event of man's temptation and the first sin. Both are crucial to understanding what God has revealed regarding the emergence of his image—the human person.

In the poetic and beautiful picture offered us in Genesis 2, the second creation account portrays the creation of man as an artistic endeavor on the part of God, the divine artist. In it, man is fashioned from mud, but is given the breath of life through which he becomes a living being (Gn 2:7). The man whom God creates is clearly different from the animals that surround him in the visible world. The man names those animals, and also finds none of them to be a suitable partner for him (Gn 2:18–22), showing his uniqueness and his qualitative superiority over the animals.

The account also speaks of God's creation of the first woman from the man: "The Lord God cast a deep sleep on the man, and while he was asleep, he took out one of his ribs and closed up its place with flesh. The Lord God then built into a woman the rib that he had taken from the man" (Gn 2:21–22). The glory of the woman God created is revealed in the man's response to her: "This one, at last, is bone of my bone and flesh of my flesh!" (Gn 2:23). As we saw in Chapter Nine, man and woman are each willed by God and destined for unity with one another.

Adam and Eve

The second creation account also notes a certain peace and tranquility in the first human couple. In fact, the text tells us that "they felt no shame" although they both were naked (Gn 2:25). This beautiful situation is quickly darkened through a moral tragedy. *Sin*, freely committed disobedience against God, enters the picture when the man and woman eat of the fruit of the tree God had forbidden them to eat (Gn 3:1–6). The event is followed by a scene in which the man and woman hide themselves from God and each other by covering their nakedness (Gn 3:7–8). When God confronts them, he describes the consequences of their sin—suffering and death await them due to their disobedience (Gn 3:14–19).

THE CHURCH'S INTERPRETATION OF GENESIS 2–3

What do these divinely inspired narratives reveal to us about the origins of humanity? The Church, established by Christ to teach the truth God has revealed through him, gives us clear guidance in how to understand the meaning of the story of man's creation and fall.

The first and most basic truth revealed in this story is that God willed the human race; in fact, humanity is the central reason for God's creation of the universe. As the Second Vatican Council proclaimed, man is "the only creature on Earth that God has willed for its own sake;"[15] "God created everything for man," echoes the *Catechism*.[16] This can be seen in Genesis 2–3 in the special attention and care which God gives to man in comparison to all the other animals.

The second key truth revealed in Genesis 2–3, as well as in other places in Sacred Scripture, is that all humans have a common origin. Humanity is a unity—a single family. The woman described in the story is called Eve "because she became the mother of all the living" (Gn 3:20). All the peoples of the Earth of all times are truly brothers and sisters, even while we recognize the variety that exists among us. Hence the Church has always rejected *racism*, or "unjust discrimination on the basis of a person's race," as a "violation of human dignity and a sin against justice."[17]

A third truth revealed in Genesis 2–3 is something we have already recognized but should repeat: man is not purely physical but also spiritual. The breath of life which God blows into the nostrils of the first man refers to man's soul, which is created directly by God at the origin of every human life and is imperishable.

A fourth truth is that God not only made man good, as he did the other animals, but also established him in a friendship with himself, in harmony with the Creator and with the rest of creation. The Church teaches that Adam and Eve were holy, created in a state in which they had perfect freedom from any slavery to "the pleasures of the senses, covetousness for earthly goods, and *self-assertion*," which is the tendency to place one's self at the center of one's life and priorities without reference to God or others. This inner harmony which results from harmony with God and results in harmony with each other is called *original justice*. As long as the man and the woman remained without sin, God promised them that, by a special preternatural gift, they would also be free from suffering and death.[18]

But this blissful state was lost through sin on the part of our first parents in an event which is called *the Fall*. This sad event, though expressed in figurative language in Genesis 3, really took place at the beginning of human history:

SECOND VATICAN COUNCIL PROCLAIMED, MAN IS "THE ONLY CREATURE ON EARTH THAT GOD HAS WILLED FOR ITS OWN SAKE;" "GOD CREATED EVERYTHING FOR MAN," ECHOES THE *CATECHISM*. THIS CAN BE SEEN IN GENESIS 2–3 IN THE SPECIAL ATTENTION AND CARE WHICH GOD GIVES TO MAN IN COMPARISON TO ALL THE OTHER ANIMALS.

Man, tempted by the devil, let his trust in his Creator die in his heart and, abusing his freedom, disobeyed God's command. This is what man's first sin consisted of. All subsequent sin would be disobedience toward God and lack of trust in his goodness. In that sin man *preferred* himself to God and by that very act scorned him. He chose himself over and against God, against the requirements of his creaturely status and therefore against his own good.[19]

This sin, freely committed by our first parents at the instigation of the devil, resulted in the loss of original holiness and original justice, of interior harmony and the proper direction by the spiritual soul— i.e., reason and will—of the body's inclinations, and the loss of the harmony between man and woman, and between humanity and the rest of creation. "*Death makes its entrance into human history.*"[20] But, worst of all, our friendship with God is broken. We are bereft of the greatest love of all.

As a consequence, man's history becomes "inundated by sin."[21] The state of separation from God caused by the Fall, called *Original Sin*, is passed down to all generations from our first parents, who pass on human nature as it has been affected by sin, transmitting it in a fallen state. In the words of the *Catechism*, "[Original Sin] is a sin 'contracted' and 'not committed'"—a state and not an act."[22] Human nature has been wounded by Original Sin, but not totally corrupted; the image of God has been disfigured and stained but still remains.[23]

Two final aspects are important to recognize—the unity of man and woman from their creation and the doctrine of *monogenism*.

In regard to the first, we encounter a surprising but beautiful aspect of the second creation account: the creation of the woman from the man. As we have already seen, the story recounts a physical relation between the body of Eve and that of Adam (Gn 2:21–22). There are numerous references to this event in Scripture, the Fathers of the Church, and in the teaching of the Magisterium. In particular, the story is described as a *prefiguration*, a foreshadowing that prophesies a future event. The future event it points to is the formation of the Church, which is the Bride of Christ: "Just as Eve was formed from the rib of Adam as he slept, so the Church was born from the pierced heart of Christ asleep in death on the Cross."[24]

From Christ's side flowed Blood and water (Jn 19:34), Eucharist and Baptism, which together form the Church, which is spiritually "the mother of all the living" and therefore the "new Eve." This close connection to the crucifixion of Christ, and thus to the very heart of God's Revelation and of our salvation, makes the formation of Eve from Adam a vitally important aspect of Scripture's account of the origins of humanity. However, the *Catechism* does not clarify whether this is an aspect of the story which is to be understood *only* as a symbolic foreshadowing of the birth of the Church or whether it is also historical and therefore to be taken literally. Regardless of whether it is literal or symbolic, this passage communicates powerful truths about the complementarity and equal dignity of man and woman and the union of Christ and the Church, his Bride.

The final issue regards Adam and Eve as parents of the whole human race. *Monogenism* is the doctrine that "the whole human race is descended from Adam and Eve."[25] As noted above, this doctrine is affirmed in several places in Scripture, such as in Acts 17:26 where the Apostle Paul declares that God "created the whole human race from one single stock." Indeed, if Original Sin is passed on through generation, from parents to children, then the possibility of many couples at the origins of the human race (called *polygenism*) does not seem possible, because it would leave open the possibility that some human beings did not fall, or that they suffer Original Sin even though they were unrelated to Adam, which would be an injustice that an all-good God would never have inflicted upon humanity.

In fact, Pope Pius XII declared the theory of polygenism to be one that is not apparently capable of being harmonized with the truth that Original Sin is passed to all humans through descent from Adam. In his own words:

> The faithful cannot embrace the opinion which maintains that either after Adam there existed on this Earth true men who did not take their origin through natural generation from him as from the first parent of all, or that Adam represents a number of first parents.[26]

In summary, through the Bible and the Catholic Church's teaching, God reveals the following about the origins of humanity:

- humanity is willed by God;

- humanity is created as a unity with a common origin;

- humanity is created spiritual, with the first human beings created directly by God in a sinless state of interior and exterior harmony;

- the interior and exterior harmony of humanity was shattered by a free act of sinful disobedience in a real historical event at the beginning of human history.

Finally, the creation of the first woman from the first man and the descent of all humanity from the first couple are also part of Sacred Scripture and Church teaching.

With the truth of Divine Revelation planted firmly in our minds, we are prepared to look at the data science has contributed to understanding the origins and development of the human species.

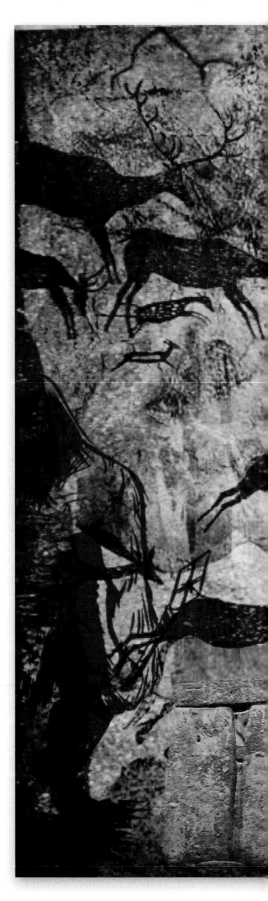

D. The Origins of Humanity According to Evolutionary Biology

HUMAN PRE-HISTORY AND EARLY HISTORY ACCORDING TO PALEOANTHROPOLOGY

The long historical panorama offered by *paleoanthropology*, the branch of biology that focuses on the study of human evolution, including pre-humans, is fascinating and complex. It is also controversial in many of its details; among experts in the field, there is still a great deal of dispute. The following sketch offers the major details, a bird's-eye-view of human evolution.[27]

In this bird's-eye-view, one question interests us the most when it comes to the relationship between faith and paleoanthropology—where is the *human threshold*, i.e., the place where human rationality first occurs? We will rely on what we have already learned about humanity to guide us.

The place where our sketch begins is the birthplace of the Dikika Baby—the *Great Rift Valley* of Africa, a vast valley created by massive subterranean forces about 20 million years ago. Its formation separated the plains of the eastern African continent from the tropical jungles of the western central part. The combination of scattered valleys and open spaces created a situation favorable to the development of *bipedalism*, the primate ability to move about on two limbs rather than four.[28]

Here, four to five million years ago, the earliest hominids developed, starting off the evolutionary family line that would ultimately lead to human beings. These primates, called the *Australopithecines*, had the rudimentary ability to walk on two feet, and were not much different in brain capacity from modern apes. It is to this species of primate that the Dikika Baby belonged, as did the famous Lucy fossil, which was discovered in 1974 and dated to 3.2 million years ago.

From the Australopithecines emerged *Homo habilis*, the next stage of the evolutionary journey, approximately 2–2.5 million years ago. Members of *Homo habilis* had a larger brain capacity and also a significant level of *manual dexterity*, the ability to use their hands. The tools they made consisted of pebbles chipped down to their cores and the flakes that had come off of those pebbles. These remnants have a random appearance, "as if the maker was not holding any design in mind and was content to accept whatever shape of stone nature might produce."[29]

The next stage begins 1.7 million years ago, with *Homo ergaster.* *H. ergaster* was capable of a whole new level of tool-making, including the making of spear-like stones, meat-cutting cleavers, and sharp picks. Anatomical evidence suggests that *Homo ergaster* was the first hominid to develop pair-bonding and a family structure in which fathers protected and provided for the mothers of their children.[30] *Australopithecus* and *Homo habilis* probably looked more like apes than like humans, with long arms and fur-covered bodies. *H. ergaster*, by contrast, had an external nose and may have been largely furless, a genetic change due in large part to the dry, hot climate of eastern Africa.[31]

Shortly after *Homo ergaster*, *Homo erectus* emerged. Along with an increase in cranial capacity, *Homo erectus* shows a jump, although only a small one, in sophistication. *H. erectus* may have been the first to mount stones on wooden handles, replacing the hand-axes of *H. ergaster*. From one lineage of *H. erectus*, about 400,000–300,000 years ago, *Homo neanderthalis* emerged in Europe, where it remained until extinction.[32] Most scientists consider *H. neanderthalis* as a different branch of the evolutionary tree than that of modern humans, based on genetic analysis of a piece of DNA from *Homo neanderthalis*. The evidence of *Homo neanderthalis* disappears in layers of sediment datable to around 35,000 years ago.

Around 200,000 years ago, the strand of *Homo erectus* which remained in Africa developed the skull size and skeleton of modern humans. This new strand on the hominid tree, *Homo sapiens*, did not at first exhibit much difference from the other hominids of what is called the *African Middle Stone Age*, which lasted from 250,000–50,000 years ago. In fact, *Homo erectus*, *Homo neanderthalis*, and early *Homo sapiens* show very little difference from each other, and a common lack of creativity: *Homo erectus* made almost no improvement or innovation in its tool making over tens of thousands of generations; and, only 100,000 years ago, early "anatomically modern" *Homo sapiens* was still using the same kind of tools as *H. erectus*.[33] But at the end of this period, as recently as 45,000 years ago, but perhaps as far back as 77,000 years ago, everything changes. In the words of Nicholas Wade:

> There is a new set of stone tools, more carefully crafted to attain specific shapes. There are complex tools made of bone, antler, and ivory. The bringers of the new culture made personal ornaments, of materials made of punctured teeth, shells and ivory beads. They played bird-bone flutes. Their missile technology was much improved. They were avid hunters who could take down large and dangerous game. They buried their dead with rituals. They could support denser populations. They developed trade networks through which they obtained distant materials.[34]

ANATOMICAL EVIDENCE SUGGESTS THAT *HOMO ERGASTER* WAS THE FIRST HOMINID TO DEVELOP PAIR-BONDING AND A FAMILY STRUCTURE IN WHICH FATHERS PROTECTED AND PROVIDED FOR THE MOTHERS OF THEIR CHILDREN.

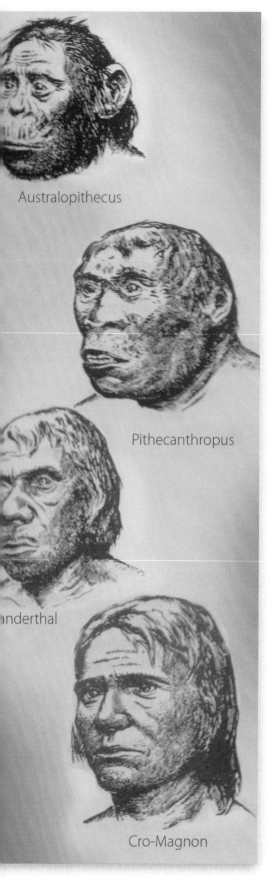

Australopithecus

Pithecanthropus

...nderthal

Cro-Magnon

The remnants of *Homo sapiens* from this period show unmistakable signs of technology and culture. They created tools with the intention of preserving and improving them. They developed and applied techniques characterized by continuity and progress over generations. Certain artifacts show the capacity for *symbolism*, the designation of a meaning to "a sign, sound, or object" that allows that sign, sound, or object to represent something other than itself. This last fact is especially significant because the capacity for symbolism is also the capacity for language.

There is no doubt that verbal language had developed among them. They clearly demonstrated "self-consciousness, self-determination, and therefore freedom," including an understanding of time and an orientation toward the future.[35]

In particular, *Homo sapiens* demonstrated *transcendence over evolution and its processes*. Once they were able to plan and to communicate through language, *Homo sapiens* could "climb over" the demands of the environment, creating a culture which acted as a border zone between their habitat and their society. Then, just as now, the members of *Homo sapiens* "are born, live, and grow up within culture," whatever that culture may be, and their relationships with the environment exist due to their culture. Through culture, they cease to be governed by purely biological rules, even though biological rules remain an essential part of their existence.[36]

According to most experts, the fully developed form of the human being bearing all the characteristics described above emerged from one line of *Homo sapiens* in a single location in Africa. The original ancestral population from whom all today's human beings are descended numbered around 5,000 individuals living in an area about the size of Rhode Island.[37] In fact, geneticists have even discovered that all human beings alive today carry genetic material from one male and one female member of the original ancestral population.[38] The development of *Homo sapiens* must have been explosive—by 35,000 years ago they had settled on every continent (except, of course, Australia). The foundations of human history and human society were in place, although recorded history would not begin until around 3000–3500 BC (about 5,000–5,500 years ago).

INVESTIGATING ORIGINS: WHERE IS ADAM?

In the long history described above, where is the "human threshold" to be located? That is, where in the fossil record do we find unmistakable signs of rationality that indicate a spiritual soul? When does the primate, the mere animal, become a human being? As we have already discussed, to be a human being means to be a rational animal. And further philosophical reflection shows that this implies that human beings have a spiritual soul that is "immaterial" and therefore imperishable, having a spiritual soul that cannot be reduced to the brain or to any other part of the body. To be human means to have the capacities of intellect and freedom, which are the twin pillars upon which the human imaging of God rest.

In the fossil record, the earliest creatures with this status are those who produced the artifacts found in connection with the later *Homo sapiens* period, around 50,000 years ago.

The reason for this judgment is simple. Animals cannot do things for which they do not have the capacity. Artifacts like the artistically designed ones described above require rationality. Therefore their producers were not animals; they had to be human. *Homo sapiens*, unlike their primate ancestors such as the Dikika baby or their hominid cousins, *Homo neanderthalis*, are truly made in the image of God.

There are a few other issues that we should note before continuing to the theological issues. The first is the possibility of error. The process involved in dating prehistoric artifacts is not perfect and therefore, further scientific research may show a different picture—for example, a later or an earlier dating than the one mentioned here. However, there is no doubt that the human race appeared at least 50,000 years ago.

Theologically, there is no reason why we should be troubled by the discovery that human history is much longer than people had realized. Some might wonder why God left human beings to wait so long for salvation. But, of course, each individual at any point in that long history was in the same situation as any other individual prior to the coming of Christ. In the words of Dennis Bonnette, "Each such human being would begin and end life awaiting the Redeemer's coming. The longer period is no worse for the individual person than the shorter."[39] Moreover, it should be remembered that the human population for most of prehistory was extremely small. 50,000 years ago the world's human population is believed to have been only several *thousand* and at the end of the prehistoric period still only several million, compared to about 150 million at the time of the Roman Empire and six *billion* today. The total number of pre-historic humans was therefore a small fraction of the total number of people who have ever lived, and presumably much smaller still compared to the number of people who will ever live.

Nor should we be scandalized by the fact that our pre-human relatives, *Homo erectus* and *Homo neanderthalis*, looked different than modern humans. It is true that lower foreheads and significantly protruding brows gave them a different facial appearance than our own. But size, facial features, and cranial capacity differ widely even today among contemporary humans. Physical appearance is not the decisive element of human nature—the presence of a rational soul, exhibited in genuine acts of rationality, is what makes an animal a rational animal, a human being.[40] This separates our pre-human relatives much more decisively from human beings than does any difference of appearance.

THE MAIN PHILOSOPHICAL QUESTION ABOUT THE EVOLUTIONARY ORIGINS OF HUMANITY IS SIMPLE AND STRAIGHTFORWARD: WHERE IN HISTORY IS THE HUMAN THRESHOLD?

A PURELY MATERIAL PROCESS CANNOT PRODUCE A SPIRITUAL REALITY. THEREFORE, ADAM COULD NOT RECEIVE AN IMMORTAL SOUL FROM HIS PRIMATE PARENTS.

So the issue of the dating of the human threshold is not one that puts the Christian Faith and paleoanthropology into conflict. But does Church teaching reveal any conflict between the findings of paleoanthropology and divine Revelation?

E. Theology on the Cutting Edge of Paleoanthropology

The main philosophical question about the evolutionary origins of humanity is simple and straightforward: where in history is the human threshold? But there are more questions when we deal with the theological issues related to the Christian Faith. As we consider each question, we will engage in some theological speculation about the origins of humanity, seeking a more profound understanding of Divine Revelation.

FROM PRIMATE TO MAN: ADAM'S ENSOULMENT

The first important theological question has to do with the process of the divine creation of humanity—how did pre-human primates (which John Paul II called "antecedent living forms") become spiritual human beings? Divine Revelation eliminates one answer right away—namely, that the reaching of the human threshold was purely natural, an effect of material causes alone. Because the human soul is immaterial (not made of matter), it cannot be produced by a material creature or any purely material process, such as biological reproduction.

God directly creates every spiritual soul; as the *Catechism of the Catholic Church* declares, the soul is not "produced" by the parents.[41] Reason confirms this fact—a purely material process cannot produce a spiritual reality. Therefore, Adam could not receive an immortal soul from his primate parents, just as we cannot receive one from our human parents. God had to bestow a soul upon him, just as he does with each of us.

How could such a transformation occur? Obviously, the whole act of ensoulment on the part of God is a great mystery, both as it regards the first humans and every act of ensoulment that follows in human history. Let us first approach the question from the perspective of the body and its evolution.

In terms of the body, the picture paleoanthropology offers is one of a gradual process of increasing brain size and ability, which ultimately produces biologically modern *Homo sapiens* around

100,000–200,000 years ago. But it seems that at least 50,000 years passed before truly human *Homo sapiens* appeared. Reason, based on evolutionary science, suggests that, at that time, an evolutionary adaptation must have occurred which, thanks to Divine Providence, made our first parents fully ready to be elevated to the level of spiritual creatures.

As to the nature of this evolutionary adaptation which made the transition to full humanity possible, modern science may offer a helpful clue. Science knows of situations where a tiny step produces a large qualitative change called *phase transitions*. An everyday example is the liquefying of water. If the temperature is a trillionth of a degree (or even much less) *below* the melting point, the H_2O is solid ice with a crystalline structure. If the temperature is raised to a trillionth of a degree (or even much less) *above* the melting point, it becomes liquid water, and has very different properties. The important point is that an imperceptible change can result in altogether different behavior. The brain is so complex that it is easy to imagine a kind of phase transition happening there also. Perhaps the last of the *Homo sapiens* before true man were on a physical level only slightly, even imperceptibly, different from true humans. In the case of Adam and Eve, a tiny evolutionary change could have made a major difference in mental capability and enabled them to receive spiritual souls from God.

What could such a transformation be like? Obviously, we pass into the realm of divine mystery whenever we deal with such a question. But our Christian Faith does give us an analogy, one with deep roots in Sacred Scripture and Tradition—the conferring of supernatural life in Baptism. As the *Catechism* states, "Baptism not only purifies from all sins, but also makes the neophyte 'a new creature,' an adopted son of God, who has become a 'partaker of the divine nature,' member of Christ and co-heir with him, and a temple of the Holy Spirit."[42] Yet we know that reception of this sacrament does not annihilate or replace our human nature—we remain the same human being after being baptized as before.

The same is true of ensoulment. When Adam and Eve were ensouled, the human race came into being, a race that did not shed its animal nature as it had evolved up to that point, but that lifted it up to a higher level, while preserving all that was ever there. In the same way, when we are reborn into the New Adam through Baptism, we become part of that New Creation by being transformed, by being given a new and higher kind of life—the supernatural life of grace, which is a sharing in the divine life—while preserving the kind of life we had before.

Recognizing that humans evolved from earlier animals helps complete the picture of human history given us through Divine Revelation. From this new perspective, we can see three great

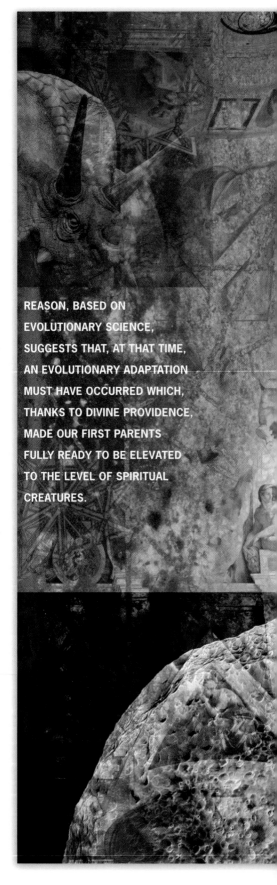

REASON, BASED ON EVOLUTIONARY SCIENCE, SUGGESTS THAT, AT THAT TIME, AN EVOLUTIONARY ADAPTATION MUST HAVE OCCURRED WHICH, THANKS TO DIVINE PROVIDENCE, MADE OUR FIRST PARENTS FULLY READY TO BE ELEVATED TO THE LEVEL OF SPIRITUAL CREATURES.

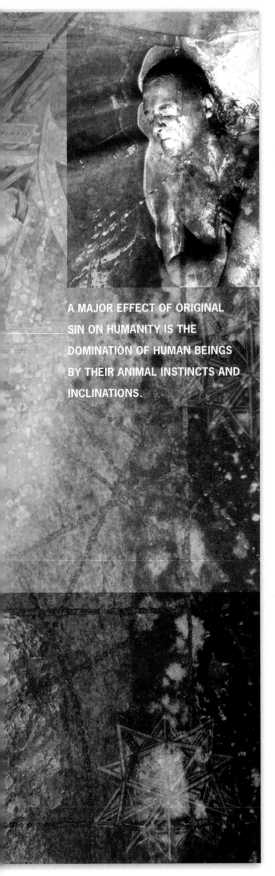

A MAJOR EFFECT OF ORIGINAL SIN ON HUMANITY IS THE DOMINATION OF HUMAN BEINGS BY THEIR ANIMAL INSTINCTS AND INCLINATIONS.

transformations. In the case of the first Adam, animal is raised up to rationality and freedom, in which the spiritual and truly human makes its appearance in the visible world. In the second transformation the human, with his spiritual nature, is raised up by receiving the divine life, i.e., the supernatural life of grace. This happens through the New Adam, Christ. Finally, this redeemed man is glorified and enters into eternal life.

The first two stages happen in this world, in this physical universe. The third stage will involve entering a new realm of existence that cannot be imagined, a radical transformation of our physical selves in a way that has no parallel in the first two transformations. No dramatic physical change takes place in the first two transformations, but regarding the third, St. Paul teaches that "eye has not seen, and ear has not heard, nor has it entered the human heart, what God has prepared for those who love him"[43] This last and dramatic transformation is foreshadowed by Eucharistic transubstantiation, in which the earthly realities of bread and wine are converted, utterly transformed, into a divine reality. What we shall be cannot be contained fully in this world of matter, space, and time, and thus can only be present here in a hidden way, sacramentally, in the Eucharist.

THE FALL: UNCOVERING SIN BENEATH THE SANDS OF TIME

What about the Fall? Is it possible to discover something of original holiness and justice in the fossils and artifacts left behind by early humans? The fossil record offers no indication of any unusual, extraordinary artifacts that could prove that, somewhere at the dawn of human rationality, the first two human beings were sinless. But a little reflection reveals that we should not expect to find such an artifact.

As we learned earlier in this chapter from Genesis 3 and from Church teaching, the sinfulness of humanity began with a real act committed by our first parents, which is described in Genesis 3: 1–7. This means that the period of human sinlessness, of original integrity and original holiness, was an imperceptible glimmer that happened within the lifespan of one couple. Original integrity and holiness may very well have been lost as quickly as they were received. Such a moment would quickly perish from human memory, especially considering that human life became inundated by sinful tendencies, separation from God, suffering, and death.

In fact, a major effect of Original Sin on humanity is the domination of human beings by their animal instincts and inclinations. After all, we call the event of the first sin the *Fall*, implying that human beings, once elevated by God to rationality and freedom (indeed to a supernatural level of rationality and freedom), fell (though not entirely) from that state—rationality and freedom remained, but the special gifts and the supernatural grace of God were lost.

It seems likely that Adam and Eve fell into a state much like the pre-human primates from which they had been elevated. In the words of St. Thomas Aquinas, "…when man turned his back on God, he fell under the influence of his sensual [bodily] impulses… [after the Fall] he is likened to beasts that are led by the impulse of sensuality… a deviation from the law of reason."[44]

This leads to a tragic situation that is well described by the theologian Fr. Henri Rondet, S.J.:

> Man has been left to his nature; but it is precisely this that is the paradox and stumbling block. Death, suffering, ignorance, the revolt of the senses—all this is in fact natural, since man is made of flesh and spirit. But what is *natural* to an animal organism becomes *unnatural* for a soul made in the image of God.[45]

Given that this is the nature of Original Sin, we should be surprised to find anything other than what we do find in the paleoanthropological data—a long, slow climb for humanity that is burdened, even today, with failures, crimes, and ignorance. If man had not fallen, he would surely have made swift progress toward the peak of his potential. But due to sin, a very different state of affairs emerged—man makes slow, painful steps toward humane civilization and responsible mastery over the world and often takes major steps backwards. Even today, many live in conditions that hearken back to the Stone Age; even in advanced cultural centers such as American cities, violence and degradation haunt human existence.

Some scientists suggest that such evil is simply part of human nature. They ask how "sin and death" can be the result of the Fall when clearly we find lust, aggression, killing, and death among animals for hundreds of millions of years before humans came along. Moreover, it is clear that our own sexual drive and aggressive impulses are inherited from our animal forebears and "bred into us." How then can they be the result of a sin that took place only after humans appeared?

The answers are simple. The Church has always taught that Adam's immortality was a *preternatural gift*. Naturally speaking, Adam and Eve would have been mortal even before the Fall, but they were offered a gift that was "outside their nature," which is what the traditional term "preternatural" means. Due to sin, God withdrew this gift and allowed man to revert to his natural subjection to death. As far as sexual drive and aggressive impulses, these are not in themselves sinful, of course. As long as they are properly directed by reason there is no sin—the same drives which are involved in lust and aggression are also involved in true sexual love and in athletics, respectively. But Original Sin resulted in *concupiscence*, which is the disordering of our nature whereby our reason and will are weakened

ADAM AND EVE WERE OFFERED A GIFT THAT WAS "OUTSIDE THEIR NATURE," WHICH IS WHAT THE TRADITIONAL TERM "PRETERNATURAL" MEANS. DUE TO SIN, GOD WITHDREW THIS GIFT AND ALLOWED MAN TO REVERT TO HIS NATURAL SUBJECTION TO DEATH. ORIGINAL SIN RESULTED IN *CONCUPISCENCE*, WHICH IS THE DISORDERING OF OUR NATURE WHEREBY OUR REASON AND WILL ARE WEAKENED AND NOT IN FULL CONTROL OF OUR EMOTIONAL IMPULSES.

The pagan god Thor

and not in full control of our emotional impulses. Thus the sin of lust is not the same thing as sexual attraction; it is sexual attraction without the guidance of reason and love.

ONE MAN, ONE WOMAN: MONOGENISM AND PALEOANTHROPOLOGY

What about monogenism? The unity of the human race is presupposed throughout Sacred Scripture and Church teaching. As Pius XII pointed out, due to the fact that Original Sin is passed on to all humanity through procreation, it does not seem possible that more than one truly human couple can be located at the beginning of human history.

There is no doubt today that *Homo sapiens* is a single species and that all human beings are genetically almost identical. But most scientists would find it hard to accept the idea that *Homo sapiens*—considered as *a biological species*—began with just a single "pair of human beings, male and female, from whom we are all descended through natural generation."[46] Evolutionary biologists understand the evolution of a new species as occurring through gradual changes taking place in a whole population, rather than by the sudden appearance of one or two individuals that are qualitatively different from what went before.[47] Do science and faith contradict each other here?

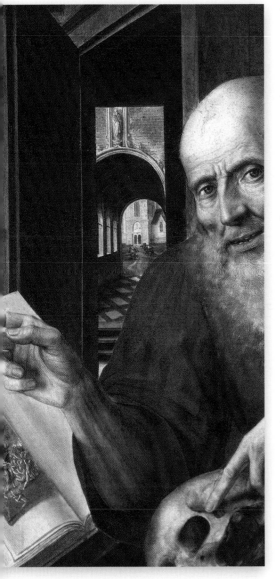

St. Jerome

One might be tempted to think so, but the insightful observations of geneticist and Jesuit priest Paulinus Forsthoefel and Catholic theologian David Liberto can help us see why there is no contradiction. According to Forsthoefel, the evolution of the human body, i.e., of the primate *non-human* ancestors of humanity, would have occurred according to the mode most evolutionists envision—through the evolution of a whole population. But the origin of *true humans*—that is, beings endowed with a spiritual soul—would have occurred only in two members of that population: "God's intervention focused on one pair (Adam and Eve) to give rise to mankind…" He concludes that "the origin of *proto-humans* [pre-human primates] involved polygenism, but the origin of true humans involved monogenism."[48]

Liberto makes the same point by distinguishing between formal and material polygenism when it comes to the first human beings. *Material polygenism* refers to the fact that the early *Homo sapiens* from which true humans descend according to the body formed an ordinary breeding population. But in terms of actual humans, i.e., primates who were transformed by God into spiritual human beings made in his image and likeness, there were only two. This is in no way incompatible with Divine Revelation. *Formal polygenism*, the idea that God elevated more than two to rationality, is a more troublesome idea, one that is not apparently capable of being harmonized with the truth that Original Sin is passed to all humans through descent from Adam.[49]

The idea of monogenism poses another problem: if Adam and Eve were truly the first parents of all human beings, then with whom did their descendents propagate the species? Let's consider three possibilities: a) the marrying of siblings; b) interbreeding with biologically human but not spiritually ensouled members of the ancestral population; and c) formal polygenism.

Regarding the first possibility, i.e., the marrying of siblings, the prohibition against this practice in modern society may not always have been the case in early history. For example, Scripture recounts how Abraham married his half-sister Sarah. While sexual relations or marriages between parents and children are clearly intrinsically evil, the taboo against brother-sister marriage seems to depend on circumstances that hold now, but would not have necessarily been the case in the beginning. In society, sexual union serves the proliferation of genetic differences and the expansion of the circle of friendship. While incest now violates this purpose, brother-sister unions in the second generation of man may have served precisely this end.

The second possibility is more problematic. While the other anatomically modern humans would have been almost indistinguishable from true humans on a biological level, they were not spiritual human beings made in the image and likeness of God. While the darkened minds of the children of Adam and Eve may have lost awareness of the great "ontological discontinuity" between themselves and the creatures with whom they lived, any union between them that may have occurred would most certainly have been contrary to the law of nature and the will of God.

As to the third possibility, Pope Pius XII called for caution and restraint, asserting that polygenism in the formal sense could never be embraced unless it could also be reconciled with the doctrine of Original Sin:

> When, however, there is question of another conjectural opinion, namely polygenism, the children of the Church by no means enjoy such liberty. For the faithful cannot embrace that opinion which maintains that either after Adam there existed on this earth true men who did not take their origin through natural generation from him as from the first parent of all, or that Adam represents a certain number of first parents. Now it is no way apparent how such an opinion can be reconciled with that which the sources of revealed truth and the documents of the Teaching Authority of the Church propose with regard to Original Sin, which proceeds from a sin actually committed by an individual Adam and which, through generation, is passed on to all and is in everyone as his own.[50]

None of the theological proposals I have suggested in this section should be mistaken for definitive Church teaching. It is not required of Catholics to believe that Baptism is the best analogy for the

The Holy Family by Bartolome Murillo

ensoulment of Adam, nor that Catholics hold that the occurrence of a phase transition was the reason that the ensoulment of Adam occurred when it did. Theological speculations such as these are attempts to illumine such mysteries, not to offer a once-for-all explanation. Most importantly, they help us see that paleoanthropology and the Christian Faith are not incompatible.

F. From the Dikika Baby to the Christ Child: The Theological Implications of Human Evolution

The great Christian author C.S. Lewis offers a beautiful summary of the picture faith and science combine to give us of the dawn of humanity:

> For long centuries, God perfected the animal form which was to become the vehicle of humanity and the image of himself. He gave it hands whose thumb could be applied to each of the fingers, and jaws and teeth and throat capable of articulation, and a brain sufficiently complex to execute all of the material motions whereby rational thought is incarnated. The creature may have existed in this state for ages before it became man: it may even have been clever enough to make things which our modern archaeologists would accept as proof of its humanity. But it was only an animal because all its physical and psychical processes were directed to purely material and natural ends. Then, in the fullness of time, God caused to descend upon this organism, both on its psychology and physiology [i.e., its bodily processes], a new kind of consciousness which could say "I" and "me," which could look upon itself as an object, which knew God, which could make judgments of truth, beauty, and goodness, and which was so far above time that it could perceive time flowing past...

> But sooner or later [these creatures] fell. Someone or something whispered that they could become as gods... They wanted some corner in the universe of which they could say to God, "This is our business, not yours." But there is no such corner. They wanted to be nouns, but they were, and eternally must be, mere adjectives. We have no idea in what particular act, or series of acts, the self-contradictory, impossible wish found expression. For all I can see, it might have concerned the literal eating of a fruit, but the question is of no consequence.[51]

Are there any important benefits offered by seeing the divine act of creating humanity through the lens of paleoanthropology? Here are a few that come to mind:

The loving patience of God:

To admit that God's preparation of the body of man took millions of years may seem scandalous to some. But actually, the process reveals something much like the time taken to prepare an artistic masterpiece. Everything had to be just right for man's creation—the delay came not on the part of God, but on the part of creation itself, which took time to be matured to the level at which it could become spiritual.

Matter had to be allowed to mature, starting all the way back at the Big Bang, to the point where its organization and potential had been realized just so. At that moment, the soul was infused and man was created. A great painting or even just a great meal takes a lot of time to prepare. How much longer should the preparation for the summit of the visible universe take?

The unity of creation:

The prospect that man evolved from earlier living creatures infuriates some Christians who fear that it is an attack on human uniqueness and dignity. But it actually reveals a marvelous truth—that all of creation is intimately related. From non-living matter evolved the simplest living organisms, from the simplest life eventually came animals, from the animals came man, in whom the animal is united to spirit so as to bring together the two vast realms of reality.

And finally, in the fullness of time, "the Word became Flesh and made His dwelling among us" (Jn 1:14). The coming of God in the flesh in Jesus completes the process God created and guided to unite all things to each other and to himself.

God unites to himself a human nature and, therefore, the whole universe! Now we await the final moment—"When, finally, all has been subjected to the Son, he will then subject himself to the One who made all things subject to him, so that God may be all in all" (1 Cor 15:28).

The need for humility and for the Eucharist:

Our connection to the Dikika Baby is not simply a matter of curiosity. It also reveals our constant need for God's help in order to be not only made in his image, but also to live out our lives in his likeness—to act like the all-good God in whose image we are made.

According to paleoanthropology, science places us in a direct descent from animals. We carry animal instincts and

THE COMING OF GOD IN THE FLESH IN JESUS CHRIST COMPLETES THE PROCESS GOD CREATED AND GUIDED TO UNITE ALL THINGS TO EACH OTHER AND TO HIMSELF. IN CHRIST, GOD UNITES TO HIMSELF A HUMAN NATURE AND, THEREFORE, THE WHOLE UNIVERSE!

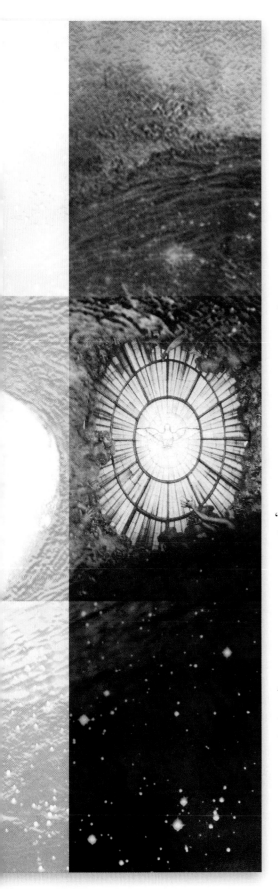

inclinations, and after the Fall our weakened reason tends to follow these animal inclinations in a sub-human way, or indeed often diverts these inclinations into de-humanizing directions. Therefore, we should constantly be reminded of our need for salvation and grace. "Lead us not into temptation" should be ever on our lips.

But along with this prayer, we should often use our lips for another reason—to receive the new life of the one who created us and redeemed us. The greatest way to do this is by receiving him, Body, Blood, Soul, and Divinity in the Eucharist. In receiving Christ in his bodily reality, our souls are strengthened to be what God made us to be—animals transformed into the image of God, living out our physical lives in a truly spiritual way. Christ is the perfect image of God, and when we receive him, we receive the power to live the life for which he made us.

The Dikika Baby's probable physical relationship to you, to me, to all humans, and therefore even to the humanity of Christ, reveals all three of these dimensions of the truth about humanity and creation in a breathtaking way. If continued scientific research bolsters this connection, we have a reason not to doubt, but to say with the psalmist, "I praise you, Lord, for I am fearfully and wonderfully made. Wonderful are your works!" (Ps 139:14).

G. Conclusion

"What our senses fail to fathom, let us grasp through faith's consent." This wonderful prayer of St. Thomas Aquinas regarding the Real Presence of Christ in the Eucharist is very applicable to our glimpse back to the origins of humanity. Many things we encountered here are difficult to understand. But our reason and our faith both tell us that in humanity we encounter something absolutely new in the history of the visible universe. With the eyes of faith, we see undeniable truths which transcend science but which are nonetheless obvious to reason.

Although our senses may not perceive God's loving plan and action in the Dikika Baby, let us grasp through faith that all things work together for God's purposes. And as we adore the Eucharist, which is Christ giving himself to us in a way that is strange and unrecognizable to eyes without faith, let us apply the same faith to open our minds to the wonderful and strange history that leads from the Dikika Baby to our own precious and irreplaceable lives.

Supplementary Reading

The Emergence of the Image: Modern Science and the Origins of Humanity

1. "ON HUMAN ORIGINS AS REVEALED BY SCIENCE AND FAITH"

(excerpted from International Theological Commission, Communion and Stewardship: Human Persons Created in the Image of God. Internet. Available from http://www.vatican.va/roman_curia/congregations/ cfaith/cti_documents/rc_con_cfaith_doc_20040723_communion-stewardship_en.html; accessed April 2, 2007.)

62   The endeavor to understand the universe has marked human culture in every period and in nearly every society. In the perspective of the Christian Faith, this endeavor is precisely an instance of the stewardship which human beings exercise in accordance with God's plan. Without embracing a discredited concordism, Christians have the responsibility to locate the modern scientific understanding of the universe within the context of the theology of creation. The place of human beings in the history of this evolving universe, as it has been charted by modern sciences, can only be seen in its complete reality in the light of faith, as a personal history of the engagement of the triune God with creaturely persons.

63   According to the widely accepted scientific account, the universe erupted 15 billion years ago in an explosion called the "Big Bang" and has been expanding and cooling ever since. Later there gradually emerged the conditions necessary for the formation of atoms, still later the condensation of galaxies and stars, and about 10 billion years later the formation of planets. In our own solar system and on earth (formed about 4.5 billion years ago), the conditions have been favorable to the emergence of life. While there is little consensus among scientists about how the origin of this first microscopic life is to be explained, there is general agreement among them that the first organism dwelt on this planet about 3.5–4 billion years ago. Since it has been demonstrated that all living organisms on earth are genetically related, it is virtually certain that all living organisms have descended from this first organism. Converging evidence from many studies in the physical and biological sciences furnishes mounting support for some theory of evolution to account for the development and diversification of life on earth, while controversy continues over the pace and mechanisms of evolution. While the story of human origins is complex and subject to revision, physical anthropology and molecular biology combine to make a convincing case for the origin of the human species in Africa about 150,000 years ago in a humanoid population of common genetic lineage. However it is to be explained, the decisive factor in human origins was a continually increasing brain size, culminating in that of Homo sapiens. With the development of the human brain, the nature and rate of evolution were permanently altered: with the introduction of the uniquely human factors of consciousness, intentionality, freedom and creativity, biological evolution was recast as social and cultural evolution.

70   With respect to the immediate creation of the human soul, Catholic theology affirms that particular actions of God bring about effects that transcend the capacity of created causes acting according to their natures... Catholic theology affirms that the emergence of the first members of the human species (whether as individuals or in populations) represents an event that is not susceptible of a purely natural explanation and which can appropriately be attributed to divine intervention. Acting indirectly through causal chains operating

Supplementary Reading

from the beginning of cosmic history, God prepared the way for what Pope John Paul II has called "an ontological leap... the moment of transition to the spiritual." While science can study these causal chains, it falls to theology to locate this account of the special creation of the human soul within the overarching plan of the triune God to share the communion of trinitarian life with human persons who are created out of nothing in the image and likeness of God, and who, in his name and according to his plan, exercise a creative stewardship and sovereignty over the physical universe.

2. "HUMAN ENSOULMENT"

(excerpted from Paulinus Forsthoefel, S.J., Religious Faith Meets Modern Science [New York: Alba House, 1994], pp. 100–104)

...Though part of the material world and subject to its laws, human beings have an immaterial aspect.... Divine Revelation as given especially in the Scriptures makes it clear that humans are essentially superior to other animals because they have spiritual souls....

Each human as he or she exists is a unit. We must not conceive [of a human being] as a body inhabited and directed by the soul as something completely separate. Rather we must think of each person as a unit in which the material aspect we see (the body) owes its vital properties to the spiritual aspect we cannot see or touch (the soul)....

If the human soul is immaterial, it cannot owe its existence to matter. We must conclude, therefore, and the Christian faith teaches us, that whenever a human soul comes into existence, it is God, the Supreme Being, who creates it and that out of no preexisting material.... Precisely when the human soul is created by God... is not clear.... Catholic theologians today think that the human soul is created by God when the male and female gametes unite to form the zygote, the single cell which proliferates to form the embryo and its supporting membranes. Speculation on the part of some holds that this takes place about 14 days later, when the primary axis of an embryo is laid down.

This last view has support in the idea that as long as twinning is possible, the human soul is not yet present. Only after definitely only one or more embryos are developing from the original zygote would the human soul or souls be created. The official teaching of the Catholic Church in the matter is that life—human life—begins at the moment of conception and, therefore, any attempt to destroy that life (e.g., by use of the "Morning-After Pill") is morally wrong: "Even if a doubt existed concerning whether the fruit of conception is already a human person, it is objectively a grave sin to risk murder" (*Acta Apostolicae Sedis* 66 (1974) 730–744).

What then is the role of the parents in generating their child? Are they merely the "parents" of the body and therefore not really of their child as a human being? They are not generating only a body, not even only a human body. They are

Supplementary Reading

generating a particular human person with such and such characteristics inherited from them. In doing this, they require divine cooperation in achieving a result superior to the possibilities of their own causality, a rational human person with a spiritual soul. This result would not occur without the parents' generative activity. They can be truly called and are the parents of their child.... God should be thought of as the "ground", the ultimate basis of the parents' causality enabling them to generate a rational being with a soul, endowed with their heredity... This discussion has been intended to show that the account of the evolutionary origin of modern Homo sapiens is incomplete if it restricts itself to the factors proposed by the natural scientist, viz., genetic variation and natural selection. Incomplete because the account necessarily ignores the spiritual aspect of every human person, that each person has an immortal non-material soul which cannot be the effect of the unaided natural factors proposed by natural scientists. But not false if the account admits that it is only explaining the origin of man as a part of the animal world....

Up to the origin of the first true human with a spiritual soul, no special creative activity of God would be required. Previous to this point in human evolution the generation of more and more advanced hominids would require no activity of God beyond that necessary for the origin of any other animal....

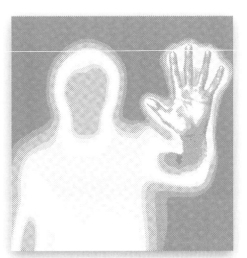

To sum up, the Christian believer and the natural scientist need not be in contradiction in how they interpret human evolution. They explain and interpret it at different levels. The natural scientist (anthropologist) tries to explain human evolution in terms of natural factors accessible to natural science and may not be able to detect any plan or purpose behind it. The Christian believer, having access to information from Divine Revelation, sees God working through these natural factors to produce a being capable of knowing, loving and serving God and of sharing His own Divine Life.

3. "HUMANI GENERIS"

(Encyclical of Pope Pius XII, 1950)

36   For these reasons the Teaching Authority of the Church does not forbid that, in conformity with the present state of human sciences and sacred theology, research and discussions, on the part of men experienced in both fields, take place with regard to the doctrine of evolution, in as far as it inquires into the origin of the human body as coming from pre-existent and living matter—for the Catholic faith obliges us to hold that souls are immediately created by God. However, this must be done in such a way that the reasons for both opinions, that is, those favorable and those unfavorable to evolution, be weighed and judged with the necessary seriousness, moderation and measure, and provided that all are prepared to submit to the judgment of the Church, to whom Christ has given the mission of interpreting authentically the Sacred Scriptures and of defending the dogmas of faith. Some however, rashly transgress this liberty of discussion, when they act as if the origin of the human body from pre-existing and living matter were already completely certain and proved by the facts which have been discovered up to now and by reasoning on those facts, and as if there were nothing in the sources of Divine Revelation which demands the greatest moderation and caution in this question.

Supplementary Reading

37   When, however, there is question of another conjectural opinion, namely polygenism, the children of the Church by no means enjoy such liberty. For the faithful cannot embrace that opinion which maintains that either after Adam there existed on this earth true men who did not take their origin through natural generation from him as from the first parent of all, or that Adam represents a certain number of first parents. Now it is no way apparent how such an opinion can be reconciled with that which the sources of revealed truth and the documents of the Teaching Authority of the Church propose with regard to Original sin, which proceeds from a sin actually committed by an individual Adam and which, through generation, is passed on to all and is in everyone as his own

Study Guide

The Emergence of the Image: Modern Science and the Origins of Humanity

VOCABULARY

Define the following terms:

 1. Dikika Baby
 2. Pius XII (evolution)
 3. *Humani generis*
 4. Pre-existent Matter
 5. Living Matter
 6. John Paul II (evolution)
 7. Epiphenomenalism
 8. Ontological
 9. Benedict XVI (evolution)
11. Second Creation Account
12. Sin
13. Racism
14. Original Justice

15. The Fall
16. Original sin
17. Monogenism
18. Prefiguration
19. Polygenism
20. Pius XII (polygenism)
21. Paleoanthropology
22. Human Threshold
23. Great Rift Valley
24. Australopithecines
25. Bipedalism
26. *Homo habilis*
27. *Homo ergaster*

28. *Homo erectus*
29. *Homo neanderthalis*
30. *Homo sapiens*
31. African Middle Stone Age
32. Symbolism
33. Ensoulment
34. Phase Transition
35. Baptism
36. Preternatural Gift
37. Concupiscence
38. Material Polygenism
39. Formal Polygenism

Study Guide

STUDY QUESTIONS

1. What lesson does 1 Samuel 16:7 offer those who wish to understand the relationship between science and faith in regard to the origins of humanity?

2. Explain the principles established by Pius XII for a Catholic understanding of evolution. What ideas are compatible with the Catholic doctrine of creation? Which ideas are not?

3. Explain the principles established by John Paul II for a Catholic understanding of evolution. What ideas are compatible with the Catholic doctrine of creation? Which ideas are not?

4. According to John Paul II, what kind of theories of evolution are not compatible with the Christian Faith?

5. Describe the nature of the ontological leap at the origins of humanity as they are described by John Paul II?

6. What key limits does John Paul II identify for the sciences in their investigation of the evolutionary origins of humanity?

7. Can science help at all in following the passage into the spiritual realm that occurred at man's origins, according to John Paul II?

8. List and briefly explain the elements of the Church's interpretation of Genesis 2–3.

9. Why did Pius XII reject polygenism as an idea of human origins?

10. Why is the story of Eve's creation from Adam in Genesis 2:21–22 important to the Christian Faith?

11. Briefly describe the historical panorama offered by paleoanthropology regarding human origins.

12. What is the significance of culture in understanding the origins and development of the human species?

13. Explain why this text identifies the human threshold in relation to the artifacts found in layers of rock datable to 50,000 years ago.

14. Is the potentially long history of humanity suggested by paleoanthropology an obstacle to faith? Why or why not?

15. Is the seeming difference in resemblance between Homo erectus and Homo neanderthalis versus modern humans a reason to reject the evolutionary origins of humanity? Why or why not?

16. Briefly explain the effects of Baptism, and then explain why the conferring of supernatural life in Baptism is a fitting analogy for ensoulment.

Study Guide

17. What facts about the Fall must be taken into account when considering the long history of humanity suggested by paleoanthropology? Does the paleoanthropological picture contradict the doctrine of the Fall and Original sin?

18. How can sin and death be the result of the Fall when we find evidence of lust, aggression, killing, and death among the animals?

19. Describe the difference between formal and material polygenism. Which is compatible with the Catholic Faith, and why?

20. If the paleoanthropological picture of human pre-history and early history is accurate, what insights into God, creation, and humanity are underlined by it? How is faithful adoration of the Real Presence of Christ in the Eucharist similar to our glimpse into the paleoanthropological picture of human origins and early history?

Endnotes

1. Christopher P. Sloan, "Dikika Baby," *National Geographic* (11/2006)
2. Ibid.
3. Pius XII, *Humani generis*, 36.
4. John Paul II, "Humans are Spiritual and Corporeal Beings" (April 16, 1986).
5. Ibid.
6. Idem, "Magisterium is Concerned with the Question of Evolution for It Involves the Conception of Man," Message to the Pontifical Academy of Sciences (October 22, 1996), 4.
7. Ibid., 4.
8. Ibid., 4.
9. Ibid., 5.
10. Ibid., 6.
11. Ibid., 6.
12. Ibid., 6.
13. "Pontiff: Evolution Does Not Exclude a Creator," in *Zenit: The World Seen from Rome Daily Dispatch*, July 27, 2007. Internet. Available from www.zenit.org; accessed July 31, 2007.
14. Benedict XVI, Inaugural Homily (April 24, 2005).
15. Vatican II, *Gaudium et spes*, 24; cf. CCC 356.
16. CCC 358; cf. GS 12 § 1; 24 § 3; 39 §1.
17. CCC "Glossary"; cf. CCC 1935.

18. CCC 400.
19. Ibid., 397–398.
20. Ibid., 400.
21. Ibid., 401.
22. Ibid., 404.
23. Ibid., 405.
24. Haffner, *Mystery of Creation*, 70.
25. Ibid., 71.
26. Pius XII, *Humani generis*, 37.
27. The two major sources for this section are Fiorenzo Facchini, "Man, Origin and Nature," in G. Tanzella-Nitti, P. Larrey and A. Strumia, ed., INTERS—*Interdisciplinary Encyclopedia of Science and Religion*,. Internet. Available from http://www.inters.org; accessed April 12, 2007; and Nicholas Wade, *Before the Dawn: Recovering the Lost History of Our Ancestors* (Penguin: New York, 2006).
28. Facchini, "Man, Origin and Nature."
29. Wade, 19.
30. Ibid., 21.
31. Ibid., 22.
32. Ibid., 27–28.
33. Ibid., 29.
34. Ibid., 30.
35. Facchini, "Man, Origin and Nature."

36. Ibid.
37. Wade, 58–60.
38. Ibid., 52–56.
39. Bonnette, 184.
40. Ibid., 165–167.
41. CCC 366.
42. CCC 1265; cf. 1 Cor 6:19.
43. 1 Cor 2:6.
44. St. Thomas Aquinas, ST I–II. 91. 6.
45. Henri Rondet, *Original sin: The Patristic and Theological Background* (New York: Alba House, 1972), 166–167.
46. Bonnette, 147.
47. Ibid., 170.
48. Forsthoefl, 36.
49. David Liberto, "A Reply to Fr. Dietzen," *Clarion Herald* (10/22/03).
50. *Humani generis*, 37.
51. C.S. Lewis, *The Problem of Pain* (New York: Simon and Schuster, 1996), 68–71.

Conclusion

Miracles: Signs and Wonders at the Crossroads of Faith and Science

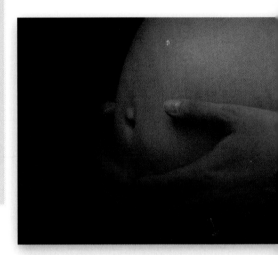

THE BISHOP ADVISED ELISABETH TO JOIN HIM IN PRAYING FOR THE INTERCESSION OF *GIANNA BERETTA MOLLA*, A MOTHER WHO HAD DIED TO SAVE THE LIFE OF HER UNBORN CHILD.

A. An Unexpected Physician

From the outside looking in, the beginning of the year 2000 might have seemed to be a wonderful time in the life of Elisabeth Comparini Arcolino. A Brazilian mother of three children, Arcolino had recently learned that she was pregnant with her fourth child and was living out the many joys of her motherhood while awaiting the expansion of her family.

But during an emergency visit to the hospital in the sixteenth week of her pregnancy, Elisabeth's happiness was shattered by horrifying and tragic news. Her baby's placenta had torn, rupturing the vital biological lifeline that conveys nutrition, fluids, and even oxygen from a mother to her unborn child. The tear had resulted in a total loss of amniotic fluid, the watery substance that creates the unborn baby's necessary growth environment. She was told the sad but undeniable truth: the baby had absolutely no chance of survival. She was then advised by the doctor to have an abortion.

At that very moment, in one of those chance occurrences we have learned to call providence, Bishop Diogenes Matthes was at the hospital visiting a friend. He was summoned to Elisabeth's room, where he urged her to consult another physician. But there was a slight problem with his advice, at least for eyes without faith: the bishop recommended a physician who had died thirty-eight years earlier!

What the bishop had advised Elisabeth was that she join with him in praying for the intercession of *Gianna Beretta Molla*, an Italian

St. Gianna Beretta Molla with two of her four children.

The Arcolino family at the canonization of St. Gianna. Elisabeth is third from left; Gianna Arcolino is fifth from left in the arms of her father.

wife, mother, and physician who had died to save the life of her own unborn child. In late 1961, Molla was newly pregnant when she learned that she had a tumor in her uterus that was threatening her own life and the life of her baby. Rather than have an abortion, or even a morally acceptable hysterectomy, she chose the path riskiest to herself and safest for her baby—an operation to remove the tumor. Her desire to save the baby was fulfilled, but only at the sacrifice of her own life—Molla died on April 28, 1962, at the age of thirty-nine, due to complications related to the surgery that had made it possible to carry her baby to term.

Already, one miracle had been attributed to Gianna Molla, and due to her remarkable love and witness as a Catholic mother, she had been declared Bl. Gianna by Pope John Paul II in 1994. This meant that she was one miracle short of sainthood, giving Bishop Matthes his idea: "You don't kill life inside the mother," the bishop told Elisabeth. "This is the time for Bl. Gianna Beretta Molla to intercede for the life you are carrying." At home the bishop began praying to Molla, saying, "The time for your canonization has arrived. Intercede to the Lord for the grace of a miracle and save the life of this little baby."[1]

Elisabeth took the bishop's advice, and began to ask Gianna for her intercession. She turned out to be the specialist Elisabeth needed. Despite the lack of amniotic fluid, and in an event completely without scientific explanation, Elisabeth delivered a healthy baby girl by Caesarean section on May 31, 2000. She and her husband named their child Gianna Marie, after the woman of faith and of science on whose prayers they had relied.[2]

The event of the Arcolino pregnancy and delivery had ramifications far beyond their family. Only four years later, on May 16, 2004, the Arcolino family, including their miracle child, traveled to Rome along with thousands of other pilgrims for Molla's canonization. There they joined Pietro, the elderly husband of Gianna Molla, as well as her children, including the daughter for whom Gianna had given her life. Gianna Beretta Molla, believer, scientist, and pro-life hero, is now St. Gianna Molla. She has joined the ranks of the extraordinary men and women throughout history who have been recognized by the Church as saints.

The story of the Arcolino family and their heavenly physician brings us to our final stop on our journey to rediscover faith on the frontiers of science—the rare but amazing phenomena of miracles. In the encounter between faith and science, miracles reveal the absolute necessity of both in understanding the world God created. Miracles stand at the crossroads of faith and science, revealing both to be true paths to knowledge and insight about history and the universe.

B. Miracles: Discovering the Borderline between Nature and the Supernatural

DEFINING MIRACLES

Throughout this text there have been references to miracles and the miraculous. Each time, these references have uncovered some important characteristics of miracles. But never have we exactly defined a miracle. To do so now we will use the definition offered by the French theologian René Latourelle. According to Latourelle, a *miracle* is "a religious wonder that expresses, in human beings and the universe, a special and utterly free intervention of God, who uses it to give human beings a sign of the presence of his message of salvation in the world."[3] Recalling the Arcolino family miracle, we can see that each of these elements was present:

> *A religious wonder*: What happened to the Arcolino baby was something that transcended the ordinary course of things, which in this case would have been the baby's death. But this escape from death was not a simple wonder; it was one related directly to the prayers made by Elisabeth Arcolino, her bishop, and others. The miracle was an intervention of God related to petitions offered by them in faith, petitions offered within the communion of saints that mysteriously links those in Heaven (in this case, Gianna Beretta Molla) to those on earth (baby Gianna Arcolino and her mother Elisabeth). It came after humble, trusting, persevering prayer; it came from the mediation of Christ shared with his holy and heroic servant, the pro-life, pro-baby hero St. Gianna. In this event we can clearly see a harmony between the wonder of the baby's miraculous cure and the calling on God, through St. Gianna, to which God responded. This is the nature of all miracles; they are not simply wonders, but *religious wonders*.

> *A special and free intervention of God*: As we saw earlier, God continuously acts in the world to bring about the fulfillment of his plan. But he does so as a general rule through the secondary causality of creatures within the laws of nature, laws studied by science. A miracle is quite different than this normal course of divine providence. A miracle is a singular (i.e., one-time) intervention of God for an express purpose; in such an intervention, God is not acting through the fixed laws of nature, but in a way above and beyond nature that has an effect within nature.

> The Arcolino healing did not occur through nature, the way a cut or a successful surgery heals. The body has no power to produce new

A MIRACLE IS A RELIGIOUS WONDER THAT EXPRESSES A SPECIAL AND UTTERLY FREE INTERVENTION OF GOD THAT IS A SIGN OF HIS MESSAGE OF SALVATION IN THE WORLD.

A MIRACLE IS A ONE-TIME INTERVENTION OF GOD FOR AN EXPRESS PURPOSE IN WHICH HE ACTS ABOVE AND BEYOND NATURE WITH AN EFFECT WITHIN NATURE.

THE ARCOLINO PREGNANCY
MIRACLE WAS A MIRACLE
PREGNANT WITH MEANINGS—
A DIVINE SIGN.

amniotic fluid for a pregnancy once it has been lost, and medical doctors are unable to create synthetic fluid to replace it. In other words, human biology and its natural processes were not the cause of this healing. But human biology was not violated by God either; it was simply made to respond directly to the loving will of the God who designed it in the first place.

A sign of God's message of salvation: The Arcolino healing miracle was not simply a mysterious, inexplicable blessing for the baby and her family. It was also a picture that painted a thousand words, an action that taught many things at once.

First, the healing made known that God's salvation is true and real. It showed God's love and care for all human beings, including the unborn, a very important message for our age in which many societies (including the United States) have legalized the destruction of unborn children for all nine months of pregnancy. Finally, it confirmed the heroic holiness and the presence in Heaven of Gianna Molla so that the Church could recognize her for the assistance that she can offer to the Church's members on Earth.

God, the greatest teacher, taught several messages all at once in this marvelous event. The Arcolino pregnancy miracle was, quite fittingly, a miracle *pregnant* with meanings. In short, it was a *divine sign*.

The joy, astonishment, shock, surprise, and even fear that such a miracle can cause is obvious. But for some, the response to any miracle is total denial. Even some believers have claimed that miracles are an old superstition that should be left behind by modern people. Are miracles marvels or mirages, reasonable or superstitious? To answer that question, let us look at the main objections used to deny the existence of miracles.

MIRACU-LESS MENTALITIES: ANSWERING THE MAIN OBJECTIONS TO MIRACLES

Objections to the possibility of miracles always take one of two forms. Either miracles are denied because they are supposedly contrary to God or because they are supposedly contrary to nature. The second kind of objection is the most common kind, so let us consider the main examples of it.

Objections to Miracles from the Perspective of Nature

Objection #1: The rarity of miracles reveal that they are impossible. Many believe that miracles cannot occur because they have never directly experienced one. Such a person concludes that, because miracles do not happen regularly or normally, they are scientific impossibilities.

But this claim oversteps the boundaries of logic. The infrequency of miracles is part of their wonder; a miracle is what it is precisely because it does not regularly occur in nature!

Just because miracles involve the transcendence by God of the regular course of nature and its laws does not mean that they cannot occur. Our experience of the normal workings of nature does not tell us that these regular workings cannot be superseded. And yet a miracle, by definition, is just such a superseding.

A miracle is always the direct intervention of God who created and holds in being the laws of nature within the sphere of the physical universe governed by those laws. In fact, to believe in a miracle one must also believe in the regular course of nature and in its laws! A religious wonder would not be wonderful if one did not believe that it was an exception to the rule. A firm believer in miracles, therefore, must also be a firm believer in the consistency and regularity of the universe. Belief in miracles always requires belief in the laws of nature, something that belief in miracles shares in common with science.[4]

Objection #2: Miracles cannot happen because the laws of nature are unbreakable. Those who hold this position insist that breaking the laws of nature would be self-contradictory, much like attempting to draw a square circle. On the basis of this they conclude that a miracle is an impossible absurdity.

However, a miracle is not the breaking of any of the laws of nature. *The presence of a miracle changes the situation, not the laws that would apply if there were no miraculous intervention by God.*

Let us consider an analogy to the transcendent nature of miracles. Suppose you placed a five dollar bill in your glove compartment this morning and then locked it. When you come back this afternoon, you will not be surprised to find that five dollar bill exactly where you left it. But if you open your glove compartment and find a one hundred dollar bill where the five dollar bill used to be, it means that some new factor is involved; in short, someone very generous has been inside your car!

In the same way, a miracle is not the breaking of any of the laws of nature. Rather, it is the intervention of the supernatural in nature. The laws of nature are not violated, they are simply bracketed. When a miracle occurs, nature reacts by receiving the miraculous exception, which comes from outside it, by immediately taking over where it left off. C.S. Lewis, who wrote a masterly book about miracles, has this to say about "nature's reaction" to the miraculous:

> If events ever come from beyond nature altogether... be sure she will rush to the point where she is invaded, as the defensive forces [of the body] rush to a cut in our finger, and there hasten to accommodate the newcomer. The moment it enters her realm

THE OCCURRENCE OF A MIRACLE CHANGES THE SITUATION, NOT THE LAWS THAT WOULD APPLY IF THERE WERE NO MIRACULOUS INTERVENTION BY GOD.

C.S. Lewis

MIRACLES ARE THE
FORESHADOWING OF THE
GRAND FINALE OF THE DRAMA
OF HISTORY AND THE UNIVERSE
WITHIN THE COURSE OF NATURE
WHICH ITSELF IS LEADING UP TO
THAT FINALE

it obeys all her laws. Miraculous wine will intoxicate, miraculous conception will lead to pregnancy... miraculous bread will be digested. The divine art of miracle is not an art of suspending the pattern to which events conform but of feeding new events into that pattern.[5]

Objection #3: Miracles offend our sense of fitness and uniformity in history and the universe. The history of science is one in which scientists have tackled the seeming oddities and irregularities in nature precisely in order to show that they are not in fact irregularities, but that they follow a real pattern. "Giving in" to the existence of miracles seems to some people to knock the wind out of science, to make it sit down and give up on its very important quest to find the regular patterns in nature. Miracles do not "fit" the norm, and so they are rejected.

But the answer to this objection can be found in a deeper question—why does science put such faith in the uniformity and regularity of nature? We have already seen that this conviction arose in an atmosphere of belief in the Creator within a Christian society. Centuries of faith in God's power and rationality produced this expectation of uniformity and order in the universe. In the words of C.S. Lewis, "men became scientific because they expected Law in Nature, and they expected Law in Nature because they believed in a Legislator [a Law-Giver]."[6] But to admit such a God is also to admit the possibility of miracles. Belief in science and belief in miracles are like twin brothers that were separated in childhood. They have the same mother (belief in God) and they need to be reunited.

As one can see, the universe and its laws hold no real obstacle to the possibility of miracles. But some argue against miracles from a different and very surprising perspective—they hold that God would never perform them, that miracles are "out of character" for God, contrary to God's nature. Let us look at this objection.

An Argument against Miracles from the Character of God

Objection #4: Some of those who reject the possibility of miracles do not doubt that God is capable of performing miracles. But, they maintain, God would never do so. He would never interrupt the steady rhythm and progress of his creation. Their objection is this: why would God, who is perfect, need to interfere with his creation? And in the answer to this objection we find the greatest surprise of all about miracles.

God would not interfere with nature if it were the final stage, the last event of his work among creatures. But if history and the universe as we know it are themselves caught up in a drama of unimaginable scope, then miracles are the foreshadowing of the grand finale within the course of nature which itself is leading up to that finale.

To understand this, C.S. Lewis invites us to consider novel writing.[7] If you are writing a story in which characters are in a completely ordinary plot, and they end up in a tragedy or a complicated mess, then it would be wrong for the author to intervene with something wondrous and strange that comes out of the blue, because that is not what one expects in a normal plot. But what if an author is writing a novel in which the wondrous and strange is really at the heart of the author's story? Then you would have an entirely different situation.

In the first kind of novel, fairies or superheroes making an appearance would turn a good novel into a bad novel. But in the second case, the absence of fairies or superheroes would make it a bad novel!

If God's plot, his storyline for humanity is just about nature in its uniformity and regularity, then miracles really would be bad form. But God has revealed to us that nature, as we know it, is not the final act in his great novel. It is being taken over by a new kind of reality, a higher one that goes beyond it and even makes it possible. Therefore, miracles are more like the twists in the tale of history and the universe which move history and the universe towards their conclusion.

The Arcolino pregnancy involved one such revealing of the deeper plot that God is unfolding for our sake. Ultimately, the whole play will be revealed to be about the amazing rescue of those who, like little Gianna Arcolino, are condemned to death. But we must go to the Christian Faith, located in Scripture and Church teaching, if we want to know just what kind of death and just what kind of grand rescue we are talking about.

If miracles are the plot twists of God's great book—history and the universe—the plot twists which bring the novel to its magnificent and surprising conclusion, then it becomes obvious who the central character is—the man whose very existence was a miracle, whose life was packed with miracles, and whose earthly life ended with the greatest miracle of all. If miracles are the heart of God's story, then Jesus of Nazareth is clearly its hero and central figure. In our next section, let us look at his life from the perspective of miracles, and in doing so we will see the whole relationship between miracles and science coming into focus.

Calling of the First Disciples

C. Meeting the Man of Miracles on the Frontiers of Faith and Science

THE INCARNATION

MIRACLES ARE THE PLOT TWISTS IN GOD'S GREAT DRAMA, AND JESUS CHRIST, THE MAN OF MIRACLES WHOSE VERY EXISTENCE WAS A MIRACLE, IS THE CENTRAL CHARACTER.

If miracles are the most important plot twists in the great story of the universe, then the Incarnation, the fact that the Son of God assumed human nature, body and soul, in order to achieve our salvation and reunion with God, is the heart of the story, the turning-point which leads to its climax.

From our Christian Faith we know that Jesus Christ, who from eternity is truly God, became true man in his Incarnation.[8] In the holy words of St. Paul, "in the *fullness of time* God sent forth his Son, born of woman" (Gal 4:4). The phrase "*fullness of time*" reveals to us that what happened in the womb of Mary is the central event of all of history. C.S. Lewis shows us how the Incarnation gives a new dimension to the things we see all around us in the natural world:

> In this descent [of God's Son] . . . everyone will recognize a familiar pattern: a thing written all over the world. It is the pattern of all vegetable life. It must belittle itself into something hard, small, and deathlike, it must fall into the ground: thence the new life re-ascends. It is the pattern of all animal generation too. There is descent from the full and perfect organisms into the spermatozoon and ovum, and in the dark womb a life at first inferior in kind to that of the species which is being produced: then the slow ascent to the perfect embryo, to the living, conscious baby, and finally to the adult . . . The pattern is there in nature because it was first there in God.[9]

The Incarnation reveals that all the "descent" around us points to the miracle in which God himself descends to us in order to re-ascend with us for our salvation.

THE EARTHLY LIFE OF JESUS

In his earthly life, Jesus, the Incarnate Son of God, performs many miracles. But these miracles were performed with a purpose. If we are looking at them in order to learn about the meaning of the universe, it helps to divide them into two types, both of which have a message for us.

First, Jesus performs some miracles that have effects which are natural. Second, he performs other miracles that have effects which are supernatural. Both types of miracles performed by Jesus have something to tell us about the meaning of the story of the universe.

The nature miracles of Jesus: The most common miracles Jesus performed are miracles in which he did suddenly what God does through nature generally and globally. That is, in certain miracles, Jesus did "small and up-close" what God does "large and everywhere." In his book on miracles, C.S. Lewis describes a few important examples.[10]

For instance, Jesus converts water into wine at the wedding feast at Cana in Galilee (Jn 2:1–11). Yet God, through the laws of organic chemistry and plant biology which he designed, changes water into wine in vineyards constantly throughout the world. At Cana,

IN THE NATURE MIRACLES HE PERFORMED, JESUS DID "SMALL AND UP-CLOSE" WHAT GOD DOES "LARGE AND EVERYWHERE;" "FOCUSING FOR US WHAT THE GOD OF NATURE HAS ALREADY DONE ON A LARGER SCALE."

God Incarnate "makes wine in a moment": everywhere else, God makes wine through gradual, natural laws. The miracle is the shortcut, as it is when he multiplies loaves and fish.

Jesus' healing miracles are the same. Thanks to science, doctors have been able to find ways to assists our bodies in healing, such as antibiotics and laser surgery. That strange, powerful energy of healing is already in us; the treatment only simulates those powers or removes obstacles to healing.

But in his healings, Jesus, God Incarnate, does quickly and flawlessly what the body does slowly and imperfectly; in him, "the power that always was behind all healings puts on a face and hands."[11]

Jesus, God Incarnate, also shows dominion over wind and sea; he tells them "calm, be still" and they obey (Mt 8:23–27). But God made nature in such a way that it has both storminess and calm weather; ultimately, God stills all storms by making the world in such a way that storms ultimately move on or dissipate. Once again, Jesus does up-close on a small level what God does always and everywhere.

In all of these cases, we see the same thing—Jesus "focusing for us what the God of Nature has already done on a larger scale." He reveals that he is the God who created and sustains the universe, not merely a king, but *the* King; nature's king and our king. Jesus' miracles give us a key to understanding the meaning of the universe; that it was created by God for God's purposes.

But the real plot twist is in the second kind of miracle, the miracles in which Jesus does things which never happen in the normal course of nature. We turn to look at those miracles now:

"The Miracles of the New Creation": In his public ministry Jesus also performs miracles which have effects that are entirely new and supernatural, such as when he raises the dead and walks on water. These miracles reveal that the nature studied by science and experienced by us is simply one stage or one act in God's play. Another new "nature" is being forged by God, "a new heavens and a new Earth" (Rv 21:1–5). Jesus' walking on water shows that in this new creation, matter will be made obedient to spirit in a way which we can scarcely begin to imagine. The raising of Lazarus or of the widow's son from death reveals that a great and glorious and irreversible resurrection of all the dead is coming in God's plan.[12]

One such miracle (which Jesus only performed once) is one of the most important of the "New Creation" miracles: the Transfiguration. Following Scripture, the *Catechism of the Catholic Church* describes this event as an astonishing moment experienced directly only by three chosen witnesses: Peter,

JESUS ALSO PERFORMED MIRACLES WHICH POINT TO THE TRANSFORMATION OF HUMANITY AND OF ALL CREATION, SUCH AS WHEN HE RAISED THE DEAD AND WALKED ON WATER.

IN THE RESURRECTION, GOD'S PERFECT PLOT FOR THE STORY OF THE UNIVERSE IS REVEALED. BEYOND HUMAN IMAGININGS, PHYSICAL REALITY IS GOING TO BE REMADE, RE-ENERGIZED IN A WAY THAT IS COMPLETELY FILLED WITH GOD'S PRESENCE.

James, and John: "Jesus' face and clothes become dazzling with light, and Moses and Elijah appear, speaking of his departure, which he was to accomplish at Jerusalem.[13] A cloud covers him and a voice from heaven says: 'This is my Son, my Chosen; listen to him.'"[14]

What does this miracle reveal? Nothing less than the greatest mystery of all—the glorification of Jesus' humanity in the Resurrection, as well as our own glorification when "he 'will change our lowly bodies to be like his glorious body.'"[15] This miracle points to the final miracle by which God announces the beginning of the final chapter of nature as we know it, which will be the general resurrection of all human beings— the "resurrection of the body."[16]

THE RESURRECTION

All of Jesus' "New Creation" miracles foreshadow, in some way, the miracle of the Resurrection. After suffering the agony of betrayal, a physical torture, a separation from all whom he loved, death, and descent into Hell, the third day after his execution found him alive and among his disciples in a way that they could never have foreseen. He is clearly beyond the ordinary limits of human bodily life; he is not limited by space and time any longer. But he can still eat food, can touch, and be touched. Therefore, the *Catechism of the Catholic Church* declares, "Christ's humanity can no longer be confined to Earth and belongs henceforth only to the Father's divine realm[17] . . . in his risen body he passes from the state of death to another life beyond time and space. At Jesus' Resurrection his Body is filled with the power of the Holy Spirit: he shares the divine life in his glorious state, so that St. Paul can say that Christ is 'the man of heaven.'"[18]

In the Resurrection, God's perfect plot for the story of the universe is revealed. Beyond human imaginings, physical reality is going to be remade, re-energized in a way in which it is completely filled with God's presence. In the words of C.S. Lewis,

> There will be no room to get the finest razor-blade of thought in between Spirit and Nature. Every state of affairs in the New Nature will be the perfect expression of a spiritual state and every spiritual state the perfect informing of, and bloom upon, a state of affairs; one with it as the perfume with a flower or the "spirit" of great poetry with its form.[19]

In summary, we see that all the miracles of Jesus have a message to share with us. They are not merely for show. They are not there to violate nature or to cancel it out, but to signal its transformation in a new and glorious reality that God has prepared for those who love him. They are clues to the meaning of the universe.

D. The End of the End: Christ, the Savior of Science

The Miracle of Jesus Christ, as well as the miracles performed by him, bring our study of faith and science to a close. We now see science as the study of nature as one part of a reality that reaches far beyond nature, the study of a stage that exists to focus our attention on the actors and on the Author whose loving hand and creative mind unfolds their story. Nature is given to us to foreshadow the coming of a greater reality that awaits us.

Therefore, of all the acts of faith which the Church calls us to perform, one of them is most fitting to the believer who also wishes to be a scientist. That act of faith is Eucharistic Adoration.

In the Adoration of the Eucharist, we do in prayer what all scientists, knowingly or unknowingly, are doing in their research—gazing upon a reality whose appearance veils a reality much deeper and more amazing than appears at first glance. In the consecrated Host, we see nature's God in the guise of a creature; in the microscope, the scientist sees a nature that belongs to God and will be transformed by him. In both cases, one must see beyond the surface to see the truth.

Pope John Paul II, Eucharistic Benediction

As we end our text, let us heed the words and receive the blessing Pope John Paul II gave to the young scientists of the world:

> To you young scientists belongs the future of the dialogue between faith and science: I urge you to carry it forward with sincerity and humility. Strive for excellence in your scientific endeavors, and keep your minds and hearts ever open to the different channels which lead us to a better understanding of ourselves and the universe in which we live. May God, whose infinite love and wisdom fashioned the heavens and established the moon and stars, ever guide you into his grace and peace.[20]

Amen!

IN THE CONSECRATED HOST, WE SEE NATURE'S GOD IN THE GUIDE OF A CREATURE; IN THE MICROSCOPE, THE SCIENTIST SEES A NATURE THAT BELONGS TO GOD AND WILL BE TRANSFORMED BY HIM. IN BOTH CASES, ONE MUST SEE BEYOND THE SURFACE TO SEE THE WHOLE TRUTH.

Supplementary Reading

Miracles: Signs and Wonders at the Crossroads of Faith and Science

1. "THE MIND OF THE MAKER: C.S. LEWIS ON THE FITNESS OF MIRACLES"

(excerpted from C.S. Lewis, Miracles: How God Intervenes in Nature and Human Affairs *[New York: Macmillan, 1960], pp. 98–99).*

How a miracle can be no inconsistency, but the highest consistency, will be clear to those who have read Miss Dorothy Sayers' indispensable book, *The Mind of the Maker*. Miss Sayers' thesis is based on the analogy between God's relation to the world, on the one hand, and an author's relation to his book on the other. If you are writing a story, miracles or abnormal events may be bad art, or they may not. If, for example, you are writing an ordinary realistic novel and have got your characters into a hopeless muddle, it would be quite intolerable if you suddenly cut the knot and secured a happy ending by having a fortune left to the hero from an

unexpected quarter. On the other hand there is nothing against taking as your subject from the outset the adventures of a man who inherits an unexpected fortune. The unusual event is perfectly permissible if it is really what you are writing *about*: it is an artistic crime if you simply drag it in by the heels to get yourself out of a hole. The ghost story is a legitimate form of art; but you must not bring a ghost into an ordinary novel to get over a difficulty in the plot. Now there is no doubt that a great deal of the modern objection to miracles is based on the suspicion that they are marvels of the wrong sort; that a story of a certain kind (Nature) is arbitrarily interfered with, to get the characters out of a difficulty, by events that do not really belong to that kind of story. Some people probably think of the Resurrection as a desperate last moment [attempt] to save the Hero from a situation which had got out of the Author's control.

The reader may set his mind at rest. If I thought miracles were like that, I should not believe in them. If they have occurred, they have occurred because they are the very thing this universal story is about. They are not exceptions (however rarely they occur) nor irrelevancies. They are precisely those chapters in this great story on which the plot turns. Death and Resurrection are what the story is about; and had we but eyes to see it, this has been hinted on every page, met us, in some disguise, at every turn... If you have hitherto disbelieved in

Supplementary Reading

miracles, it is worth pausing a moment to consider whether this is not chiefly because you thought you had discovered what the story was really about?—that atoms, and time and space and economics and politics were the main plot? And is it certain you were right? It is easy to make mistakes in such matters. A friend of mine wrote a play in which the main idea was that the hero had a pathological horror of trees and a mania for cutting them down. But naturally other things came in as well; there was some sort of love story mixed up with it. And the trees killed the man in the end. When my friend had written it, he sent it to an older man to criticize. It came back with the comment, "Not bad. But I'd cut out those bits of *padding* about the trees." To be sure, God might be expected to make a better story than my friend. But it is a very *long* story, with a complicated plot; and we are not, perhaps, very attentive readers.

2. "A FINAL LOOK AT FAITH AND SCIENCE: RULES FOR THEIR RELATIONSHIP"

(excerpted from Paul Haffner, Mystery of Creation *[Herefordshire, UK: Gracewing, 1995], pp.175–177. Fourteen Theses on Relations Between Science and Religion).*

1. There is no intrinsic contradiction between Christian Faith and natural science.

2. Science is of itself insufficient for human growth in understanding and human development.

3. As science and technology progress, human civilization will not reach a type of earthly utopia.

4. Scientific progress is part of human and spiritual progress....

5. Just as grace perfects nature in a dynamic partnership, so also is Christian Faith like a guiding star which leads science to a deeper and more perfect understanding of its role within human experience....

6. Science cannot be regarded as having such autonomy that its applications and philosophy may be followed, even if they contradict faith, morals, and the dignity of the human person.

7. The Magisterium of the Church can and should pronounce on scientific issues which have a bearing on faith or morals or have implications for other aspects of the Christian life....

8. The Church does benefit from an understanding of the scientific milieu and mentality, and this is necessary for the more [effective] communication and diffusion of the Gospel of Christ.

9. It would be rash, necessarily and immediately, to attribute to God that which is still inaccessible to science, for if and when science has achieved a discovery of the said areas, the power of God may appear to be reduced. (This is the 'God of the gaps' error.)

10. It is an error to hold that in the order of created things there is, immediately manifested to the human intellect, something divine in itself, such that it belongs to the divine nature.

11. Science arrives at the truth, but not at all of the truth, so that not even all that which is in the natural order is its proper subject. Natural science will never be able to penetrate all the secrets of nature to the extent that the cosmos would fail to evoke in man a sense of mystery.

Supplementary Reading

12. Notwithstanding our increasing pure and applied knowledge in science and technology, leading to a greater understanding of the laws of nature and their control, it would be an error to exclude immediate and direct intervention of God in his creation in a miraculous way; for although we are bound by the laws of nature, God is not.

13. The mediation of philosophy, and especially of metaphysics, is required in relating Christian Faith and natural science.

14. Among the chief implicit presuppositions of science are that the material entities observed are real, existing independently of the observer, that these entities have a coherent rationality, and being governed by consistent laws form a consistent whole....

Study Guide

Miracles: Signs and Wonders
at the Crossroads of Faith and Science

VOCABULARY

Define the following terms:

1. Gianna Beretta Molla

2. Miracle

3. Religious Wonder

4. Nature Miracles

5. New Creation Miracles

6. Incarnation

7. Transfiguration

8. Resurrection (Jesus)

9. General Ressurection

10. Eucharistic Adoration

STUDY QUESTIONS

1. Explain Latourelle's identification of every miracle as a religious wonder, using the Arcolino pregnancy miracle as an example.

2. What are the implications of the fact that a miracle is always a special and free intervention of God?

3. Explain Latourelle's identification of every miracle as a sign of God's message of salvation, using the Arcolino pregnancy miracle as an example.

4. Are miracles scientifically impossible? Why or why not?

5. Why does the recognition of any event as a miracle also involve a recognition of the laws of nature studied by science?

6. Are miracles a violation of the laws of nature? What do miracles reveal about nature?

7. Do miracles really offend a proper sense of the fitness and uniformity of the universe? Why or why not?

8. How are belief in science and belief in miracles related to each other?

9. What does the presence of miracles in human history reveal about God and his plan? Use novel writing to explain.

10. What is the significance of the Incarnation? How does it reveal the true meaning of the natural process of the generation of living things?

11. What is the meaning of the nature miracles of Jesus? What do they reveal?

12. What is the meaning of the New Creation miracles of Jesus? What do they reveal?

13. Describe the special significance of the Transfiguration for understanding God's plan for history and the universe.

14. What will the general resurrection, as revealed in Jesus' Resurrection, involve for the natural world?

15. Why is Eucharistic Adoration an excellent form of prayer for scientists?

Study Guide

PRACTICAL EXERCISES\

1. Research the miracles that have occurred at Lourdes and have been approved by the Church. Apply Latourelle's definition of a miracle to the event. How does it measure up to the standard set by Latourelle?

2. Have you or anyone you know ever experienced an event that seemed miraculous? Apply Latourelle's definition of a miracle to the event. How does it measure up to the standard set by Latourelle? If it does not, why should God still be given thanks for it?

3. Pope John Paul II is currently being considered for beatification by the Church. Pray the following prayer for his cause for sainthood:

O Blessed Trinity, We thank you

for having graced the Church with Pope John Paul II

and for allowing the tenderness of your Fatherly care,

the glory of the Cross of Christ,

and the splendor of the Holy Spirit, to shine through him.

Trusting fully in your infinite mercy

and in the maternal intercession of Mary,

he has given us a living image of Jesus the Good Shepherd,

and has shown us that holiness is the necessary measure

of ordinary Christian life and is the way of achieving eternal communion with you.

Grant us, by his intercession,

and according to your will, the graces we implore,

hoping that he will soon be numbered among your saints. Amen.

Endnotes

1. "A Pro-Life Icon to be Canonized: Gianna Molla Gave Her Life for Her Unborn Daughter," *Zenit: The World seen from Rome* (http://www.zenit.org/english/visualizza.phtml?sid=53575).
2. Ibid.
3. René Latourelle and Rino Fisichella, eds., *Dictionary of Fundamental Theology* (New York: Crossroad, 1994), 702.
4. C.S. Lewis, *Miracles: How God Intervenes in Nature and Human Affairs* (New York: Macmillan, 1978), 45-48.
5. Ibid., 59-60.
6. Ibid., 106.
7. Ibid., 98-99.
8. CCC 461.
9. Lewis, *Miracles*, 112.
10. Ibid., 132-142.
11. Ibid., 140.
12. Ibid., 150-151.
13. Lk 9:31.
14. CCC 554; Lk 9:35.
15. CCC 556; cf. Phil 3:21.
16. Cf. CCC 997-1001.
17. Cf. Mt 28:9; 16–17; Lk 24:15, 36; Jn 20:14, 17, 19, 26; 21:4.
18. Ibid., 645–646; cf. 1 Cor 15:35–50.
19. Lewis, *Miracles*, 161.
20. John Paul II, "Address to Participants in the Fifth Summer School in Astrophysics," Vatican Observatory (July 7, 1995): 4.

Art and Photo Credits

Cover

Lyndon Studio, Downers Grove, Illinois USA

Introduction

iv *Roman Coin with Christogram;* AG Archives

Chapter 1

2   *Two Wings,* Geoff Yerke

5   (center) *Copernicus's De Revolutionibus Orbium Caelestium, 1543*; William Pyle Philips Collection of Rare Books

5   (bottom) *Astronomer Copernicus: Conversation with God,* Jan Matejko; Frombork, Poland

6   (*Title Page*) *Atlas Historique Tome IV,* Henri Chatelain; Amsterdam, 1719

10 *Science and the Arts* (detail), Adriaen Van Stalbemt; Museo del Prado, Madrid, Spain; Archivo Oronoz

12 *Adoration of the Saints and Angels,* Jacinto Gomez; Museo del Prado, Madrid, Spain; Archivo Oronoz

15 *Abraham and Isaac*; Rembrandt Hermitage Museum, St. Petersburg, Russia

16 Engraving from Tycho's *Astronomiæ instaurata mechanica*, published in Wansbeck in 1598; High Altitude Observatory (website)

Chapter 2

21 *Crossroads,* Geoff Yerke

22 *Visible Invisible,* Geoff Yerke

23 (top) *Sistine Chapel Ceiling* (detail), Michelangelo; Vatican

23 (center) *The Ptolemaic system of celestial motion;* Harmonia Macrocosmica, 1661

24 (center) *Doubt,* Geoff Yerke

24 (bottom) *Carl Sagan;* public domain

25 *The Face of Jesus*; based on the Shroud of Turin

26 (center) *Plato and Aristotle* (detail) from *The School of Athens*, Raphael; Stanza della Segnatura, Palazzi Pontifici, Vatican

26 (bottom) *Feet of Clay*, Geoff Yerke

27 (top) *Tree of Science,* Geoff Yerke

27 (center) *Cardinal Schönborn;* public domain

28 (top) *Euclid of Alexandria*; public domain

28 (bottom) *Stephen Jay Gould*; public domain

29 (top) *Sir Isaac Newton*; from Wikimedia Commons; public domain

29 (bottom) *St. Thomas Aquinas*; public domain

33 (top left) *Flower of Science,* Geoff Yerke

35 *Frontpage of Dialogo di Galileo Galilei Linceo* (Galileo in conversation with Ptolemy and Copernicus); from Dialogo di Galileo Galilei; Florence, 1632; *The Origins and Growth of Physical Science*, Penguin Books

36 *Dialogo di Galileo;* public domain

286

Art and Photo Credits

Chapter 3

38   *Ancient of Days,* William Blake; British Museum, London, 1794

39   *Moses*, Michelangelo; San Pietro in Vinculo, Rome, 1513–1515

39   (top) *Spiral Galaxy*; public domain

40   (center) *Dialogo di Galileo;* public domain

40   (bottom) *Albert Einstein;* public domain

41   *Prophet Amos,* Gustave Doré; The Doré Gallery of Bible Illustrations

44   *The Confusion of Tongues,* Gustave Doré; The Doré Gallery of Bible Illustrations

46   (top) *Ezra Thanks God for His Help;* www.breadsite.org

47   *Whore of Babylon*, unknown artist; public domain

48   *Prophet,* unknown artist, c. 600 BC; public domain

49   (top) *Picture of Old Testament;* public domain

49   (bottom) *Portrait of Archbishop Ussher*, public domain

50   (top) *Old Testament;* unknown artist; public domain

51   (bottom) *Writing on the Wall,* The woodcut illustrations by Julius Schnorr von Carolsfeld (copied from "Das Buch der Bucher in Bildern" Verlag von Georg Wigand, Liepzig, 1908); public domain.

53   (top) *Clio*; Greek Museum of History

54   (bottom) *The Babylonian Captivity*; unknown artist; public domain

55   *Hevelius' 150-foot-long refractor*; public domain

57   *Original sketches of the Moon,* Galileo Galilei, c. 1610; public domain

62   *The Tower of Babel,* Pieter Bruegel the Elder; Kunsthistorisches Museum, Vienna

Chapter 4

64–5   *Galileo Galilei showing medicean planets,* unknown artist; public domain

67   (top) *St. Paul in Ephesus,* Eustache le Sueur; Louvre, Paris

67   (bottom) *Pontifica Academia Scientiarum*; public domain

68   (top) *Cistercian Monks,* Francisco Zurbaran; Sanchez Muniain Collection, Madrid; Archivo Oronoz

68–9   *Devises et Emblemes Anciennes et Modernes;* public domain

70   (top) *Nicholas Oresme*; public domain

70   (bottom) *Nicholas of Cusa*; public domain

71   (top) *A diagram of an armillary sphere,* Christoph Clavius

71   (bottom) *A chart of sunspots,* Christoph Scheiner; public domain

72   (top) *Illustrated Manuscript*; *Missal;* Archivo Oronoz

72–3   *Pentecost,* Francisco Zurbaran; Cádiz Museum, Cádiz, Spain; Archivo Oronoz

73   (bottom) *Marin Mersenne;* public domain

74   (bottom) *Steno's shark teeth from Elementorum myologiæ specimen,* Niels Stensen (Steno)

75   Portrait of Bl. Nicholas Steno, Justus Sutterman, Uffizi Gallery, Florence, c. 1670

76   (top) *Pietro Angelo Secchi;* public domain

76   (center) *Sketch of Fr. Secchi's Telescope;* public domain

76   (bottom) *Fr. Georges Lemaître with Albert Einstein;* public domain

77   *John Paul II,* public domain

Art and Photo Credits

Art and Photo Credits

All uncredited images were created by Lyndon Studio using personal images or from public domain.

Index

Index

Index